THE SELECTED LETTERS
OF EZRA POUND

1907-1941

BY EZRA POUND

ABC OF READING
A LUME SPENTO AND OTHER EARLY POEMS
THE CANTOS (NUMBERS 1–95)
THE CANTOS OF EZRA POUND (1–117)
THE CLASSIC NOH THEATRE OF JAPAN
COLLECTED EARLY POEMS OF EZRA POUND
CONFUCIUS (ENGLISH VERSIONS)
THE CONFUCIAN ODES
CONFUCIUS TO CUMMINGS (WORLD POETRY ANTHOLOGY)
DRAFTS AND FRAGMENTS OF CANTOS CX-CXVII
EZRA POUND AND MUSIC
GAUDIER-BRZESKA
GUIDE TO KULCHUR
LITERARY ESSAYS
LOVE POEMS OF ANCIENT EGYPT (TRANSLATED WITH NOEL STOCK)
PAVANNES AND DIVAGATIONS
PERSONAE
POUND/JOYCE: LETTERS & ESSAYS
SELECTED CANTOS
SELECTED LETTERS 1907–1941
SELECTED POEMS
SELECTED PROSE 1909–1965
THE SPIRIT OF ROMANCE
THRONES (CANTOS 96–109)
TRANSLATIONS
WOMEN OF TRACHIS (SOPHOKLES)

THE SELECTED LETTERS OF

EZRA POUND

1907-1941

EDITED BY D. D. PAIGE

A NEW DIRECTIONS PAPERBOOK

This book was originally published in 1950 as *The Letters of Ezra Pound,
1907-1941*, by Harcourt Brace Jovanovitch, Inc., to whom the author, editor
and publisher are grateful for unusual assistance in making this new edition
possible.

Manufactured in the United States of America
First published as New Directions Paperbook 317 in 1971
Published simultaneously in Canada by McClelland & Stewart, Ltd.

New Directions Books are published for James Laughlin
by New Directions Publishing Corporation,
333 Sixth Avenue, New York 10014

SECOND PRINTING

Preface

These are the letters of a serious and humorous man—we might almost say, so serious a man that he had to be humorous too. But it would be foolish to say that, partly because we know that seriousness does not always lead to laughter, and partly because in Pound's case the two things are impossible to separate. He was not the one thing and then the other; he was both things from the start, he had a genius in him that kept him playful in his grimmest hours, and merry when he was most wroth. To read these letters is certainly to be amused in the grand manner; but at the same moment it is to witness an anger that could last for thirty years, and it is to listen while important theories of art are being stated.

The art of poetry was the thing. Pound's anger, commencing in 1910 or thereabouts, rose out of his conviction that nobody thought there *was* such an art—no editor, no publisher, no critic, and even no poet. Hence for him the inanity of verse in that dim day. It was not as well written as prose, said Pound. It had to be overhauled. "Learn your art thoroughly," he wrote William Carlos Williams from London. He asked Harriet Monroe whether she understood what her responsibilities were as editor of a magazine of poetry: "Can you teach the American poet that poetry *is* an *art*, an art with a technique, with media, an art that must be in constant flux, a constant change of manner, if it is to live? Can you teach him that it is not a pentametric echo of the sociological dogma printed in last year's magazines? . . . I may be myopic, but during my last tortured visit to America I found no writer and but one reviewer who had any worthy conception of poetry, The Art. . . . Honestly, whom do you know . . . who takes the Art of poetry seriously? As seriously that is as a painter takes painting? Who Cares? Who cares whether or no a thing is really *well* done? Who in America believes in perfection and that nothing short of it is worth while? . . . What, what honestly, would you say to the workmanship of U.S. verse if you found it in a picture exhibit??????"

The "U.S. verse" was undoubtedly deliberate—absurd vocables, answering at once the question whether all that Pound had in mind was a new and better American poetry. He did have that in mind, of course, but there was a special meaning in his further question to Miss Monroe: "Are you for American poetry or for poetry? The latter is more important, but it is important that America should boost the former, provided it don't mean a blindness to the art. The glory of any nation is to produce art that can be exported without disgrace to its origin." If Pound was an expatriate, he was one who never forgot his own point of origin; but he was one who never deviated from his conviction that art has its universal province. "Being the best magazine in America," he wrote, "is *not* good enough. . . . There is this country [England]. . . . There is also an absolute standard." As for the poets of America, they struck him as rather too proud of being nothing but Americans. "You know perfectly well," he lectured Miss Monroe, "that American painting is recognizable because painters from the very beginning have kept in touch with Europe and dared to study abroad. Are you going to call people foreigners the minute they care enough about their art to travel in order to perfect it? Are the only American poets to be those who are too lazy to study or travel, or too cowardly to learn what perfection means?"

Perfection, and study in the interest of perfection—he never abandoned that program. The public might care nothing about it, and the universities might be so indifferent to it that teachers thought of little except the need to prevent students from learning more than they themselves had learned; but Pound would keep at it night and day. And night and day, for thirty years, he did. To some young poet who wrote him for criticism and advice—and innumerable young poets sought him out, in London, in Paris, in Italy—he replied not only with strictures upon weak lines but with lists of books to read. The young person didn't know enough; didn't know, for instance, the classics of poetry. Pound had his own notion of what the classics were. Virgil was not one of them; Sophocles was not; and the beginner in question had better stay away from the English poets. There were good English poets, but it had been a bad thing for people to suppose there were no others. There was always Homer; there was Dante; there was Heine; and here and there in ancient and medieval literature, tucked away from professors' eyes, there was many a master, little or big, whom it might make all the difference if one knew. The thing to do was to get busy and root around in the poetry of the whole world, East and West. "The one use of a man's knowing the classics," he wrote to Margaret Anderson, "is to prevent him from imitating the false classics. . . . The classics, 'ancient and modern,' are precisely the acids to gnaw through the thongs and bulls-hides with which we are tied by our schoolmasters. They are the antiseptics. They are almost the only antiseptics against the contagious imbecility of mankind. I can conceive an intelligence strong enough to exist without them, but I cannot recall having met an incarnation of such intelligence. . . . The strength of Picasso is largely in his having chewed through and chewed up a great mass of classicism."

Pound, in other words, was more serious than most living teachers of literature; and he was a lot more fun. He was certainly profane, and he was absolutely informal; but nobody could miss his meaning or fail to respect it. Anything so personally stated was bound to be true for the speaker, especially since he didn't spare the persons he liked best. "Epstein is a great sculptor," he wrote his mother. "I wish he would wash, but I believe Michel Angelo *never* did, so I suppose it is part of the tradition." "Bill Wms.," he once remarked to Margaret Anderson, "is *the* most bloody

inarticulate animal that ever gargled." As for the persons he despised—
"diseased dodderers," "literary hencoops"—well, they naturally caught the
heaviest of it. Not only persons, either; there were the American universities, and on at least one occasion there was "that sodden mass of half-
stewed oatmeal that passes for the Brit. mind."

His devotion to poetry was immense and unwearied. He himself might
groan under the burden of an ever-growing correspondence and an ever-
expanding battle area of criticism and propaganda, but his ideas could not
be dampened down. His humor was what saved his strength and kept him
going; hyperbole rewarmed him to his work, and epithet rejoiced him
even while he staggered. His war was for a "hardness" that had been lost
in poetry, an edge and sense and brevity such as classics have. The classics,
"ancient and modern." He didn't care which. He knew *The Waste Land*
was a classic before anyone else did; he knew Robert Frost was one; he
knew Joyce was, in prose. The art was all, whether living or dead men
practiced it. "Poetry must be *as well written as prose*. . . . No words
flying off to nothing. . . . Rhythm must have meaning. . . . There must
be no cliches, set phrases, stereotyped journalese. . . . Objectivity and
again objectivity, and expression . . . nothing that you couldn't, in some
circumstance, in the stress of some emotion, actually say. . . . I have
always wanted to write 'poetry' that a grown man could read without
groans of ennui, or without having it cooed into his ear by a flapper. . . .
Damn it all I want the author talking to the one most intelligent person he
knows, and *not* accepting any current form, form of story, form of anything. Hang it all, how the hell does one say what I'm trying to get at."

Sooner or later he did say it, and he was more than defending Imagism
or free verse. He was defending the art of poetry. Also, he was helping
good poets to prevail. If his correspondence contained nothing but the
letters to Eliot about *The Waste Land* it would be worth reading—it
would be, in fact, one of the fundamental documents in modern literature.
Concerning Eliot he had never had any doubt since he spent six months
persuading Harriet Monroe to print "The Love Song of J. Alfred Prufrock." His affection for the poetry and his fidelity to the man make one
of the finest stories we can read. In 1922 he was canvassing America and
Europe for contributions to a fund that would keep Eliot free from the
work and worry that had him "at the last gasp." There were others, too,
but Eliot should be first. "There is no organized or coordinated civilization left, only individual scattered survivors. . . . Only those of us who
know what civilization is, only those of us who want better literature,
not more literature, better art, not more art, can be expected to pay for
it. No use waiting for masses to develop a finer taste, they aren't moving
that way. . . . Darkness and confusion as in Middle Ages; no chance of
general order or justice; we can only release an individual here or there.
. . . It is for us who want good work to provide means of its being done.
We are the consumers and we demand something fit to consume. In the
arts quantity is nothing, quality everything." The project did not develop
beyond a point, but Pound, then as ever, was doing all that one man
could do to provide a situation for poetry where none seemed to exist.

A situation for poetry—the phrase, like the problem, is peculiar to our time. For Pound there was not merely the fact that most editors and publishers were "swine"; there was the more abysmal fact that a dense and maddening ignorance prevailed with respect to the rudiments of the art. Nobody cared whether poetry was good or not—as good as it could be, in however few men's work. Nobody read it with diligent attention and damned it when it was derelict. "A man can get more for doing rotten writing than he can for doing rotten chemistry." Promising poets lost their promise in the absence of criticism that would help them as surgery helps ailing men: lost their promise, and increased their output. "A man is valued by the abundance or the scarcity of his copy," De Gourmont had said; and Pound added: "The problem is how, how in hell to exist without over-production." He set a higher value upon scarcity than either scarcity or abundance in itself deserves; quantity is really as irrelevant as he insisted it was, though he sometimes lost sight of this; yet he was right in the main, at least just then; and he was fearfully right in the judgments he made upon most of his contemporaries. He never set up as a critic in the impressive way Eliot did. "Criticism shd. consume itself and disappear," he once told Laurence Binyon—that is, it should be content to lead others to where excellence might be found and leave them there with only some notes or an anthology in their hands. Pound was never quite sure that Eliot had done well to become even the most influential critic of his age. He didn't make literature sound "enjoyable"; he wasted time on "dull subjects," and sometimes he made the worse appear the better work. Pound in his own mind was first of all a poet; and last of all he was a poet still, with only the most practical sort of interest in helping his friends clean house so that all of them might live and work in peace and self-respect.

His criticism, such as it is, concentrates so much upon the problems of language that we can wonder how he read the *Poetics* of Aristotle, which he was always recommending. Aristotle treated of language but also of other things: of story, of idea, of character, of morals, of manners. Pound was not indifferent to these, but like most critics since Wordsworth and Coleridge he gave his chief attention to "the word," with the result that we do not learn from him how modern poetry might become wiser and deeper as well as harder and finer. For him the age was so sunk in barbarism that the first step out was the only step to try—make poetry readable once more, he seemed to suggest, and then we can decide what it shall say. If he was wrong in his initial assumption, it is a pity that the assumption limited him as it did; he *is* limited, whatever the reason, though within his limits he is valuable as intelligence and character make any man valuable. He was curiously without vanity, or jealousy, or the will to go on saying something merely because he had said it once. He had the liberality of a prince without the purse; he had resolution; and he had patience. "*Why* the hell I was born patient, gord alone knows. You mightn't think it, but when I lose patience something is *lost*. It ain't that thur waren't any." Also, of course, he had a temper. "I have never known anyone worth a damn who wasn't irascible," he said, and left us to under-

stand that it was but one part of his humanity. He was human somewhat
as Artemus Ward was, whose style he perpetuated. He was not cold
like Yeats, of whom he wrote to Iris Barry: "Only after five years of
acquaintance does he learn to distinguish one member of the race from
another member. He has not my Chaucerian busy-ness and curiosity concerning minute variants in human personality." "I should probably like
G.K.C. personally if I ever met him." But he made no haste to meet
Chesterton, disapproving as he did of the man's ideas and religion.

The Ezra Pound of these letters was a distinguished person, and the
letters themselves are distinguished—for their fun, their fanaticism, and
their underlying horse-sense. It was high time that they be published, if
only to restore an age now gone for good, and a dominant figure in it
who also is gone though he is not dead. He ran out of bounds in his
pursuit of a society where artists might live—that, as much as anything,
explains his assault upon the society that had asked him to starve—and for
most purposes he is permanently beyond reach. We need not argue the
rightness of his being so, or the wrongness, or the relevance, or the justice,
in order to estimate the quality of the work he did for poetry in his
prime. That is its own story, and these letters tell it perfectly. It is to be
hoped that readers exist whom nothing can prevent from listening to its
own faraway, fantastic, hotheaded, and quixotic words.

MARK VAN DOREN

Contents

II. *The Little Review*

PART TWO: PARIS (1921-1924)

PART THREE: RAPALLO (1925-1941)

Introduction

If Pound had any reputation as a letter-writer before 1915, and he probably had, it was a private reputation amongst his friends. When in that year Harriet Monroe printed a few of his letters in *Poetry* (Chicago) as hints to youthful talents, she made public another aspect of his genius. His correspondence immediately began to acquire, deviously and, as it were, subterraneously, an enviable reputation. It grew alike privately and publicly, fed in the former instance by the passing about of letters and in the latter by their scrappy publication in literary magazines, until it became for about five years nearly as well-established as his legitimate reputation.

But as Pound's interest in those magazines waned or became diverted and the editors no longer received letters to print in their back pages under "Correspondence," the public part of that fame came, in the years immediately following, almost to be forgotten. As for the private part· he lost interest in certain of the young with whom he had corresponded prior to 1920; and he moved to Paris. There the post-war young American or Briton sought him out in person rather than by letter. And the scope of his correspondence fell off thereby.

When T. S. Eliot wrote of him, in the January 1928 number of *The Dial*, "his epistolary style is masterly," the statement was almost a revelation to a later generation. A few years afterwards, Margaret Anderson, one of the editors of *The Little Review*, published her autobiography. She remarked that Pound's letters, flowing torrentially from London, bearing blasts and blesses as startling as those in *BLAST* and accompanying the manuscripts of Eliot, Lewis and Joyce, might themselves have filled an exciting number of the magazine. As earnest whereof she printed about a dozen of them. They bore out her statement and Eliot's as well. Such meagre evidences—to which one must add those letters which Miss Monroe printed in her autobiography—were about all that appeared in print.

But Pound's really firm and unshakable epistolary eminence came less from the printed letters, one suspects, than from the direct reading of the originals. After he settled in Rapallo, his private correspondence became, in fact, public in extent as it had always been in interest. By the Thirties it had taken on Napoleonic proportions and he began to keep a file of carbon copies of his letters—"otherwise I couldn't remember what I wrote to this or that bloke." And the list of correspondents was indeed various, for in addition to letters from old friends and contemporaries there came, for the most part unsought, letters from instructors of history, from diplomatic officials, from classical scholars, from politicians, from professors of economics—from those of them, that is, who wanted frank speaking along lines of unofficial thought.

Above all, letters arrived from "les jeunes"—as he never tired of calling them—from batch after batch of them. Fifteen and twenty years after those great days when he got himself, Eliot, Lewis and Joyce into the pages of a single magazine, each succeeding generation still considered him as one of them, with, perhaps, a slight edge of experience, and still sought him out. From as far off as Japan! The tone of his prose criticism, with its coruscations, its ellipses, its dogmatisms, its gay carnival air, its unwillingness to enjoy the safety gravity offers, its violence against entrenched stupidity and its championings of fresh writers—all that simply encouraged them to approach him. A tremendous lure!

A little magazine was to be started in Nebraska or London? It had to have Pound's coöperation, or at least his blessing. Forthwith a letter to Rapallo. One disagreed with the lists in *How to Read?* A letter to Rapallo. One had written a forty page poem which no editor wished to print? A letter to Rapallo. Under such circumstances, given certain tastes, desires and perceptions, it became difficult not to meet someone who corresponded with Pound. He wrote, one formed the impression, to anyone.

Consequently you would one day meet a young man who had received a letter from Pound or possibly had borrowed it from a friend of the recipient. He would show a largish, square-shaped envelope, addressed in blue ink with a sputtering pen and with a small blue stamp in the corner. You would extract the sheets, unfold them. At the top, framed in a heavy rectangle, the Gaudier sketch of Pound. And then, as highly individual as another person's hand might be, two or three pages of typewriting, with marginal interpolations in pen. The letter might begin: "Dear F/ Yrz/ to hand. Partly horse sense an' pawtly NUTS." And then continue with a distinction between the ownership of the means of production and the proper distribution of the fruits thereof, the whole being, perhaps, an exhortation to a leftist to consider the ideas of Douglas and Gesell as implements to Communism. Scattered through the letter might be scraps of literary advice: "IF you are nuvvelizing, READ H/J// Learn HOW to do it/ or one WAY of doing it// No excuse for iggorunce." Or: "Poetical prose??? Hell// The great writing in either p or p consists in getting the SUBJECT matter onto paper with the fewest possible folderols and antimacassars. When the matter isn't real, no amount of ornament will save it. The inner structure IS the poetry. And the prose-powtry stunt is merely soup/ lacking the rhythmic validity of verse. (By which I don't mean the cuckoo-clock of traditional British metric.) Great writer (Hardy) has forgotten he exists. Got his mind on what he is TELLING."

All of which was nothing like one's previous experience of letters. I do not mean in the abbreviations, the deliberate misspellings, the capitalizations and the use of slanted lines for much of his punctuation. One recollects that at the time they scarcely bothered one; one was too interested in what he was saying. Pound scattered such dicta with incredible profusion, in letter after letter, with no apparent exhaustion of idea or of "the glittering phrase" to contain it. The impression may be incorrect, yet one holds it firmly, that it would be difficult to find more than two dozen pages of Keats' or Shelley's or Swift's correspondence that would have an other than biographical interest. The same seems true of Byron's letters; but those, in their racy informality of style and their brusque changes of subject, bear some resemblance to Pound's. But that is as close as one can come to congeners. The simple fact remains that Pound's letters are unique.

He came, a sort of flaming Savonarola, into a literary world which, as Wyndham Lewis has pointed out, preferred brilliant amateurism to a professional concern for the arts. Pound saw the dangers to perfection inherent in such an attitude. To him art was not something one could practice a certain number of hours a day, with Saturdays and Sundays "off." Art was instead a kind of life, a life which kept one's "private life," in the most ordinary sense, to a minimum.

This attitude is clear throughout his letters. He very rarely writes gossip or sends news of himself. As one goes through thousands of pages of letters, one remains impressed instead by his sustained devotion—I was about to say to art—to humanity. He justly believed that humanity deserved the best—in art, in ethics, in an economic system that would insure the just distribution of goods. It was kept from the best by a few simians who maintained themselves in offices of power only because the really first-rate men had not concerned themselves with approaching those who controlled the offices. A naive attitude, perhaps, but we find it expressed again and again in his letters. In such spirit he wrote to Harriet Monroe on October 22nd, 1912: "I'm the kind of ass that believes in the public intelligence. I believe your 'big business man' would rather hear a specialist's opinion, even if it's wrong, than hear a rumour, a dilutation." I shall return later to this aspect of Pound's correspondence. For the moment, I wish to emphasize its impersonal quality. His letters do not concern themselves with "private life"—with what he scornfully calls "laundry lists"—but with the health of the arts. For that reason they have at times a messianic tone. Considering the stakes at hazard, one doesn't wonder!

He was not, of course, the only man who held art in such seriousness, but he was so constituted that he had not only abundant energies but a civic sense acute to a degree which possibly only Americans can understand. When Harriet Monroe wrote him late in 1931 that she planned to retire, visit her sister in Cheefoo and allow *Poetry* to die, he replied:

The intelligence of the nation more important than the comfort or life of any one individual or the bodily life of a whole generation.
It is difficult enough to give the god dam amoeba a nervous system.
Having done your bit to provide a scrap of rudimentary ganglia amid the wholly bestial suet and pig fat, you can stop; but I as a responsible intellect do not propose (and have no right) to allow that bit of nerve tissue (or battery wire) to be wrecked merely because you have a sister in Cheefoo or

because there are a few of your friends whom it would be pleasanter to feed
or spare than to shoot.

As he recognized, the health of the arts, of economic ideas, could not be
the concern of a single person. He had to form, in so far as the power was
vouchsafed him, an *avant garde:* in a military as well as in the literary
sense. He had to produce a generation that would battle for the arts with
the same vigour and tenacity with which he battled. The personal letter
was his means of contact, and his high aim determined its extent.

The editor, when naming off to Pound those from whom to solicit
letters for this edition, mentioned Jules Romains and got the following
reply: "Nothing there. It was not necessary to repeat to Romains. He was
active." And indeed, Pound's best letters are those to people from whom
he had to remove some sort of inertia, whether of simple physical action
or of ignorance, and not, as one might think, to old friends and colleagues
like Joyce, Eliot and Lewis. They had their own jobs to do and their own
ways of doing them. Discussion on these points was out of the question,
for they are what make those personalities interesting artists.

The bulk and interest of his letters to Harriet Monroe testify to no
physical inertia on her part. She was active enough. But he had to overcome in her an inertia of ignorance. It was sometimes difficult for her to
understand quite simple things. In a note to his article entitled "The Renaissance: I, The Palette" printed in the February 1915 number of *Poetry,*
Pound had written: "I have not in this paper set out to give a whole history of poetry. I have said, as it were, 'Such poets are pure red . . . pure
green.' Knowledge of them is of as much use to a poet as the finding of
good colour is to a painter." To this note Miss Monroe appended hers, in
which she declared that there was pure color in Poe's "Helen," in "Kubla
Khan," in "La Belle Dame Sans Merci" and concluded with: "But certain
Shakespearean songs and sonnets would be the basis of my palette." Pound
wrote her with some irritation: "Your note is bewrying. The whole point
of a 'palette' is that it has *various* pure colours. Shx. lyrics—maximum of
their own tone or colour—yes. But 'basis of palette' is a foolish expression."

Pound had to overcome as well her narrow conception of poetry. In
later years he wrote her frankly about her limitations: "(They) can be
pardoned *to you,* but not tolerated in themselves, or for themselves." Fortunately she possessed enormous good-will and courage. If, in the years
1912-1917, she at the beginning rebelled against printing H.D., Frost, and
Eliot, she could ultimately be convinced by those letters issuing first from
10 Church Walk and later from 5 Holland Place Chambers. Even if—as in
the case of Eliot—it took six months! Doubtless she printed the best of
what came to her hand independently of Pound's influence, but for years
the average measure of *that* verse can be taken from the following lines
chosen at random from a 1913 issue of *Poetry:*

> Stream, stream, stream
> Oh the willows by the stream;
> The poplars and the willows
> And the gravel all agleam!

But those lines measure not only *Poetry;* they measure as well the magazine verse of the time. And the established magazines did not, of course,
print Pound or Eliot or H.D. or Frost. That glory was Miss Monroe's.
It would be saying too much that Pound thrust greatness upon her; but
one wonders, had he not been there with that acute civic sense, with
those prodding letters—?

His correspondence with the young falls into the category of letters to
inactive persons. The young were learning; they stood at the verge of
action. Pound undertook, like an inspired pedagogue, to set them into
action fully armed with a knowledge of their personalities. He spent a
great deal of time and energy on them, even on those who showed little
talent, for they, too, might prove of use. "I don't lay as much stock," he
wrote Miss Monroe in 1931, "by teachin' the elder generation as by
teachin' the risin', and if one gang dies without learnin' there is always
the next. Keep on remindin' 'em that we ain't bolcheviks, but only the
terrifyin' voice of civilization, kulchuh, refinement, aesthetic perception."
And he did teach the rising generations. Those who produced, produced;
those who did not produce at least reminded others what that terrifyin'
voice was.

In his four decades of activity, he received many hundreds of pages of
manuscript from the young, together with appeals for criticism. A prospect of labors that might have staggered a professional instructor of composition! But Pound assumed such fatigues as though they were duties.
When he discerned any talent, he replied with page after page of detailed
suggestions. When he did not perceive any interest in the work he said so
with what must have been a stunning frankness, as in a letter of 1933: "I
don't think there is any chance for *any* yng. feller making a dent in the
pubk. or highly select consciousness by means of pomes writ in the style
of 1913/15. An thet's flat and no use my handlin you with gloves."

Although most of his criticism was highly specific, he recognized that
thereby a danger inhered in it: that of impressing his own tone and personality upon the manuscripts submitted to him. (In his criticisms of the
work even of elder men, whose personalities might be presumed to be
fixed, he refrained from too much verbal suggestion. When he felt it
necessary, as in his word by word examination of Binyon's translation of
the *Purgatorio*—here reduced to one-third its original length—, he would
produce something (say a pseudo-Chaucerian pair of lines) out of tone
with the rest of the manuscript, so that the writer would be stimulated
to a new solution independent of Pound's.) With his young "students"
(there seems to be no other word), he allayed the danger by giving them
reading lists that would serve to develop their own personalities and, at the
same time, answer certain problems of expression and thereby relieve the
pressure upon himself. In 1916 he put Iris Barry through a formidable
regimen. He was evidently pleased with the result, for the reading lists
and suggestions in that series of letters later became the basis of his *How
to Read*.

He considered that his function was to save the young time and error,
and his aim, as he put it, to turn proselytes into disciples. After the publi-

cation of *How to Read*, he referred his correspondents to that pamphlet.
If they had read it and had pursued, in so far as they were able, the recommended readings, he offered advice and put them in touch with others
of his correspondents, generally those of the same city or college. And
sometimes a young man so introduced would come weeping back in the
next letter that he did not agree with X or Y, whom he had met through
Pound. A letter like that could make him explode into:

If you are looking for people who agree with you!!! How the hell many
points of agreement do you suppose there were between Joyce, W. Lewis, Eliot
and yrs. truly in 1917; or between Gaudier and Lewis in 1913; or between me
and Yeats, etc.?

If you agree that there ought to be decent writing, something expressing the
man's ideas, not prune juice to suit the pub. taste or *your* taste, you will have
got as far as any "circle" or "world" ever has.

If another man has ideas of *any* kind (not borrowed clichés) that irritate
you enough to make you think or take out your own ideas and look at 'em,
that is all one can expect.

He constantly urged the young to form groups. It was very difficult. He
would seldom bring them to understand that "it requires more crit. faculty
to discover the hidden 10% positive, than to fuss about 90% obvious
imperfections," or that, above a certain level, differences—of taste, of viewpoint, of technique, of material, of belief—*ought* to exist. They generally
proved much less resilient than Miss Monroe. He once persuaded her to
allow Louis Zukofsky to edit a number of *Poetry*, the "Objectivist Number." After the act, somewhat appalled at the result, she wrote Pound
that the number did not seem to "record a triumph" for that group.
Pound agreed, but insisted that the point of the number was that the
mode of presentation was good editing: "The zoning of different states
of mind, so that one can see what they are, is good editing." And he continued: "*Get* some other damn group and see what it can do. What about
the neo-Elinor-Wylites? . . . Or the neo-hogbutcher-bigdriftites?"

Both the editorial and the propaedeutic advice of his letters formed a
part of his vast effort to create a milieu in which art could exist. Conscious,
as I have indicated, that it was not a job for a single person however great
his energies, he usually called into service existing institutions. For they
had, after all, an organization and contact with a part of the public. In
his great magazine ventures—*Poetry, The Egoist,* and *The Little Review*—
he employed already established facilities in order to provide space for
serious writers and to divert money to them. If, before 1917, *The Little
Review* did not print the best work available, it had shown at least an
attitude with which Pound could sympathize. He had simply to convince
the editors of the importance of printing Eliot or Lewis or Joyce or some
new poet who had sought him out in London or who had written from
some remote township in, say, Indiana.

But there was a job ancillary to that of providing a means of circulation
for contemporary writers, that of cleansing stables. He went at it with a
flaming American zeal, as John Brown had gone at slavery or Carrie
Nation at rum. Unlike them, he did not seek to destroy out of hand, for

his letters reveal that he thought well of nearly all organizations and institutions, from magazines through universities to governments—in their ideal forms. A bad magazine or university or government had merely departed from its ideal; perhaps because time had gone on and left it struggling for aims that were no longer valid, perhaps because it had been warped. The first of these did not bother him much. Such institutions, while they lent a faintly musty odor of decayed thought to the ambience, would die without his help. What moved him to decided action was the warped institution, which he assumed might function properly but for ignorance at the top, and consequently he bent his efforts to educating it.

This would seem to be an excess of optimism. But he partakes of that American trait. Consider, for example, one of his earliest attempts to reform an institution. In 1916 he wrote to Professor Felix Schelling of the University of Pennsylvania suggesting that the English faculty institute a "fellowship given for creative ability regardless of whether the man had any university degree whatsoever." He went on to name Carl Sandburg as a candidate for such a fellowship. Professor Schelling replied with what Pound regarded as the epitaph for the American university system: "The university is not here for the exceptional man." Pound apparently learned, for when in 1929 that university wrote asking him for money, he added the following postscript to an already negative answer: "All the U. of P. or your god damn college or any other god damn American college does or will do for a man of letters is to ask him to go away without breaking the silence." But five years later in reply to a letter from Professor Schelling he wrote: "You ain't so old but what you cd. wake up. And you are too respected and respectable for it to be any real risk. They can't fire you *now*. Why the hell don't you have a bit of real fun before you get tucked under?" A last act of repentance as the curtain falls!

Or consider, again, that he was not at all awed by the magnitude of an economic reform that he had undertaken. Letters went out to friends and acquaintances, senators and M.P.'s, with astonishing fluency. Here, perhaps, he may have lost a sense of proportion, but the matter was of desperate urgency. He saw Europe drifting towards a war that could have been avoided by a simple currency reform. Under such conditions, nothing that promised alleviation was too remote for him to try. In 1934 he wrote to Salvador de Madariaga, an old acquaintance of his from London days, asking him to introduce the theories of Douglas in the Cortes of the new Spanish republic. After all, why not? Serious things were at stake, and Spain *had* given evidence that she wanted economic justice for her people. The peak of his optimism is reached in a letter of September 25, 1935, to John Cournos. "Are you," he wrote, "in touch with any of these Rhooshun blokes you write about in *Criterion?* As there is no way of getting one grain of sense into Communists *out*side Russia, would there by any way of inducing any Rhoosian intelligentsia to consider Douglas and Gesell?"

Sanguine perhaps, but not comic. The well-being of millions of people depends upon mankind's adopting a system of economic justice. Pound's eagerness to approach every person or organization that gave any promise, however slight, of moving toward that ideal is the gauge of his seriousness.

He never sentimentalized over humanity; in fact, its obtuseness frequently irritated him. Nevertheless, what strikes one in nearly every letter he wrote is his sustained devotion to it.

The present book owes its being to that devotion. It is one effort more to communicate with an epoch.

If the editor has managed by the arrangement and selection of these letters to illuminate Pound's own work and to convey the history of the chief artistic developments of the past forty years, in so much as these touched Pound, he will have succeeded in his aim. There remains the portrait of the artist's personality. That emerges perforce; it is none of the editor's doing.

The letters have come from various sources: from the recipients themselves, from collectors and from libraries. The loss of many letters to political confiscations, bombings, and climatic conditions—those, for example to Aldington, Dulac, Hemingway and Rodker—suggests that this collection has not been made too soon. Such early letters as are lost may be presumed to be completely lost. Those of later years can often be supplied by carbon copies, to which Mr. Pound has generously given the editor access. These carbon copies have been used to fill in gaps left by the editor's inability to get in touch with correspondents or with executors or to spare time-claimed correspondents the fatigue of searching out the originals. In all cases he has sought the permission of correspondents or executors to use the carbons. When he has not received replies, he has nevertheless used the letters.

A Note on the Editing

Deletions. Deletions have been indicated by the following symbols: — — — — indicates that one to twenty-five words or thereabouts have been dropped; −/−/ indicates that more than fifty words have been dropped. The first of these symbols occurs frequently with proper names, and in such juxtaposition generally indicates that the person's address has been deleted. All other deletions have been made in order to avoid repetitions or to eliminate material of little general interest. In each letter the editor has aimed to keep deletions to a minimum and to present the whole letter.

Suppressions. Names have been suppressed according to the following scheme: (a) initial letter followed by periods, used when a harsh critical comment, untempered by favourable remarks in other letters, is made about a living artist; (b) final letter preceded by dots when the comment is not critical or when the name stands as a symbol of evil; (c) letters followed by a long dash when complete suppression is desirable.

Notes. The editor has tried to avoid an excess of footnotes and where possible has interpolated explanatory matter in the text between brackets.

Punctuation, Spelling and Emphases. As has been indicated by several quotations above, these are anything but normal, and they have put the editor in considerable dilemma, for to hold to the letter would have made the book intolerable to read, while to set all things aright would have missed some of Pound's epistolary savor. The editor has accordingly compromised. The slanted line is replaced by more normal marks of punctuation, but regularization has been avoided. Misspellings have been corrected. Plays on spelling have been thinned out (but not eliminated) only when they have come so thickly as to retard the reader. These changes are very few. Pound's emphases in his typed letters came more and more to be indicated by capitals instead of by underlinings—evidently to avoid the loss of time in going back and underlining a word. But even capitalized words are sometimes doubly and triply underlined in ink. The editor has indicated these capitalizations by italics when the words have not been re-emphasized, and by small capitals when they have been.

The general aim has been to present a volume that can be read consecutively with as little eye fatigue as possible. The editor alone is responsible for these prettyings up. In short, the excellencies of the book are Mr. Pound's and the faults the editor's.

Thanks are due to Mr. and Mrs. Pound and to the following individuals and institutions: Charles Abbott, Director, Lockwood Memorial Library, University of Buffalo; John Alden, Curator of Rare Books, University of Pennsylvania Library; Richard Aldington; Margaret Anderson; Mary Barnard; Agnes Bedford; Cecily Binyon; William Bird; Judith Bond, Curator, Harriet Monroe Collection, University of Chicago Library; Basil Bunting; Montgomery Butchart; Lena Caico; Sarah Perkins Cope; John Cournos; Hubert Creekmore; E. E. Cummings; John Drummond; Edmund Dulac; Ronald Duncan; T. S. Eliot; Arnold Gingrich; Douglas Goldring; W. W. Hatfield; Ernest Hemingway; Hilaire Hiler; Houghton Library, Harvard University; Sisley Huddleston; Glenn Hughes; Langston Hughes; Joseph Darling Ibbotson; Maria Jolas; Norah Joyce; Katue Kitasono; James Laughlin; A. W. Lawrence; Wyndham Lewis; H. L. Mencken; Fred R. Miller; Marianne Moore; F. V. Morley; Gerhart Münch; The New York Public Library; N. H. Pearson; Laurence Pollinger; John Rodker; Olga Rudge; Peter Russell; John Scheiwiller; Henry Swabey; René Taupin; Harriet Shaw Weaver; T. C. Wilson; Donald Wing; and the Yale University Library.

D. D. PAIGE

PART ONE

LONDON

1907-1920

1 9 0 7

1: To Felix E. Schelling

Wyncote, Pa, 16 January

My dear Dr. Schelling: I have already begun work on "Il Candelaio" which is eminently germane to my other romance work and in which I have considerable interest.

On the other hand, since the study of Martial there is nothing I approach with such nausea and disgust as Roman life (Das Privatleben). Of course if you consider the latter of more importance, I shall endeavor to make my hate do as good work as my interest.

1 9 0 8

2: To William Carlos Williams

London, 21 October

Dear Bill: Glad to hear from you at last.

Good Lord! of course you don't have to like the stuff I write. I hope the time will never come when I get so fanatical as to let a man's like or dislike for what I happen to "poetare" interfere with an old friendship or a new one.

Remember, of course, that some of the stuff is dramatic and in the character of the person named in the title.

The "Decadence," which is one of the poems I suppose in your index expurgatorius, is the expression of the decadent spirit as I conceive it. The Villonauds are likewise what I conceive after a good deal of study to be an expression akin to, if not of, the spirit breathed in Villon's own poeting. "Fifine" is the answer to the question quoted from Browning's own "Fifine at the Fair."

Will continue when I get back from an appointment.

And once more to the breech.

I am damn glad to get some sincere criticism anyhow. Now let me to the defence. It seems to me you might as well say that Shakespeare is dissolute in his plays because Falstaff is, or that the plays have a criminal tendency because there is murder done in them.

To me the short so-called dramatic lyric—at any rate the sort of thing I do—is the poetic part of a drama the rest of which (to me the prose part) is left to the reader's imagination or implied or set in a short note. I catch the character I happen to be interested in at the moment he interests me, usually a moment of song, self-analysis, or sudden understanding or revelation. And the rest of the play would bore me and presumably the reader. I paint my man as I *conceive* him. Et voilà tout!

Is a painter's art crooked because he paints hunch-backs?

I wish you'd spot the bitter, personal notes and send 'em over to me for inspection. Personally I think you get 'em by reading in the wrong tone of voice. However, you may be right. Hilda [Doolittle] seems about as pleased with the work as you are. Mosher is going to reprint. W. B. Yeats applies the adjective "charming," but they feel no kindly responsibility for the morals and future of the author.

As for preaching poetic anarchy or anything else: heaven forbid. I record symptoms as I see 'em. I advise no remedy. I don't even draw the disease usually. Temperature 102⅜, pulse 78, tongue coated, etc., eyes yellow, etc.

As for the "eyes of too ruthless public": damn their eyes. No art ever yet grew by looking into the eyes of the public, ruthless or otherwise. You can obliterate yourself and mirror God, Nature, or Humanity but if you try to mirror yourself in the eyes of the public, woe be unto your art. At least that's the phase of truth that presents itself to me.

I wonder whether, when you talk about poetic anarchy, you mean a life lawlessly poetic and poetically lawless mirrored in the verse; or whether you mean a lawlessness in the materia poetica and metrica. Sometimes I use rules of Spanish, Anglo-Saxon and Greek metric that are not common in the English of Milton's or Miss Austen's day. I doubt, however, if you are sufficiently au courant to know just what the poets and musicians *and* painters are doing with a good deal of convention that has masqueraded as law.

Au contraire, I am very sure that I have written a lot of stuff that would please you and a lot of my personal friends more than *A L[ume] S[pento]*. But, mon cher, would a collection of mild, pretty verses convince any publisher or critic that *I* happen to be a genius and deserve audience? I have written bushels of verse that could offend no one except a person as well-read as I am who knows that it has all been said just as prettily before. Why write what I can translate out of Renaissance Latin or crib from the sainted dead?

Here are a list of facts on which I and 9,000,000 other poets have spieled endlessly:

1. Spring is a pleasant season. The flowers, etc. etc. sprout, bloom etc. etc.
2. Young man's fancy. Lightly, heavily, gaily etc. etc.
3. Love, a delightsome tickling. Indefinable etc.
   A) By day, etc. etc. etc. B) By night, etc. etc. etc.
4. Trees, hills etc. are by a provident nature arranged diversely, in diverse places.
5. Winds, clouds, rains, etc. flop thru and over 'em.

6. Men love women. (More poetic in singular, but the verb retains the same form.)

(In Greece and Pagan countries men loved men, but the fact is no longer mentioned in polite society except in an expurgated sense.) I am not attracted by the Pagan custom but my own prejudices are not materia poetica. Besides I didn't get particularly lascivious in *A.L.S.* However, in the above 6 groups I think you find the bulk of the poetic matter of the ages. Wait—

7. Men fight battles, etc. etc.

8. Men go on voyages.

Beyond this, men think and feel certain things and see certain things not with the bodily vision. About this time I begin to get interested and the general too ruthlessly goes to sleep? To, however, quit this wrangle. If you mean to say that *A.L.S.* is a rather gloomy and disagreeable book, I agree with you. I thought that in Venice. Kept out of it one tremendously gloomy series of ten sonnets—à la Thompson of the *City of Dreadful Night*—which are poetically rather fine in spots. Wrote or attempted to write a bit of sunshine, some of which—too much for my critical sense—got printed. However, the bulk of the work (say 30 of the poems) is the most finished work I have yet done.

I don't know that you will like the *Quinzaine for this Yule* any better.

Again as to the unconstrained vagabondism. If anybody ever shuts *you* in Indiana for four months and you don't at least *write* some unconstrained something or other, I'd give up hope for your salvation. Again, if you ever get degraded, branded with infamy, etc., for feeding a person who needs food,[1] you will probably rise up and bless the present and sacred name of Madame Grundy for all her holy hypocrisy. I am not getting bitter. I have been more than blessed for my kindness and the few shekels cast on the water have come back ten fold and I have no fight with anybody.

I am amused. The smile is kindly but entirely undiluted with reverence.

To continue. I am doubly thankful for a friend who'll say what he thinks —after long enough consideration to know what he really thinks—and I hope I'm going to be blessed with your criticism for as long as may be.

I wish you'd get a bit closer. I mean make more explicit and detailed statements of what you don't like.

Bitter personal note??? "Grace Before Song"—certainly not.

---

[1] Pound spent the winter of 1907 at Wabash College, Crawfordsville, Indiana, where he taught French and Spanish. After having read late one night, he went into town through a blizzard to mail a letter. On the streets he found a girl from a stranded burlesque show, penniless and with nowhere to go. The centennial history of the college records that he fed her and took her to his rooms where she spent the night in his bed and he on the floor of his study. Early in the morning he left for an eight o'clock class. The Misses Hall, from whom he rented the rooms, went up after his departure for the usual cleaning. They were maiden ladies in a small mid-Western town and had let those rooms before only to an elderly professor. They telephoned the president of the college and several trustees; the affair thus made public, only one outcome was possible.

"La Fraisne"—the man is half- or whole mad. Pathos, certainly, but bitterness? I can't see it.

"Cino"—the thing is banal. He might be anyone. Besides he is catalogued in his epitaph.

"Audiart"—nonsense.

"Villonaud for Yule." "Gibbet"—personal???

"Mesmerism"—impossible.

"Fifine"—ditto.

"Anima Sola." "Senectutis"—utterly impossible.

"Famam Librosque"—self-criticism, but I don't see it as bitter.

"Eyes"—nonsense.

"Scrip. Ig."—ditto.

"Donzella Beata"—ditto.

"Vana." "Chasteus." "Decadence"—writ. in plural; even if not it is answered and contradicted on the opposite page.

"The Fistulae"—nonsense.

Where are they? I may be the blind one.

Now to save me writing. Ecclesiastes 2:24; Proverbs 30:19. This is the arrant vagabondism. The soul, from god, returns to him. But anyone who can trace that course or symbolize it by anything not wandering. . . .

Perhaps you like pictures painted in green and white and gold and I paint in black and crimson and purple?

However, speak out and don't become "powerless to write that you don't like." There is one thing sickly-sweet: to wit, the flattery of those that know nothing about the art and yet adore indiscriminately.

To your "ultimate attainments of poesy," what are they? I, of course, am only at the first quarter-post in a marathon. I have, of course, not attained them, but I wonder just where you think the tape is stretched for Mr. Hays, "vittore ufficiale," and Dorando Pietri, hero of Italy. (That was by the way delightful to get in Italy and to get here one of the men who arranged the events, one of the trainer sort who said Pietri would have never got there if he hadn't been helped.[1]) I wish, no fooling, that you would define your ultimate attainments of poesy. Of course we won't agree. That would be *too* uninteresting. I don't know that I can make much of a list.

1. To paint the thing as I see it.
2. Beauty.
3. Freedom from didacticism.
4. It is only good manners if you repeat a few other men to at least do it better or more briefly. Utter originality is of course out of the question. Besides the *Punch Bowl* covers that point.

Then again you must remember I don't try to write for the public. I can't. I haven't that kind of intelligence. "To such as love this same beauty that I love somewhat after mine own fashion."

Also I don't want to bore people. That is one most flagrant crime at this

[1] During the 1908 Olympic Games in England, Pietri collapsed two or three times in the last ten metres of the 5,000-metre race. As he arose in final effort and staggered toward the tape, an enthusiastic timekeeper rushed onto the track and supported Pietri for three metres, to break the tape. Pietri was disqualified.

stage of the world's condition. 19 pages of letter ought to prove that. I am hopeless. "Ma cosi son io." Your letter is worth a dozen notes of polite appreciation. Eccovi, an honest man. Diogenes put to shame.

Write now that the bars are down and tear it up. You may thereby help me to do something better. Flattery never will.

My days of utter privation are over for a space. — — — —

P.S. The last line page 3 of *A.L.S.*[1] ought to answer some of your letter.

1 9 0 9

3: To William Carlos Williams

London, 3 February

Deer Bill: May I quote "Steve" on the occasion of my own firing: "Gee!! wish I wuz fired!" Nothing like it to stir the blood and give a man a start in life. Hope you shine the improving hour with poesy.

Am by way of falling into the crowd that does things here.

London, deah old Lundon, is the place for poesy.

Mathews is publishing my *Personae* and giving me the same terms he gives Maurice Hewlett. As for your p'tit frère. I knew he'd hit the pike for Dagotalia. When does he come over? I shall make a special trip to Ave Roma immortalis to rehear the tale of "Meestair Robingsonnh."

If you have saved any pennies during your stay in Neuva York, you'd better come across and broaden your mind. American doctors are in great demand in Italy, especially during the touring season. Besides, you'd much prefer to scrap with an intelligent person like myself than with a board of directing idiots. — — — —

4: To William Carlos Williams

London, 21 May

I hope to God you have no feelings. If you have, burn this *before* reading. Dear Billy: Thanks for your Poems. What, if anything, do you want me to do by way of criticism?

?Is it a personal, private edtn. for your friends, or??

As proof that W.C.W. has poetic instincts the book is valuable. Au contraire, if you were in London and saw the stream of current poetry, I wonder how much of it you would have printed? Do you want me to criticise it as if [it] were my own work?

I have sinned in nearly every possible way, even the ways I most condemn. I have printed too much. I have been praised by the greatest living

[1] "For I know that the wailing and bitterness are a folly."

poet. I am, after eight years' hammering against impenetrable adamant, become suddenly somewhat of a success.

From where do you want me to show the sharpened "blade"? Is there anything I know about your book that you don't know?

Individual, original it is not. Great art it is not. Poetic it is, but there are innumerable poetic volumes poured out here in Gomorrah. There is no town like London to make one feel the vanity of all art except the highest. To make one disbelieve in all but the most careful and conservative presentation of one's stuff. I have sinned deeply against the doctrine I preach.

Your book would not attract even passing attention here. There are fine lines in it, but nowhere I think do you add anything to the poets you have used as models.

If I should publish a medical treatise explaining that arnica was good for bruises (or cuts or whatever it is) it would show that I had found out certain medical facts, but it would not be of great value to the science of medicine. You see I am getting under weigh.

If you'll read Yeats and Browning and Francis Thompson and Swinburne and Rossetti you'll learn something about the progress of Eng. poetry in the last century. And if you'll read Margaret Sackville, Rosamund Watson, Ernest Rhys, Jim G. Fairfax, you'll learn what the people of second rank can do, and what damn good work it is. You are out of touch. That's all.

Most great poetry is written in the first person (i.e. it has been for about 2000 years). The 3rd is sometimes usable and the 2nd nearly always wooden. (Millions of exceptions!) What's the use of this?

Read Aristotle's *Poetics*, Longinus' *On the Sublime*, De Quincey, Yeats' essays.

Lect. I. Learn your art thoroughly. If you'll study the people in that 1st lecture and then reread your stuff—you'll get a lot more ideas about it than you will from any external critique I can make of the verse you have sent me.

Vale et me ama!

P.S. And remember a man's real work is what *he is going to do*, not what is behind him. Avanti e coraggio!

I. *Poetry: A Magazine of Verse*

5: To Harriet Monroe

London, [*18*] *August*

Dear Madam: I *am* interested, and your scheme as far as I understand it seems not only sound, but the only possible method. There is no other magazine in America which is not an insult to the serious artist and to the dignity of his art.

But? Can you teach the American poet that poetry *is* an *art*, an art with a technique, with media, an art that must be in constant flux, a constant change of manner, if it is to live? Can you teach him that it is not a pentametric echo of the sociological dogma printed in last year's magazines? Maybe. Anyhow you have work before you.

I may be myopic, but during my last tortured visit to America I found no writer and but one reviewer who had any worthy conception of poetry, The Art. However I need not bore you with jeremiads.

At least you are not the usual "esthetic magazine," which is if anything worse than the popular; for the esthetic magazine expects the artist to do all the work, pays nothing and then undermines his credit by making his convictions appear ridiculous.

Quant à moi: If you conceive verse as a living medium, on a par with paint, marble and music, you may announce, if it's any good to you, that for the present such of my work as appears in America (barring my own books) will appear exclusively in your magazine. I think you might easily get all the serious artists to boycott the rest of the press entirely. I can't send you much at the moment, for my *Arnaut Daniel* has gone to the publisher, and the proofs of *Ripostes* are on my desk, and I've been working for three months on a prose book. Even the *Ripostes* is scarcely more than a notice that my translations and experiments have not entirely interrupted my compositions.

I sincerely hope, by the way, that you mean what you say in your letter —that it isn't the usual editorial suavity of which I've seen enough—for I am writing to you very freely and taking you at your word.

Are you for American poetry or for poetry? The latter is more important, but it is important that America should boost the former, provided it don't mean a blindness to the art. The glory of any nation is to produce art that can be exported without disgrace to its origin.

I ask because if you do want poetry from other sources than America I may be able to be of use. I don't think it's any of the artist's business to see whether or no he circulates, but I was nevertheless tempted, on the verge of starting a quarterly, and it's a great relief to know that your paper may manage what I had, without financial strength, been about to attempt rather forlornly.

I don't think we need go to the French extreme of having four prefaces to each poem and eight schools for every dozen of poets, but you must keep an eye on Paris. Anyhow I hope your ensign is not "more poetry"! but more interesting poetry, and *maestria!*

If I can be of any use in keeping you or the magazine in touch with whatever is most dynamic in artistic thought, either here or in Paris—as much of it comes to me, and I *do* see nearly everyone that matters—I shall be glad to do so.

I send you all that I have on my desk—an over-elaborate post-Browning "Imagiste" affair and a note on the Whistler exhibit. I count him our only great artist, and even this informal salute, drastic as it is, may not be out of place at the threshold of what I hope is an endeavor to carry into our American poetry the same sort of life and intensity which he infused into modern painting.

P.S. Any agonizing that tends to hurry what I believe in the end to be inevitable, our American Risorgimento, is dear to me. That awakening will make the Italian Renaissance look like a tempest in a teapot! The force we have, and the impulse, but the guiding sense, the discrimination in applying the force, we must wait and strive for.

6: To Harriet Monroe

London, [*24*] *September*

Dear Miss Monroe: — — — — I've just written to Yeats. It's rather hard to get anything out of him by mail and he won't be back in London until November. Still I've done what I can, and as it's the first favor or about the first that I've asked for three years, I may get something—"to set the tone."

Also I'll try to get some of the poems of the very great Bengali poet, Rabindranath Tagore. They are going to be *the* sensation of the winter. . . . W.B.Y. is doing the introduction to them. They are translated by the author into very beautiful English prose, with mastery of cadence.

I shall leave the "literati" to themselves—they already support themselves very comfortably—unless there is someone whose work you particularly want. . . . We must be taken seriously at *once*. We must be *the* voice not only for the U.S. but internationally. . . . I think we might print one French poem a month. *My idea of our policy is this: We support American poets—preferably the young ones who have a serious determination to produce master-work. We import only such work as is better than that produced at home. The best foreign stuff, the stuff well above mediocrity,*

or the experiments that seem serious, and seriously and sanely directed toward the broadening and development of The Art of Poetry.[1]
And "TO HELL WITH HARPER'S AND THE MAGAZINE TOUCH"!

7: To HARRIET MONROE

London, October

Dear Harriet Monroe: — — — — I've had luck again, and am sending you some *modern* stuff by an American, I say modern, for it is in the laconic speech of the Imagistes, even if the subject is classic. At least H.D. has lived with these things since childhood, and knew them before she had any book-knowledge of them.

This is the sort of American stuff that I can show here and in Paris without its being ridiculed. Objective—no slither; direct—no excessive use of adjectives, no metaphors that won't permit examination. It's straight talk, straight as the Greek! And it was only by persistence that I got to see it at all.

8: To HARRIET MONROE

London, 13 October

Dear Miss Monroe: I don't know that America is ready to be diverted by the ultra-modern, ultra-effete tenuity of Contemporania.[2] "The Dance" has little but its rhythm to recommend it.

"The Epilogue" refers to *The Spirit of Romance* to the experiments and paradigms of form and metre—quantities, alliteration, polyphonic rimes in *Canzoni* and *Ripostes*, and to the translations of *The Sonnets and Ballate of Guido Cavalcanti*, and *The Canzoni of Arnaut Daniel* (now in publisher's hands). It has been my hope that this work will help to break the surface of convention and that the raw matter, and analysis of primitive systems may be of use in building the new art of metrics and of words.

The "Yawp" is respected from Denmark to Bengal, but we can't stop with the "Yawp." We have no longer any excuse for not taking up the complete art.

You must use your own discretion about printing this batch of verses. At any rate, don't use them until you've used "H.D." and Aldington, s.v.p.

[1] The italics were added by Pound in 1937, when this and several other letters were printed in Harriet Monroe's autobiography.
[2] A series of his poems published in *Poetry* (Chicago), April 1913.

9: To Harriet Monroe

London, 22 October

Dear Harriet Monroe: — — — — I'm willing to stand alone. . . . I make three enemies in a line—"Noyes, Figgis, Abercrombie." . . . I raise up for Abercrombie passionate defenders (vid. R. Brooke in the next *Poetry Review*). Even Brooke can find little to say for Noyes, and nothing for Figgis.

Until someone is honest we get nothing clear. The good work is obscured, hidden in the bad. I go about this London hunting for the real. I find paper after paper, person after person, mildly affirming the opinion of someone who hasn't cared enough about the art to tell what he actually believes.

It's only when a few men who know, get together and *disagree* that any sort of criticism is born. . . . I can give you my honest opinion from the firing line, from "the inside." I'm the kind of ass that believes in the public intelligence. I believe your "big business men" would rather hear a specialist's opinion, even if it's wrong, than hear a rumor, a dilutation. My own belief is that the public is sick of lukewarm praise of the mediocre. . . .

It isn't as if I were set in a groove. I read any number of masters, and recognize any number of kinds of excellence. But I'm sick to loathing of people who don't care for the master-work, who set out as artists with no intention of producing it, who make no effort toward the best, who are content with publicity and the praise of reviewers. I think the worst betrayal you could make is to pretend for a moment that you are content with a parochial standard. You're subsidized, you don't have to placate the public at once. . . .

Masefield was acclaimed. Nobody dared to say one word the other way. The people who cared were puzzled. Here was something strange—one liked his plays, or his sea-ballads, or something. . . . One lady said, "It's glorified Sims." Several people liked "the end." *Et ego* suggested that he would probably be the Tennyson of this generation. One man said: "He will appeal to lots of people who don't like poetry but who like to think they like poetry." . . .

If one is going to print opinions that the public already agrees with, what is the use of printing 'em at all? Good art can't possibly be palatable all at once. . . .

Quiller-Couch wrote me a delightful old-world letter a week ago. He hoped I did not despise the great name Victorian, and he wanted to put me in the *Oxford Book of Victorian Verse*. This is no small honor—at least I should count it a recognition. Nevertheless he had hit on two poems which I had marked "to be omitted" from the next edition of my work, and I've probably mortally offended him by telling him so. At least I haven't heard from him again. This is what happens if you've got a plymouth-rock conscience landed on predilection for the arts. . . .

If a man write six good lines he is immortal—isn't that worth trying for?

Isn't it worth while having *one* critic left who won't say a thing is *good* until he is ready to stake his whole position on the decision? . . .

Twenty pages a month is O.K.—there's that much good stuff written. You don't want the Henry Van Dyke kind—I'll write personally to anyone you do want. — — — —

The French laugh, but it's not a corrosive or hostile laughter. In fact, good art thrives in an atmosphere of parody. Parody is, I suppose, the best criticism—it sifts the durable from the apparent. — — — —

I've got a right to be severe. For one man I strike there are ten to strike back at me. I stand exposed. It hits me in my dinner invitations, in my weekends, in reviews of my own work. Nevertheless it's a good fight.

10: To Harriet Monroe

London, December

Dear Miss Monroe: Yes, the "Related Things" is more to my fancy. I had no intention of trying to exclude you from your own magazine but you know as well as I do that you could have written the "Nogi" in four lines if you'd had time to do so.

I've sent the 30 dollars to Tagore.

For GORD's sake don't print anything of mine that you think will kill the Magazine, but so far as I personally am concerned the public can go to the devil. It is the function of the public to prevent the artist's expression by hook or by crook. Ancora e ancora. But be sure of this much that I won't quarrel with you over what you see fit to put in the scrap basket.

I am, however, sending you a series of things [1] herewith which ought to appear almost intact or not at all.

Given my head I'd stop any periodical in a week, only we are bound to run five years anyhow, we're in such a beautiful position to save the public's soul by punching its face that it seems a crime not to do so. — — — —

P.S. Yes, do chuck out "the last one"—whichever it may be [2]—it's probably very bad.

1 9 1 3

11: To Homer L. Pound

London, January

Dear Dad: — — — — A deal of dull mail this A.M. Wrote yesterday or day before, didn't I? At least I can't think of anything much that's new.

---

[1] The "series of things" were additions to the "Contemporania" poems.
[2] "The Epilogue," *vide supra*, p. 11.

Note from Tagore who has retired to Urbana, Ill., where, as he says, his friends "out of their kindness of heart" leave him pretty much alone.

There is a charming tale of the last Durbar anent R.T. One Bengali here in London was wailing to W.B.Y. "How can one speak of patriotism of Bengal, when our greatest poet has written this ode to the King?" And Yeats taxing one of Rabindranath's students elicited this response. "Ah! I will tell you about that poem. The national committee came to Mr. Tagore and asked him to write something for the reception. And as you know Mr. Tagore is very obliging. And all that afternoon he tried to write them a poem, and he *could* not. And that evening the poet as usual retired to his meditation. And in the morning he descended with a sheet of paper. He said 'Here is a poem I have written. It is addressed to the deity. But you may give it to the national committee. Perhaps it will content them.' "

The joke, which is worthy of Voltaire, is for private consumption only, as it might be construed politically if it were printed.

Well, I've got to get on to affari.

12: To Alice Corbin Henderson

London, March

Dear A.C.H.: I enclose some more Tagore for the May number. The one marked "10" has gone to *The Atlantic*, but if they haven't yet accepted it you can use it. It will save time for you to write them direct. Say that you are going to use it unless they reply "by return post that they are."

Have just discovered another Amur'kn [Robert Frost]. Vurry Amur'k'n, with, I think, the seeds of grace. Have reviewed an advance copy of his book, but have run it out too long. Will send it as soon as I've tried to condense it—also some of his stuff if it isn't all in the book.

13: To Harriet Monroe

London, March

Dear H.M.: Congratulations on March. While it contains nothing wildly interesting, it contains nothing, or rather no group of poems, which is wholly disgusting. I think the average "feel" of the number is as good as you've done.

My prose is bad, but on ne peut pas pontifier and have style simultaneously. I didn't set out for a literary composition or an oration. Still I wish I'd done it a bit better—not that I care about convincing fools. A formal treatise decently written would have taken forty pages anyhow.

I'm glad you're going to print "Bill," i.e. Wm. Carlos Williams.

McCoy needs licking worse than anyone else in March. The Davis person has a tendency toward seeing things, also howling need of training.

Noyes adapts "Bringing in the Sheaves" less amusingly than Lindsay did
"The Bloody Lamb," also Alfred still lolls on the Kipple.

Goethe is dead (in the physical sense).

"I am called liberty" does not make a fetching termination to a poem.

Neither is there any valuable denouement in ending, full close, maximum
impression desirable, etc., strong pull, "years" and "tears." Harmless rime,
but to use it as "ornament" on return to the "tonic" especially after he had
spent a little thought on his rimes earlier in the poem. No, Mr. Torrence,
vous n'êtes pas artiste. −/−/

Good god! isn't there one of them that can write natural speech without
copying clichés out of every Eighteenth Century poet still in the public
libraries? God knows I wallowed in archaisms in my vealish years, but
these imbeciles don't even take the trouble to get an archaism, which might
be silly and picturesque, but they get phrases out of just the stupidest and
worst-dressed periods.

> *Oft in the stilly night I dallied in the glade*
> *On the banks of the Schuylkill as often I strayed.*

The Davis person has caught up with 1890, like Kennerly, only she plys
the Celtic oar.

I think you are probably taking the best of what comes in, but I do now
and then have a twinge of curiosity about what is being cast out.

Honestly, besides yourself and Mrs. Henderson, whom do you know
who takes the Art of poetry seriously? As seriously that is as a painter
takes painting? Who Cares? Who cares whether or no a thing is really
well done? Who in America believes in perfection and that nothing short
of it is worth while? Who would rather quit once and for all than go on
turning out shams? Who will stand for a level of criticism even when it
throws out most of their own work?

I know there are a lovely lot who want to express their own personalities, I have never doubted it for an instant. Only they mostly won't take
the trouble to find out what is their own personality.

What, what honestly, would you say to the workmanship of U.S. verse
if you found it in a picture exhibit?????

I want to know, we've got to get acquainted somehow. I don't think I
underestimate the difficulty of your position.

I think so far as possible you and Mrs. Henderson should do all the prose
that is done at your end. Unless you find someone with special knowledge
on some special topic. The editorial staff ought by now to be assuming a
"tone," a more or less uniform tenor—with an occasional protest from without, if WITHOUT dares to dispute with us. − − − −

Oh well. Honestly, "They," the American brood, have ears like elephants
and no sense of the English language. And as for Amur'k'n, Geo. H. Lori-
mer and Geo. Ade speak it better than they do. To say nothing of the
G-lorious O. Henry deceased. And I think you are doing very well with
them.

Bynner is at least aware of life as apart from brochures. Yet he himself
is most aptly described in just that ultimate term "brochure." And his tone

of thought smacks of the pretty optimism of McClure and E. W. Wilcox. If America should bring forth a real pessimist—not a literary pessimist—I should almost believe.

14: To Harriet Monroe

London, March

Dear H.M.: Sorry I can't work this review [1] down to any smaller dimensions! However, it can't be helped. Yes it can. I've done the job better than I thought I could. And it's our second scoop, for I only found the man by accident and I think I've about the only copy of the book that has left the shop.

I'll have along some of his work, if the book hasn't used up all the best of it. Anyhow, we'll have some of him in a month or so.

I think we should print this notice at once as we ought to be first and some of the reviewers here are sure to make fuss enough to get quoted in N.Y.

The *Current Gossip* (God what a sheet!!!!) seems to have taken Tagore hook and all. *Current Opinion* (March number). However, it serves as illustration of what I said a while back. These fools don't KNOW anything and at the bottom of their wormy souls they know they don't and their name is legion and if once they learn that we do know and that we are "in" first, they'll come to us to get all their thinking done for them and in the end the greasy vulgus will be directed by us. And we will be able to do a deal more for poetry indirectly than we could with just our $5,000 per annum.

And for that reason we can and must be strict *and* INFALLIBLE and the more enemies we make, up to a certain number, the better, for there is nothing reviewers like better than calling each other liars. The thing is to herd the worst fools into the opposition at the start and then the rest can occupy their combative impulses in slaying them.

15: To Harriet Monroe

London, March

Dear H.M.: I hear that the *International* is going to start on Vildrac and Romains. If they haven't printed their stuff (mere translations and probably bad), I think it our sacred duty to forestall them by printing that D!!d rigamarole of C.V.'s at once.

Oh, oh, oh, this vulgar haste for journalistic priority, and from sanctified me!!! at that. However we've got to be IT, first in the hearts of our countrymen, etc.

[1] His review of Robert Frost's *A Boy's Will* in *Poetry* (Chicago), May 1913.

Frost seems to have put his best stuff into his book, but we'll have something from him as soon as he has done it, "advanced" or whatever you call
it. Lawrence has brought out a vol. He is clever; I don't know whether to
send in a review or not. We seem pretty well stuffed up with matter at
the moment. (D. H. Lawrence, whom I mentioned in my note on the
Georgian Anthology.) Detestable person but needs watching. I think he
learned the proper treatment of modern subjects before I did. That was in
some poems in *The Eng. Rev.;* can't tell whether he has progressed or
retrograded as I haven't seen the book yet. He may have published merely
on his prose rep.

P.S. Who the deuce is Elsa Barker? Says she has 5000 lines in her last
vol., which sounds suspicious. Otherwise, personally agreeable with a
Christian Science voice.

16: To Harriet Monroe

London, 30 March

Dear Miss Monroe: I'm deluded enough to think there is a rhythmic system in the d—— stuff, and I believe I was careful to type it as I wanted it
written, i.e., as to line ends and breaking *and capitals*. Certainly I want the
line you give, written just as it is.

> *Dawn enters with little feet*
> *   like a gilded Pavlova.*

In the "Metro" hokku, I was careful, I think, to indicate spaces between the
rhythmic units, and I want them observed.

Re the enclosed sheet from your letter.[1] It never occurred to me that
passage A. would shock anyone. If you want to take the responsibility for
replacing it with asterisks, go ahead.

Personally I think it would weaken it to say "Speak well of John Wanamaker who pays his shop-girls 5 dollars per week, and of others who do
the same." Child labour needs a villanelle all to itself.

Passage B. honi soit! Surely the second line might refer to the chastest
joys of paradise. Has our good nation read the Song of Songs? No, really,
I think this ought to stay. The tragedy as I see it is the tragedy of finer

---

[1] Miss Monroe had objected to the following passages:
  A. *Speak well of amateur harlots,*
     Speak well of disguised procurers,
     Speak well of shop-walkers,
     Speak well of employers of women.
                              (from "Reflection and Advice")
  B. *Go to those who have delicate lusts*
     Go to those whose delicate desires are thwarted.
                              (from "Commission")
  C. *O how hideous it is*
     To see three generations of one house gathered together.
                              (from "Commission")

desire drawn, merely by being desire at all, into the grasp of the grosser animalities. G—d! you can't emasculate literature utterly. You can't expect modern work to even look in the direction of Greek drama until we can again treat actual things in a simple and direct manner.

Morte di Christo! Read the prefaces to Shelley written just after his death, where the editor is trying to decide whether Shelley's work is of sufficient importance to make up for his terrible atheism!!!

As to passage C.: A poem is supposed to present the truth of passion, not the casuistical decision of a committee of philosophers. I expect some time to do a hymn in praise of "race" or "breed," but here I want to say exactly what I do say. We've had too much of this patriarchal sentimentality. Family affection is occasionally beautiful. Only people are much too much in the habit of taking it for granted that it is always so.

In my opinion B. and C. ought to stand. A. I don't care about. —/—/

The "Pact" and the "Epilogue" could go. I should certainly substitute the enclosed "Salutation" for the "Epilogue," and for the Whitman if there isn't room for both.

I can't remember quite what I've sent you and what I haven't, but I won't trouble you now with other alternative pieces.

I shall send you two or three pages of very short poems later, if you survive the April number. I'm aiming the new volume for about the Autumn.

Again to your note: "Risqué." Now really!!! Do you apply that term to all nude statuary? I admit the verse "To Another Man on his Wife" might deserve it, but you're not including that. Surely you don't regard the Elizabethans as "risqué"? It's a charming word but I don't feel that I've quite qualified.

As to getting out a number that will please me; I think it is a possible feat, tho' I'd probably have to choose the contents myself. When you do finally adopt my scale of criticism you will, yes, you actually will find a handful of very select readers who will be quite delighted, and the aegrum and tiercely accursed groveling vulgus will be too scared by the array of delightees to utter more than a very faint moan of protest.

I want the files of this periodical to be prized and vendible in 1999. Quixotic of me! and very impractical?

The good Hessler once assured the seminar that it might as well agree with me in the first place because it was bound to do so in the end out of sheer exhaustion. You may pay my respects to the U.S.A. at large and assure them that this truth is of even wider application. Or Veritas parevalebit as I should have said some centuries ago.

I do hope you'll print my instructions to neophytes [1] (sent to A.C.H.) soon. That will enable our contributors to solve some of their troubles at home.

Oh well, enough of this, if I'm to catch the swiftest boat.

[1] "A Few Don'ts by an Imagist," *Poetry* (Chicago), March 1913, *Vide* "A Stray Document," *Make It New.*

17: To Harriet Monroe

Sirmione, 22 April

Dear H.M.: God knows *I* didn't ask for the job of correcting Tagore. He asked me to. Also it will be very difficult for his defenders in London if he takes to printing anything except his best work. As a religious teacher he is superfluous. We've got Lao Tse. And his (Tagore's) philosophy hasn't much in it for a man who has "felt the pangs" or been pestered with Western civilization. I don't mean quite that, but he isn't either Villon or Leopardi, and the modern demands just a dash of their insight. So long as he sticks to poetry he can be defended on stylistic grounds against those who disagree with his content. And there's no use his repeating the Vedas and other stuff that has been translated. In his original Bengali he has the novelty of rime and rhythm and of expression, but in a prose translation it is just "more theosophy." Of course if he wants to set a lower level than that which I am trying to set in my translations from Kabir, I can't help it. It's his own affair.

Rec'd £28, with thanks, salaams etc.

Dell is very consoling. It's clever of him to detect the Latin tone.[1]

I don't doubt that the things Frost sent you were very bad. But he has done good things and whoever rejected 'em will go to hell along with *Harper's* and *The Atlantic*. After my declaration of his glory he'll have to stay out of print for a year in order not to "disappoint" the avid reader. Serieusement, I'll pick out whatever of his inedited stuff is fit to print—when I get back to London. —/—/

18: To Isabel W. Pound

Venice, May

Dear Mother: Your remarks on "low diet and sedentary life" are ludicrously inappropriate—if that's any comfort to you. As to the cup of joy I dare say I do as well as most in face of the spectacle of human imbecility.

As to practicality. I should think with the two specimens you hold up to me, you'd be about through with your moralization on that subject. Surely the elder generation (A.F. and T.C.P.) attended to this world's commerce with a certain assiduity, and camped not in the fields of the muses.

I don't suppose America has more fools per acre than other countries, still your programme of the Ethical Society presents no new argument for my return.

All Venice went to a rather interesting concert at "La Fenice" on

---

[1] The reference is to the epigrams in "Contemporania." Floyd Dell had written of them in the Chicago *Evening Post*, 11 April 1913.

Wednesday; and I also, thanks to Signora Brass, for the entrance is mostly by invitation.

I don't know whether you remember the very beautiful 18th century theatre, but it's a place where you might meet anyone from Goethe to Rossini.

I enclose what I believe to be a Donatello madonna and an interior which I don't think you saw. At least I wasn't with you if you did see it.

I can't be bothered to read a novel in 54 vols. Besides I know the man who translated *Jean Christophe*, and moreover it's a popular craze so I suppose something *must* be wrong with it.

Have you tried Butler? *Way of All Flesh* and his *Diary* (I think that's what they call it).

I shall go to Munich next week and thence to London.

P.S. The Doolittles are here, père et mère. Also Hilda and Richard.

19: To Harriet Monroe

London, May

Dear H.M.: I've been so fortunate as to get some prose from Hueffer. It is in a way excerpts from a longer essay and even so it is really too long, but he is willing to let us have it as it stands and count it as twelve (or ten, we ought to call it 12) pages.[1] I think we ought even to print a few pages extra rather than cut it much, as it will be a considerable boost to our prose dept.

Have just sent it to typist by special messenger. Hope it will come in time for Aug. as I'd rather have it there than with my lot of stuff in Sept. However that must be as it may. It can't go in later than Sept. as it is going into a book here. The thing will be all the prose in the number except the very brief notices. But it will be the best prose we've had or are likely to get.

Clear the decks for it, s.v.p. . . .

20: To Homer L. Pound

London, 3 June

Dear Dad: Thanks for your cheerful letter. If there is any joy in having found one's "maximum utility," I should think you might have it, with your asylum for the protection of the unfortunate. As for T.C., it is rather fine to see the old bird still holding out, still thinking he'll do something, and that he has some shreds of influence.

I'll try to get you a copy of Frost. I'm using mine at present to boom him and get his name stuck about. He has done a "Death of the Farm Hand"

---

[1] "Impressionism," *Poetry* (Chicago), September 1913.

since the book that is to my mind better than anything in it. I shall have that in the *Smart Set* or in *Poetry* before long.

Whitman is a hard nutt. The *Leaves of Grass* is the book. It is impossible to read it without swearing at the author almost continuously. Begin on the "Songs of Parting"—perhaps on the last one which is called "So Long!", that has I suppose nearly all of him in it.

We had a terribly literary dinner on Saturday. Tagore, his son and daughter-in-law, Hewlett, May Sinclair, Prothero (edt. *Quarterly Rev.*), Evelyn Underhill (author of divers fat books on mysticism), D. and myself.

Tagore and Hewlett in combination are mildly amusing. (I believe Hewlett's *Lore of Persephone* is good, but haven't yet seen it.)

Tagore lectured very finely last night. I enclose a note from Koli Mohon Ghose, who has been translating Kabir with me. The translation comes out in the Calcutta *Modern Rev.* this month.

Prothero is doing my article on troubadours in the *Quarterly,* as I think I wrote.

Am finishing the *Patria Mia,* book, for Seymour and doing a tale of Bertrans de Born.

Hope Aug. *Poetry* will have some stuff by a chap named Cannéll whom I rooted up in Paris, a Philadelphian.

W. R[ummel] is playing at Mrs. Fowler's Friday, before his pub. concert.

W. G. Lawrence down from Oxford yesterday. Good fellow, going out to India next winter.

Am playing tennis with Hueffer in the afternoons.

I'm promised that I shall meet De Gourmont and Anatole France, in-time, next time I go to Paris; that also pleases me.

"Ortus" means "birth" or "springing out" same root in "orient." "Strachey" is actually the edtr. of *The Spectator,* but I use him as the type of male prude, somewhere between Tony Comstock and Hen. Van Dyke. Even in America we've nothing that conveys his exact shade of meaning. I've adopted the classic Latin manner in mentioning people by name.

Love to you and mother. Salutations to the entourage. Cheer up ye' ain't dead yet. And as Tourgeneff says, most everything else is curable.

21: To Harriet Monroe

London, 13 August

Dear H.M.: Right-O. I am eased in my mind about the Hueffer matter. If, yes it's jolly well IF, the poets would send in that sort of stuff. F.M.H. happens to be a serious artist. The unspeakable vulgo will I suppose hear of him after our deaths. In the meantime they whore after their Bennetts and their Galsworthys and their unspeakable canaille. He and Yeats are the two men in London. And Yeats is already a sort of great dim figure with its associations set in the past. — — — —

I'm sending you our left wing, *The Freewoman*. I've taken charge of the literature dept. It will be convenient for things whereof one wants the Eng. copyright held. I pay a dmd. low rate, but it might be worth while as a supplement to some of your darlings. So far Johns and Kilmer are about the only ones I care to welcome.

Orage says he has written you giving grounds for declining to exchange. I can do nothing more. Am beginning a series of articles in *The New Age* next week, on "The Approach to Paris."

Will tell *The Freewoman* to exchange. They will.

Miss Lowell is back from Paris, and pleasingly intelligent.

Yours, after a morning of trying to write prose. Disjecta membra.

22: To Harriet Monroe

London, 13 August

Dear H.M.: Here is the Fletcher. I'd like to use the full sequence. I suppose that's hopeless to suggest.

Of course my *Lustra* lose by being chopped into sections and I suppose J.G.F. will have to suffer in like manner. Anyhow, do hack out ten or a dozen pages in some way that will establish the tone and in some way present the personality, the force behind this new and amazing state of affairs.

Am sending the review of him and the Frost poem shortly.

Of course one of Fletcher's strongest claims to attention is his ability to make a *book*, as opposed to the common or garden faculty of making a "Poem," and if you don't print a fairish big gob of him, you don't do him justice or stir up the reader's ire and attention.

23: To Harriet Monroe

London, 23 September

Dear H.M.: Lawrence, as you know, gives me no particular pleasure. Nevertheless we are lucky to get him. Hueffer, as you know, thinks highly of him. I *recognize* certain qualities of his work. If I were an editor I should probably accept his work without reading it. As a prose writer I grant him first place among the younger men.

I want you to use a bunch of Fletcher's things before you use Lawrence. In fact I send these things along only on the supposition that they won't delay Fletcher's appearance. I should be glad however, if you would choose what you want, at once, and return the rest. Lawrence ought to have five or six pages. Fletcher ditto or more.

Upward is a very interesting chap. He says, by the way, that the Chinese stuff is not a paraphrase, but that he made it up out of his head, using a certain amount of Chinese reminiscence. I think we should insert a note to that effect, as the one in the current number is misleading.

24: To Harriet Monroe

London [? *September*]

Dear Miss Monroe: Heaven knows this is the briefest and hastiest of summaries. And the facts—are old enough.

Yet you are dead right when you say that American knowledge of French stops with Hugo. And—dieu le sait—there are few enough people on this stupid little island who know anything beyond Verlaine and Beaudelaire—neither of whom is the least use, pedagogically, I mean. They beget imitation and one can learn nothing from them. Whereas Gautier and de Gourmont carry forward the art itself, and the only way one can imitate them is by making more profound your knowledge of the very marrow of art.

There's no use in a strong impulse if it is all or nearly all lost in bungling transmission and technique. This obnoxious word that I'm always brandishing about means nothing but a transmission of the impulse intact. It means that you not only get the thing off your own chest, but that you get it into some one else's. Yrs. ever pedagogically. — — — —

25: To Alice Corbin Henderson

London, October

Dear Mrs. Henderson: I wonder if Miss Monroe can get my memento into the "notes and announcements" section—right away. I know the *Mercure* is held as old-fashioned but Duhamel's notes would be very good for Sterling and various others if they could be got to read 'em. The sooner we get this intercommunication working, the better.

Postscript. varii:

Dear Mrs. Henderson: I don't see where we're to find space for that prose of Cournos', but it *is* his own and is at least direct treatment of life. And he is a good chap who has risked physical comfort for the good of his soul in leaving a steady job.

Frances Gregg has done a permissible poem. I've told her to send it direct with whatever else she thinks decent.

I wonder if *Poetry* really dares to devote a number to my *new* work. There'll be a *howl*. They won't like it. It's absolutely the *last* obsequies of the Victorian period. I won't permit any selection or editing. It stands now a series of 24 poems, most of them very short.

I'd rather they appeared after H.M. has published "The Garden" and whatever else of that little lot she cares to print, as a sort of preparation for the oncoming horror. There'll probably be 40 by the time I hear from you. It's not futurism and it's not post-impressionism, but it's work contemporary with those schools and to my mind the most significant that I have yet brought off.

BUTT they won't like it. They won't object as much as they did to Whitman's outrages, because the stamina of stupidity is weaker. I guarantee you *one* thing. The reader will not be *bored*. He will say ahg, ahg, ahh, ahhh, but-bu-bu-but this isn't Poetry.

Six years ago, there wasn't an editor in the U.S. who would print so staid and classic a work as "La Fraisne."

This series of poems is PREposterous. I refer you to the article "The Open Door" in the Nov. number.

I expect a number of people will regard the series as pure *blague*. Still, I give you your chance to be modern, to go blindfoldedly to be modern, to produce as many green bilious attacks throughout the length and breadth of the U.S.A. as there are fungoid members of the American academy. I announce the demise of R. U. Johnson and all his foetid generation.

26: To AMY LOWELL

London [*? November*]

Dear Miss Lowell: I'd like to use your "In a Garden" in a brief anthology *Des Imagistes* that I am cogitating—unless you've something that you think more appropriate.

As to the enclosed: J.G. apparently did go walking, but it don't seem to have taken him long.

Most of my intervening activities will be conveyed to you in print.

The gods attend you.

27: To HARRIET MONROE

London, 7 November

Dear H.M.: Re your letter of Oct. 13th etc. There is no earthly reason why *Poetry* shouldn't "*reach* England." "England" is dead as mutton. *If* Chicago (or the U.S.A. or whatever) will slough off its provincialism, if it will begin to be aware of Paris (or of any other centre save London), if it will feed on all fruit, and produce strength fostered on alert digestion— there's no reason for Chicago or *Poetry* or whatever not being the standard.

We've a better list of contributors than any English magazine of poetry (which ain't saying much—but still——).

There's a very decent notice of us in *La Vie des Lettres*.

Until "we" accept what I've been insisting on for a decade, i.e., a universal standard which pays no attention to time or country—a Weltlitteratur standard—there is no hope. And England hasn't yet accepted such a standard, so we've plenty of chance to do it first.

I'm trying to say as much in *The Quarterly Review*, but heaven knows if I'll succeed. (They've printed my "Troubadours.")

I'm asking Hueffer for more prose, you seemed to like it.

About the change of format. Unless you can go on being subsidized after the end of the 5 years, I think one must seriously consider it. I don't want a great wodge of prose, but about double what we have at present.

Again and again and again. The *gods* do not care about lines of political geography. If there are poets in the U.S.??? Anyhow, they oughtn't to be poisoned in infancy by being fed parochial standards.

Galdos, Flaubert, Tourgenev, see them all in a death struggle with provincial stupidity (or Jammes in "La Triomphe de la Vie"). All countries are equally damned, and all great art is born of the metropolis (or *in* the metropolis). The metropolis is that which accepts all gifts and all heights of excellence, usually the excellence that is *tabu* in its own village. The metropolis is always accused by the peasant of "being mad after foreign notions."

By the way *The Glebe* is to do our Imagiste anthology. There'll be various reprints from *Poetry*.

Re the rest: All I want is that the "American artist" presuming that he exist shall use not merely London, but Paris, London, Prague or wherever, as a pace-maker. And that he cease to call him champion for having done 100 yds. in 14 seconds merely because there's no one around to beat him (world's record being presumably $98\frac{5}{100}$).

28: To Isabel W. Pound

London, November

Dear Mother: I plan to spend my birthday largesse in the purchase of four luxurious undershirts. Or rather I had planned so to do; if, however, the bloody guardsman who borrowed my luxurious hat from the Cabaret cloak room (*not* by accident) does not return the same, I shall probably divert certain shekels from the yeager.

Upward's *Divine Mystery* is just out, Garden City Press, Letchworth. His *The New Word* has been out some time; the library may have the anonymous edtn.

My stay in Stone Cottage will not be in the least profitable. I detest the country. Yeats will amuse me part of the time and bore me to death with psychical research the rest. I regard the visit as a duty to posterity.

Current Opinion is an awful sheet. Merely the cheapest rehash of the cheapest journalistic opinion, *ma chè!* No periodical is ever much good. Am sending the *Quarterly* which is at least respectable. I hope you don't think I *read* the periodicals I appear in.

I am fully aware of *The New Age's* limitations. Still the editor is a good fellow—his literary taste — — — — is unfortunate. Most of the paper's bad manners, etc. . . . .

I seem to spend most of my time attending to other peoples' affairs, weaning young poetettes from obscurity into the glowing pages of divers rotten publications, etc. Besieging the Home Office to let that ass K—— stay in the country for his own good if not for its. Conducting a literary kindergarten for the aspiring, etc., etc.

Richard and Hilda were decently married last week, or the week before, as you have doubtless been notified. Brigit Patmore is very ill but they have decided to let her live, which is a mercy as there are none too many charming people on the planet.

Met Lady Low in Bond St. Friday, "returned from the jaws of death," just back.

The Old Spanish Masters show is the best loan exhibit I have yet seen. The post-Impressionist show is also interesting.

Epstein is a great sculptor. I wish he would wash, but I believe Michel Angelo *never* did, so I suppose it is part of the tradition. Also it is nearly impossible to appear clean in London; perhaps he does remove some of the grime.

Anyhow it is settled that you come over in the Spring. If dad can't come then, we'll try to arrange that for the year after. I shall come back here from Sussex (mail address will be here all the time, as I shall be up each Monday). You will come over in April; at least you will plan to be here for May and June. Once here you can hang out at Duchess St. quite as cheaply as you could at home.

I shall go to a Welsh lake later in the season instead of going to Garda in the Spring. Having been in the country thru' the winter I shall probably not need spring cleaning.

If I am to get anything done this day, I must be off and at it.

Love to you and dad.

29: To Amy Lowell

Coleman's Hatch, 26 November

Dear Miss Lowell: I agree with you that "binding" is better than "a-binding" and that "Harriet" is a bloody fool. Also I've resigned from *Poetry* in Hueffer's favour, but I believe he has resigned in mine and I don't yet know whether I'm shed of the bloomin' paper or not.

I'm deaved to death with multifarious affairs. I think Duhamel on schools was amusing but more needed in Paris than here, where yr. humbl. svt. is the only person with guts enough to turn a proselyte into a disciple.

W.B.Y. and I are very placid in the country.

Do send on yr. poemae. Perhaps I can pick some paragraphs out of the Duhamel when I get a breathing space. Will use some of the last batch, prose also—with a substitution of "paragraphs" for "pages." If there are translations you might mark what from. Or if your own you might say so. — — — —

30: To Harriet Monroe

Coleman's Hatch, 8 December

Dear H.M.: All right, but I do not see that there was anything for me to have done save resign at the time I did so. I don't think you have yet tried to see the magazine from my viewpoint.

I don't mind the award as it seems to be Yeats who makes it, or at least "suggests," and as you have my own contrary suggestion for the disposal of the money made before I knew Lindsay had been otherwise provided for.

For the rest, if I stay on the magazine it has got to improve. It's all very well for Yeats to be ceremonious in writing to you, a stranger, and in a semi-public letter. Nobody holds *him* responsible for the rot that goes into the paper.

I am willing to reconsider my resignation pending a general improvement of the magazine, and I will not have my name associated with it unless it does improve.

31: To William Carlos Williams

Coleman's Hatch, 19 December

Deer Bull: Thanks for your good letter. Almost you make me think for a moment that I might come to America. Dolce nido, etc. There are still a half dozen people there.

I suppose you've seen Demuth about *The Glebe*—if not take my introduction to Alfred Kreymborg — — — —. They ought to do yr. book. They're doing the anthology.

I am very placid and happy and busy. Dorothy is learning Chinese. I've all old Fenollosa's treasures in mss.

Have just bought two statuettes from *the* coming sculptor, Gaudier-Brzeska. I like him very much. He is the only person with whom I can really be "Altaforte." Cournos I like also. We are getting our little gang after five years of waiting. You must come over and get the air—if only for a week or so in the spring.

Richard is now running the *N[ew] F[reewoman]* which is now to appear as *The Egoist*. You must subscribe as the paper is poor, i.e. weak financially. The *Mercure de France* has taken to quoting us, however. It is the best way to keep in touch.

I wish Gwen could study with Brzeska.

Yeats is much finer *intime* than seen spasmodically in the midst of the whirl. We are both, I think, very contented in Sussex. He returned $200 of that award with orders that it be sent to me—and it has been. Hence the sculptural outburst and a new typewriter of great delicacy.

About your "La Flor": it is good. It is gracious also, but that is aside the point for the moment. Your vocabulary in it is right. Your syntax still strays occasionally from the simple order of natural speech.

I think I shall print "La Flor" in *The Egoist*.

I think "gracious" is the word I should apply to it also as a critic. It is dignified. It has the air of Urbino. I don't know about your coming over. I still think as always that in the end your work will hold. After all you have the rest of a lifetime. Thirty real pages are enough for any of us to leave. There is scarce more of Catullus or Villon.

You may get something slogging away by yourself that you would miss in The Vortex—and that we miss. It would be shorter perhaps if one of us would risk an Atlantic passage.

Of course Gwen ought to come over. I haven't heard from her for long, and from V. only a news paper cutting.

Damn! Why haven't I a respectable villa of great extent and many retainers?

Dondo has turned up again after years of exile. He is in Paris, has met De Gourmont. We printed a page of his stuff, verse, in *The N.F.* last week. I think he will do something.

If you haven't had that paper, send for back numbers since Aug. 15th.

Cournos has just come in. Shall mail this at once.   .

32: To Isabel W. Pound

Slowgh (more or less), 24 December

Dear Mother: Am down here for a week with the Hueffers in a dingy old cottage that belonged to Milton. F.M.H. and I being the two people who couldn't be in the least impressed by the fact, makes it a bit more ironical.

I can't remember much of what has been going on. Tea with your Mrs. Wards in the Temple on Sunday.

Yeats reading to me up till late Sat. evening, etc.

Richard gone to Italy.

Dined with Hewlett sometime or other last week.

Have written about 20 new poems.

3 days later:

Impossible to get any writing done here. Atmosphere too literary. 3 "Kreators" all in one ancient cottage *is* a bit thick.

Xmas passed without calamity.

Have sloshed about a bit in the slush as the weather is pleasingly warm. Walked to the Thames yesterday.

Play chess and discuss style with F.M.H.

Am not convinced that rural life suits me, at least in winter.

Love to you and dad. Greetings of the season to Aunt Frank.

1914

33: To Amy Lowell

Coleman's Hatch, 8 January

Dear Miss Lowell: No, of course I'm not outraged or enraged or en-wrothed—only there's no use my trying to keep up correspondences.

I expected your stuff to have appeared (Poems) in *The Egoist* on Jan 1st, but I have given up direct control and so now I find they won't be in until Feb. 1 or 15. They're all going in, I believe.

The cerebralist hasn't come off, so don't bother with it.

Yes, I resigned from *Poetry* in accumulated disgust, and they axed me back. And I consented to return "on condition of general improvement of the magazine"—which won't happen—so I shall be compelled to resign permanently sometime or other.

For instance C. Y. Rice in the Dec. number. Can? I? go on leaving my name on a paper so that it misleads some guileless Frenchman to believe that that is a "des meilleurs poètes anglais"?????

I think J.G.F.'s in same no. shows up very well.

The trouble with yr. prose was that the *Mercure* reserves "translation rights" and it couldn't have gone in without *fracas*.

I don't however believe that there's much use your sending in French clippings. The new staff is so much nearer Paris. And *ergo*. . . . However, I think we'd like a brief essay on "America the lost continent," "The Barren West," "The gt. occidental desert."

Until you come over again and make some sort of arrangement, I don't believe there's much use in your bothering.

Yeats sails on the 29th. I don't know his Boston date but I have impressed you on his mind from time to time. Do you want him "to dine" only, or "to stop"? —/—/

34: To Isabel W. Pound

Coleman's Hatch, January

Dear Mother: It is rather late in the day to go into the whole question of realism in art. I am profoundly pained to hear that your prefer Marie Corelli to Stendhal, but I can not help it.

As for Tagore, you may comfort yourself with the reflection that it was Tagore who poked my "Contemporania" down the Chicago gullet. Or at least read it aloud to that board of imbeciles on *Poetry* and told 'em how good the stuff was.

I do not wish to be mayor of Cincinnati nor of Dayton, Ohio. I do very well where I am. London may not be the Paradiso Terrestre, but it is at least some centuries nearer it than is St. Louis.

I believe Sussex agrees with me quite nicely.

35: To Harriet Monroe

London, 20 January

—/—/ *Postscript:* As for your recent number, I would protest against the substitution of "Bêl" for "Christ" in Mr. Aldington's "Lesbia."[1] Mr. Aldington is sufficiently devout but there is no need to pretend that everyone subscribes to a bastard faith devised for the purpose of making good Roman citizens, or slaves, and which is thoroughly different from that originally preached in Palestine. In this sense Christ is thoroughly dead. If one is trying to express the passing of the gods, in poetry that expression is distinctly weakened by the omission of the one god or demi-god who is still popularly accepted.

A hundred years ago the cast of the Venus de Medici at the Philadelphia Academy of Fine Arts was kept in a carefully closed cupboard and shown only to those "who especially desired to see it." There was one day per week reserved for ladies.

If Mr. Aldington believes more in Delphos than in Nazareth, I can see no reason for misrepresenting his creed. For centuries our verse has referred to "The False Mahound" and thereby done violence to the feelings of the countless faithful who alone maintain an uninterrupted prayer to their prophet.

Mr. Allen Upward, whom you have printed to your honour, was, as proconsul in Nigeria, always careful to explain to the natives that Christianity was NOT the universal religion of England and that there were many who looked upon it as a degrading superstition. I know that he performed at least one "miracle" by means of a gnostic gem, and reconverted at least one Mohammedan.

36: To Harriet Monroe

London, 31 January

Dear H.M.: Here is the Japanese play for April.[2] It will give us some reason for existing. I send it in place of my own stuff, as my name is in

---

[1] The lines originally read

> *And Picus of Mirandola is dead;*
> *And all the gods they dreamed and fabled of,*
> *Hermes and Thoth and Christ are rotten now,*
> *Rotten and dank.*

[2] *Nishikigi,* printed May 1914.

such opprobium we will not mention who did the extracting. Anyhow
Fenollosa's name is enough.

These plays are in Japanese, part in verse, part in prose. Also I have
written the stuff as prose where the feet are rather uniform. It will save
space and keep the thing from filling too much of the number.

There's a long article with another play to appear in *The Quarterly*. This
Nishikigi is too beautiful to be encumbered with notes and long explanation. Besides I think it is now quite lucid—my landlady and grocer both
say the story is clear *anyhow*. Fenollosa, as you probably know, is dead. I
happen to be acting as literary executor, but no one need know that yet
awhile.

I think you will agree with me that this Japanese find is about the best
bit of luck we've had since the starting of the magazine. I don't put the
work under the general category of translation either. It could scarcely
have come before now. The earlier attempts to do Japanese in English are
dull and ludicrous. That you needn't mention either as the poor scholars
have done their bungling best. One can not commend the results. The
best plan is to say nothing about it. This present stuff ranks as re-creation.
You'll find W.B.Y. also very keen on it.

37: To Amy Lowell

London, 2 February

Dear Miss Lowell: Yeats sailed Saturday, with your name and address
carefully glued into his address-book. — — — —

I suppose *The Egoist* will run another six months. I don't think an
American correspondent would save it; you can no more interest London
in the state of the American mind than you could interest Boston in the
culture of Dawson or Butte, Montana.

Your note would be O.K. in Boston, but here I don't think it more than
echoes the general opinion of every expatriate that any inhabitant has met.
You refer to things like Schauffler which no one has heard of. It could
well appear in *Poetry* where it would cause a little salutary irritation. Here
it would merely be lost. I think *The Egoist* might well use something
solider and more "reaching."

Yes, I thought Fletcher came up very well in *Poetry*.

Etc. Interruptions. . . .

May as well send this before it gets mislaid.

38: To Amy Lowell

London, 23 February

Dear Miss Lowell: It is too late to monkey with the Anthology.

Do you want to edit *The Egoist?* Present editrix writes me this A.M.

that she is willing to quit. (This is in confidence.) Of course there is a string to it. The paper made enough in the first six months to pay for the next three. It is assured up to June. That is, I think, fairly good when one considers what it usually takes to get a paper started. I think they have been timid. I think it would have paid better to pay an occasional "selling" contributor than to trust too much to voluntary work. With any sort of business management the thing ought to pay its expenses, or at least to cost so little that it would be worth the fun. A clever manager could make it a property (perhaps).

If the idea amuses you, you should make arrangements for American distribution before you come over.

At present the paper is printed at Southport. An editress and editorial secretary are paid, also useless office rent in London. Richard could perfectly well do all that for another ten dollars a month. I don't know how many subscriptions your name is good for in Boston. We've had posters well about, and the sales increase, very slowly, but still the thing is creeping on.

If you want that sort of lark you could at least have a run for your money.

If the damn thing took to buying contributions and possibly to selling in the U.S.A. at 5 cents a copy (doubtful????? about this) it might be made solid. Of course one would fire Carter and Ricketts and the sex problem.

If the thing were run seriously, I would, I think, get almost anyone to write for half-rate for a while at least. There would be a certain amount of creative work. And also a column of fortnightly information for the provincial reader, for it is useless to try to circulate a paper that implies that all its readers live in London and know everything that's on.

The Spectator and *New Age* etc. pretend to supply a "complete culture" to every reader. It is a bore to the office, but I think it essential to sales.

People who solidly subscribe to a paper year after year MUST feel that they don't need to subscribe to any other.

Anyhow. Thah it is.

39: TO AMY LOWELL

London, 11 March

Dear Miss Lowell: Thanks for clippings. I don't know anything more about "The Fountain." I handed over the bunch of mss. and told 'em to print the lot. I don't know at which stage the Fountain leaked; anyhow I haven't got it, and you are at liberty to use it. Also to reprint anything that has appeared in *The Egoist*.

Les Imagistes may get a theatre ("Little" or "Savoy") chucked at their heads, the proposed date is May 26, but it isn't yet settled. I'd like you to appear and read some Fort or Jammes.

July is too late. However the whole thing may be transferred or deferred till Autumn so I can't feel justified in urging you to change the date of your departure from Abyssinia.

Yeats WAS in Chicago, I dare say his mastery of rhythmic simultaneity isn't yet sufficiently complete to let him "Chi" and "Bost" on the same day.

40: To Amy Lowell

London, 18 March

Dear Miss Lowell: — — — — Re *The Egoist*. Of course you won't get it for nothing unless Miss Marsden can keep her corner or some corner to let loose in. She has her own clientele who look for her.

About the policy and mistakes, you realize that nothing is paid for (save the verse sometimes); Aldington and Miss Marsden and a couple of clerks get a guinea a week. If people are writing for nothing they only do so on condition that they write as they dammmm please. Also one can't afford time to write carefully.

I'm responsible for what I get into the paper but I am at present nearly, oh we might as well say quite, powerless to keep anything out. I don't think I'd come to Boston save for a salary or guarantees that would equal the present gross cost of the paper, or at least the "expenses."

On the other hand I don't give a hang where the thing is printed or who runs it. Of course a strong staff is important . . . essential. It won't come for being whistled for.

You can "run" a paper in Boston and have a staff here. To wit me and Hueffer and anybody you've a mind to pay for.—'Arriet, as you know, has that recommendation. Only she will try to pick out contributors for herself which is usually, from the point of view of internationality or English circulation, fatal. My flair is also at the service of anybody. That may be a drawback. At least I'm getting jolly tired of pushing other people's stuff.

I'll send your letter on to Miss Marsden anyhow.

I don't see why you shouldn't live half the year in London. After all it's the only sane place for any one to live if they've any pretense to letters.

Two days interruption——

Guess there wasn't much more than a signature to add.

I can't answer all of your questions as I don't own the paper. All I can say is that I think you could make it go and that I'll back you if you try it.

I think everything in your letter perfectly sound.

41: To Amy Lowell

London, 23 March

Dear Miss Lowell: *The Egoist* has just had £250 chucked as its head to do as it likes with, so I'm afraid there's no chance of your getting it in July to do as *you* like with. Still I dare say you'll find some way of amusing yourself when you arrive. I'm not sure a·quarterly wouldn't be cheaper and more effective, and you could edit that from Boston quite easily.

Also a quarterly staff is at hand in Hueffer, Joyce, Lawrence, Flint, and myself on this side and you and your crowd on the other. I should also develop some more intimate connection with Vienna and Florence. We could have whoever we liked for special articles or stories, but I think Lawrence and Joyce are the two strongest prose writers among les jeunes, and all the rest are about played out. And we could have anything Yeats happened to do. And we should, I think, print a reasonable amount of French, or else *reprint* a ten to twenty page selection from some French poet in each number. This would be cheaper than trying new stuff and we could get the man's whole work before us instead of depending on the scraps he happened to submit.

The French departments of the U.S. universities, or the Modern Language Association or the Alliance Française ought to back us up in such an endeavour to promote international understanding. The whole three of 'em ought to be tackled.

42: To Harriet Monroe

London, 28 March

Dear Miss Monroe: –/–/ No, the Fenollosa play can't wait. It won't do any harm to print it with the Yeats stuff in May. Every number ought to be at least as "sublimated" as such a number will be. If we can't stay that good we ought to quit.

The Hueffer can't possibly wait past June. Both he and V[iolet] H[unt] have done nothing but fuss and plague me about the delay supposedly till June ever since I got the thing from them, and "printing it in America is just like burying it" and he has turned down Monro of *Poetry and Drama* when said H.M. tried to buy the thing from him. That was out of friendship for me and because I had insisted on his waiting for English publication until after we had printed the poem.

It is excessively inconvenient not to get the play done in April.

I have just come back from Blunt's, he is giving us a batch of stuff for July. I dare say he will send back the cheque for it; he seldom or never accepts payment. And that will either help you out of deficits or give you another prize for Johns or someone who needs it.

The Blunt stuff, glory of the name etc. ought to build up our position with the older French reviews and "solidify" us in other quarters. Besides it is good of its kind. And Macmillan is soon to bring out a collected edition of him.

If I could be sure of even three or four good stiff numbers I might make some sort of stand for a restart here, or even an English "publication" of *Poetry*, but the thing flopped so before that there has been no use "talking it up." Of course, circulating a magazine takes energy and a lot of time, and for a person in my position it is purely impossible unless the magazine really "means" what I mean and keeps up the sort of pace I believe in.

Of course, until you do put out something "that will circulate in England," no author of any standing will give, or expect to give, you anything but American serial rights on a poem. However. I've chewed over that sufficiently.

About the dates I propose for printing, I dare say I seem arbitrary BUT I get stuff that no one else (save possibly Hueffer, and in many cases not even Hueffer) could possibly get you. I do this by use, or abuse as you like, of the privilege of personal friendship or acquaintance. If added to that there is to be constant worry about dates of publication etc. delays, etc. I simply can not go on with it, it is too wearing to a set of nerves that have received few favors from circumstance. These people can't be treated like novices sending uninvited contributions to *Harper's*.

Hang it all, the only way to sell a specialized magazine like *Poetry* is to pack it full FULL of good stuff. You sent up the sales with the number containing Yeats and myself a year or more ago. It ought to have kept on going up at a steady rate. It would do twice as much good to everybody concerned. Even the rotten poetasters that I object to having in at all might get as much for one page as they now do for two or three and they'd get corresponding advance in prestige. How can the bloomin provincial poet be expected to keep a pace unless we set it? If you'd only have some faint trace of confidence in the American poet's ability to hit the trail.

If "the public" once got convinced that you meant business . . . that you weren't waiting for laggards . . . and trying to run an ambulance corps for the incapable . . . aihi ai ai ai !!! bopp!!!

"Sublimated number" be hanged. I dare say I'm vague and etc. but what I've been wanting all along is some such standard as that Yeats-Fenollosa number would be. Print it and don't fall below it. Don't accept till things hit at least that level, don't promise, leave the files open till the very going to press on the chance that a really good thing may come in. Then if nothing does come in use up some of your dead wood.

Precedent: that rotten *Poetry and Drama*, established itself solely by Flint's French number which everybody had to get; it was the first large article on contemporary stuff. — — —

P.S. Hang it all, I wrote something to you or to somebody month and months ago about that damn *Glebe* thing.

Of course if you think any of the people I've sent in have the faintest notion that you think the stuff is your "absolute property" you are wholly mistaken. A clever author like Newbolt or Masefield only gives his publishers "leave to print."

No, the *Glebe* does not get the stuff for nothing. They pay a royalty on sales the same as any other publisher would. I did not and do not regard 'em as a periodical. The book is issued as a monthly series, but it is issued bound at the same time as what I suppose to be a separate book. I have mucked in the filthy matter for the sake of a few young writers who need money and that oblique means to it, reputation. If the unpunchable God had any respect for my finer feelings . . .

Anyhow, I've begged the Hueffer and given my own stuff for lower payment than I should have otherwise received for it, and paid one man an advance for his poem. Why in hell do I bother? . . .

September is *impossible* for Hueffer, he has already refused another fine offer.

For God's sake if you've got a lot of second-rate stuff on hand and accepted, for god's sake get some one to *pay* the authors and then return the stuff to them. It would be better to take the money out of *Poetry's* own fund and recoup on sales or go smash if necessary. Anything better than water down the quality with stuff that "looks pale beside." . . .

43: To Harriet Monroe

London, April

Dear H.M.: The author of the enclosed, H—— P——, his wife and infant are I believe starving or thereabouts. I have helped him and I suppose I should do so still, but I'm "strapped." He tried to start a magazine here on another man's promises and he has got into such a mess that I don't think anyone else here will do anything for him.

The poor devil had been keeping his poems for his own magazine or I suppose I should have had them to go over before.

Can you send him a cheque for the poem at once and print it when you have relieved the present congestion?

Or does some supporter want to take him on: he has something in him, enough at least to make him worth keeping on the planet a few months longer.

The last I had of him was to send him a telegraph order to buy food, then he disappeared, ashamed to ask for more, and I heard nothing until his wife found my address among his papers and wrote from Leicester (he had been in London).

44: To Amy Lowell

Coleman's Hatch, 30 April

Dear Miss Lowell: — — — — By all means "Astigmatize" me, très honoré.

Joyce is the author of that *Portrait of the Artist as a Young Man* now in *The Egoist*, and he is also in the Imagiste book.

We can consider what French stuff is worth using when you come over, and jaw about possibilities.

Fletcher looking "real hearty" to my amazement the last time I saw him.

I am on my head with Fenollosa notes and the expectable disturbances of such a season. —/—/

45: To Harriet Monroe

London, 23 May

Dear H.M.: —/—/ Cut out any of my poems that would be likely to get you suppressed but don't make it into a flabby little Sunday School lot like the bunch in the November number. Now WHO could blush at "Lesbia Illa"?????????? WHO???

Anyway I haven't any new things that will mix with the lot I've sent in. You can leave out the footnote to "[A Study in] Aesthetics."

The Hueffer good? Rather! It is the most important poem in the modern manner. The most important single poem that is.

As for my only liking importations, that's sheer nonsense. Fletcher, Frost, Williams, H.D., Cannéll and yrs. v.t. are all American. You know perfectly well that American painting is recognizable because painters from the very beginning have kept in touch with Europe and dared to study abroad. Are you going to call people foreigners the minute they care enough about their art to travel in order to perfect it? Are the only American poets to be those who are too lazy to study or travel, or too cowardly to learn what perfection means? —/—/

Blunt hasn't sent in his stuff, and I won't stir him up, if you don't much want him. I don't care about giving people the sort of stuff that they want, or using stuff in the old manner. If he remembers on his own account he will have to go in in my place.

Rodker ought to go in fairly soon, not later than Sept.

As for importations. You know what a man's painting is like when he has never been out of, say Indiana, and has never seen a good gallery.

And what is there improper in "The Father"?

Am I expected to confine myself to a Belasco drawingroom? Is modern life, or life of any period, confined to polite and decorous actions or to the bold deeds of stevedores or the discovery of the Nile and Orinoco by Teethidorus Dentatus Roosenstein? Are we to satirize only the politer and Biblical sins? Is art to have no bearing on life whatever? Is it to deal only with situations recognized and sanctioned by Cowper? Can one presuppose a public which has read at least some of the classics? God damn it until America has courage enough to read Voltaire it won't be fit for pigs let alone humans. —/—/

46: To Amy Lowell

London, [?13] July

Dear Miss Lowell: *BLAST* dinner on the 15th as I phoned this P.M.

Upward in yesterday. Will be glad to come to *your* dinner.

Richard will come to call on you Friday and help you make what preparations and invitations you want. (H.D. will come too, but don't mention it as she is in retreat from all social appearances, feigning indisposition. This information is private.) If Friday P.M. don't suit you, will you write and name some other day? He is at no. 8 in this building.

47: To Amy Lowell

London, 1 August

Dear Miss Lowell: It is true that I might give my sanction, or whatever one wants to call it, to having you and Richard and "H.D." bring out an "Imagiste" anthology, provided it were clearly stated at the front of the book that "E.P. etc. dissociated himself, wished success, did not mind use of title so long as it was made clear that he was not responsible for contents or views of the contributors." BUT, on the other hand that would deprive me of my machinery for gathering stray good poems and presenting them to the public in more or less permanent form and of discovering new talent—of which the already discovered will be constantly jealous and contemptuous (especially R.A.), will fuss etc.—or poems which could not be presented to the public in other ways, poems that would be lost in magazines. As for example "H.D.'s" would have been, for some years at least.

The present machinery was largely or wholly my making. I ordered "the public" (i.e. a few hundred people and a few reviewers) to take note of certain poems.

You offer to find a publisher, that is, a better publisher, if I abrogate my privileges, if I give way to, or saddle myself with, a dam'd contentious, probably incompetent committee. If I tacitly, tacitly to say the least of it, accept a certain number of people as my critical and creative equals, and publish the acceptance.

I don't see the use. Moreover, I should like the name "Imagisme" to retain some sort of a meaning. It stands, or I should like it to stand for hard light, clear edges. I can not trust any democratized committee to maintain that standard. Some will be splay-footed and some sentimental.

Neither will I waste time to argue with a committee. I have little enough time for my own work as it is. And all things converge to leave me all too little for the part I should like to give to actual creation, rather than to criticism, journalism etc.

If anyone wants a faction, or if anyone wants to form a separate group, I think it can be done amicably, but I should think it wiser to split over an aesthetic principle. In which case the new group would find its name automatically, almost. The aesthetic issue would of itself give names to the two parties.

Your proposition was not that you would find a publisher and that you would prefer the stuff to be selected by a committee or by each contributor, but that such an anthology would be published and that I could come in or go hang. At least that was my impression which may have been inexact. We may both have rushed at unnecessary conclusions.

48: To Amy Lowell

London, 12 August

Dear Miss Lowell: I think your idea most excellent, only I think your annual anthology should be called *Vers Libre* or something of that sort. Obviously it will consist in great part of the work of people who have not taken the trouble to find out what I mean by "Imagisme." I should, as I have said, like to keep the term associated with a certain clarity and intensity.

A number of your contributors object to being labeled. Vers libre seems to be their one common bond. Also if you use such a title (or anything similar) there need be no bothersome explanation of my absence.

I think the annual will be very good for all concerned. I trust I shall not as you say "take any one with me"; I have no desire to prevent anyone else's participation in the project. Also I will refrain from publishing another anthology in America before 1916 if you think it likely to clash in any way with yours. This offer is a little inconvenient as I had written to that side of the water before you spoke to me of Macmillan. However I recognize that the Aldingtons prefer Macmillan and I don't want them to incur any uncertainty about having their poems published together in 1915.

If you want to drag in the word Imagisme you can use a subtitle "an anthology devoted to Imagisme, vers libre and modern movements in verse" or something of that sort. I think that will be perfectly fair to everyone.

49: To Douglas Goldring

London, 18 September

Dear Goldring: Those people in Chicago have at last printed two of your poems. I suppose you'll get paid in a day or so.

I like your "Loredan" now I see it in print. Though the interjected "Alice" rhyming with palace, and the last line of "Hill House" still stick in my craw.

If you think it worth while to subject some more things to my captious and atrabilious eye, I should be glad to see another lot of your stuff. I have no means of guaranteeing that *Poetry* will print anything under six month's time, but I will try to hurry them as much as possible.

P.S. I should like to make up 5 or 6 pages of your stuff, but we have so many points of disagreement that I'll need a large lot to select from if I am to do so.

50: To Harriet Monroe

London, 30 September

Dear H.M.: 1. Received with thanks, £18/10, receipt enclosed.

2. Enclosed also the first fruits of sin with Masefield. I have answered to the effect that if they will delay publication until Nov. 1st I will do what I can for them but the bloody *Philip the King* is a play not a poem *and* it is 54 pages long. I send you copy herewith under separate cover. You can arrange as you like with Reynolds. – – – – If they delay, and if it is impossible to print the whole play, which has *no* division into acts, there is one alternative, i.e. that of printing the Messenger's speech and part of an endless dialogue between Philip and the Infanta. It would be perhaps simpler to wait until J.M. has something else for us.

So far as the public is concerned it would be better to print the whole play or nothing. If Heinemann does not delay publication, Reynolds would probably sell you the play for a few pounds, butt. . . . You could print the play, and have nothing else in the number, either prose or verse.

3. I was jolly well right about Eliot. He has sent in the best poem I have yet had or seen from an American. Pray god it be not a single and unique success. He has taken it back to get it ready for the press and you shall have it in a few days.

He is the only American I know of who has made what I can call adequate preparation for writing. He has actually trained himself *and* modernized himself *on his own.* The rest of the *promising young* have done one or the other but never both (most of the swine have done neither). It is such a comfort to meet a man and not have to tell him to wash his face, wipe his feet, and remember the date (1914) on the calendar.

51: To Amy Lowell
[postcard]

London, 2 October

Congratulations.
Why not include Thomas Hardy? [1]

52: To H. L. Mencken

London, 3 October

Dear Mr. Mencken: So far I only find novels. All more than 30,000 words. I enclose a poem by the last intelligent man I've found—a young

[1] See Letter No. 56.

American, T. S. Eliot (you can write to him direct, Merton College, Oxford). I think him worth watching—mind "not primitive."
His "[Portrait of a] Lady" is very nicely drawn.

53: To Harriet Monroe

London, October

Dear H.M.: Here is the Eliot poem.[1] The most interesting contribution I've had from an American.
P.S. Hope you'll get it *in* soon.

54: To Harriet Shaw Weaver

London, 12 October

Dear Miss Weaver: Here is some copy for which I take no responsibility. Rodker has some reason or other for wanting his essay printed as soon as possible. He always has. Miss Heyman's article might precede Rodker's. Please do not put it next to mine.

I shall have a rather longish article, that is about a page to a page and a half, announcing the College of Arts.[2] I may be a bit late with it, but I particularly want it in. Said affair may be of a good deal of use to *The Egoist*: it can't be of immediate use.

[1] "The Love Song of J. Alfred Prufrock," not printed until June 1915.
[2] This article became the basis of the following prospectus:
"It has been noted by certain authors that London is the capital of the world, and 'Art is a matter of capitals.' At present many American students who would have sought Vienna or Prague or some continental city are disturbed by war. To these The College of Arts offers a temporary refuge and a permanent centre.
"We draw the attention of new students to the fact that no course of study is complete without one or more years in London. Scholarly research is often but wasted time if it has not been first arranged and oriented in the British Museum.
"The London collections are if not unrivalled at least unsurpassed. The Louvre has the Venus and the Victory but the general collection of sculpture in the Museum here is, as a whole, the finer collection. The National Gallery is smaller than the Louvre but it contains no rubbish.
"Without chauvinism we can very easily claim that study in London is at least as advantageous as study elsewhere, and that a year's study in London by no means prevents earlier or later study in other capitals.
"The American student coming abroad is usually presented with two systems of study, firstly, that of 'institutions' for the most part academic, sterile, professorial; secondly, instruction by private teachers often most excellent, often the reverse.
"The College of Arts offers contact with artists of established position, creative minds, men for the most part who have already suffered in the cause of their art.
"Recognizing the interaction of the arts, the inter-stimulus, and inter-enlightenment, we have gathered the arts together, we recommend that each student shall undertake some second or auxiliary subject, though this is in all cases left to his own inclination. We recognize that certain genius runs deep and often in one groove only, and that some minds move in the language of one medium only. But this does not hold true

For the rest I think *The Egoist* can very well "suspend publication during duration of war." That is better than shutting up shop altogether. From a practical point of view it is hopeless to try to *increase* the sales of *The Egoist* during war time. The staff might be put on half pay if any one wants to do it, but . . . the finishing up of things has not come suddenly. Everyone has known that December would see at least "a suspension" unless the unexpected occurred. If we "suspend during duration of war" there will be reasonable colour to any efforts one might make, after wartime,

---

for the general student. For him and for many of the masters one art is the constant illuminator of another, a constant refreshment.

"The college prepares two sorts of instruction; one for those who intend a career in some single art, who desire practical and technical instruction, a second for those who believe that learning is an adornment, a gracious and useless pleasure, that is to say for serious art students and for the better sort of dilettanti.

"The cost of instruction will vary from £20 to £100, depending on how much the student wishes to do himself and how much he wishes to have done for him. We recognize that the great majority of students now coming to Europe are musical students, the next most numerous class are painters and sculptors; we nevertheless, believe that there are various other studies which would be pursued if student knew where to go for instruction.

"We try not to duplicate courses given in formal institutions like the University of London, or purely utilitarian courses like those of Berlitz. London is itself a larger university, and the best specialists are perhaps only approachable in chance conversation. We aim at an intellectual status no lower than that attained by the courts of the Italian Renaissance.

"Our organization is not unlike that of a University graduate school, and is intended to supplement the graduate instruction in 'arts.' This instruction is offered to anyone who wants it, not merely to those holding philological degrees.

"A knowledge of morphology is not essential to the appreciation of literature, even the literature of a forgotten age or decade.

"M. Arnold Dolmetsch's position in the world of music is unique, and all music lovers are so well aware of it, that one need not here pause to proclaim it. Painting and sculpture are taught by the most advanced and brilliant men of our decade, but if any student desires instruction in the earlier forms of the art, instruction in representative painting awaits him. The faculty as arranged to date, though it is still but a partial faculty, is perhaps our best prospectus."

Among the members of the faculty were the following: Henri Gaudier-Brzeska, Wyndham Lewis, Edward Wadsworth, Edmund Dulac, Reginald Wilenski, Arnold Dolmetsch, Felix Salmond, K. R. Heyman, Ezra Pound, John Cournos, Alvin Langdon Coburn.

The prospectus continues:

"As a supplement to the various courses in arts and crafts, we point out the value of individual research in, and study of, the various collections of the South Kensington and British Museums. We will endeavour to save the student's time by giving general direction for such work, and initiation in method, apart from the usual assistance offered by the regular Museum officials.

"In certain rare cases, the American college student, desiring more than his degree, will find it possible to spend his Junior or Sophomore year in London and return to his own University for graduation. Those desiring to do this should of course submit to us their plans of study, together with a clear statement of their requirements for graduation at the home college. Such students will have to possess rather more than average intelligence.

"If intending to take graduate work for higher degrees, they may, however, find that this form of recess will give them a distinct advantage over their colleagues, such

to recommence. Also, one could begin quite awhile AFTER without damage. Pardon, if I am running out of my own province and giving needless advice.

55: To Harriet Monroe

London, 12 October

GET SOME OF WEBSTER FORD'S[1]
STUFF FOR "POETRY"

Dear H.M.: Please observe above instructions as soon as possible. *Poetry* is really becoming more or less what one would like to have it.

I will send in a letter in a day or so, NOT an article, replying to your heresies. Why you deny the name of science or art to everything the public don't know, is beyond me.

As to Amy's advertisement. It is, of course, comic. On the other hand, it is outrageous. It is what one would expect of a lying grocer like ....n, I don't suppose she is much to blame. STILL, for us to print it in *Poetry* is wrong, even if it does pay a few dollars.

I have always objected to the Berg Essenwein[2] ad but this is a point beyond it. If it dealt with biscuits or a brand of sardines ......n and possibly the magazines publishing the adv. would be liable to prosecution.

56: To Amy Lowell

[Pasted to the top of the first page is an advertisement of Amy Lowell's *Sword Blades and Poppy Seed*, reading: "Of the poets who to-day are doing the interesting and original work, there is no more striking and unique figure than Amy Lowell. The foremost member of the 'Imagists'—a group of poets that includes

as fully to compensate for the inconvenience and derangement of undergraduate studies. It is always open to them to fill in routine courses by application to the University of London (that is to say, ordinary mathematics or classics), pursuing said courses in conjunction with their special work with the College of Arts.

"(*End of Prospectus.*)

"Remarks.—The college should come as a boon to various and numerous students who would otherwise be fugging about in continental pensions, meeting one single teacher who probably wishes them in the inferno, and dependent for the rest on fellow boarders and public amusements.

"Secondly, it would seem designed to form itself into a centre of intelligent and intellectual activity, rather than a cramming factory where certain data are pushed into the student regardless of his abilities or predilections." . . .

[1] Webster Ford was E. L. Masters' penname.

[2] Co-author of *The Art of Versification,* offered in the back pages of *Poetry*.

William Butler Yeats, Ezra Pound, Ford Madox Hueffer—she has won wide recognition for her writing in new and free forms of poetical expression."]

London, 19 October

Dear Miss Lowell: In view of the above arrant charlatanism on the part of your publishers, I think you must now admit that I was quite right in refusing to join you in any scheme for turning Les Imagistes into an uncritical democracy with you as intermediary between it and the printers.

While you apologize to Richard, your publishers, with true nonchalance, go on printing the ad in American papers which we would not see, save by unexpected accident.

I think you had better cease referring to yourself as an Imagiste, more especially as *The Dome of Glass* certainly has no aspirations in our direction.

I suppose you will really stop this ad sometime or other. Now that you have presented yourself to the ignorant in so favorable a light, it won't so much matter. W.B.Y. was perhaps more amused than delighted.

I don't suppose any one will sue you for libel; it is too expensive. If your publishers "of good standing" tried to advertise cement or soap in this manner they would certainly be sued. However we salute their venality. Blessed are they who have enterprise, for theirs is the magazine public.

P.S. I notice that the canny ......n in his ad refrains from giving a leg up to any of the less well known members of the school who might have received a slight benefit from it.

57: To Harriet Monroe

London, 9 November

Dear H.M.: Your letter—the long one—to hand is the most dreary and discouraging document that I have been called upon to read for a very long time.

Your objection to Eliot is the climax. No—you are not at liberty to say that she is Mrs. F. M. Hueffer. You are especially requested to make no allusion to the connection.

I think that is all that needs an immediate answer. —/—/

58: To Harriet Monroe

London, 9 November

Dear H.M.: No, most emphatically I will not ask Eliot to write down to any audience whatsoever. I dare say my instinct was sound enough when

I volunteered to quit the magazine quietly about a year ago. Neither will I send you Eliot's address in order that he may be insulted.

Now about news, I don't quite know what you can use. The stuff I had in mind was material for write-ups of Lewis, Epstein, Brzeska and any other good stuff that might turn up. You said you couldn't criticize stuff you hadn't seen. However I'll get you some photos if you think you can make anything of it.

The general theory of the new art is, I think, made fairly clear in my article "Vorticism" appearing in the September no: *Fortnightly Review*.

I don't think I can get photos from Epstein unless you really want to use them.

Now about topics of the moment. There is an exhibit of Rodin at the South Kensington museum, good of its kind but it does look like muck after one has got one's eye in on Epstein's Babylonian austerity. And Brzeska's work, for all that he is only 22, is much more interesting.

Would it be any use to you to have photos of the better Rodin's? A couple are fine and some of 'em make me sick. Slime. No form.

Brzeska by the way is at the front, French army. 7 out of his squad of 12 were killed off a few weeks ago, when scouting. He has killed two "boches." The dullness in the trenches for the last weeks has bored him so that he is doing an essay on sculpture for the next number of *BLAST*. Also he has done a figure, working with his jacknife and an entrenching tool.

The exhibition of Modern Spanish Art at the Grafton is a fit exhibit to hang where the show of the Royal Society of portrait painters hung recently. MUCK. If it weren't in "aid of the Prince of Wales fund" one would be inclined to sue for one's shilling. On what pretence is it modern! Most of the stuff that has any tendency at all is an archaism of one sort or another. The preface to the catalog which I now look at for the first time is as silly as the show, all anchored about 1875 and amateurish.

Picasso is not mentioned. Even Picabia is a large light in comparison with their twaddle.

The one thing that stands out is the work of Nestor Martin *Fernandez della Torre*. (This is not a fad.) Fernandez has four things, two pictures and two black and white things. The two pictures are very different superficially. Coburn and I did the show together and these things scattered about were the only things of interest.

He paints hard and clear. As canvases of the masters of Leonardo's time might have looked when *new*. It is as if he had learned from Van Gogh and, in the portrait of the young man "Joselito," been younger and more gentle. In the woman's portrait "La maja del abanico" it is as if he had tried to combine the Van Gogh hardness with the splendour, the ornateness, of Seville or of the Renaissance period.

The two drawings of dances are good, but not sufficiently so to make one remember him apart from the show, had they not been seen with the paintings.

Wadsworth, a young painter, not nearly so important as Lewis, but good, might interest you, as he has a bee for industrial centres and harbours. He is doing woodcuts at the moment. I suppose I could get you a couple, or at least get you impressions of some sort that would give you an idea, if it's any use.

I've mentioned Wadsworth, Epstein, Brzeska and Lewis in hurried scribbles in *The Egoist*. Do you see it? I think it is sent in as an exchange, but am not sure.

May Sinclair's last book, *The Three Sisters*, is the best she has done. She is just back from Belgium, went out with Red Cross, supposedly as a secretary or something, but has been pulling wounded off the field, and making Belgian interpreters run autos into more dangerous places than they like, etc. She has kept her name out of the papers so far, although everybody else has been appearing in large photos.

Wadsworth, along with Augustus John and nearly everybody, is drilling in the courtyard of the Royal Academy, in a regiment for home defence.

I was in a huge studio building, I should say the largest, in Chelsea, and every man, save one "sculptor" who makes monuments, had volunteered.

Wyndham Lewis, whose decorations of the Countess of Drogheda's house caused such a stir last autumn (and they weren't very good either) is now decorating the study of that copious novelist and critic, Mr. Ford Madox Hueffer. *And*, as I intimated in my note this morning, *no*, for gawd's sake don't connect Violet Hueffer with F.M.H. There have been enough suits for libel etc. I can't go into the inner history at this moment, but refrain from bracketing the two names.

I wonder if any of this is of the slightest use to you. Remember I don't know the least thing about what newspapers use. I once did two book reviews but that is the extent of my services to the daily press so you'll have to guide me more or less.

Getting pictures would be fairly simple, in the case of Rodin or Fernandez. I suppose I'd have to buy the prints??

Conrad was reported lost either in Poland, or going thither at the outbreak of the war. I don't happen to have heard recent news of him. Cunninghame Graham volunteered, after having lived a pacific socialist. He is to be sent off to buy remounts, as he is over-age and knows more about horses than anyone else except Blunt.

Blunt has brought out a two volume collected edition. Also they say he has barred his front door and put up a sign "BELLIGERENTS WILL PLEASE GO ROUND TO THE KITCHEN." I dare say he is watching Egypt at the present.

Ricketts has made the one mot of the war, the last flare of the 90's: "What depresses me most is the horrible fact that they can't *all* of them be beaten." It looks only clever and superficial, but one can not tell how true it is. This war is possibly a conflict between two forces almost equally detestable. Atavism and the loathsome spirit of mediocrity cloaked in graft. One does not know; the thing is too involved. I wonder if England will spend the next ten years in internal squabble *after* Germany is beaten. It's all very well to see the troops flocking from the four corners of Empire. It is a very fine sight. But, but, but, civilization, after the battle is over and everybody begins to call each other thieves and liars *inside* the Empire.

They took ten years after the Boer War to come to. One wonders if the war is only a stop gap. Only a symptom of the real disease.

However this isn't news. I'll write you about the proposed College of Arts in a day or so. I am too tired this evening, and the new prospecti haven't come in.

I don't think you can use either that mot of Ricketts nor Blunt's jape. These things get public and make trouble.

Blunt's collected edition and that rotten book of Masefield's are the book news. If that sort of thing is any use to you, or if America don't get it as soon as we do, I'll keep an eye on publishers' announcements for you. You didn't say *what* sort of news you could do with.

Fletcher is fleeing to the U.S.A. on Oct. 14th. I trust the Poetry Society will turn out to meet him. Rodker wants to know if he could get work there.

Tuesday, 10 November

The proof of the College of Arts prospectus has just come and I enclose it. I was going to ask A.C.H. to give it publicity but I guess you can use it as news quite as well. It is, obviously, a scheme to enable things to keep on here in spite of the war-strain and (what will be more dangerous) the war back-wash and post bellum slump. BUT it embodies two real ideas:

A. That the arts, INCLUDING poetry and literature, should be taught by artists, by practicing artists, *not* by sterile professors.

B. That the arts should be gathered together for the purpose of inter-enlightenment. The "art" school, meaning "paint school," needs literature for backbone, ditto the musical academy, etc.

I was going to ask A.C.H. to boom it, because I think it can be made a valuable model, or starting point for a much bigger scheme for Chicago. This thing here is done by artists *in spite of* the rich, but Chicago should be able to do a really big thing, if, as they seem able to do, they can get money and the creative people working together. My third "Renaissance" article will outline something. With three year fellowships, life-endowment, etc.

You see also, that while the vorticists are well-represented, the College does not bind itself to a school. Vide Dolmetsch, Robins and in less degree Dulac and Coburn.

Also the College should be of very real service to American students, I have seen enough of them to know.

By the way, Dolmetsch's forthcoming book ought to be good for a column.

1 9 1 5

59: To Harriet Monroe

Coleman's Hatch, January

Dear H.M.: There are two ways of existing in la vie littéraire. As De Gourmont said some while since: "A man is valued by the abundance or the scarcity of his copy." The problem is *how*, how in hell to exist without over-production. In the Imagist book I made it possible for a few poets who were not over-producing to reach an audience. That delicate operation was managed by the most rigorous suppression of what I considered faults.

Obviously such a method and movement are incompatible with effusion, with flooding magazines with all sorts of wish-wash and imitation and the near-good. If I had acceded to A.L.'s proposal to turn "Imagism" into a democratic beer-garden, I should have undone what little good I had managed to do by setting up a critical standard.

My dissociation with the forthcoming *Some Imagist Poets* book, and my displeasure, arises again from the same cause, which A.C.H. aptly calls "the futility of trying to impose a selective taste on the naturally unselective."

A.L. comes over here, gets kudos out of association. She returns and wants to weaken the whole use of the term imagist, by making it mean *any* writing of vers libre. Why, if they want to be vers-librists, why can't they say so? But no, she wants in Lawrence, Fletcher, her own looser work. And the very discrimination, the whole core of significance I've taken twelve years of discipline to get at, she expects me to accord to people who have taken fifteen minutes' survey of my results.

My problem is to keep alive a certain group of advancing poets, to set the arts in their rightful place as the acknowledged guide and lamp of civilization. The arts must be supported in preference to the church and scholarship. Artists first, then, if necessary, professors and parsons. Scholarship is but a hand-maid to the arts. My propaganda for what some may consider "novelty in excess" is a necessity. There are plenty to defend the familiar kind of thing. — — — —

60: To Harriet Monroe

Coleman's Hatch, January

Dear H.M.: — — — — Poetry must be *as well written as prose*. Its language must be a fine language, departing in no way from speech save by a heightened intensity (i.e. simplicity). There must be no book words, no periphrases, no inversions. It must be as simple as De Maupassant's best prose, and as hard as Stendhal's.

There must be no interjections. No words flying off to nothing. Granted one can't get perfection every shot, this must be one's INTENTION.

Rhythm MUST have meaning. It can't be merely a careless dash off, with no grip and no real hold to the words and sense, a tumty tum tumty tum tum ta.

There must be no cliches, set phrases, stereotyped journalese. The only escape from such is by precision, a result of concentrated attention to what is writing. The test of a writer is his ability for such concentration AND for his power to stay concentrated till he gets to the end of his poem, whether it is two lines or two hundred.

Objectivity and again objectivity, and expression: no hindside-before-ness, no straddled adjectives (as "addled mosses dank"), no Tennysonianness of speech; nothing—nothing that you couldn't, in some circumstance, in the stress of some emotion, actually say. Every literaryism, every book word, fritters away a scrap of the reader's patience, a scrap of his sense of your sincerity. When one really feels and thinks, one stammers with simple speech; it is only in the flurry, the shallow frothy excitement of writing, or the inebriety of a metre, that one falls into the easy—oh, how easy!—speech of books and poems that one has read.[1]

Language is made out of concrete things. General expressions in non-concrete terms are a laziness; they are talk, not art, not creation. They are the reaction of things on the writer, not a creative act *by* the writer.

"Epithets" are usually abstractions—I mean what they call "epithets" in the books about poetry. The only adjective that is worth using is the adjective that is essential to the sense of the passage, not the decorative frill adjective.

Aldington has his occasional concentrations, and for that reason it is always possible that he will do a fine thing. There is a superficial cleverness in him, then a great and lamentable gap, then the hard point, the true centre, out of which a fine thing may come at any time.

Fletcher is sputter, bright flash, sputter. Impressionist temperament, made intense at half-seconds.

H.D. and William C. Williams both better emotional equipment than Aldington, but lacking the superficial cleverness. Ought to produce really fine things at great intervals.

Eliot is intelligent, very, but I don't know him well enough to make predictions.

Masters hits rock bottom now and again. He should comb the journalese out of his poems. I wish Lindsay all possible luck but we're not really pulling the same way, though we both pull against entrenched senility. — — — —

[1] 1937. It should be realized that Ford Madox Ford had been hammering this point of view into me from the time I first met him (1908 or 1909) and that I owe him anything that I don't owe myself for having saved me from the academic influences then raging in London.—*E.P. January* 1937. Footnote from Harriet Monroe's *A Poet's Life.*

Sandburg may come out all right, but he needs to learn a *lot* about *How to Write*. I believe his intention is right.

Would to God I could see a bit more Sophoclean severity in the ambitions of mes amis et confrères. The general weakness of the writers of the new school is looseness, lack of rhythmical construction and intensity; secondly, an attempt to "apply decoration," to use what ought to be a vortex as a sort of bill-poster, or fence-wash. Hinc illae lachrymae. Too bad about Amy—why can't she conceive of herself as a Renaissance figure instead of a spiritual chief, which she ain't.

Ebbene—enough of this.

61: To Harriet Monroe

Coleman's Hatch, 31 January

Dear H.M.: Poe is a good enough poet, and after Whitman the best America has produced (probably?). He is a damn bad model and is certainly not to be set up as a model to any one who writes in English. – – – –

Now as to Eliot: "Mr. Prufrock" does not "go off at the end." It is a portrait of failure, or of a character which fails, and it would be false art to make it end on a note of triumph. I dislike the paragraph about Hamlet, but it is an early and cherished bit and T.E. won't give it up, and as it is the only portion of the poem that most readers will like at first reading, I don't see that it will do much harm.

For the rest: a portrait satire on futility can't end by turning that quintessence of futility, Mr. P. into a reformed character breathing out fire and ozone.

Fletcher is no great judge of anything. He has a lawless and uncontrolled ability to catch certain effects, mostly of colour, but no finishing sense.

I will let the unfortunate Ficke pass without complaint if you get on with "Mr. Prufrock," in a nice quiet and orderly manner. I assure you it is better, "more unique," than the other poems of Eliot which I have seen. Also that he is quite *intelligent* (an adjective which is seldom in my mouth).

Yeats has sent five poems to his agent with note that they should be submitted to you; there are three here (in his desk) which will be sent either direct or through the agent.

I know Poe wrote other poems besides "Et le corbeau dit jamais plus." I have bought them pomes, also Chivers's pomes. I note: "yore," "own native," "Wont to roam," "Naiad airs," "yon," even in the cameo; and they are bad for the budding. Also inversion and periphrasis: "bore" out at end of line for rhyme; and slight over-alliteration. These things one doesn't bother over so far as the gen. public is concerned and one accepts the inner force of a poem, but it would be treacherous and dishonest to let them pass in a thing set up *as a model*. They are things that one may do by accident or through inability but they are not things that one should intend. – – – –

62: To H. L. MENCKEN

Coleman's Hatch, 18 February

Dear Mr. Mencken: As I wrote I am "cleaned out" of verse by a book and two big batches of poems in *Poetry* and *BLAST*.

I send all that I have. I did it this morning.[1] I think it has some guts, but am perhaps still blinded by the fury in which I wrote it, and still confuse the cause with the result.

Have sent word to various people that you want good stuff. Aldington for light verse, W. L. George, Hueffer, May Sinclair, etc. Will see D. H. Lawrence. Frost is in America, dull perhaps, but has something in him. I have told him to see you or write. I should be glad if you could use his stuff. . . . He has reality.

The prose writer I am really interested in is James Joyce. He is in Austria; therefore I can't write to him but you might. — — — — His *Dubliners*, a book of short stories, has succeeded since I first wrote to him. *The Egoist* is using a long novel [2] of his as a serial. It's damn well written.

E. L. Masters — — — — (has written as "Webster Ford") has some punch but writes a little too much, and without sufficient hardness of edge. He is worth watching and printing. He and Eliot seem to me for the moment the most hopeful American poets—closer the thing. — — — —

63: To JOHN QUINN

[In *The New Age* of 21 January, Pound had published an article on Jacob Epstein in which he had written that the sculptor had "pawned his 'Sun God' and two other pieces" for sixty pounds. And he continued: "One looks out upon American collectors buying autograph mss. of William Morris, faked Rembrandts and faked Van Dykes." On 25 January, John Quinn wrote to Pound protesting against that sentence as a reflection upon himself. Quinn went on to point out that he had given up collecting manuscripts; that he collected modern art and not faked Rembrandts and Van Dykes and, indeed, had canvases by Matisse, Picasso and Derain; that he was responsible for the new tariff law which broke up the market in faked old masters. He inquired about the possibility of getting some good work by Gaudier-Brzeska and, finally, suggested that Pound might write for *The New Republic*.]

London, 8 March

My dear John Quinn: Thanks, apologies and congratulations. If there were more like you we should get on with our renaissance.

I particularly congratulate you on having shed your collection of mss.

---

[1] An unpublished poem "1915: February."
[2] *A Portrait of the Artist as a Young Man.*

and having "got as far as Derain." (Mind you, I think Lewis has much more power in his elbow, but I wouldn't advise a man to buy "a Lewis" simply because it was Lewis. Out of much that I do not care for there are now and again designs or pictures which I greatly admire.) However, there are few such reformed characters as yourself, and I might have as well said, "medals given to John Keats for orthography, first editions of eighteenth century authors," instead of "mss. of Wm. Morris," which allusion would not have dragged you into it and would have left the drive of my sentence about the same. I might have gone on about the way Morgan and a certain old friend of his, whose niece I knew in Paris, used to buy, but Morgan is such a stock phrase (and besides he has done some good in America by bringing in Old Masters). Then there's Ricketts now showing Old Masters, collected for Davis I think it is. There are a lot of heads at the fair.

I have still a very clear recollection of Yeats père on an elephant (at Coney Island), smiling like Elijah in the beatific vision, and of you plugging away in the shooting gallery. And a very good day it was. – – – –

As to fake Rembrandts, etc., I carried twenty "Rembrandts," "Van Dykes" and "Velasquez" out of Wanamaker's private gallery at the time of his fire some eight years ago. I know that they aren't the only examples in the U.S., so my sentence was by no means a personal one. My God! What Velasquez! I also know a process for Rembrandts: one man studies the ghetto and does drawings, one the Rembrandtesque method of light and shade and manner and does the painting, and a third does the "tone of time." However, that's a digression. Let me go at your letter as it comes.

I haven't seen much of Epstein of late. He and Lewis have some feud or other which I haven't inquired into, and as Lewis is my more intimate friend I have not seen much of Jacob, though I was by way of playing for a reconciliation. Jacob told me some time ago that the "Sun God" was in hock. He told me, just before the war, it was still in hock. I heard from W.B.Y., after I had written the article and after it was in print, that you had bought "an Epstein" ("an Epstein," not half a dozen.) – – – –

By the way, if you are still getting Jacob's "Birds," for God's sake get the two that are stuck together, not the pair in which one is standing up on its legs.

However, let me apologize for my ignorance and make an end of it.

I congratulate you on the tariff law. Have they, I wonder, done as well by the writers as by the painters? I wrote to the President (for all the jolly sort of good that sort of thing does). I have to pay a duty if I am in America and want a copy of one of my own books, printed in England. You can't get a book printed in America unless it conforms to the commercial requirements. Rennert [1] had to pay some huge duty on his *Life of Lope de Vega*, which is a standard and which got him into the Spanish Academy. Only an English firm would risk the publication. The American law as it stands or stood is all for the publisher and the printer and all against the author, and more and more against him just in such proportion as he is before or against his time. If you are near the councils of the powers I

---

[1] Hugo Rennert, once professor in Romance languages at the University of Pennsylvania.

would be glad to make out a fuller statement. This detail is one of the causes of American authors' coming abroad and of the funereal nature of all serious American periodicals. The printing is supposed to be so costly that it is impossible to publish in America, especially in periodicals which are, as are a few in London and Paris, largely in the control of writers or in which they have influence.

Henry IV took off the octroi from books coming into Paris some centuries since, because they made for the increase of learning, and it is high time America followed suit. The absurd tariff (25% it was) *and* the egregious price the American booksellers stick on a foreign book, unnecessarily, "because of the tariff," are just enough to prevent sales. Example, I caught a publisher selling my *Spirit of Romance* at 2½ dollars. No fool would pay that for a six shilling book. Besides, that damn swindler had bought the book at 3 shillings by special arrangement so as to be able to sell it at the English price (I being paid as at 3/). These are merely personal instances, but it is the sort of thing that goes on and keeps books by living authors out of the U.S., and the tariff, which is iniquitous and stupid in principle, is made an excuse. *All* books ought to be on the free list, but more especially all books of living authors, and of those the non-commercial books, scholarship and belles lettres, most certainly.

About GAUDIER-BRZESKA: I naturally think I've got the two best things myself, though I was supposed by his sister to have bought the first one out of charity because no one else would have it. The second one is half paid for by money I lent him to get to France with. He is now in the trenches before Rheims. However, there is, or was, a charming bas-relief of a cat chewing its hind foot, and there are the "Stags," if you like them. However, money can't be of much use to him now in the trenches. I send him a spare pound when I have it to finish up my payment on the "Boy with a Coney." But when he comes back from the trenches, if he does come, I imagine he will be jolly hard up. In the meantime I will find out exactly what is unsold and let you know about it. Coburn is doing a photo of one of my own things of Brzeska's and I hope it will interest him enough to go on and do a portfolio, in which case you will be able to make your selection from the best possible photographs.

At any rate, I will write to Gaudier at once and see what he has, and where it is, and how much he wants for it, and if there is anything that I think fit to recommend I think Coburn will probably photograph it for me. Then there will be no waste in dealer's commissions.

Which brings me back to another hobby. Speaking of 30,000 dollars for two pictures, I "consider it immoral" to pay more than 1,000 dollars for any picture (save, perhaps, a huge Sistine ceiling or something of that sort). Your Puvises are big pictures so it don't hit you. But NO artist needs more than 2,000 dollars per year, and any artist can do two pictures at least in a year. 30,000 dollars would feed a whole little art world for five years.

My whole drive is that if a patron buys from an artist who needs money (needs money to buy tools, time and food), the patron then makes himself equal to the artist: he is building art into the world; he creates.

If he buys even of living artists who are already famous or already making £12,000 per year, he ceases to create. He sinks back to the rank of a consumer.

A great age of painting, a renaissance in the arts, comes when there are a few patrons who back their own flair and who buy from unrecognized men. In every artist's life there is, if he be poor, and they mostly are, a period when £10 is a fortune and when £100 means a year's leisure to work or to travel, or when the knowledge that they can make £100 or £200 a year without worry (without spending two-thirds of their time running to dealers, or editors) means a peace of mind that will let them work and not undermine them physically.

Besides, if a man has any sense, the sport and even the commercial advantage is so infinitely greater. If you can hammer this into a few more collectors you will bring on another Cinquecento.

(In sculpture I might let the price run over £200, simply because of the time it takes to cut stone. Drill work is no damn good. Both Gaudier and Epstein cut direct, and there may be months of sheer cutting in a big bit of sculpture, especially if the stone is very hard.) Gaudier does mostly small things, which is sane, for the sculpture of our time, save public sculpture, ought to be such as will go in a modern house.

About *The New Republic*, I am afraid it is not much use. – – – – I saw and lunched with Lippmann when he was over here, but he didn't seem disposed to take any of my stuff. A poet, you know!!! Bad lot, they are. No sense of what the public wants. Even Cournos, who isn't exactly modern, met Lippmann and said: "You've heard of English stodge? Well, there's one stodge that's worse. That's American stodge."

Even *The New Age* has nipped my series in the middle because I have dared to write an article praising an American writer of vers libre, one Edgar Masters. They say it's an insult to their readers to praise vers libre after they have so often condemned it. (God knows most vers libre is bad enough. Still, Masters has something in him, rough and unfinished, ma!) If you told Croly of *The New Republic* that I was an art critic he might believe you, but he'd think me very bad for his paper. The fat pastures are still afar from me. And I have a persistent and (editorially) inconvenient belief that America has the chance for a great age if she can be kicked into taking it. (Whereanent some remarks in *The Dial*, here enclosed).

64: To Harriet Monroe

London, [? March]

Dear H.M.: – – – – You are in the same state as the late medieval critics who insisted that Paul wrote good Greek because he was an inspired Christian. We now know he neither wrote good Greek nor represented the teaching of the original Christian. No matter.

You say you understand and then you just don't. Whatever talent Poe may have had, or anybody may have had, the only stuff to use as a model is stuff that is without flaws, or stuff in which we see the flaws so clearly that we may avoid them.

Laws do not begin with the man who puts them in print; whatever "laws of imagisme" are good, have been good for some time.

One condemns a fault in Poe, not because it is in Poe. It is all right for Poe if you like, but it is damn bad for the person who is trying uncritically to write like Poe. (Incidentally no one who has tried to write like Poe (verse: leave his prose out of it for the present) has done anything good. Personally I think an ambition to write as well as Poe a low one: an ambition to write like Villon or Stendhal a great ambition.)

And there is no use implying that I lack reverence for great writers. My pantheon is considerable, and I do not admire until I have thought; that is to say I do not admire until I [have] tested. One has passing enthusiasms: one finds in time lasting enthusiasms.

I don't condemn any man who has made lasting or even more or less durable art. But can't you ever see the difference between what is "good," and good enough for the public, and what is "good" for the artist, whose only respectable aim is perfection?

I don't think Pindar any safer than Poe. "Theban Eagle" be blowed. A dam'd rhetorician half the time. The infinite gulph between what you read and enjoy and what you set up as a model.

"The difference between enthusiastic slop and great art"—there's a text to preach on in your glorious unfettered desert for the next forty years.

Now about the [Catholic] Anthology: I believe Mathews is to publish it though I haven't the matter in writing. He says, "yes." (Admitted he hasn't seen the contents, still I think the thing is fairly sure.) I have now got about all the people I can use. — — — —

I have written to Sandburg, chosen two of his poems and want a few more.

I have already commended Masters at the top of my lungs, but if he gets facetious he can follow Bret Harte to the dung heap. As a matter of fact, I think he keeps his ideal of form pretty constantly before him, though I dare say he gets little encouragement. (Yes, my American mail is "in" this morning.)

Bodenheim I am afraid I can't use this time,[1] I've got to keep some balance in the book. Nor yet Bynner. Nor Lindsay; he's all right, but we are not in the same movement or anything like it. I approve of his appearance in *Poetry* (so long as I am not supposed to want what he wants), but not in anything which I stand sponsor for as a healthy tendency. I don't say he copies Mennetti; but he is with him, and his work is futurist. And anyhow I shall be unremittingly damned for putting so much American stuff into the *Anthology* (which I don't mind, but I decline to suffer for what I don't believe in). Jingles and Bret Harte. The easy thing.

You constantly think I undervalue élan and enthusiasm. I see a whole country rotted with it, and no one to insist that "form" and innovation are

---

[1] But some of Bodenheim's poems were used, under the signature "M.B.," as it was decided that his full name might be objectionable at a time when England was at war with Germany.

compatible. Most of the people who have heard of good writing are all anchored at '76 and have forgotten it. Dam 'em.

65: To H. L. Mencken

London, 17 March

Dear H. L. Mencken: I am glad Wilkinson has turned out something acceptable. I came down with influenza within ten hours of getting back to London, so have not been able to do or find anything until yesterday.

Cournos has translated a novelette from Sologub; you don't want translations, but you do want novelettes so it might do at a pinch rather than nothing. His stuff is now with Constable; but if they have no objection to its being used in a magazine before they do the book, I have asked him to give you a shot at it. — — — —

I will try also to get a complete ms. of Joyce's novelette-length story now running in *The Egoist*. They won't mind its appearing in the *S.S.* here if you don't. It had appeared in *The Egoist* in such snippets, and *The Egoist* has so few readers that I don't think it would matter, and a lot of people (oh well, no, not a lot, I suppose, in the large sense of lot but some) who want the whole story would buy the *S.S.* to get it. The use of it in the *S.S.* might however cut into the firm who want it for book form. I can't tell yet. We'll see if you want it before we begin worrying.

This is the first day I have had energy to go through my mss. I find the enclosed which have not been published. I have made clean copies of the best. I see reasons for an editor's being reluctant. Still, Yeats likes "The Temperaments." He says I have achieved the true Greek (he should say Roman) epigram. (Besides Bastidides is such a perfect portrait of a certain distinguished author who wouldn't recognize it, that I should greatly regret not giving it, sometime, to the light of day.)

Sometimes I think "Before you Were" has some guts. I don't know whether you will like it.

I have signed "Bishop Golias" with a nom-de-plume as it is so far out of the style of my present work, and I think a man ought only to print one style at a time. FOR GOD'S SAKE DON'T LOSE THAT PARTICULAR MS. AS I DON'T know whether I have another copy, and I am still too tired to make out another.

I am afraid the two poems, "Prayer to a Lady," and its companion piece lose a little force unless your audience know that Atys cut out his testicles in a fit of religious enthusiasm.

However, here's the bloody lot, and if any of it is of use to you, so much the better.

Joyce is evidently beginning to be "the common man" (commercially even), for H. G. Wells' agent wrote in to say that H.G. had put him on to Joyce, and that he wanted to handle his stuff.

That is, I think, the sum of the London news that I have gathered in the few days I've been up and about, save that we'll have out another *BLAST* soon, and that if you touch art, even en passant, Lewis (Wyndham Lewis) and Gaudier-Brzeska are great artists though their stuff is still so far from the public comprehension that I don't expect many people to believe me when I say so. Quinn has, however, written here to know if he can get a good statue by Brzeska; and whatever Picasso has done or is about to do in New York, I think Lewis will be able to go beyond it. I don't know what you intend about covers and posters for the *S.S.* but if you can get a man with a great future whose work is VISIBLE, mehercule! and at the same rates, probably, as you would pay a nobody, it might in the long run pay, merely as advertising.

I don't know whether you have seen my article on Vorticism in *The Fortnightly Review* for last Sept. It is a moderately clear introduction. In any case you might keep in mind the fact that Vorticism is not Futurism, most emphatically NOT. We like Cubism and some Expressionism, but the schools are not our school. Even though they are equally distant from Manet or from Alma Tadema.

66: To Harriet Monroe

London, 10 April

Dear Harriet: No! Had I spent more than 1 minute 38 seconds on the parody on Lindsay—more per similar section of the poem—we had neither of us achieved the result, the élan, the free bravura, the fecundity, the felicity, the obvious rag-time of the cadence: jig jilly jig jilly jig, etc. Perfectly good humoredly. He is better than most, than any one else of your lot except Ford and Sandburg who are trying harder.

Lindsay's top ambition is obviously Kipling, which is all well and good so far as it goes. Effervescence, futurism, it is very "horrid" of me not to be enthusiastic about it, as I am for even the botches of some of the more constipated authors.

The rural sarcasm of Indianapolis: [1] dear editor must have been smoking cigarettes illicitly. Has discovered the old trick of turning the picture upside down. Thoughtful man. Future before him. – – – –

Do get on with that Eliot.

67: To H. L. Mencken

London, 18 April

Dear Mencken: Here, at last, is the satire.[2] If Nathan thinks it is too long, I have not the slightest objection to his printing it as prose, though I believe with the loose rhythm it will read more quickly if the rhymes come at the ends of lines.

---

[1] The Indianapolis *News* of March 11, 1915, had printed Pound's "Dogmatic Statement Concerning the Game of Chess" with the order of the lines reversed.

[2] "L'Homme Moyen Sensuel," published in *Pavannes and Divisions.*

Also I don't mind your cutting it, if you like—especially the 1st three pages, but I can't shorten it any more, and am inclined to think it would be better, as it was in an earlier version, set down looser and longer. Note that the guts of all satire (*Don Juan*, for instance) are in the digressions, à propos de bottes, and that a *Don Juan* canto is about the shortest length convenient for such digression. Note that they run from 800 to 1600 lines. Well, I have done my job in a fourth part of that, i.e. about 240 lines.

My business instinct, such as it is, makes me think the most advantageous thing all round would be to boom it as THE satire, "best since Byron." New York is accustomed to a new Keats and a new Shelley once a fortnight and one might vary the note. It is not such an awful lie, if one considers that nobody has written satire, in the best English iambic tradition since God knows when. Hood was sheer larks. Bret Harte merely advised the virtuous American to beware of the dangerous oriental Chinee. Arlington Robinson in "Miniver Cheevy" satirizes one love eccentric. Nobody has taken on the whole caboodle.

If it goes, I can turn you out an installment every two or three months and it ought to focus some stray attention on the *S.S.* – – – –

I think that my statements in the present whoop are *intelligible*. That's the intention. I have made my quiet classical remarks elsewhere, but here I want " 'em to know that they are being spoken to." I think there is very little that won't be understood.

Anyhow, something has got to be done with it, printed as prose *or* as verse. With occasional expunging if you like, though why bother? CALL it literature, lay weight on the traditional excellence and it will go. Point out that Byron uses that naughty word "syphilis" and that I don't. Observe that "whore" and "Jesus" are left blank (sic . . . , . . . ,).

As to the best form. A long, really long narrative like *Juan* is probably the best, but I am perfectly willing to recognize the exigencies of the *S.S.* and make each rip self-contained, as this one is.

Also it is no stronger than some things you've printed. However . . . And it will rhyme when spoken by the most catarrhal kitchen-canary (and only then). – – – –

I think there are one or two couplets that ought to melt even the stern heart of Nathan. And you might remind him that long poems can be popular *provided they aren't too poetic*. And we might cite examples even among our contemporaries.

Part of the trick is a hurrying rhythm. Which was absent from your "Hot water bag" poem, which by the way I liked very much and meant to have sent my compliments via you to the author.[1]

Anyhow, in the present poem, I've taken off more trimmings than I should have, in a vain strife for a useless brevity.

God be with you.

Of course I don't expect the same rate per line for a lark of this length, as Wright paid for short poems. Comfort the treasurer.

Also the word *calor* is not a misprint for color, page 4.

[1] "Certainly, It Can Be Done," by John Sanborn, *The Smart Set*, April 1915, pp. 389 ff.

68: To Harriet Monroe

London, [?25] April

Dear H.M.: Rupert Brooke is dead in the Dardanelles. I have some of his work, and will send the Post Mortem in a day or so, probably tonight. So it will reach you in time for the June number. As even if you had got the news by cable there would have been no time to do an appreciation in time for the May number.

He was the best of all that Georgian group.

69: To H. L. Mencken

London, 2 May

Dear Mencken: I am sending you an unbound vol. of some stories by Goldring; they were published under another name and had a fair bit of notice.

As nearly as I can tell such stories as "Lily May," "A London Dawn," "Savoir Faire," "Watch Night Service," "Life Wins," are just about the stuff your public wants. In "Life Wins," though it obviously "rings a bell" in the last paragraph, he has got a curious English quality. I doubt if the story could have been written in any other country (that is, however, an aside). "Lily May" seems to me very good. The problem before the house is HOW MUCH do you pay? Goldring says the stories take him a hell of a time to write.

The cheque you sent him was not, so to speak, magniloquent (I know it's war time, so this is not a growl), anyhow you might send a tariff for stories of 2000, 4000, 7000 words. I judge by Wilkinson's cheque that £25 is the rate for the long story. (?Can you pay more for long (25,000) stories (novellettes) by special people with some rep., or don't it pay to bother? 25,000 words is an unsalable length *after* a writer has done a story of that size, so I'm not sure that you would gain much in offering a higher rate. On the other hand it is not everyone who will write for £1000).

Your question about sending cheques via me. It don't in the least matter. As I explained to Wright, I can't take 20 cents or 10 dollars either, from a man across a tea table, especially when we are all rather impecunious together, and most of the people I send in are friends or at least acquaintances.

If you find an opening for my pamphleteering and polemical stuff, you can put me next to it, or if you see a comfortable salaried job you can remember my existence, or when you are again flush, in the days of a future peace you can send a bouquet to cover time and postal expenses if I have found you enough good stuff to warrant it. As I told Wright, it is quite impossible for me to set up as a literary agent. In the meantime don't worry about the matter.

Wright, I think, took Hueffer's first year and a half of *The English Review* as his model, and the quality of *The Eng. Rev.* then depended, I think, very largely on the sort of personal touch between the office and writers, and that sort of personal touch is about all I can help you with. The fact that some editor actually wants the best he can get is a very considerable comfort to me; perhaps we had better let it go at that.

A chap named Lynch is coming in tomorrow. I shall probably have him send something to you. (Utility rather than grace, I am afraid; however, he may be good.)

I have, by the way, sent a sort of circular letter de rebus omnibus to various young writers in the U.S. Orrick Johns may bring it in for your perusal when it reaches him in the course of the circuit. There is a certain amount of work that ought to be put through: tariff ought to be taken off books, the people who insist on regarding America solely as a monument to John Quincy Adams, the pilgrim fathers, Geo. W. and Co., ought to be prodded, etc. Hope the note won't bore you to death. It is badly written, but for a private circulation I couldn't take the time to rewrite it. – – – –

70: To Harriet Monroe

London, 17 May

My gawddd! This IS *a* ROTTEN *number of Poetry.*
Dear H.M.: It is, honestly, pretty bad. [Marianne Moore's] titles are nice. Beach is punk. A little bad Yeats will set us up a bit.

Thanks, very much, for the kindness of the adv. of my stuff. If you repeat it, could you take out that silly quotation from the *Telegraph's* first review of *Personae* (A.D. 1909), and substitute the *Times'* more measured speech re *Cathay*, i.e. the passages I have outlined in ink?

I am sending a Manifesto via Johns, Williams, Masters, etc., which I want you to print (no charge!). Also I wish you could draw proofs of it and send one to each of the signatories as I want them each to print it somewhere.

I am not asking you, A.C.H., Mencken, Kreymborg or Dell to sign it as it is largely against the old magazines, and I don't think anyone in an editorial position ought to sign a manifesto definitely against other editors. It looks too much like boosting one's own show.

H—— is a drivvelling ass, but kindly and amiable. S—— is worse, for he not only pours out amateurish blither, but he is a rich man who does NOTHING—god damn nothing—for the arts, recognizes no obligation, and on top of it tries to "earn a living," which meant he hogs a minor job which would be a living to some other man, but which wouldn't pay for the gasoline in S——'s automobile. Blithering sow. To see him sitting in this room on my perfectly good furniture trying to get up nerve enough to spend £5 on a bit of sculpture, it's enough to make a cat spew.

His name might appear on a list of guarantors, but it should appear no where else.

I have, as you see, re-marked the *Times* cutting. As a general position it is a good thing to have it in print. How the devil the *Times* got on, got as wide awake as to admit what I have been hammering on for five years, completely mystifies me. The phrase "talking seriously and without parade," is one of the best dicta on good poetry that has appeared in my time. — — —

Is literature limited to Christianity?

Above subject for chaste debate in the American parliament.

Oh well, it's a hell of a thing to be an editor or to be in any way responsible for the prog. of letters. Yours in sympathy.

71: To FELIX E. SCHELLING

London, June

Dear Dr. Schelling: Thank you for your note and for the monograph on professors. I have read with interest your remarks on "time for digestion," "buildings," "wasted time of the intelligent" etc. and heartily concur. I always wonder when the creative element will be recognized; when the mind of the student is to be recognized as, at least potentially, dynamic, and not solely as a receptacle.

As for the Chinese translations, they have been approved by one or two people who know some of the originals. They are, I should say, closer than the *Rubaiyat*, but then the ideographs leave one wholly free as to phrasing. I mean, instead of "hortus inclusus" you have a little picture of an enclosure with two or three stalks of [illegible ideograph] grass and a flower (very much abbreviated) inside. Or for "to visit, or ramble" you have a king and a dog sitting on the stern of a boat. 逰 (No, I don't make them nicely. I haven't a brush. The two top dabs are ripples or drops for the water.) This charming sign does not occur in *Cathay*. It is merely an exquisite example of the way the Chinese mind works.

Of course, all the ideographs are not as amusing. Fenollosa has left a most enlightening essay on the written character (a whole basis of aesthetic, in reality), but the adamantine stupidity of all magazine editors delays its appearance. I had hoped to be able to write you of a new periodical which should do in English what the *Mercure* does in France, and where one might find "Little Eyasses" and other matters which are interesting and not, in the worst sense, philology. However, it is still merely vision.

Gaudier-Brzeska has been killed at Neuville St. Vaast, and we have lost the best of the young sculptors and the most promising. The arts will incur no worse loss from the war than this is. One is rather obsessed with it.

P.S. Have you seen Hueffer's *When Blood is Their Argument?*

P.P.S. If you are interested in the Fenollosa papers, you will find a lot of stuff in *The Drama* for May.

72: To Harriet Monroe

London, [August]

Dear H.M.: Bridges' new booklet is privately printed, but he has given me permission to quote the poems.[1] It amounts practically to making a free contribution, I suppose. I think the two poems quoted in full are quite good, yes very good, especially the short one. And the cadence of the other is exquisite. I suppose I shall have to wait till he dies before I can do an appreciative character sketch. — — — —

I send also the three jems of Eliot for September, and a forthcoming "Cousin Nancy" which may do to fill the second page.[2]

73: To the Editor of the Boston *Transcript*

London, [August]

Dear Sir: I don't know that it is worth my while to call any one of your reviewers a liar, but the case has its technical aspects and the twistings of malice are, to me at least, entertaining.

I note in *Current Opinion* for June a quotation from your paper to the effect that my friend Robert Frost has done what no other American poet has done in this generation "and that is, unheralded, unintroduced, untrumpeted, he won the acceptance of an English publisher on his own terms" etc.

Now seriously, what about me? Your (?negro) reviewer might acquaint himself with that touching little scene in Elkin Mathews' shop some years since.

Mathews: "Ah, eh, ah, would you, now, be prepared to assist in the publication?"

E.P.: "I've a shilling in my clothes, if that's any use to you."

Mathews: "Oh well. I want to publish 'em. Anyhow."

And he did. No, sir, Frost was a bloated capitalist when he struck this island, in comparison to yours truly, and you can put that in your editorial pipe though I don't give a damn whether you print the fact.

You might note *en passant* that I've done as much to boom Frost as the next man. He came to my room before his first book *A Boy's Will* was published. I reviewed that book in two places and drew it [to] other reviewers' attention by personal letters. I hammered his stuff into *Poetry*, where I have recently reviewed his second book, with perhaps a discretion that will do him more good than pretending that he is greater than Whitman. E. L. Masters is also doing good work.

[1] The poems are quoted in Pound's review of the booklet, *Poetry*, October 1915.
[2] Only three of the four were printed: "The Boston Evening Transcript," "Aunt Helen," and "Cousin Nancy," *Poetry*, October 1915.

You understand I don't in the least mind being detested by your under-strappers, but I think you owe it to the traditions of the *Transcript* to keep them within the bounds of veracity.

Of course, from the beginning, in my pushing Frost's work, I have known that he would ultimately be boomed in America by fifty energetic young men who would use any club to beat me; that was well in my calculation when I prophesied his success with the American public and especially with the American reviews, and I rejoice to see that it has caught on.

But your critic's statement is caddish. Moreover, I think it unwise that you should encourage that type of critic which limits the word "American" to such work as happens to flatter the parochial vanity. It is not even Chauvinism. It is stupid.

74: To Harriet Monroe

London, 25 September

Dear Harriet: — — — Itow tells me he is going to America next week. I have given him a note to you. I am very fond of him, though I mostly detest the Japs, i.e., the moon-faced thin-minded sort. This man is a samurai, more like an American Indian to look at, the long face you see in some of the old prints.

I don't know whether *Drama* or A.C.H. or anyone can get him anything in Chicago. He has a good engagement in N.Y. His arm work is very interesting—better than the Russians—; foot work not so good. He himself a fine fellow. — — — —

Don't know that there is much news. Hueffer up in town on leave yesterday. It will be a long time before we get any more of his stuff, worse luck. He is looking twenty years younger and enjoying his work.

Yeats still in Ireland. Eliot back here, thank God. Monro discovered "Prufrock" on his unaided own and asked me about the author when I saw him last night. I consider that Harold is dawning. He was very glad to hear that T.S.E. was in the forefront of our [*Catholic*] *Anthology*. It was a great waste to let the "Portrait of a Lady" go to *Others*, but I was in a hurry for it to come out before the *Anth.* as you know. — — — —

75: To Harriet Monroe

London, 2 October

Dear H.M.: I have cabled my vote for Eliot. As you might have known.

I see no other possible award of the prize. And besides, something ought to be done to atone for the war-poem scandal.[1]

---

[1] A special prize for a war poem was awarded to "The Metal Checks" by Louise Driscoll, *Poetry*, November 1914.

Of the people worth keeping up, Masters and Williams have professions. Masters' *Spoon River* appeared elsewhere and the poem he sent us is not of any special importance. Johns would be my second choice, but his work in this volume of *Poetry* is hardly solid enough. Still it would be better to give the prize to him than to a yahoo. Cannéll has a good poem; H.D. has two small verses: but it would be imbecile to compare Cannéll's stuff to Eliot's, and H.D.'s is less important (in this vol. *certainly*). Lindsay . . . Oh gawd!!! Besides he has had a prize, and I don't suppose he is any more eligible than I am. Sandburg had the prize last year.

No, if your committee don't make the award to Eliot, God only knows what slough of ignominy they will fall into—reaction, death, silliness!!!!!!

Bodenheim shows promise in some mss. sent me, but he has nothing in this year's *Poetry*, and besides he is young enough to wait. Ajan is not American, besides he is not as good as Eliot, not anywhere near. You can take Hueffer's commendation of Eliot to back up mine, if it is any use to you. Even Monro's Devonshire Street occiput has been pierced.

Eliot's poem is the only eligible thing in the year that has any distinction.

The average of the year has been perhaps better than the two years before, but there has been no particularly notable work. Except "Prufrock" (and, si licet, "The Exile's Letter").

The things to be avoided are, naturally, an award to Amy, Skinner, Fletcher, Lindsay or Aiken. Or even Ficke. If you don't give the £40 to Eliot, for God's sake award it to *yourself*.

However, De Gourmont is dead and the world's light is darkened. I write this expecting the worst. I will send in an obituary of De Gourmont.

76: To HARRIET MONROE

London, 12 October

Dear H.M.: — — — — Buncumb about Brooke!

A. There is no mention of Brooke in *BLAST*.

B. The verse referred to was written months before his death, and *BLAST* was supposed to go to press in December. I am not responsible for Lewis' times and seasons.

C. The verse contains nothing derogatory. It is a complaint against a literary method. Brooke got perhaps a certain amount of vivid poetry in life and then went off to associate with literary hen-coops like Lascelles Abercrombie in his writings.

Brooke would have been amused by the lines, at least I hope and suppose he was man enough to have been entertained by them. If he wasn't, God help him in limbo.

Now that his friends have taken to writing sentimental elegies about his long prehensile toes, it might seem time for him to be protected by people like myself who knew him only slightly.

If he went to Tahiti for his emotional excitements instead of contracting diseases in Soho, for God's sake let him have the credit of it. And for God's sake if there was anything in the man, let us dissociate him from his surviving friends.

Something ought to be done to clear him from the stain of having been quoted by Dean Inge, and to save him from friends who express their grief at his death by writing such phrases as (yes, here it is verbatim):

"in fact Rupert's mobile toes were a subject for the admiration of his friends."

That, madame, is the sort of detractor upon whose evidence you complain of me. — — — —

77: To Douglas Goldring

London, [?22] November

Dear Goldring: I have had some cables from Q. He says he has fair hopes of success with the magazine.

I don't know of anyone who wants to pay for their own publication. I have written to one man in America to send on his poems. He wouldn't expect to be paid anything, but I doubt if he could put up much or anything.

Eliot has about 15 or 20 poems. He would let you have them if I suggested it, but then he has no money and besides he oughtn't to be asked to pay. He can obviously get published when he is really ready. A small book of M.M. might strike.

Elkin is now in such a funk over the title of the anthology that he'd probably let you have special rates if you stocked a lot of it.

I wonder if you couldn't make some sort of profit in taking on approval, or on sale, large orders, say 200 copies of good books that haven't gone. Joyce's *Dubliners* hasn't sold. If you had a decent traveller you might develop the system. It wouldn't be the same, quite, as buying remainders. You would, without paying anything down, undertake to push good stuff, stuff that you believed in, stuff the publisher couldn't sell himself, or isn't selling, and that he would let you have at half rates, or something of that sort.

It would need brains in selecting stuck books with some *go* in them, *ma chè*.

It wouldn't need capital on your part, which seems to be your difficulty.

I shall be at Yeats' this evening (18 Woburn Blds. next St. Pancras Church). He goes to Ireland tomorrow. Perhaps if you get this in time you'll look in there.

You might stir up an interest, or get a marked individuality as a firm, by my suggested scheme. I don't know. . . . Various authors might be willing to back you to some extent.

I don't suppose my Guido Cavalcanti is any use to anyone. The sheets are mostly at the binders where they were left by Swift and Co.'s demise. I could let you have them for next to nothing if they are any possible use to you. The binders want 2½ d. a copy (in sheets) for their lien, but I dare say they'd take less. I could let you have them flat for what I have to pay the binder, and wait until you have sold some before you pay me anything. You needn't take but a couple of hundred to begin on. If you are amind to print a new title page and call it a new edition ? at 1/ (the first edtn. was 3/6) price?????, as we think fit, I may be able to find some decent press notices . . . probably lost *ma chè*. . . .

For god's sake don't touch it unless you think there's a chance for you to make something.

It seems to me you might do a Poetry Bookshop minus the Abercrombie element. However let's wait until we can talk.

If you don't show up this evening, perhaps you could drop in some evening during the week? Wednesday par example?

To HARRIET MONROE

London, 1 December

Dear H.M.: Of course the Brooke matter was an error. Ma chè! It can't harm anyone but me, and it can't hurt me much ("where I live"). Besides it is as much the fault of *BLAST* as mine; Lewis ought to have got the magazine out sooner. However, admitting it is an error, I by no means consider it a felony, and I am not going into mourning. Other young men have gone, and will go, to Tahiti, and they will write Petrarchan verses, and they will be envied their enthusiastic princesses.

No one has ever swarmed up a cocoanut tree on *my* account, though I have heard the second person singular of the personal pronoun. And they are not black in Tahiti, only a faint pinkish chocolatine colour, "a very beautiful people" as Manning says.

Yes, the prizes [1] were peculiarly filthy and disgusting, the £10 to H.D. being a sop to the intelligent. However, I knew it would happen. I know just what your damn committee *wants*.

As to T.S.E. the "Prufrock" IS more individual and unusual than the "Portrait of a Lady"! I chose it of the two as I wanted his first poem to be published to be a poem that would at once differentiate him from everyone else, in the public mind.

I am sending on some more of his stuff in a few days, I want to see him and talk it over first. Thank God he has got a job in London after Xmas.

Re Frost: I must again insist that I did not send that letter to *The Transcript* but to the editor as a private citizen. I think however that the charge of my being jealous of Frost ought to be nailed, perhaps even at the disclosure of state secrets. . . . However, I am sorry if it annoyed you. But I DO get wroth at the difficulty I have in getting stuff printed in *Poetry* now and again. I didn't know it was the coon I was answering, nor did it

---

[1] The Helen Haire Levinson Prize of $200 was awarded to Vachel Lindsay for "The Chinese Nightingale"; a guarantor's prize of $100 was awarded to Constance Lindsay Skinner for "Songs of the Coastdwellers."

enter my head that *The Transcript* was a hostile organ. I thought they had always treated me fairly well, otherwise I should not have written them at all.

Most certainly I did not write the letter to Braithwaite. He isn't the editor of *The Transcript*!!!! Good heavens!!! — — — —

Little Bill (i.e. W.C.W. as distinct from Big Bill, W.B.Y.) writes that Amy is roaring around a good deal. He also says that she and Fletcher are to be united in wed-lock, but this seems too perfect a consummation for me to believe it without further testimony.

Well, I must dust out of this. Keep on moving, remember that poetry is more important than verse free or otherwise. Be glad you have a reckless competitor in N.Y. (*Others*) to keep you from believing that scenery alone and unsupported is more interesting than humanity. Really geography is not the source of inspiration. Old Yeats père has sent over such a fine letter on that subject. I hope to print it sometime, or see it printed.

I really must stop. Am arranging new channel of communication with Paris, etc., etc., etc.

1 9 1 6

79: To Harriet Monroe

Coleman's Hatch, 21 January

Dear H.M.: Jan. to hand. A.C.H. by far the best of it. The "One City Only," as you know, I like. The Sarasate poem, with its memory of Spanish metre, is also good.

Rodker had a mood, has not quite caught it. F—— W—— is muck of the last variety, maudlin, philanthropistic, sloppy sentimentality. "Blanche [of the Quarter]." I once knew a fine upstanding woman who had faced strikers, lived her own life in vigorous probity, and had what we can call by no other name than a "fine character," rather the old "spartan sort," her language also was normal. But in contemplating the sort of female that writes "Blanche" 's she said: "Matter with 'em? Matter with 'em!!! They ought to be caught once and raped."

I do not agree in the case of the W—— female. She should be eliminated. She has *no* excuse, travel won't save her. Life in the "monde yanqui polonais" won't save her, travel will not develop her wits. Blowing about her tolerance!!!!!!!!!! Gosh.

If Untermeyer had read my original imagist outlines he'd see that Heine is one of the very people on whom one wished to focus attention. It is Heine vs. the rhetoricians that one wants. I haven't the back files down here, but I think I have definitely indicated Heine as one of the lights. However let the Killkennies slaughter each other. — — — —

F—— W—— is a fine example of what W.B.Y. has called in painting "the mangel-wurzel period." Vide pictorial correspondence Anne Estelle Rice (Tapioca).

Yeats and Hueffer both seem grumped about your anth. [*The New Poetry*]. You *did* ask 'em for pretty big sections . . . and despite signs of improvement (chiefly Masters, who will be read here), the possibility of being printed along with a great exposition of transpontine talent does not yet lure the developed mind. I doubt if I can do anything about it. F.M.H. is taken up with his soldiering and one only sees him when he's on leave.

I hope you are not including all the contributors to *Poetry* in the anth. . . . However, I shall be interested to see the result.

I believe, if *Spoon River* goes well enough, and IF you print more E.M. you might—or he might, if he *are* not too beastly occupied—get his English publisher Werner Laurie, to circulate *Poetry* properly in England. — — — —

And what the hell is the use of people writing about (page 203) people being "sodden with drink and capable too of the highest flights of the soul"? "Mr. Jones not only kept a horse but a yellow canary." Is Amy's book any good? She has read a reasonable amount and ought to know the subject, but her weakness for Fort is a febrile symptom. Still she got started before Fort went so to rot and it is hard to drop an enthusiasm. She ought to be a great service to her contemporaries. Ma chè. . . .

80: To Harriet Monroe

Coleman's Hatch, January

Dear H.M.: Joyce has at last sent some poems. He says he sends 3 and only encloses 2. I shall try to get typed copies from him. "Flood" is, I think, worth printing. Can you manage to pay him *at once?*

Perhaps you can use both the poems. He is a writer who should be kept up. And it is the war that has put him out of his job in Trieste (this last is NOT an aesthetic reason). — — — —

It is an outrage that he shouldn't have got something from his books by now. Which isn't our fault. Ma chè.

81: To Harriet Shaw Weaver

Coleman's Hatch, [February]

Dear Miss Weaver: I agree with you. If Lewis' novel [*Tarr*] begins in April, my article should go into March, with a rather full announcement that the novel is to start in April, and that a new "bust out" is expected.

I think sample copies of both March and April might be sent to the list of names I have sent you, unless you think that too lavish. It *might* pay. I don't know. The prod plus the curiosity about the novel. . . .

I shall not send in any copy for April, as I think all possible space ought to be given Lewis in that number. My eleven further articles can be sent in as you wish, or if you wish. You can announce that I am to contribute during the coming year, or not, as you like, in the March number along with the other announcements. It may please as many as it will displease.

Perhaps Madame Chiolkowska might also make some announcement. She might give her stuff a new name or something. She is usually interesting, I don't suggest any real change in the nature of her copy, but she might start a "New Series" or something, just to make it look as if the spring house-keeping were thorough and vigorous.

I think Aldington might be put onto Prose Authors of the Renaissance. Poggio, Aretino, Sannazarro, Erasmus' dialogues, etc. I don't want to interfere with any of his plans, but if he is ever to do a book on that period it might be of use to him to get his general material into shape, and a series of this sort with some biographical matter might be made rather human and interesting. One might go back as far as Petrarcha. I haven't read his prose, but there may be more snap in it than in his verse. The articles should be informative rather than controversial. I believe Poggio's travels are interesting if anyone could be persuaded to dig out the right selections. At least it would be "off the war" without being too precious. The historic background is interesting if he will take the trouble to "get it up."

About Madame Ciolkowska, *if* she could find, say six writers each worth a full article, it might have a bit more grip, and be a better start for a "new series." It can't be denied that Paris is rather dead just at present. I wonder if there were any interesting "heavy" books brought out just before the war????

Oh well, enough of this.

82: To Harriet Monroe

Coleman's Hatch, [*February*]

Dear H.M.:   LESBIAD. NO. HELL NO.

I began reading it carefully, pleased that someone should try the impossible, knowing the immense difficulty. I meet three attempts at the "Vivamus, mea Lesbia." Not much Catullus and a lot of muck added. Then I come to positively the *worst* travesty of the "Ille me par esse deo videtur" that has *ever* been perpetrated. In this poem Catullus changed, and made possibly a little more austere, Sappho's "PHAINETAI MOI KENOS ISSOS THEOISIN."

Even Landor turned back from an attempt to translate Catullus. I have failed forty times myself so I do know the matter. *But* there are *decent* and *dignified* ways of failing, and this female has not failed in any respectable way.

The most hard-edged and intense of the Latin poets should *not* be cluttered with wedding-cake cupids and clichés like "dregs of pain," etc., etc., ad. inf. Pink blue baby ribbon.

You need not communicate my opinion to the female.—There's no use cutting up a writer unless there is some chance of doing them some good.

I think it would be a mistake to review a book of so little worth as this is, however nicely printed. It shows neither merit nor promise, there is not enough good to make it profitable to point out the faults.

As for "mood transcriptions," nothing could possibly be further from Latin feeling than this bake-shop decoration. God! she's no better than Storer, probably not so good.

Now another matter. Talking with Yeats yesterday, he said it is "ridiculous for *Poetry* to sell at six pence, you ought to charge a shilling." This point is perhaps worth considering. — — — —

P.S. Forty years of hard labour *might* teach the Catullus female something but I doubt it.

83: To Harriet Monroe

London, 5 March

Dear H.M.: I had a long letter from [T. Sturge] Moore which I have destroyed. I have to some extent pacified him as you see by this card.

But I wish you could realize the uncomfortable position you place me in by reducing the rates of payment without informing me. I am not intimate with Moore and therefore it is all the worse. Or rather I don't know which is worse in dealing with these older men who have been accustomed to certain consideration: to have an intimacy clouded as by the reduction on Hueffer and the scandalous shift later, or to be put de puntos with a man whom I meet rather frequently at W.B.Y.'s but with whom I have always a slight disagreement.

Again the anthology crops up (in his first letter which I destroyed). Of course, *here* people get paid for lending poems to anthologies. Where one is breaking the way, as I was in *Des Imagistes*, or trying to bring in new people as in the *Cat. Anth.*, there is no money. But America has no standing here, and if you write for free contributions, you must at least write as if you were asking and not conferring a favor. Perhaps you did. Neither, considering the awful rabble that has been admitted to *Poetry*, can you expect men of position here to be eager to appear in a book simply qualified as an anthology from *Poetry*, or whatever it is you tell them.

As to rates, less than ten dollars per page is *not* a good rate. One gets ten or fifteen dollars for a sonnet in plenty of places, and *Poetry* gets much more than 14 lines to a page . . . AND the less commercial the man, the less will he be bothered with fuss. — — — —

OF COURSE I dare say his damn poem *is* only eight pages long. . . . Ma chè Christo!!

Still: either *Poetry* IS Maecenas, upholding a principle that poetry ought to be decently paid, or else it is a sheet begging for favours . . . which last it, of course, is not. BUT nothing is more enraging to a writer than to receive less than he has been led to expect (even if it is only ten cents less) for a job.

As W.B.Y. writes to his sisters: "Are you a convent, or are you not?"

Another detail you might remember is that every Englishman has once or twice or twelve times in his life been cheated by one or more of our compatriots. (I myself more times, and I should never trust an American voluntarily and consciously until I had known him some time.) This is of course unfair to the 99 just men in the hundred, but it takes so little to stir up all the memory these people have of "American business," that these small misunderstandings are very difficult for me to deal with.

What I want, and what would be best for the magazine would be for me to be able to *select* from Moore's mss.—from anybody's—and to know when he had done a really fine thing and then get it. This of course CAN'T be done after strained relations. No one in England will submit stuff for editorial selection—at least no one worth anything. The present political degradation of our country will not help things.

Being the best magazine in America is NOT good enough (that you know perfectly well). There is this country—intelligently selective even when not creative (at least more intelligently selective than ours). There is also an absolute standard. — — — —

P.S. The fact that there's an awful slump in Eng. poetry just at this moment is all the more reason why we should go on trying to maintain our contention that we print the best of it. Moore isn't a colossus but still he isn't a yahoo like Chesterton, etc., etc.

We ought to have had that incomprehensible thing of H.D.'s in the March *Egoist* and there were two decent things by R.A. in the *Poetry Journal* some time ago. When do we get some *Masters*??? Mind you, I thought the last *Poetry* (Feb.) fairly solid and the prose stuff uniform. (Yes, quite apart from Sandburg on me.) I thought the standard of criticism in the number good, and without the howlers that so often annoy me. — — — —

84: To Kate Buss

London, 9 March

Dear Miss Buss: It is always pleasant to know that one has a reader. As my American royalties amount to about one dollar 85 cents per year, I am naturally surprised to discover, or have revealed to me, the presence of so rare a phenomenon, habitat U.S.A.

I have forwarded your request for books to Mathews. Now unfortunately Mrs. Henderson wrote to me or him only a fortnight ago, I suppose about you, and I think from a note of Mathews' which I have mislaid that he, like the sap-headed imbecile that he is, has sent your lot of books to the infernal chasm of the Boston *Transcript*. If you don't receive them in a week or so, or if they don't turn up unlabeled at the *B.T.* office (in which case they will probably be given to the janitor), I think you had best write to Mathews. — — — —

I enclose announcements of part of my immediate activity and will put the photo either in this envelope or another, depending on its size when I find it. (I am just back from Sussex and still littered with the débris of Gaudier's studio, so it may be a long process—the finding.) It is the most recent, probably the most disagreeable, and slightly resembles Mr. Shaw, which I do not.

Re Gaudier-Brzeska: leaflet explains itself.

Re *Egoist:* Am trying to put a little life into it again. If I succeed in getting a little cash I shall properly revive it. Lewis' novel is entertaining, and I am much pleased with their sporting intention of publishing Joyce's novel in despite of all fools, printers, censors, etc., whatsoever. It, the novel, is a very fine piece of work, and I hope you will review it also when it finally comes out.

Of course American publishers ought to be stirred up into doing such things. They are rather weak in the back, also they skulk behind the beastly tariff on books, which you and the rest of the inhabitants should not sleep until you get rid of. It is as bad as a second Wilson.

Further announcement:

CERTAIN NOBLE PLAYS OF JAPAN
FROM THE MANUSCRIPTS OF ERNEST FENOLLOSA
SELECTED AND FINISHED BY EZRA POUND
WITH AN INTRODUCTION BY W. B. YEATS

Now being published by the Cuala Press (10/6). I expect proofs any day. I dare say they'll send you a review copy if you write to them for it. — — — — But if you want "copy" you'd better save it for an article on the new theatre, or theatreless drama, about which there'll be a good deal to say soon, as Yeats is making a new start on the foundation of these Noh dramas.

My occupations this week consist in finally (let us hope) dealing with Brzeska's estate; 2, getting a vorticist show packed up and started for New York; 3, making a selection from old father Yeats' letters, some of which are very fine (I suppose this will lap over into next week), small vol. to appear soon; 4, bother a good deal about the production of Yeats' new play.

This letter as a pure prose composition may suffer slightly in consequence.

Biographical or otherwise: Born in Hailey, Idaho. First connection with vorticist movement during the blizzard of '87 when I came East, having decided that the position of Hailey was not sufficiently central for my activities—came East behind the first rotary snow plough, the inventor of which vortex saved me from death by croup by feeding me with lumps of sugar saturated with kerosene. (Parallels in the life of Fracastorius.) After that period, life gets too complicated to be treated coherently in a hurried epistle. It is very hard to compose on this topic.

Bibliography is in *Who's Who*, I think; at least it is right in the English *W.W.* I can't keep track of the others.

Small Maynard in Boston are supposed to have published two of my books, a selection of poems and an ill-starred *Guido Cavalcanti* (I dare say they will send you a review copy of that, or them, if you ask). I wish *someone* would put a little dynamite under them for it is slightly ridiculous that the .oooooooooooooooooooooo% of the great American public which wants my work should have to send to England for five or six small books instead of decently purchasing *one* volume inclusive and up to date in the U.S.

I shan't publish again here until after the war, so with the exception of *Cathay*, there is nothing newer than *Ripostes* that is available. I don't know why all the spirit of adventure in these matters should be confined to a few round sleepy little old men in this city. Besides Coburn has done such a classic effigy that even Yeats thinks it ought to placate the public and console them for the verses to follow. He complains now that my stuff gives him no asylum for his affections. (That is intimate conversation and not for quotation save indirectly.)

I have told Mathews to send you also a *Cat. Anth.* [*Catholic Anthology*]. The Jesuits here have, I think, succeeded in preventing its being reviewed in press (at least I have seen no review during the past months). Poor Elkin wailing, "Why, why will you needlessly irritate people?"

E.P.: "Elkin, did you ever know Meynell to *buy* a book?"

E.M.: "n n n n n-no, I ddddon't know that he ever did. He always wants me to be giving him books. He he he said, 'You won't sell a copy, sir, you won't sell a COPY,' banging the table with his fist."

(That you can quote, anywhere you like.)

I think the decent papishes are just as much pleased as anyone else, and have just as clear vision of the firm of ———— as anyone else has. Having forged the donation of Constantine (some years since) they now think the august and tolerant name belongs to them, a sort of apostolic succession.

I know I should be more grave in view of events on the continent, but I can't spend all my time writing obituaries; which seems about all there is at the moment. I shall try to finish a brief "Henry James" for the May *Egoist*.

What have I left out? Do keep an eye out for Joyce and also for T. S. Eliot. They are worth attention.

The *Poetry* with your Armenian stuff hasn't yet arrived.

Interruption of two hours. It is now too late to go on with this. ————

P.S. I am afraid this is a very helter-skelter sort of reply, but short histories of one's life are difficult impromptu.

85: To John Quinn

London, 10 March

Dear Quinn: Lewis has just sent in the first dozen drawings. They are all over the room, and the thing is stupendous. The vitality, the fullness of the man! Nobody knows it. My God, the stuff lies in a pile of dirt on the man's floor. Nobody has seen it. Nobody has *any* conception of the volume and energy and the variety.

Blake, that W.B.Y. is always going on about!!!! Lewis has got Blake scotched to a finish. He's got so much more *in him* than Gaudier. I know he is seven years older. Ma chè Cristo!

I have certainly GOT to do a Lewis book to match the Brzeska. Or perhaps a "Vorticists" (being nine-tenths Lewis, and reprinting my paper on Wadsworth, with a few notes on the others).

This is the first day for I don't know how long that I have envied any man his spending money. It seems to me that Picasso alone, certainly alone among the living artists whom I know of, is in anything like the same class. It is not merely knowledge of technique, or skill, it is intelligence and knowledge of life, of the whole of it, beauty, heaven, hell, sarcasm, every kind of whirlwind of force and emotion. Vortex. That is the right word, if I did find it myself. — — — —

In all this modern froth—that's what it is, froth, 291, Picabia, etc., etc., etc., Derain even, and the French—there isn't, so far as I have had opportunity of knowing, ONE trace of this man's profundity.

Brzeska's "Jojo" sits impassively before me, flanked by a pale mulatto, and something (blue drawing) in spirit like Ulysses in a storm passing the Sirens. If any man says there is no romance and no emotion in this vorticist art, I say he is a liar. Years ago, three I suppose it is, or four, I said to Epstein (not having seen these things of Lewis, or indeed more than a few things he had then exhibited), "The sculpture seems to be so much more interesting. I find it much more interesting than the painting."

Jacob said, "But Lewis' drawing has the qualities of sculpture." (He may have said "all the qualities" or "so many of the qualities." At any rate, that set me off looking at Lewis.)

What the later quarrel with Jacob is, I do not know, save that Jacob is a fool when he hasn't got a chisel in his hand and a rock before him, and Lewis *can* at moments be extremely irritating. (But then, damn it all, he is quite apt to be in the right.)

Oh well, enough of this. You'll soon have the stuff before you.

86: To Harriet Shaw Weaver

London, 17 March

Dear Miss Weaver: I personally should prefer the Joyce novel without an introduction by anyone. However, that is a practical point outside my jurisdiction.

As for early or late in the season, I think that is all nonsense in connection with a book of this sort. If it were to be sold by Smith and the other barrators, or if it were to go through the usual channels of corruption there would be some reason for consulting their times and seasons. But a book like this which the diseased and ailing vulgar will not buy can take its own course.

If all printers refuse (I have written this also to Joyce) I suggest that largish blank spaces be left where passages are cut out. Then the excisions can be manifolded (not carbon copies, but another process) by typewriter on good paper, and if necessary I will paste them in myself. The public can be invited to buy with or without restorations and the copyright can be secured [on] the book as *printed*. That is to say the restorations will be privately printed and the book-without-them "published."

And damn the censors.

Joyce is ill in bed with rheumatism, and very worried, and I hope for his sake, as well as for the few intelligent people who want the book, that it can manage to come out.

Professional people never have any real knowledge about what an unusual book will do, and when cornered they usually confess it, so I don't think their advice about times and seasons is worth much. And par example, the "practical" Pinker was able to do less than I was, and was very glad of my aid in getting the mss. even read.

Let me know when you want copy for May number, s.v.p.

P.S. Pardon haste of this note but I *am* really hurried.

Can you come to tea with us sometime when I get a spare hour? I will write.

87: To Wyndham Lewis

London, March

Dear Lewis: I have cabled Quinn, written to Miss Weaver, and had up Pinker's office on the phone. They say he won't be back today (I phoned at 2.15, it is now 2.25). His secretary says Joyce's ms. is now at Werner Laurie's. I don't think that matters, but . . . , no, I don't think it matters save that V's pull will be strengthened or weakened according as W.L. likes or dislikes the Joyce.

P.S. Perhaps old Stg. Moore could do something with the Royal Lit. Fund.

88: To Harriet Shaw Weaver

London, 30 March

Dear Miss Weaver: I find that the name and address of Kreymborg's publisher is John Marshall, 331 Fourth Ave., New York, U.S.A.

I have just written him direct a very strong letter re Joyce, advising him to print the Joyce in preference to my book,[1] if his capital is limited. I can't go further than that.

I advise you to send *him* (i.e., mail to him not to Kreymborg) at once the leaves of *The Egoist* containing the novel *and also* the bits the printer cut out. He may as well have it all, and at once while my letter is hot in his craw.

[1] *This Generation,* never published.

My other letter was to Kreymborg for Marshall, I think the two letters ought to penetrate some one skull.

89: To IRIS BARRY

[Pound had seen some of Iris Barry's poems in Harold Monro's magazine, *Poetry and Drama*. On 2 April he wrote to Miss Barry, asking if he might see more of her work and suggesting that some might be used in *Poetry*.]

London, 17 April

Dear Miss Barry: It is rather difficult to respond to your request for criticism of your stuff. I am not quite satisfied with the things you have sent in, still many of them seem to have been done more or less in accordance with the general suggestions of imagisme, wherewith I am too much associated. The main difficulty seems to me that you have not yet made up your mind what you want to do or how you want to do it. I have introduced a number of young writers (too many, one can't be infallible); before I start I usually try to get some sense of their dynamics and to discern if possible which way they are going.

With the method of question and answer: Are you very much in earnest, have you very much intention of "going on with it," mastering the medium, etc.? Or are you doing vers libre because it is a new and attractive fashion and anyone can write a few things in vers libre? There's no use my beating about the bush with these enquiries. I get editorial notes from odd quarters blaming me that I have set off too many people.

I can send on your stuff to Chicago as it is, if you like. I should prefer to see more of it first, if that is convenient.

Coming to details. In "Impression," I don't think "dissolved" is just the right word, though I recognize that you may have been aiming at a sort of restraint or under-emphasis which *can* be effective.

In "The Fledgling," "emancipated from the home" seems to me a definitely Fabian Society or cliché phrase, you might have used it with " " marks in an ironic passage, but the rest of this poem is grave, and the reiteration of "The fire is nearly out, the lamp is nearly out" in the first 2 and last 2 lines seems to me very effective. In fact, the poem seems to me to be good, and all its words in one tone, homogeneous, in key, save this one Latin, doctrinaire term.

I am not sure that the sonnet "The Burial" isn't the best of the lot. Not that I like it best.

The Sapphic affair seems to spoil itself by a touch of trifling. I may be wrong. I think both passion and sensuousness are really without humour. One can be ironic and critical of their defects, or one can be gravely in sympathy. I can't recall any effective poetry that does not comply with one or other of the cases??????

Some of the things seem to me "just imagistic," neither better nor worse than a lot of other imagistic stuff that gets into print. If I am to hurl a new writer at the magazine with any sort of conviction I must have qualche cosa di speciale, I must have at least three or four pages of stuff which "establish the personality." At least I am not interested in the matter unless I can do that. I simply forward some mss. without comment.

In some of the "regular" stuff, you fall too flatly into the "whakty whakty whakty whakty whak," of the old pentameter. Pentameter O.K. if it is interesting, but a lot of lines with no variety won't do.

I don't see what you gain by the form "maked" in "Biography"??

Re cadence: "Some loving thoughts still linger here with me," seems rather a flat hobby horse sort of movement, that we've all heard till we're dead with it. So many of your pentameter lines seem all in one jog, whereas the metre skillfully used *can* display a deal of variety.

With some of the things, as I said, there is nothing to distinguish you from a lot of neo-imagists, and there are too d'd many neo-imagistes just at present.

"Monstrance" seems to me a beastly literary, magazine-poetry sort of word. Enough to spoil any mood.

No, hang it all, the stuff in *Poetry and Drama* (Dec. 1914) seems to me to have more passion and considerably more individuality than anything you have sent me in this sheaf.

"That . . . which . . . " etc. in "Persian Desert" line 5 seems a little clumsily arranged.

(Of course if a thing moves one, all this minutiae is no matter, or not much matter, but a series of these minute leakages will sink a poem, or a group of poems.) As to this particular poem, I can't read it so as to make the final cadence really a close or ending. (That may be my dulness, but I don't get the rhythm. The last line seems to me to be a tripping little line, gaily running tatatati, four very short little vowels, the soft "owl" and then the long *ie.*)

I think you might get a certain edge or cut of sensuousness, passion whatever you like to call it, and which would relieve the very gentle sort of impressionism-imagisme of "Picture," which is quite nice as it is, but not different from a poem I received last week.

It is so dashed hard to find poems different from the poems rec'd last week, and the beastly magazine gets *so* depressing if one doesn't find them.

I don't know whether any of these suggestions are any use to you, or whether you want to "have another go" at any of the poems you have sent in.????? In any case I should like to see a large mass of your stuff, if there is a larger mass. (If there isn't or if there isn't going to be . . . it is not much worth my while arguing with an edittor.) Though in any case I would send on to Chicago some or all the mss. you have sent in, if you wish it. Several of the things would do to fill up a group of things if there were a few more salient poems to fire it.

On second thought I return you the poems which interest me least (five of them).

There is a newer American publication, which alas does not pay its contributors, but which would print some of those I am keeping if *Poetry* refused. BUT I want a larger lot of poems to look through before I send any off.

My present feeling is that "nothing is worth while save desire" and I am sick of verse without it. Or else there is a bitterness which shows the trace of desire, that also can make good verses, but placidity is a drug, at least for the season.

Ah well, you may have got a worse overhauling than you wanted, but one can't criticize and be tactful all at once. And at any rate, I shan't have kept you waiting six months for an answer.

90: TO HARRIET MONROE

London, 21 April

Dear H.M.: April number depressing. Re March: I didn't mean you to print *that* letter to you,[1] and not to *Poetry*, that you quoted. What I did want printed was the note on *The Dial*, and I repeat for the 444444444444-44th time that I can not see any sense in your keeping on terms with these old dodderers, treacherous decrepit old beasts who would, you know perfectly well, stab you in the back the first chance they got, and suppress us all together.

However, on the positive side:

I think—both because it would be a good thing in itself, and since there has been such a deluge of rhetoric and slush spilled over new verse, and since you have printed excerpts from my not very compact or well-phrased letter—that:

It would be a good thing to reprint my original "Don'ts," with the addition of a few notes, emendations or additions. An 8 or ten or 12 page pamphlet for ten cents. It would certainly pay its expenses, and it could be more widely dispersed than a bound volume of *Poetry* at 1.50 would be likely to be. It would be much better than my writing new articles pointing out the various sorts of silliness into which neo-imagism or neogism is perambulating, which latter could with difficulty escape allusions to Amy and Fletcher, etc. etc.

The first anthology was designed to get printed and published the work of a few poets whose aim was to write a few excellent poems, perhaps not enough for even the slenderest volume, rather than the usual magazine thousands of E—— B——, the futurist diarrhoea, rhetorical slush, etc.

That first type of poet is the one worth caring for. I do not think the present methods of the neoists are in any way designed to further or foster the "few perfect" things against Chestertonian or Paul Fortian sloppiness. The general copying of a few of the most superficial characteristics of the first group of writers does no more good to American poetry than the former slavery to the *Century-Harper's* ginger-bread, stucco, paste-board ideal. You will remember that the "Don'ts" were originally intended as a

[1] Letter No. 83, p. 70, was printed in *Poetry*, March 1916.

slip to be sent with returned mss. so the idea of a pamphlet is not so far off the original intention.

Production in England at present very low. I — — — — have had in some stuff from Iris Barry, have sent back part and told her to let me see a larger mass. I think one can get a four or five page group from her, ultimately.

Eliot has been worried with schools, etc. (i.e. teaching, not schools of verse or porpoises). He is to come in next week to plan a book, and I will then send you a group of his things. — — — —

91: To Iris Barry

London, 24 April

Dear Miss Barry: Don't bother to type mss. for me if you have so little free time; your hand is fairly legible. . . . Still, one does sometimes see a poem better in typescript, but don't bother to make new copies.

"Impression": "dissolve" is bad not only because it is, as I think, out of key with what goes before but because it really means a solid going into liquid, and when you compare that to pear-petals falling, you blur your image. Conceivably, crystals suspended in liquid might dissolve quickly, but if they fell they would slip away slowly through the water. At least the word bothers me. "Faster" may be the hitch; one doesn't always get the real trouble at the first shot, but one can sometimes tell about where it lies. You might say "Then we drifted apart" or forty other things; the phrase "friendship was dissolved" is I think newspaperish, and then it is passive and your comparison is active: "petals fall"; "was dissolved."

(You are quite right, it is much easier to go at such points in talk than by letter. However.)

It isn't so much "getting a better word" very often as doing a new line.

Your practice with regular metres is a good thing; better keep in mind that [it] is practice, and that it will probably serve to get your medium pliable. No one can do good free verse who hasn't struggled with the regular; at least I don't know anyone who has.

In *"The Fledgling"*: I don't see why you don't say simply "escape" instead of "be emancipated." The "for ever" in your "gone for ever" emendation seems to me a little in excess of the real emotion (which is desire to get free, rather uncalculating)????? At least it is a little out of key with the rest of the words . . . as I feel it.

Re *"Girls"*: I think you are right, it is not the best you can do, and you had better take a new canvas.

Re *"Monstrance"*: You are out of my depth. I don't in the least know what to say about a word that has a Catholic association. If it has, it will probably make the word or the poem right to Catholic readers.——?? Is there any way of making it carry to non-Catholic readers to whom "monstrance" gives a sort of mood-breaking jolt? Ars longa.

In *"Nocturne"*: I wonder if you are right to jump from "slipped" in the first strophe, to "remember" in the second. I shouldn't say "His young head crowns," inversion with no special meaning or reason.

"In the Desert": The "that stirs which" can be avoided in a dozen ways. "Wind steps through the darkness" (possibly too violent).

The thing I notice in your emendations is that you stick very tight to the form or arrangement of words you have already used. Better get the trick of throwing the whole back into the melting-pot and recasting all in one piece. It is better than patching.

A new line or a new word may demand the rewriting of half a poem to make it all of a piece.

Re metre: What they call "metre" in English means for the most part "iambic." They have heard of other metres and tried a few, but if the music of the words and the feel of the mood are to have any relation, one *must* write as one feels. It may be only an old hankering after quantitative verse that is at the bottom of it. All languages I think have shown a tendency to lengthen the foot in one way or another, as they develop.

Well, send on what you've got and I will go through it.

92: To Iris Barry

London, 2 May

Dear Miss Barry: No, there's no hurry about retouching the rest of the verses. I can't place them anywhere to any advantage until the first lot comes out in *Poetry*, not, that is, unless by a very rare chance we bring out another *BLAST*. Not that this is any reason why you shouldn't send them (i.e. the verses attacked) or the new ones to me whenever you feel like it, only there is no external or mechanical cause of haste.

If you can't escape your Birmingham, you had better get Karl Appel's *Provenzalische Chrestomathie* out of the university library. German publication not likely to be got for you through a bookseller, but the university ought to have it. (There is a university in B. isn't there?) I'll lend you what's left of my copy if there isn't.

And really you mustn't send me large books of stamps. In my strictly quasi-editorial capacity, I may have used about six, which I remove for the sake of companionability.

93: To Iris Barry

London, May

Dear Miss Barry: If you have a passion for utility, and if by any chance you intended to get my new volume of poems *Lustra* when it comes out, then do for God's sake order your copy at once and UNABRIDGED.

The idiot Mathews has got the whole volume set up in type, and has now got a panic and marked 25 poems for deletion. Most of them have already been printed in magazines without causing any scandal whatever, and some of them are among the best in the book. (It contains *Cathay*, some new Chinese stuff and all my own work since *Ripostes*.)

The scrape is both serious and ludicrous. Some of the poems will have to go, but in other cases the objections are too stupid for words. It is part printer and part Mathews.

At any rate if you were going to want the book, do write for it at once, *unabridged*.

The printers have gone quite mad since the Lawrence fuss. Joyce's new novel has gone to America (AMERICA!) to be printed by an enthusiastic publisher. Something has got to be done or we'll all of us be suppressed, à la counter-reformation, dead and done for.

P.S. Elkin Mathews — — — — called in Yeats to mediate and Yeats quoted Donne at him for his soul's good. I don't know what will come of it.

94: To HARRIET MONROE

London, 5 June

Dear H.M. So long as you put the "Cabaret" question on the grounds of expediency and the assininity of your guarantors, or in fact on any ground save the desire of the editor for the candy box, I suppose I must submit. I enclose the only other poem I have ready, to go with the inoffensive selection you already have. FOR GOD'S SAKE print 'em at once.

My next contribution will probably be a 40 page fragment from a more important opus.

I approve of your trying to use the larger things (re Head etc.); but Drama is a dam'd form, tending nearly always toward work of secondary intensity, though the tendency doesn't always set in strong enough to wreck the work.

I am writing to W. H. Davies for some poems. I was much impressed by his reading a few days ago. I doubt very much if the things will carry in print; at least they must lose a lot by not having them done by his own voice, but there seems to be something in him, or rather in his later work. I saw the early stuff some years ago, and he hadn't then got very far.

I didn't much mind my letter to you being printed, but there were things I wanted printed much more, *and* the letter could have been much better if it had been intended for print. The very name of the U.S. president is an obscenity. I suppose it is debarred on these grounds.

My *Lustra* is all set up, and I find I have been beguiled into leaving out the more violent poems to the general loss of the book, the dam'd bloody insidious way one is edged into these tacit hypocrisies *is* disgusting.

I don't mean I have left out anything I put into the ms. Certainly the "Cabaret" is there in its entirety, etc., but the pretty poems and the Chinese softness have crept up in number and debilitated the tone.

What you object to in the "Cabaret" is merely that it isn't bundled up into slop, sugar and sentimentality, the underlying statement is very humane and most moral. It simply says there is a certain form of life, rather sordid, not gilded with tragedy any more than another, just as dull as another, and possibly quite as innocent and innocuous, vide, my singers in Venice. The thing the bourgeois will always hate is the fact that I make the people *real*. I treat the dancers as human beings, not as "symbols of sin." That is the crime and the "obscenity." E poi basta.

95: To Iris Barry

London, June

Dear Miss Barry: I am sending Bill "The Cup," "The Daughter," "La Coquette," "Biography," "Public Gardens," "Head Clerk," "Resentment." I don't imagine he will be able to use them all, but he may as well suit himself.

I make the following notes on other poems. "Wet Morning": "Too tender to have become grimed" is a weak line. I am sorry about your holidays, also you should have a chance to see Fenollosa's big essay on verbs, mostly on verbs. Heaven knows when I shall get it printed. He inveighs against "is," wants transitive verbs. "Become" is as weak as "is." Let the grime *do* something to the leaves. "All nouns come from verbs." To primitive man, a thing only is what it *does*. That is Fenollosa, but I think the theory is a very good one for poets to go by.

Try the Hon. lover in vers libre, leave the rhymes in but let them come where they will, and try leaving out the extra words (if they are extra.) Another variant would be to let the "Us" stay on at the end of the line . . . "upon." The present line-form of the poem interferes very much with the cadence, and gives a jolt where one oughtn't to be.

I think however you would find the weak spots and eliminate them if you wrote out the poem without inversions and chucking the sonnet idea.?????????

In "Complaint" chuck "Lo" and "do you think they," and then see if it will form up into anything.

If you can send back these quite soon, I will send them also along to Williams. *Others* is a harum scarum vers libre American product, chiefly useful because it keeps "Arriet," (edtr. *Poetry*) from relapsing into the Nineties.

Get loose whenever you can. I am sending "The Daughter" in preference to "The Burial"; there isn't room for both in so small a bundle. I don't think the other poems are quite good enough, or even good enough without the "quite." "In Two Months" has something in it.

Poor Mathews can't send you the unabridged *Lustra* yet as it ain't printed. However, he has been persuaded into doing 200 copies unabridged for the elect and is allowed to have the rest of the edition almost as modest as he likes—God knows, the whole thing is innocent enough, but the poor man has had an awful week of it.—I suppose he has some right to decide how he'll spend his money.

Monro is called up on Saturday so that stifled my shifting the book to the Poetry Book Shop.

96: To WYNDHAM LEWIS

London, 24 June

Dear Lewis: Judging the matter from the depths of my moderately comfortable arm chair, with the products of your brush, pen and the reproductory processes of the late publisher M. Goschen before me—or from free seats at the opera—I can not see that the future of the arts demands that you should be covered with military distinctions. It is equally obvious that you should not be allowed to spill your gore in heathen and furrin places.

I can only counsel you to endure your present ills with equanimity and not to be too ready to see malice where mayhap none is intended. Nothing exists without efficient cause. I can but ask you to contemplate the position as deeply as you are able, and that without passion, and from *all* points of view.

I should suggest that you spend your spare time with a note book, preparing future compositions. If you like I will send a copy of *Cathay* so that the colonel may be able to understand what is imagisme.

You didn't send me your address so I couldn't forward the *Egoists*, which I send herewith.

Ed. Wad[sworth] went off yesterday for Lemnos. Don't think my opening paragraphs unfeeling. I only ask you to consider all possible interpretations of fact before you rush to an emotive conclusion. I trust you will not think the remarks imply a personal bias on my part, but take them rather as a point of view which may be held by persons other than the writer.

I appear to be the only person of interest left in the world of art, London. I have had a fine row over *Lustra;* as both Mathews and the printer decline to go on with it on grounds of indecorum, I am getting 300 copies printed almost unabridged at Mathews' expense and he is to print the rest *castrato.* I have placed a Jap book with Macmillan, which is a peg up for me. The enclosed circular, with the young damsel squirming neath the jujube tree, is for your comfort. It will fill you, in the midst of your afflictions, with a sense of your own dignity, and show how badly you are needed here as a police force. However it is supposed to net me £20 which I bloody well need.

Met that pig M—— S—— at the U.S. consulate, by accident. He gave me a taxi ride and a good cigarette. He said he would be very glad to consider *Tarr* if I could get him a loan of the ms. Publication after the war.

Pinker also wanted to know if he might be allowed to vend the ms. As he has been no use re Joyce's stuff, and I have done all the work, I don't see that there is much use dealing with him. A. P. Watt fixed me up with Macmillan in about a week. I don't know whether *Tarr* is in his line.

I have not heard from Quinn re receipt of pictures. He didn't seem keen on paying for *BLAST*. He said he put up as much *as I thought he ought to*, but I did not feel it would be wise to press the matter. I should want £100 to lubricate it.

I have now £25 of his which I have asked permission to pay over to you.

For the rest, don't be more irritating to your unfortunate "superior" officers than you find absolutely necessary to your peace of mind, or at least try not to be.

And don't get wroth with the *Egoist* for cutting the novel. The sooner they get through serializing it the better, for then we can get it published decently in vol. form.

And do try to penetrate the meaning of some of this note.

97: To WYNDHAM LEWIS

London, 28 June

Dear Lewis: I still rather doubt whether you have got to the bottom of my beastly letter. The information I received, or the assurances were very definite and at the same time very general. They are hardly repeatable, and as they tacitly forbade me to make any further more meticulous enquiry, their substance was very much what I have already conveyed to you . . . but in a sort of categorical and imperial tone.

That is to say "The gods grant your prayers *to the letter*, neither more nor less. . . . Cease from troubling the gods."

I will have a copy of *Cathay* transmitted. I think I perhaps sympathize more with your desire for advancement than the tone of my last note might seem to show. I will wait for a fitting moment. Balfour between the second and third acts did not seem to me to present a favourable target. It is not his dept. and he would have been distinctly annoyed. He considered that Shelley's best work was done in his youth, etc.

Your Colonel seems more contemporary in his interests. Besides you see more of him.

I don't believe A. P. Watt would be any use re an article for the Dily Mile. The last link with Goschen is either "joined up" or evading the military. God knows I don't know how to go at a thing of this sort (article into D. *Mail*), I have never been able to get printed in any English paper save the *New Age* and *Egoist*, and the more august reviews.

The £25 malheureusement is not yours till Q. instructs me to pay it you, which won't be till he gets my letter saying I have recovered it for him.

We know not any à Beckett, but D. thinks she may have a cousin who does. She has never met the cousin.

I am bubbling at my Jap plays for MacM. If Q. is successful in N.Y. in placing various things, I may get started on the brochure concerning your glory. De Bosschère is very much impressed with "Timon," says "we have nothing like it in Paris." Not exactly news. *Ma che.*

98: To HARRIET SHAW WEAVER

London, 12 July

Dear Miss Weaver: A friend has persuaded Heinemann to read Joyce's novel for himself. I have sent on my sole set of *Egoists* but Heinemann says something is missing. Can you send him the complete ms. at once? to his private house — — — — *not* to the office.

Don't mention my name, s.v.p.

George Moore has also been reading Joyce with approbation. We'll get the thing started sometime.

99: To IRIS BARRY

London, 13 July

Dear Miss Barry: I believe the Underground runs from here to Wimbledon. At least I have a map with black lines on it, moving in that direction, and I think it implies some form of conveyance. I will enquire with due diligence. Also as to time consumed in transit. Place of arrival, whether two or six stations in Wimbledon, etc.

As to marks of identification in case there be two males loose on the platform??? Do you wish any, or will you trust purely to instinct? And I?

The "Whitman Chesterton" definition is new to me. Manning in one of his more envenomed moments once said something about "More like Khr-r-ist and the late James MacNeil Whistler every year."

It would be a shame to pass in silence for the want of a boutonnière. Perhaps a perfectly plain ebony staff, entirely out of keeping with the rest of the costume will serve. Perfectly plain, straight, *without* any tin bands, etc. at the top of it. Emphatically not a country weapon.

And what am I to look for?

100: To WYNDHAM LEWIS

London, July

Dear Lewis: Quinn has sent the other £25, which I will forward to you as soon as I hear that the address on this envelope is still the right one.

He now says he "agrees with what" I say about Lewis. He expects to make an offer for certain other works "ten or twelve or possibly 15." That is rather indefinite and I doubt if you could sue legally if he changed his mind. However!!!! Davies seems to be friendly. He offered to pay half the freight when Montrose refused. Quinn naturally wouldn't let Davis do it. Still it shows a sporting mind on the, or in the, skull of Davies. Q. thinks, or thought, in a former note that Davis might buy something.

The £25 which I now have for you finishes up the £150 of the agreement with Q. for the Kermoos etc.

I have just returned from a dam'd week by the seawaves. Eliot present. Eliot in local society. Fry, Canon, Lowes Dickenson, Hope Johnson (none of whom I met). But the ineffable pleasure of watching Fry's sylphlike and lardlike length bobbing around in the muddy water off the pier.

Met Hueffer's brother-in-law on the plaisaunce. He said a shell had burst near our friend and that he had had a nervous breakdown and was for the present safe in a field hospital. Ford's brother Oliver is in the trenches. (These small bits of news will doubtless cheer and enlighten you. Thank God I have got back to the court-suburb.)

Ed Wad has arrived in Mudros. He has written me an epistle which I will forward to you if you have not received one of your own.

P.S. Eliot, after mature deliberation, has discovered that Fry is "an ass." Eliot had walked into his landlady's bedroom, "quite by mistake," said he was looking for his wife. Landlady unconvinced. Wife believes in the innocence of his intentions. Landlady sympathetic with wife. Landlady spent Sunday placing flowers on her mother's grave. Landlady (in parenthesis) unmarried but under fifty.

Oh yes, called at Leicester gallery day before I went toward seawaves. Phillips away ill, so accomplished nothing.

101: To Harriet Shaw Weaver

London, 19 July

Dear Miss Weaver: Will you please write at once accepting Huebsch (? I think it is Huebsch) offer for the U.S.A. edition of Joyce. I will phone Pinker at once also. I have just heard that Marshall has met with personal calamities which, while they exonerate him wholly for his neglect to answer letters, will make it impossible for him to go on with anything.

Don't write to Joyce for a few days, it will only give him needless worry, and in a few days we may have a reply from Heinemann.

102: To Iris Barry

London, [?20] July

KOMPLEAT KULTURE: Schedule at 11 227 b 5 q/12/4685
The main thing being to have enmagazined some mass of fine literature which hasn't been mauled over and vulgarized and preached as a virtue by Carlyle, *The Daily Mail. The Spectator, The New Witness,* or any other

proletariat of "current opinion." This mass of fine literature supposedly saves one from getting swamped in contemporaneousness, and from thinking that things naturally or necessarily must or should be as they are, OR should change according to some patent schedule. ALSO should serve as a model of style, or suggest possibilities of various sorts of perfection or maximum attainment.

Greek seems to me a storehouse of wonderful rhythms, possibly impracticable rhythms. If you don't read it and if you can't read Latin translations from it, it can't be helped. Most English translations are hopeless. The best are in prose.

MacKail's *Select Epigrams from the Greek Anthology* (Longman's, Green, 2/) is worth reading.

There is a translation of Theocritus; I think Andrew Lang had something to do with it. Parts are readable and beautiful, especially the "Wheel of the Magic Spells." (I think it is book IV, Idyl 2.) – – – –

I don't know that one can read any trans. of the *Odyssey*. Perhaps you could read book XI. I have tried an adaptation in the "Seafarer" metre, or something like it, but I don't expect anyone to recognize the source very quickly.

Certainly the so-called "poetic" translations of Greek drama are wholly impossible.

Wharton's "Sappho" is the classic achievement. That you should find in any decent library.

I am mailing you MacKail's *Latin Literature*. It is in many ways untrustworthy and vicious, BUT MacKail has the grace really to care for the stuff he writes of. He is the poor dam'd soul of the late Walter Pater. Has written some poems which I thought, fifteen years ago, were finely chiselled. The translations from the Greek Anthology, mentioned above are O.K. I owe him a few grudges. His praise of Tacitus moved me and I ruined my English prose for five years, trying to write English as Tacitus wrote Latin. VERY BAD. However, I may have learned something by it. I now know that the genius of the two languages is NOT the same.

Catullus, Propertius, Horace and Ovid are the people who matter. Catullus most. Martial somewhat. Propertius for beautiful cadence though he uses only one metre. Horace you will not want for a long time. I doubt if he is of any use save to the Latin scholar. I will explain sometime viva voce.

Virgil is a second-rater, a Tennysonianized version of Homer. Catullus has the intensity, and Ovid might teach one many things.

The "Pervigilium Veneris" is beautiful; it is, however, MacKail's own pet infant and he is a little disproportionately lyric over its beauty.

To the best of my knowledge there is no history of Greek poetry that is worth ANYTHING. They all go on gassing about the "deathless voice" and the "Theban Eagle" as if Pindar wasn't the prize wind-bag of all ages. *The* "bass-drum," etc.

This is a very short list but you'd better do at least this much "classics" to keep you steady and to keep your general notion of poetic develop-

ment more or less shapely. Possibly you can find a French prose translation of Catullus and Propertius.

There was poetry in Egypt; I have seen a small book of interesting
translations and forgotten the name. *Cathay* will give you a hint of China,
and the "Seafarer" on the Anglo-Saxon stuff. Then as MacKail says
(p. 246) nothing matters till Provence.

After Provence, Dante and Guido Cavalcanti in Italy.

Very possibly ALL this mediaeval stuff is very bad for one's style. I don't
know that you have time to live through it and???? to survive? (If I have
survived.)

The French of Villon is very difficult but you should have a copy of
Villon and not trust to Swinburne's translations (though they are very fine
in themselves); they are too luxurious and not hard enough. Not hard
enough, I mean, if one is to learn how to write. There are dull stretches in
the "Testament" but one has to dig out the fine things.

That is enough to keep you busy for a week or so. (Or for a year or so,
as the case may be.)

I have now got to shave, out of respect to the Chinese Minister.

I have read your things and will send critique when I have energy
enough to write it. — — — —

103: To Iris Barry

London, 27 July

Dear Iris Barry: Of course I might have known you had most of Villon
by heart, but the bounds of even my knowledge are not without their
limit, AND I was probably thinking more about the actual amount of poetry
worth knowing than about what you had or hadn't imbibed. We therefore expand our apologies. You have read Villon, Ford Madox Hueffer,
the anthology *Des Imagistes*, nine verses by me, Omar Kayamm, forty-five
vols. on dissection of plants and animals, Zola, . . . enough of this. So
long as you don't adore Milton and Francis Thompson, it don't matter.

Send on the B—— as soon as you like. ONLY you *did* give the chap away
when you made the chance remark that he feared plagiarism. It is as bad
as Cannéll's being afraid to read anything for fear it would destroy his
"individuality."!!!!!!!!!! Same weakness put the other side to. If a man has
anything it can't be either taken from him or rubbed away.

To continue the schedule.

I ought perhaps to emend what I said of Tacitus. So long as one writes
poetry and NOT prose, he may do one good by stirring up one's belief in
compression, compactness. The force of phrase, and of the single line.

After Villon one can, I think, skip everything down to Heine (whom
you have also committed to memory).

If you have nothing to do and are going in for lyricism and grace there
is a side line. Charles D'Orleans and the Pleiade. And Burns is worth study
as technique in song rhythms. But I don't think this is the main line.

Théophile Gautier is, I suppose, the next man who can write. Perfectly plain statements like his "Carmen est maigre" should teach one a number of things. His early poems are many of them no further advanced than the Nineties. Or to put it more fairly the English Nineties got about as far as Gautier had got in 1830, and before he wrote "L'Hippopotame."

I don't quite know what to say about more recent French poets. Whether they aren't too likely to set one to imitation of not the best sort I am not sure. One ought to be strongly ballasted against them. I wonder if my *This Generation* will be out before you get to them. Part of it is about them. I'll give you a list of what's worthwhile, whenever you want it.

I think however you'd do yourself more good reading French prose. —???? How much have you read? How much have you read as a reader reading the story?? How much as artist analyzing the method?

As I said Sunday, I suppose Flaubert's *Trois Contes*, especially "Coeur Simple," contain all that anyone knows *about* writing. Certainly one ought to read the opening of the *Chartreuse de Parme*, and the first half or a more than half of the *Rouge et Noir*. Shifting from Stendhal to Flaubert suddenly you will see how much better Flaubert writes. AND YET there is a lot in Stendhal, a sort of solidity which Flaubert hasn't. A trust in the thing more than the word. Which is the solid basis, i.e. the thing is the basis. You have probably read the *Education Sentimentale* and *Madame Bovary*.

I really think this little list and the short list I have already sent contains the gist of the matter.

Sometime, certainly, you must have the soufflé of contemporary French poets.

Sometime before that I think you shall try a huge mass of Voltaire. I am having him *very* late. Until I get to the end of the eighth fat vol. I shan't know how much I shall want to hurl at you. Perhaps you should read all of the *Dictionaire Philosophique*. Presumably no other living woman will have done so. One should always find a few things which "no other living person" has done, a few vast territories of print that you can have to yourself and a few friends. They are a great defense against fools and against the half-educated, and against dons of all sorts (open and disguised).

Yeats and I spent our last winter's months on Landor. There is a whole culture. I don't quite know whether you will like much of it. Perhaps you had better keep it till later. I think it might get a little in the way if you try to gobble it now. It wants leisure and laziness. AND he (Landor) isn't very good as a poet save in a few places, where he is fine, damn fine, *but* he is no use as a model. One has got constantly to be thinking that "this is fine, but this is not really the right way to do it."

Your first job is to get the tools for your work. Later on you can stuff yourself up with erudition as much or as little as suits you. At forty you will probably thank god that there is something you haven't read.

And English poetry???? Ugh. Perhaps one shouldn't read it at all. Chaucer has in him all that has ever got into English. And if you read Chaucer you will probably (as I did though there is no reason why you should be the same kind of imbecile) start writing archaic English, which you shouldn't.

Everybody has been sloppily imitating the Elizabethans for so long that I think they probably do one more harm than good. At any rate let 'em alone.

Wordsworth is a dull sheep. He will do you no good though he was better than some, and if there were no French prose and nothing worth reading one might learn a little about descriptions of nature from his endless maunderings.

Byron's technique is rotten.

I am not sure however that Crabbe's *The Borough* isn't worth reading. It at least shows a gleam of sense. The man *was* trying to put down things as they were. Apart from his tagging on morals, he is safe reading. He is in some ways more modern than a lot of moderns. (He is antique nevertheless, but still he is perhaps worth an evening.)

In the main one should read French prose. When you want the modern French poets I will send on the list of the intelligent ones.

You might learn Latin if it isn't too much trouble. If it is, I shall have to read a few Latin and Greek things aloud to you, and possibly try to translate 'em.

The value being that the Roman poets are the only ones we know of who had approximately the same problems as we have. The metropolis, the imperial posts to all corners of the known world. The enlightenments. Even the Eighteenth Century is obsessed by the spectre of Catholicism, the Index, the Inquisition. The Renaissance is interesting, but the poets inferior. The Greeks had no world outside, no empire, metropolis, etc. etc.

It is best to go at the thing chronologically, otherwise one gets excited over an imitation instead of over a creation or a discovery.

What about Browning? Does he entertain you? Is it possible to read him after you have been reading Russian novels? I don't in the least think there is any reason in particular why *you* should read him now. (Same applies to Yeats. We've been flooded with sham Celticism for too long, imitations of imitations of Yeats, and of the symbolistes *ad infinitum*. Soft mushy edges.) Also Kipling has debased much of Browning's and Swinburne's coin. The hell is that one catches Browning's manner and mannerisms. At least I've suffered the disease. There is no reason why you should.

Some of the books I can mail you when you want 'em.

The whole art is divided into:

a. concision, or style, or saying what you mean in the fewest and clearest words.

b. the actual necessity for creating or constructing something; of presenting an image, or enough images of concrete things arranged to stir the reader.

Beyond these concrete objects named, one can make simple emotional statements of fact, such as "I am tired," or simple credos like "After death there comes no other calamity."

I think there must be more, predominantly more, objects than statements and conclusions, which latter are purely optional, not essential, often superfluous and therefore bad.

Also one must have emotion or one's cadence and rhythms will be vapid and without any interest.

It is as simple as the sculptor's direction: "Take a chisel and cut away all the stone you don't want." ???? No, it is a little better than that.

Don't hurry. I am not sending back your poems, because it is more important you should take in fodder. You will get a lot more from the general reading than from the inspection of a few minute and problematical flaws in your last things.

Another time also I shall send you a great mass of work by some of our CONTEMPORARIES, as an awful example of all the what-not-to-do, and the what-are-the-normal-results.

And if you CAN'T find *any* decent translations of Catullus and Propertius, I suppose I shall have to rig up something. At least we can talk them over.

What else?

Oh well, perhaps you'd better send me a list of what prose writers you've read since Zola, as a guide to my senescent feet. With little marks saying whether or no you learned anything about writing by reading 'em.

When you do want Landor, sing out, and I'll try to name the parts worth beginning on.

Spanish, nothing. Italian, Leopardi splendid, and the only author since Dante who need trouble you, but not essential as a tool. Spain has one good modern novelist, Galdos.

E basta.

104: To Iris Barry

London, August

Dear Iris Barry: Certainly send on the 3 page disclosure. Your poems are on the other side of a floor I have just stained and it is too wet and sticky to cross. You shall have them in a few days. I don't suppose you want that list of contemporary French poets yet??? You can't have got to the end of the other lists. Don't kill yourself, and remember it is August. I'm sorry about the Wharton, only, as I remember it, he does give a decent and lucid prose translation, wherewith one can follow the Greek.

I prize the Greek more for the movement of the words, rhythm, perhaps than for anything else. There is the POIKILOTHRON and then Catullus, "Collis O Heliconii," and some Propertius, that one could do worse than know by heart for the sake of knowing what rhythm really is. And there is the gulph between TIS O SAPPHO ADIKEI, and Pindar's big rhetorical drum TINA THEON, TIN' EROA, TINA D'ANDREA KELADESOMEN, which one should get carefully fixed in the mind. I'll explain viva voce if this metatype-phosed Greek is too unintelligible.

It is perhaps a sense of Latin that helps or seems to have helped people to a sort of superexcellent neatness in writing English—something different from French clarity. It may be merely from the care one takes in following the construction in an inflected language.

If you are panting for the Frenchmen, they are, with all sorts of qualifications and restrictions, Rémy de Gourmont, De Régnier (a very few poems), Francis Jammes, Jules Romains, Chas. Vildrac, TRISTAN CORBIÈRE, Laurent Tailhade, Jules Laforgue, (dates all out of order), Rimbaud. I'll make out a list of books, when you are really ready, also send you L'Effort Libre anthology of the younger men. There's no hurry about returning the things you have.

When verse bores you or is too great a strain you are ever at liberty to study De Maupassant, and to consider the excellent example which Flaubert set us in sitting on De M's head and making him write, and De M's excellent example in doing what he was told. . . . In describing such and such a concierge in such and such a street so that Flaubert would recognize which concierge when he next passed that way, etc. . . . Consider the wagon full of young ladies in "La Maison Tellier."

That is the way to write poetry.

Macmillan has started setting up my Jap play book.

That imbecile Mathews will never finish with Lustra. I have just rec'd four large cheques for vorticist pictures sold in America . . . and shall have to turn them over to the artists!!!!!!!!!!

I think I did tell you to read the Rouge et Noir and the Chartreuse de Parme for relaxation. If you haven't already done so.

I believe I am to have another batch of Chinese mss. turned over to me.

That's all the letter you can expect until you return one.

105: To IRIS BARRY

London, 24 August

Beautiful Evelyn Hope: By all means write your autobiography. I would suggest that you do it as a series of letters to me. Under seal. It will be much easier than trying to write it all at a sitting, and it will keep the style simple and prevent your getting literary or attempting to make phrases and paragraphs. I know when I tried to do a novel based more or less on experience I wrote myself into a state of exhaustion doing five chapters at one sitting, arose the next day, filled reams, and then stuck. You might very likely run the same danger. If you do it as letters, it may get done. It can perfectly well be published pseudonymously, IF publishable, if long enough, good enough, etc. This will relieve the great grandchildren of the responsibility.

I believe my Russonymic would be Homerovitch.

I dare say the translation of the Odyssey WAS good if it was readable, they mostly ain't. I don't however understand anyone's admiring Gilbert Murray. Is his Hippolytus any good?

You can send on the criticisms if you like. I should like to see them, if it's too much bother to send them, or if they aren't interlocked with other matter not for my eyes. It will do me no harm to hear that "the cat, etc. . . ." Dulac has just lent me dear old Brantôme who is full of much worser scandals.

I forget what Stevenson says about Villon. I read it twelve years ago and remember nothing but the "Lodging for the Night," not the Villon essay. In the "Lodging" I suppose S. is merely making a story. People have tried to prove that V. was much more important a person in his day (socially, etc.) than is generally supposed. I don't know that there is much use trying to *know* such matters. I did a chapter on him in my *Spirit of Romance* which contains what I thought about him in 1910. But there are things much more worth your while reading.

I'll try to place your story if you've nothing better to do with it. Send on the *Chimera* or a sample copy thereof.

I have spent the day with Wang Mei, eighth century Jules Laforgue Chinois.

I will not say anything more about Stendhal, wait and see, or wait and guess. I am not absolutely cracked in the matter, though I am not surprised at your wondering: "what . . . etc."

Salammbô is dull and tedious. I am not sure that anyone can read it through, but it is necessary at least to get stuck in the attempt. Otherwise one doesn't know where one is with "Herodias." One receives no salutary instruction.

Don't despair about Greek and Latin. There is no particular haste. I have this day written my first two sentences in Chinese, on a post card to Koumé.

If you must marry, do follow your excellent ancestress's precedent. Marry and govern the state. Don't marry three servants and a villa in Birmingham. It is not a short cut to leisure.

Really one DON'T need to know a language. One NEEDS, damn well needs, to know the few hundred words in the few really good poems that any language has in it. It is better to know the POIKILOTHRON by heart than to be able to read Thucydides without trouble (Fleet Street muck that he is. The first journalist . . . at least the first we have thrust upon us.)

Interruption for food—but will send this as it is.

106: To Iris Barry

London, [August]

Dear Iris: I foresee that I shall have to read, or try to read the impossible Murray, a full set of whose translations were sent to the war library some months ago.

I am reading Brantôme and I doubt if even the opportunities afforded you in Birmingham will have produced anything capable of horrifying his readers. The fine old robustness.

No, the Stendhal is NOT a personal application (*I recommended La Chartreuse at the same time and you can't imagine I saw you on the field of Waterloo, etc. etc.*), you would have had it (*Rouge at Noir*) administered just the same were you cockney or duchess. I wish you to consider the relation of Stendhal, Flaubert, Maupassant (possibly Laforgue, but don't bother about Laforgue now).

Certainly send on the plays, I am supposed to be meeting Knoblauch next week. I have very little of my own to thrust upon him. I hear he is the Gawd of the British theatre. Shall try him with Joyce, but if he is to be harnessed I may as well have any stray bits of twine handy. (I don't of course know that I can do anything, still if your stuff is any good at all I can probably get it looked at.)

Of course I meant the *Chimera* with you in it.

Re the Murray. I am probably suspicious of Greek drama. People keep on assuring me that it is excellent despite the fact that too many people have praised it. STILL there has been a lot of rhetoric spent on it. And I admit the opening of *Prometheus* (Aeschylus') is impressive. (Then the play goes to pot.) Also I like the remarks about Xerxes making a mess of [illegible] in another Aeschylean play, forget the name. Some choruses annoy me. Moralizing nonentities making remarks on the pleasures of a chaste hymeneal relation, etc., etc. Statements to the effect that Prudence is always more discreet than rashness, and other such brilliant propositions.

I think it would probably be easier to fake a play by Sophocles than a novel by Stendhal, apart from the versification. And even there one mustn't be too gullible. Aristophanes parodies some of the tragic verse very nicely, at least I believe so. I am too damd ignorant to talk intelligently about the Greek drama. Still I mistrust it, *dona ferentes*, etc.

There are fine lines in *Phedre* though it is perhaps a labour to read it, and extremely difficult to understand how it was popular, except on the supposition. . . . Oh, on a lot of damd suppositions.

I don't *know* when *Lustra* will be done, I suppose in September.

107: To Iris Barry

London, 29 August

Dear Iris: In the main the trouble with this lot is that there wasn't enough urge behind it. I tried in vers libre to make a medium where the "bard" couldn't fake. Perhaps the game has come off. At least I don't think I can be fooled all the time. Most of the shorter verses aren't sufficiently distinguished from the other little verse of the others who appear in *Others*.

"Influence" has too many inactive words to give an effect of efficiency.

"The Old House" has a germ, but a beastly Russian called Slobagob or Sologub has done a whole novel, or at least a 30,000 word story and more or less queered the pitch.

"Warning" is a bit too Whitman. Don't throw it away, but wait till you get it better. Same with "Old House." —/—/

I have made some very rough scratches on one ms. I don't mean that I
have left a finished opusculus. It is only interrogation.

Returning to amical correspondence. Yes, I care somewhat for music.
My first friend was a painter, male, now dead. 2nd a Pyanist, naturally 15
years plus agée que moi. That was in "The States." I entered London more
or less under her wing; I was even an impressario, I borrowed the Lyceo
Benedetto Marcello in Venice for a press recitation, in the absence of Wolf-
Ferrari, author of *Das Neues Leben* and other operas, etc. Je connus the
London mondo musicale, at least the concert-hall, recital part of it. Later I
lived with Rummel several times for months at a stretch in Paris. He is a
good but no longer very productive young composer, dated alas by
Debussy. D. said that Rummel played his stuff better than he could. Both
K[itty] R. H[eyman] and Rummel are *some* musicians. My present pin-
nacle is sponged stalls at the Beecham opera. Malheureusement, I can't
offer them to my friends; the grip isn't strong enough. W.R. is in Paris,
K.R.H. back in the States.

Remains one clavichord, Dolmetsch's own handiwork—Dulac making
Arabian lutes.

P.S. Have looked at a bad trans. of Sophocles. Certainly the whole
Oedipus story is a darn silly lot of buncombe—used as a peg for some very
magnificent phrases. Superbly used.

I believe language *has* improved; that Latin is better than Greek and
French than Latin for everything save certain melodic effects—and we
don't *know* that the Greeks didn't ruin their stuff by rocking-horse reading. Though I can't believe they did. At any rate, early Greek *can* be read
with wonderful music.

108: To Iris Barry

London, [September]

Dear Iris: — — — — The portrait is there to make junior typists clasp their
hands ecstatically. Or as Yeats says: "*That'll* sell the book." Perhaps you
will find the enclosed more compendious.

I think I told you of the effect of the Coburn photo [1] on my ex-landlady:
"Oh the first that ever did you justice." Then at the doorway, depre-
catingly, "Eh, I hope you won't be offended, sir, but, eh It-is-like-the-
good-man-of-Nazareth, isn't-it, sir?"

I am glad that the effect on the junior typist is satisfactory.

2. Re Burglars, I enclose the S[mart] S[et] slip. [2]

Exeunt:

I thought for the first few pages that you really had got a good thing.

But it seems to me that the real play is to have them all go out. (Aggie is
utterly unnecessary.) But the whole family should go out one by one

[1] Frontispiece to limited edition of *Lustra*, Elkin Mathews, 1916.

[2] *The Smart Set* sent to contributors a slip listing impossible material, which included: "7.—Stories about burglars or other rogues."

through sheer boredom with "the home." There is an effect to be got from that arrangement, a much longer play than you have made.

In fact I think any play to be stageable must be 15 or 20 pages of typescript. At least Yeats made me lengthen a skit of mine before he would take it for the Abbey. (Later rejected by the manager on the grounds that its indecencies would cause a riot in Dublin.)

But I think there is a real piece of literature to be made if you send the four of them out, father last, I should think, or perhaps daughter last; it don't matter which, only it will change the nature of the satire. Still either way could be fine.

Old lady's bed would have to be visible or near door into sitting room, or dining room or whichever you call it. But she should have the finale ALL to herself. Mon escient. A clear stage to die in.

One might even call it "The Home."

109: To Iris Barry

London, 11 September

Chère Iris: I believe in everyone's having their heart's desire at the earliest possible opportunity. If they are bad they die at once; they rot in a sort of explosion. If they are good it does them no harm. If they are unusual they "amazingly overcome it."

STILL, you might have told me his name was Reginald. Why should you sent me a poet named Reginald? If you had told me his name was Reginald I should have known it was "all off" from the beginning.

Reginald will be here in one hour and forty-five minutes. By that time your letter will be safely placed in a drawer. — — — —

I should give the old lady a very short death. Either she can stagger to door, or bed can be visible and make-up can do the rest. Let jaw drop. Give her a line or two if necessary. NOT a long drawn agony, à la cinema. Sic: OLD FEMALE: "I am dying of boredom." Obit.

Re Lions: No, Yeats won't appreciate it. He will be vaguely conscious of "another" male in the room, but will forget it. Only after five years of acquaintance does he learn to distinguish one member of the race from another member. He has not my Chaucerian busy-ness and curiosity concerning minute variants in human personality.

If I despatch this instanter, the charwoman can mail it. And you shall have another after Reginald has departed.

110: To Iris Barry

London, 22 September

Dear Iris: On the whole, it is all rubbish your going to a farm. The soul is more than flesh, etc. You had better much come up to London. I am

writing to my treasured and unique ex-landlady to see if she has a room
. . . unless you have some better place to stay. I shall be back Wednesday.
You can come to tea, and be took out to see someone or other some evening, and come in to meet someone else. God knows who is in London
at the moment, and divers circles are non-extant from war. Still you can
put in your spare time somehow.

The cheapest clean restaurant with a real cook is Bellotti's, Ristorante
Italiano (NOT Restaurant D'Italie) 12 Old Compton St. I will send you
Mrs. Langley's address if I find she has a room.

Directions: for life in the capital. NOT to use the competent and de-
fensive air. (In really Lofty circles an amiable imbecility is the current
form. . . . That you won't need in the monde d'art; a naive and placid re-
ceptivity should suffice.) — — — —

I believe being a bar maid would be no obstacle, BUT one would be
obliged to conceal the fact.

As for "competent bearing and defence," it is no use. People here haven't
the time; and anyone would be perfectly willing to be friendly. Simply
the capital is "intime," instantly "intime," scarcely ever familiar.

One talks aesthetics, literature, scandal about others, political intrigue
(war, for the present, though no stranger should introduce this last topic.)

All this is very bald, but am in hurry. General instructions:

Ask questions. Everyone likes to be asked questions.

Super-strategy:

Ask questions showing knowledge of or sane interest in something of
interest to interlocutor.

All of which you know quite well already. Yours, Polonius. — — — —

III: To H. L. Mencken

London, 27 September

Dear Mencken: Have signed one copy Dreiser protest and sent it to Hersey
with brief note on the "Authors' League."

Have sent other copy to *The Egoist* to be printed as soon as possible, in
the hope that it will reach more people than I have time to see or write to.
Will print it with blank for signature.

Still the *country* U.S.A. is hopeless and may as well go to hell its own
way. Hell is a place completely paved with Billy Sunday and Ellis.

Glad you are going to start a "better" magazine. "Better" IS such a
bloody ambiguous word. Seriously I think what is wrong is simply that
neither England nor America have had an Eighteenth Century deist. I
don't believe superficial work is any good.

A society for the publication of selections of Voltaire, in five and ten
cent editions, translated, of course, into English, PLUS a general campaign
of education would be the best beginning.

Christianity has become a sort of Prussianism, and will have to go. All the bloody moral attacks are based on superstition, religion, or whatever it is to be called. It has its uses and is disarming, but it is too dangerous. Religion is the root of all evil, or damn near all.

Patient plodding "reformers" got you into the scrape, and it will take patient, plodding, unfrivolous people like myself to free the country of the curse.

It's all very well your doing the light fantastic, but *you* (*you* H.L.M.) and a lot more of your friends will have to take art and freedom more seriously before you are done with the matter. "Hell" in the person of Comstock's following, Sunday, and all the rest, will do you in, unless you get some heavy artillery.

Perhaps the new magazine is intended to be a bit more "weighty," in which case you are on the right road.

Am exceedingly worn out at the moment, so pardon lack of precision and of glittering phrase in this epistle. — — — —

112: To Harriet Shaw Weaver

London, 14 November

Dear Miss Weaver: I have just received the enclosed from Joyce. Of course I am ready to do an article or preface BUT I think I have written so much about him that it would be much more advantageous to have some other critic turned loose.

I suggest that you write to Edward Marsh (10 Downing St., S.W.). He will be flattered. His appreciation would reach a different and new circle of people. He is in a position to do much more for Joyce than I can.

If he won't write a whole article, I suggest that you get a set of testimonials, about a paragraph long. From H. G. Wells, me, Marsh, George Moore (if he will), Martin Secker (??), anyone else you can.

I can hardly add anything to what I said in *Drama*. It was about the strongest kind of statement one could make. You might quote from that article. I am not trying to get out of doing a job, but I think these things should be tried before the reader of the *Egoist* is required to hear any more "Me on Joyce."

Is the book getting printed in New York????

113: To Felix E. Schelling

London, 17 November

Dear Dr. Schelling: I keep on writing in *Poetry*, a distressful magazine which does however print the few good poems written in our day along with a great bundle of rubbish, . . . the sentence is getting out of hand . . . I keep on writing on the subject of fellowships for creation as a substitute for, or an addition to, fellowships for research.

Now that there can be no longer any suspicion of my wanting the thing
for myself, I think it may be more use to write to you than to keep on
addressing that many-eared monster with no sense, the reading public.

It is true that H—— is a barbarian wanting to erect a pyramid to his
progenitor and wholly indifferent to the curricula or intellectual status of
the university, and S—— is a barbarian interested in the Y.M.C.A. and a
parvenue system of morals.

But then NO American University has ever tried to be a centre of
thought. Pennsylvania would score if she were first to institute such a
fellowship. A fellowship given for creative ability regardless of whether
the man had any university degree whatsoever. The fellow would attend
lectures when he liked and then only, he would have no examinations for
the thought of them is poison in a man's ear, he can not hear through it.
The lute sounds like a cash register, and a cadence is weighed down with
a "job."

I have in mind a couple of youngish men whose work will stay imperfect through lack of culture. Sandburg is a lumberjack who has taught
himself all that he knows. He is on the way toward simplicity. His energy
may for all one knows waste itself in an imperfect and imperfectable argot.

Johns is another case. A year in a library, with a few suggestions as to
reading and no worry about their rent might bring permanent good work
out of either of these men.

Masters is too old and instead of rewriting *Spoon River* he has gone off
into gas. Still a year's calm would do even him some good. But his expenses are probably too heavy to make him a possible candidate.

I admit such an irregular student might be a dam'd nuisance, but he
might also be a stimulant.

Colum has I believe an endowment, but there is no library attached.

It might be a safeguard to make eligible only men who have *not* pre-
viously studied in the university.

The Wanderjahr was an excellent institution.

I don't know whether you will have time to consider this. It is perhaps
more in Weygandt's province???

Dr. Child is an ideal companion for the young barbarian but hardly, I
think, the politician to get the thing done. Weygandt's interest in contemporary literature has however always appeared typical of himself and
America. That is to say he wrote to me for free copies of my books, just
after he had come into a comfortable inheritance and at a time when I was
working my own way on the edge of starvation. But there is no reason
why he should suspect that the thought of this fellowship comes from me.
I should have had to buy his free copies and it would have cost me a
dinner.

It is dull repetition to say that every other art has its endowed fellowships. Poetry, which needs more than any other art the balance of study, is
without them. I say the balance of study because a sculptor or painter
with instinct can see a masterpiece almost instantly and a book takes time
to read. Music is difficult to decide on.

Oh well, I grow lengthy. Amities.

P.S. The English department might even apply its present fellowships in this way now and again.

Rennert's last letter to me five years ago implied that the "advancement of learning" clause had come to be interpreted "continue a professor," but there was the university ['s] personal loathing [of] me behind that decision.

II. *The Little Review*

1 9 1 7

114: To Kate Buss

London, 4 January

Dear Miss Buss: Thanks for sending me the copy of your review.

The only error seems to be in supposing that "Albâtre" was in any way influenced by Chinese stuff which I did not see until a year or two later. The error is natural as *Cathay* appeared before *Lustra*, but the separate poems in *Lustra* had mostly been written before the Chinese translations were begun and had mostly been printed in periodicals either here or in America. I think you will find all the verbal constructions of *Cathay* already tried in "Provincia Deserta."

The subject is Chinese, the language of the translations is mine—I think. At least if you compare the "Song of the Bowmen" with the English version of the same poem in Jennings' "Shi King" Part II, 1-7 (p. 180) called "Song of the Troops," or the "Beautiful Toilet" with the same poem in Giles' *Chinese Literature*, you will be able to gauge the amount of effect the celestial Chinese has on the osseous head of an imbecile or a philologist.

Omahitsu is the real modern—even Parisian—of VIII cent. China. — — —

115: To John Quinn

London, 10 January

Dear John Quinn: The Dec. number of *Seven Arts* has just arrived. I don't know whether I owe it to you or to the editor.

I have just sealed up Fenollosa's "Essay on the Chinese Written Character," to send to them. It is one of the most important essays of our time. But they will probably reject it on the ground of its being exotic.

Fenollosa saw and anticipated a good deal of what has happened in art (painting and poetry) during the last ten years, and his essay is basic for all aesthetics, but I doubt if that will cut much ice.

Seven Arts looks to me as if it were riding for a fall. A fall between two stools or two haystacks, or whatever it is things fall between.

All this desire for a compromise. Great Art is NEVER popular to start with. They (*Seven Arts*) want to be popular and good all at once?????!!!!!

The stuff they complain of is precisely the stuff (American or otherwise) that tries to please the "better" public.

Their facts are flimsy. The "cultured" man doesn't much read *Jean Christophe* (he can't), nor yet Wells. He does read Henry James, but he reads him with rigorous selection.

Nothing but ignorance can refer to the "troubadours" as having produced popular art. If ever an art was made for a few highly cultivated people it was the troubadour poetry of Provence.

The Greek populace was PAID to attend the great Greek tragedies, and it damn well wouldn't have gone otherwise, or if there had been a cinema. Shakespeare was "Lord Somebody's players," and the Elizabethan drama, as distinct from the long defunct religious plays, was a court affair.

Greek art is about as fine an example of UNINTERRUPTED decadence as one could want, and its decay keeps pace with the advance of popular power.

Seven Arts don't seem to me much better than *The Egoist*, though you needn't say so publicly, as I want the Fenollosa essay published. (Naturally, I could use it in *The Egoist*, but I want to be paid for it. It's damn well worth it.) China is fundamental, Japan is not. Japan is a special interest, like Provence, or 12-13th Century Italy (apart from Dante). I don't mean to say there aren't interesting things in Fenollosa's Japanese stuff (or fine things, like the end of *Kagekiyo*, which is, I think, "Homeric"). But China is solid. One can't go back of the "Exile's Letter," or the "Song of the Bowmen," or the "North Gate."

Yeats is still hustling about the Lane picture bequest.

116: To Harriet Shaw Weaver

London, 22 January

Dear Miss Weaver: The limerick Joyce asked me to use was my limerick on him, a very poor bit of doggerel, rhyming Joyce with "purse" (the latter pronounced "poice" in the manner of the N.Y. Bowery). I don't think his request was serious, if it was so, it [was] merely a bit of amiability on his part. At any rate the limerick won't fit in a serious manifesto.

His limerick on me shows that an amiable feeling exists between author and reviewer, and that also would weaken the force of my note.

I don't think you are right about *The Nation* and *Athenaeum*, for the following reasons:

1. The reviewing on *The Nation* has more and more fallen into the control of a gang of Irish, presumably S——'s gang, and he has already attacked Joyce's prose, rather sneeringly, and will go on doing so, presumably (jealousy).

The anonymous reviewer is usually cowardly, *also* I have before now procured civility by direct attack. Again a direct attack may make the head of a paper look up the reviews which cause it, and smack the reviewer into order. IF Wells reviews the book, the two latter effects will be intensified.

2. *The Athenaeum* is anything but "well-established." It is so groggy that it "reorganizes" about every five months. It is being held up by a silly "pigeon" back from Egypt after forty years in the desert. It has appealed for funds to its *contributors,* and talked about democratic control of its opinion. Any kick at it may help toward its extinction, which is devoutly to be hoped for.

3. I certainly don't want to include the virtuous by such a phrase as "well-established" journals.

If, however, you don't want to name names, I could consent to

"attacks from a few sheltered, and therefore courageous, anonymities"

It is well to forestall attack, and the nasty Catholics like the M—— and T—— stye are bound to attack because Joyce so allmightily wipes the floor with the "Whore of Babylon" in that chapter on the long sermon. −/−/

117: TO JOHN QUINN

London, The Evening of the 24th day January

Dear John Quinn: I am glad you really enjoyed *Lustra* and aren't going on with it merely out of esprit de corps.

I have always wanted to write "poetry" that a grown man could read without groans of ennui, or without having to have it cooed into his ear by a flapper.

Re your troubles with S., I send my commiserations and am almost moved to offer myself as a substitute. Ignorant as Ham but capable of consecutive work and of putting together an argument.

Besides, one might live in America if one had a reputable job and were not that lowest of God's creatures: a man with an ambition to write well trying to live by his pen IN the Eunited States.

AND one would be free from editors. If I ever do come to America I would rather do something of the sort than lead the dog's life of a Tagore-as-at-present, or Noyes-teaing-at-Princeton, let alone the humbler roles in the business.

Re Washington Square imitation Quartier Latin, a chap named Bruno occasionally sends me a "weekly" when he isn't grouched by my lack of admiration for it. I judge that is the superior-top-kurrust of the crowd you mean, and can get a perspective.

I am glad you liked my progenitors. They certainly had a good time seeing you and the collection. You can be quite sure Dad will descend upon you whenever he gets to New York again.

Yes, I got your Casement article, two copies. I didn't think your argument quite held together in some places, or that you on the bench would have given verdict to a barrister who had made it.

I intended to make a detailed analysis of it, and then was interrupted. I think by getting a rush order to translate a libretto AT ONCE (very lucky for me that I did get an order to do something). Beecham is a good fellow and paid in guineas, not pounds as proposed. Also he is intelligent, apart from being the only man in England who can conduct an orchestra.

People usually misinterpret him. In my long talk with him I discovered the cause, i.e. I caught him *thinking*. By GAWD, a musician *thinking, straight off his own bat*.

At any rate, the Casement matter was all over by the time I got back to your article. Then came proofs of *Noh,* and then work on a new long poem (really L O N G, endless, leviathanic).

No, Joyce hasn't a pension. He had a grant of £100 from the last government. One lump sum, not a hardy annual. I don't know whether the present regime will be as generous. However, his books are now out, and a start is made.

I think justice will be done to MacNeill as soon as the war is over, if not before. Certainly as soon as people have time and can think calmly once more. I am glad Spring-Rice is with you in this.

Don't worry over *This Generation,* and for God's sake, don't spend money on it.

If there is any spending it would be much more fun to spend it on illustrations (even in colour) for the book on Lewis.

I don't believe there's much "oil" of lucre in Pisistratan sculpture, but the blighted Greeks did a few things before Phidias, and it would be amusing to point out Greek art as one continuous decadence. The Moscophoros (alias, "The chap with the calf") is, I think, a good job (possibly better than Yakob).

My wife, trying to find a formula of words, said, "No . . . ah . . . no, Dulac *isn't* an artist."

I: "What?"

She: "No, he's something else, he is different" (that means different from Lewis, me, Gaudier, Eliot, etc.). "He is a . . . dilettante."

Which is probably the answer. He is a nice chap to dine with and probably better at conversation or anything else than at ART.

Don't worry about Lewis not understanding mild delay. Everything turned out all right.

The vorteseope isn't a cinema. It is an attachment to enable a photographer to do sham Picassos. That sarcastic definition probably covers the ground. A chap named Mountsier has seen the stuff and is doing an article on it, also on Lewis and me and Coburn. He is going to N.Y.—on the *Sun,* I think.

The show of Coburn's results comes off here in Feb. He and I are to jaw about abstraction in photography and in art, and old G.B.S. has promised to come out and perhaps chip into the jawing. The vortographs are perhaps as interesting as Wadsworth's woodcuts, perhaps not quite as interesting.

At any rate, it will serve to upset the muckers who are already crowing about the death of vorticism.

It, the vortescope, will manage any arrangement of purely abstract forms. The present machine happens to be rectilinear, but I can make one that will do any sort of curve, quite easily.

It ought to save a lot of waste experiment on plane compositions, such as Lewis' "Plan of War," or the Wadsworth woodcuts. Certainly it is as good as the bad imitators—Atkinson, and possibly some Picabia—and might serve to finish them off, leaving Lewis and Picasso more clearly defined.

Thanks again for fixing up things with Knopf.

Will say nothing about periodical until I get your next letter, save that it is very good of you to go on being interested after all my varied and divergent propositions.

Am glad the vorticist exhibit is really open. But this letter is already long enough, so I won't expatiate. Regards to Yeats Sr. and remembrances to Brodzky, and thanks again to you.

118: To Iris Barry

London, 25 January

Dear Iris: Good. Only you omit the most important detail, namely price of said room WITH BAWTH. Within reach of Whitehall plus bath spells Chelsea, the riverboard of Chelsea rich with memories of . . .

I find a bath can be dispensed with PROVIDED one have a geyser that will make the liquid for dumpable detached bath really hot. Whereas the damp coolish hot bath of a boarding house is disgusting.

A few weeks ago I found a studio with bath, for I think £40 per year, but naturally unfurnished, and probably you would have to take it for three years, and probably it is already gobbled.

Wisdom consists in getting a room cheap and having spare cash to embellish it, add gas conveniences, etc., which are paid once and for all and not a constant drain.

Alas, I was in Chelsea but yesterday. Had you written 24 hours earlier I might have enquired.

I had better get you a furnished room at 8 (eight) shillings a week, in the centre of the part of Chelsea where you will probably find what you really want (very possibly unfurnished).

Let me know exact or probable date of your arrival as soon as you know it.

Chelsea is a bit nearer Whitehall than I am here, and it (Chelsea) is not too disgustingly far from here. You might be provided with some amiable neighbors there, if discretion be exercised.

Now for the moving letter.

You do not poetize because you are suffering from your first attack of "style" or "rush of critical sense to the heart." At 18 I always thought each poem the last.

What is your attitude toward Mr. Pound? "All things are possible to labour."

Tagore got the Nobel Prize because, after the cleverest boom of our day, after the fiat of the omnipotent literati of distinction, he lapsed into religion and optimism and was boomed by the pious non-conformists. Also because it got the Swedish Academy out of the difficulty of deciding between European writers whose claims appeared to conflict. Sic. Hardy or Henry James?

Tagore obviously was unique in the known modern Orient. And then, the right people suggested him. AND Sweeden is Sweeden. It was also a damn good smack for the British Academic Committee, who had turned down Tagore (on account of his biscuit complexion) and who elected in his stead to their august corpse, Alice Meynell and Dean Inge.

Therefore his Nobel Prize gave pleasure unto the elect.

Massenet was finished God knows when. I know that I was paid, guineas not pounds as proposed, on Jan 1st and that I am for the moment solvent. Laus Dei. I think that answers the list of questions????? — — — —

119: TO HARRIET SHAW WEAVER

London, 30 January

Dear Miss Weaver: I will write to Archer and Brock, not later than tomorrow. You can then send the books to *The Times* (not to Brock); but to Archer direct, s.v.p.

Do warn Wells that there is an Irish vendetta in the senile *Nation*, AND tell him there is no reason why Joyce should be dragged into it. Joyce has never laid eyes on me and has nothing to do with my personal feuds.

I will speak to Granville, probably today. Does he send you an exchange copy? It may have slipped his mind.

Following emendations in article. Please see that revises are correct.

p. 2. *Egoist* turns publisher and produced *A Portrait* . . .

p. 9. Violent attacks from several sheltered and therefore courageous anonymities. When you tell . . .

p. 10. Now, despite the jobbing of bigots and their sectarian publishing houses, and despite the Fly-Fishers . . .

I am afraid Eliot has split with *The Westminster*, and De Bosschère also. However, I will see.

120: TO MARGARET C. ANDERSON

London, [? January]

Dear M.C.A.: *The Little Review* is perhaps temperamentally closer to what I want done??????

DEFINITELY then:

I want an "official organ" (vile phrase). I mean I want a place where I and T. S. Eliot can appear once a month (or once an "issue") and where

Joyce can appear when he likes, and where Wyndham Lewis can appear if he comes back from the war.

DEFINITELY a place for our regular appearance and where our friends and readers (what few of 'em there are), can look with assurance of finding us.

I don't know quite how much your pages carry. I don't want to swamp you.

I must have a steady place for my best stuff (apart from original poetry, which must go to *Poetry* unless my guarantor is to double his offer. Even so I oughtn't to desert *Poetry* merely because of convenience.

I have only three quarrels with them: Their idiotic fuss over christianizing all poems they print, their concessions to local pudibundery, and that infamous remark of Whitman's about poets needing an audience.)

As to policy, I don't think I am particularly propagandist. I have issued a few statements of fact, labelled two schools and there has been a lot of jaw about 'em. But an examination of files will show that I have done very little preachy writing.

A monthly should keep some tab on the few interesting books that DO appear in London and Paris.

I should count on Eliot a good deal for such current criticism and appreciation. He is in touch with various papers here and sees what is going on.

I don't know how much Joyce would send in. He is working on another novel.

Lewis is not to be counted on, NOW; by the grace of God he may come back in due season.

The young stuff here that hasn't a home would be an occasional poem from Rodker or Iris Barry and the unknown.

The rest are clustered to *The Egoist.* I got Aldington that job several years ago. He hasn't done quite as well as I expected, BUT he was very young. H.D. is all right, but shouldn't write criticism. The Lawrence-Lowell-Flint-Cournos contingent give me no active pleasure. Fletcher is all right now and again, but too diffuse in the intervals.

You advertise "new Hellenism." It's all right if you mean humanism, Pico's *De Dignitate,* the *Odyssey,* the Moscophoros. Not so good if you mean Alexandria, and worse if you mean the Munich-sham-Greek "Hellas" with a good swabian brogue.

Confucianism is not propagandist, and polytheism would only be misunderstood, so I shan't offer any or much competition on these lines. (Perhaps an essay on Confucius? On approval.)

This is to be printed straight off. (Bar of course libel, and the usual thing, or the printers' refusing ABSOLUTELY to set it up, because of its inflammability.)

If there happens to be more copy the excess would be submitted to you as any other contribution. No hard feelings if you chuck it.

I think we might criticize each other's selections in confidence with SOME freedom and directness????

(As you like . . . it is sometimes amusing . . . I don't insist . . .)

— — — —

121: To ALICE CORBIN HENDERSON

London, March

Dear A.C.H.: —— — The only thing I can see for strengthening the prose section of *Poetry* is a series of essays on French poets unknown to *The Atlantic Monthly* and the Great Generation of Pimps, beginning with Gilder and ending with the friends of H. W. Mabie.

Amy has not exhausted the subject. *Poetry* could quite well do with essays on Laforgue, Corbière, Tailhade, possibly Rimbaud, Jammes, possibly Elskamp, possibly a reminder of Malarmé, Samain, Hérédia. I would suggest that a series of this sort by me, Eliot, and De Bosschère would at least keep out a certain amount of *slop* from the prose section.

I believe you get the *Egoist*. De B. has had an enormous essay on me running through three numbers, Jan., Feb., and March still to come.

He has also what he calls a "Portrait" of me.

Even tho H. has not yet printed his poems, I shall suggest his sending this along. If she don't use me in April, she might make a number of my long poem, his poem or poems, and this "portrait." It and the essay in *The Egoist* make the first part of a book on contemporary English poets which he will publish in France after the war. *The Egoist* essay might be noted in *Poetry's* notes by way of annoying the profane. It quotes Sandburg and is altogether the most lengthy treatment I have yet had from any critic. . . . Not that it is to be accepted as gospel, but lest the forces of darkness crow and cackle too loudly.

I can't stir up De B. and Eliot to do the French essays until I know that they are wanted and that they will appear one a month in a regular series. —— — They'd make a good solid series, and also be a change. About 1500 words each, and £3 as remuneration.

The series OUGHT to be announced. It should help sales IF ANNOUNCED, otherwise it won't, as sales proceed from expectation.

My prose now lying in the office ought to be cleared up also. Lump it all into two lots, one on Davies and the other as "Notes by E.P." That'll clear the deck, get one ready to do something "in reply to the noble effort of the 60 guarantors." One ought to make a bit of a spurt in reply to 'em.

122: To JOHN QUINN

London, 18 April

Dear Quinn: *The New Republic* has come. The title "Green Sickness" and the paragraph on "mortal sin" seem to me the two back-handers in the thing. Perhaps in less degree the phrasing, "never even thought of *plot* or importance of consulting the reader."

This latter paragraph and the one on Wells give Hackett away and should not harm Joyce.

The title is a dig. Some of the other things you have marked don't seem to me vicious. His saying that the novel is "unpleasant" is balanced by the next paragraph which says it has beauty and intensity (which is more than most reviewers would do, especially if they were disappointed novelists instead of being disappointees in other walks of litterchure).

I don't much like the opening sentence. However, the tribe of Gosse all think the public has to be apologized to for the existence of genius *in any form.*

I hope you aren't going to be offended by my remarks on artists and patrons in the editorial I sent direct to Miss Anderson. I was wroth with the editorial in *Poetry* on the same topic. H. Monroe seems to think that if her Chicago widows and spinsters will only shell out she can turn her gang of free-versers into geniuses all of a onceness. Hence my remarks on the inability of patrons to create artists. I may have phrased it a bit crudely. But I think what I said is so, and that if the words are examined closely the meaning holds good.

I am rereading your article on Joyce. Do send copies to official circles. Possibly to the English ambassador in Washington. It ought to do more good than anything else I have seen on Joyce. Good also to me, *The Egoist*, Picasso, etc.

Re what you say of the book's being most intelligible to Irish Catholics, did I write you that a female married to a Belgian said the whole thing was just as true of Belgium as of Ireland (with, of course, necessary substitutions in the matter of Parnell, etc.)?

I am neither Irish nor Catholic, but I have had more mediaeval contact than most, through Dante and my Provençal. I have read a 12th Century Provençal sermon about hell—same model as the one in *The Portrait*, same old hoax.

I don't put myself up as a sample of how the book will strike most people. But I do think Joyce has done his job so well and so thoroughly that he conveys the *milieu* of the book, and that an Irish Catholic with local knowledge has very little advantage over the outsider with good grounding in literature when it comes to understanding *The Portrait*.

(That sentence is written nearly as badly as some of Hackett's.) This may not be so. My uncle-in-law couldn't understand parts of the conversation, or at least found them difficult. And he is extremely well read. It may be my having read Dante and a few paragraphs of Richard St. Victor, and Guido Cavalcanti, that makes me so much readier to take in the novel than some other people seem to be.

I wonder if he *has* read Balzac many times. I read about a dozen books of Balzac's ten years ago, but I can't read him now.

I also wonder if he has read Flaubert and the de Goncourts, or if his hardness isn't a direct development from the love of hardness bred by reading Dante, or possibly in his case, Aquinas. (I have not read Aquinas, but I have looked through a good book of scholastic logic, by something-Agricola.)

His hardness is more like *La fille Elisa* than anything of Balzac's, I think.

I enclose bibliography. I have put in the dates of a few critical articles—"pure matter of literary history." I have taken damn small part in the current muck concerning vers libre. I don't think an unessential matter of that sort would have been raised to the pitch of a Martin Luther-John Calvin church-schism but for the crass ignorance of magazine editors, critics and publishers at the time I began writing. Ignorant opposition caused a stoppage, and now follows an inundation. I think the simple table of dates may tell the story in a quiet way, if anyone wants to hear it. It is better than writing diatribes against the unstable.

Later. I have compiled the bibliography. It is in a beastly mess, but let Knopf straighten it out or retype it.

I enclose another note from Joyce which has just come. I didn't tell him the magazine was settled but only that there was good hope, and asked him to send me a note on chance. Please have Miss Anderson print either his brief note, or a notice saying he has written to say that he will collaborate at the earliest opportunity.

I think with Yeats' poems, Lewis, Joyce, Eliot, and the chance of a few "young," the *Little Review* is worth going on with.

I have added J.B.Y.'s letters to the bibliography. May as well note it, though my introduction is only a page. Still it may sell a few copies for Cuala.

Perhaps you'll be good enough to forward Joyce's question about his eyes to Gould, with the other data I sent you. That is, if Gould is still alive. Vide the end of Joyce's long letter enclosed.

More later.

123: To Harriet Monroe

London, 24 April

Dear H.M.: At last a letter from you. I am sorry you have been laid up, glad you are through with it. Glad to hear A.C.H. is better and also that something was done for her last autumn.

As to poem,[1] string it out into three numbers if that's the best you can do. Price named for magazine rights is satisfactory. Only for gawd's sake send it along as soon as possible.

Let us hope you may get over your dislike of the poem by the time the last of it is printed, you disliked "Contemporania" and even the first of Frost himself, and you loathed and detested Eliot. "Contemporania" didn't exactly wreck the magazine. You have even put some of them into the anthology.

It is disgusting of Mathews not to have sent you *Lustra*, but it may have been sunk.

You can't expect me to keep in touch with the magazine unless you

[1] "Three Cantos," published June, July, and August 1917.

write more often than once in six months. Since Alice went to New Mexico I have been wholly, or almost wholly cut off.

124: To Margaret C. Anderson

London, [ca. May]

Chère M.: All right!

Only don't go wrong about Quinn. Quinn made me mad the first time I saw him (1910). I came back on him four years later, and since then I have spent a good deal of his money. His name does not spell Tightwad. The £150 is my figure, not his.

I am not looking for a soft job, at least not in that way. Quinn is not a rich man in the American sense of the word. He has what he makes month by month, and most of it goes to the arts. I know part of what he does, and I know somewhat of how he does it. . . . Quinn wanted me to take £120 a year for myself in connection with *The Egoist* a year or so ago.

The point is that if I accept more than I *need* I at once become a sponger, and I at once lose my integrity. By doing the job for the absolute minimum I remain respectable and when I see something I want I can ask for it. I mean to say, as things stand I can ask for money when Joyce finishes his next novel or if Hueffer ever gets his *real* book finished.

If I began by blowing 1500 dollars and did no more than I shall now do with 750 I should feel a mucker and there would be nothing ahead.

My whole position and the whole backing up of my statement that the artist is "almost" independent goes with doing the thing as nearly as possible without "money."

I think also Quinn may know more than you think. He works very hard and I think rather excitedly and his talk after hours may not have the precision a sentence would have if a man had nothing to do but write art criticism and if he took a day to a paragraph.

At any rate, take a bit more time before you finally make up your mind. I wish there were one or two more like him.

I don't know whether his talk about art is like all American talk about art, but his *act* is a damn sight different.

Don't insist on his toning down his enthusiasms to a given foot rule.

Old Yeats (J.B.) describes Q. as "the kindest, most generous, most irascible" of men. I have never known anyone worth a damn who wasn't irascible.

Quinn says a number of nice things about both of you, and admires your courage and nerve and energy. This is not a grouch but a prayer. . . . I don't believe anybody else will do half or a tenth as much for us, or give us so many chances to make good after a slip. — — — —

The other thing is not to let J[ane] H[eap] cheek Quinn too much. I think he likes you both. But still I think it would be better if you saw him, than that she should. If they meet, whatever she may think of his artistic judgment, do let her remember that some of the best living artists think a great deal of it. Not merely because he buys their stuff.

125: To Edgar Jepson

London, 29 May

Dear Jepson: The damblasted trouble is that it *is* a magazine story; that it does not in every line — — — — on the magazine-reader, on the world that makes Harrison and *The English Review* possible.

If I am to make anything of a 32 page minute rag of a paper that looks like nothing at all, I cannot possibly compete with larger magazines on their own ground,—I have got to use stuff and I think exclusively stuff that in no way suggests the contents or existence of any other magazine; stuff that couldn't possibly appear, that couldn't think of appearing elsewhere.

My corner of the paper is *BLAST*, but *BLAST* covered with ice, with a literary and reserved camouflage (I mean, that's what I want: a classic and impeccable exterior: — — — — enunciated with an exquisite politeness. *BLAST* in which the exuberance has given place to external decorum of phrase.

Seccombe, Nicoll, The Authors' Club, all the — — — — inhabited by these animals and their American shadows, impeccably shattered, annihilated.

I should undoubtedly poison the lot were we not educated or deviscerated beyond that order of procedure. I stumble through a great number of words in trying to say, "your story is not satiric, but human and tragic" and that satire is such a cool and quiet word that it don't in the least express the quality of bitterness that I want, the peculiar kind of contempt for contemporary mentality, for the reading public, for the way the "world of letters" goes on.

Possibly a hyper-aesthesia, but I find no other word but "— — — —"; the sensation of being thrust head downward up to chin into the mire of an open privvy which comes upon me at the mention of the house of Murray, the *Bookman*, Seccombe, Chesterton, the whole order of these things.

New Statesman conveys a dryer, a more dusty feeling.

Certain people have felt this sort of thing about "life," I feel it about contemporary "litterchure," gensdelettres, etc.

Poetry gets out of reach of the stench, and satire is a quick-lime, or ammonia which cuts through it.

If I am to do anything with my half magazinette I have got to concentrate; at least for a while, I can use nothing which is not definitely an insult to the public-library, the general-reader, the weekly press.

On the practical side I have enough cash to pay myself, Eliot and Lewis an extremely small monthly screw. I have so little beyond that, that it is ludicrous to say how little. The first six months of it are gone already.

I think I could get you more for your story from Mencken, and get it quicker. At least I should suggest trying that if you permit or approve.

After I have definitely established the tone (how the hell does one escape that cliché), the chemical pungency of the *L.R.*, I may be able to think about general contributions.

Damn it all I want the author talking to the one most intelligent person he knows, and NOT accepting any current form, form of story, form of anything. Hang it all, how the hell does one say what I'm trying to get at.

I want it all "untanned alligator skin," and NO "make love's" and "dear angel's."

"Women's dresses, music, champagne" ne me disent rien.

126: To Margaret C. Anderson

London, [*? June*]

Dear editor: The one use of a man's knowing the classics is to prevent him from imitating the false classics.

You read Catullus to prevent yourself from being poisoned by the lies of pundits; you read Propertius to purge yourself of the greasy sediments of lecture courses on "American Literature," on "English Literature from Dryden to Addison," you (in extreme cases) read Arnaut Daniel so as not to be over-awed by a local editor who faces you with a condemnation in the phrase "paucity of rhyme."

The classics, "ancient and modern," are precisely the acids to gnaw through the thongs and bulls-hides with which we are tied by our schoolmasters.

They are the antiseptics. They are almost the only antiseptics against the contagious imbecility of mankind.

I can conceive an intelligence strong enough to exist without them, but I can not recall having met an incarnation of such intelligence. Some does better and some does worse.

The strength of Picasso is largely in his having chewed through and chewed up a great mass of classicism; which, for example, the lesser cubists, and the flabby cubists have not.

127: To Margaret C. Anderson

London, [*? August*]

Dear M.C.A.: Bodenheim has been on the grump ever since I was forced to tell him that I could not perceive much originality in his work. Neither is there. He was commendable in the first place because he was trying to take more care of his actual wording than either Masters or Sandburg. In verse having no very marked or seductive cadence, no rhyme, no qualitative measure, the actual language must be fairly near to perfection.

Also . . . Bodenheim distorts my words. I said nothing against these poets save that they hadn't opened up anything new during the past three years. Which, damn it, they haven't. I set my period at three years (definitely and deliberately). Thus H.D.'s early work, Aldington's, and Williams' "Postlude" do not come up for comparison.

I don't think any of these people have gone on; have invented much since the first *Des Imagistes* anthology. H.D. has done work as good. She has also (under I suppose the flow-contamination of Amy and Fletcher) let loose dilutations and repetitions, so that she has spoiled the "few but perfect" position which she might have held on to.

Anyhow Eliot has thought of things I had not thought of, and I'm damned if many of the others have done so. Inventive, creative, or what not.

And *The Dial*, OH *gosh*, slosh, tosh, the dial, d,i,a,l, dial. Dial—the stationary part of a clock or other chronometer. AND the *New Republic*, dessicated, stodgied copy of the dessicated *New Statesman*. WHY "new," why this passion for "newness" always confined to the title? Put there presumably to keep it out of the way. Not that one desires newness so awfully AWFULLY, goodness would suffice.

128: To H. L. MENCKEN

London, 12 August

Dear Mencken: I sent a letter to Hatteras [1] last week, in your care, asking if he had any stuff too wild for the *S.S.* I have been a bit slow getting the *Little Review* off the mark, but perhaps not so slow as would at first sight appear, as stuff has to leave here so infernally long before it gets into print in N.Y.

Apart from Yeats, I have a play by Lady Gregory, and one from Symons (not so valuable). Joyce has been in hospital ever since we started so he has been no use. But I have now got Hueffer's best ms. for 1918, and a topping story from Lewis for Dec.

I wonder if you have any stuff of your own too unComstockian for your own readers. And what about Wright?

I hope old Hatteras has impractical moments.

I suppose an exchange of ads at this stage of the game would be a pure present on your part. Still a statement that "the *S.S.* is the only magazine, American or otherwise, that ever lost 50,000 subscribers in attempting to give America better literature than she wanted" might fetch a few of our rare readers (who on the other hand probably read you (tacitly and unadmittedly in the midst of Browning societies) already).

I suppose Benefield is written out, or that anything he does would fit you perfectly well?

Hope you enjoyed Eliot in our July number. That unitarian upbringing has not been wasted.

(How many of your polysyllabic authors write under their own

[1] A pseudonym of Mencken.

names???? There can't be so many patristocratic cognomens in Manhattan.)

At any rate, if there is impractical stuff, I want it.

129: To Harriet Monroe

London, 21 August

Dear HM.: — — — — Re the Brooke. *I* didn't write about his beautiful toes, it was his "friend" who chose that theme for a dithyrambic. And some of his friends were a pretty poor lot. I don't mind the article [1] not appearing, BUT I wish I could really get you roused on the meaning of the American University and the menace of it.

The professor and his class are the only people in America who know enough to get a perspective, i.e., who could for example compare Masters and Crabbe, and get a level appreciation. They are so stuck that they, of course, don't see Masters. They are so provincial that they don't know any modern French (which in this case is the other angle from which to get a proper appreciation of Masters, i.e. apart from a rhetorical whoop, or a controversial smashing of the fools who opposed his *Spoon River Anthology*).

This sort of defence isn't balanced appreciation. It don't in the least help the next real thing that appears.

The matter ought to be gone on with, both in detail and in general—whether my tone in doing so is politic or not. Nobody else ever has the nerve to tackle this sort of thing: heaven knows it is not particularly enjoyable. In dealing with the "public" one has never said enough. There is nothing but "rubbing it in" that has the slightest effect.

I am sorry Sandburg don't like *Three Cantos*. F—— is too low in the scale of God's creatures to bother about. I can't see how anyone can see the thing in such small sections. However, the printing it in three parts has given me a chance to emend, and the version for the book is, I think, much improved. Eliot is the only person who proffered criticism instead of general objection.

I discount Sandburg's objection, by the fact that he would probably dislike anything with foreign quotations in it. Flint used to be the same (may be yet). Still one can't stop merely because some people haven't read Latin. It is the complex of the uneducated, in the same way class hatred works on the basis of money. Don't for God's sake say this to Sandburg. A decent system would give him time to loaf in a library. Which while perhaps less important than loafing in pubs, is still a part of the complete man's loafing.

Anyhow my next batch of stuff will be short poems, which, let us hope, someone will enjoy. Also one should not do the same thing all the time. The long poem is at least a change.

[1] An article protesting the award of the Henry Howland Memorial Prize for poetry to the *heirs* of Rupert Brooke.

Are you printing Alice's poems on American poets? They are the only entertaining native products I have seen for some time.

The lowest level is reached by *The Seven Arts*. Compare their August poem "The Old Courtesan" with the poem of Villon's from which Rodin named his statuette, to which the 7 *Arts* animal dedicates his muck.

The enclosed note is typical. Will you send the ass a copy of *Poetry* [Oct. 1913], with my list of French poets in it. Who the hell does she think is going to pay my board while I take two months to translate a volume of selections from contemporary French writers. She is like Weygandt who wrote for free copies of my books just after he had come into a fortune.

For sheer lack of consideration or realization give me a compatriot every time. Too bloody lazy to know anything or read anything. Why the hell can't she subscribe to *The Egoist* and read Ciolkowska, who is the only regular chronicler of French stuff. — — —

130: To John Quinn

London, 21 August

NOTHING TO ANSWER.

Dear John Quinn: 1. Dispatched Lewis' *Tarr* to Knopf yesterday, ms. complete, AT LAST. Heubsch has written to *Egoist* for it, but you said Knopf was to have first shot. However, it is just as well that there are two possible publishers in the field.

2. I forwarded your cable re *Exiles* to Joyce, as I couldn't make much of it. I haven't any copy of *Exiles*, and Pinker writes me that Joyce has told him to do something or other with his copy, and Yeats is in France so I can't get at the copy he either may or may not have (probably in Ireland). *Ergo*, I have referred the matter to Joyce himself.

3. I am worried by your cable received this A.M. re the two lines on Chesterton. Do what you like about them. Only they are part of my position, i.e., that one should name names in satire. And Chesterton is like a vile scum on the pond. The multitude of his mumblings cannot be killed by multitude but only by a sharp thrust (even that won't do it, but it purges one's soul).

All his slop—it is really modern catholicism to a great extent, the *never* taking a hedge straight, the mumbo-jumbo of superstition dodging behind clumsy fun and paradox.

If it were a question of cruelty to a weak man I shouldn't, of course, have printed it. But Chesterton *is* so much the mob, so much the multitude. It is not as if he weren't a symbol for all the mob's hatred of all art that aspires above mediocrity.

I feel very differently about Belloc, who once wanted to do the real thing, and for a long time, at least, had moments of bitterness (I think) that he had taken the journalistic turning. Still, he has left "Avril" and his translation of Bédier's *Tristan*.

Chesterton has always taken the stand that the real thing isn't worth doing. (Perhaps this is a slight exaggeration???? Complex of my own vanity??) My feeling is, perhaps, heightened by a feeling that I should probably like G.K.C. personally if I ever met him. Still, I believe he creates a milieu in which art is impossible. He and his kind.

However, I don't want to be hysterical over two lines. If you want them out or if Knopf thinks it will cost him too much to retain them, do what you think best. It is not so important that it should appear in America as here. (It has appeared in *BLAST* anyhow.)

Still, someone had to be the first to say that Hall Caine wasn't Christ returned, and Marie Corelli wasn't Flaubert, etc.

On the other hand, the lines are contemptuous, and contempt may not be a very formidable weapon. Leave the lines in the limited edition, anyhow, and do what you like with the other.

Lewis is out of hospital and back in the thick of it. Last note said he had his respirator on for two hours without break, parapet of one of his battery's guns knocked off, and general hotness. The news this A.M. is excellent.

I hope you are getting some fun out of *The Little Review*. I am. I feel I have been a bit slow in getting it off the mark, but stuff has to go from here so far in advance, and I couldn't at the start tell quite what I should be able to get hold of. AND some people simply can't be depended on to get stuff in by a given date. I have perhaps lost one number out of the first six, i.e., I should have got the stuff of the first six numbers into the first five. I am very much pleased at getting such a lot from Hueffer. Watt has written to Hardy.

Symons sent in unasked. Wanted to be with us unpaid rather than have me send his playlet to *Drama*, which I offered to do, as it isn't particularly of this generation, and as *Drama* would have paid him. — — — —

I shall send ms. of my prose collection to Knopf as soon as *The Egoist* sends me clear proofs of the "Fontenelle." That will be better for K.'s printers to work from than the sections cut from the paper.

To-Day for July has a review of J.B.Y.'s letters, joined with an attack on Bennett. I think Father will have sent you the *Times Literary Supplement* review of the letters (it is by Clutton-Brock).

Father has just sent me a copy of *Seven Arts*. I am glad there is something else.

I have been in a whirl of work for weeks. However, you'll see the results. No use discussing 'em here.

Do what you like re the "Cake of Soap." Please remember me to J.B.Y.

131: TO WYNDHAM LEWIS

London, 25 August

Dear Lewis: *Tarr* has been gathered into a lump and been sent to America. As that sentence cannot possibly pass any censor, let me say clearly "The manuscript of your novel" more or less correct (Miss S. having been through the furrin languidges) has at last been dispatched by registered post.

I have also a receipt from Barclay's for £12/12 (sent to be sure to Miss E. Pound, but passons). That's for your Egyptian drawing. I forget the name and can't be bothered looking it up. I have asked them to print the "Soldier of Humour" all in one number (*Dec.*).

As to Mayfair. I wrote you months ago that I hadn't seen anybody for ages. My letter was sent back with a statement that your whereabouts was uncertain. It was just after you had gone to hospital. My tidings were then stale, and no use.

Miss S. has sent you the letters, with request to expurgate. I'd rather you did it yourself. I am using the Preface "Inferior Religions" in Sept. and "Cantleman" in Oct. Lady Gregory's respectability in Nov. supposed to placate the reader.

I am doing a series of "Studies of Contemporary Mentality" in the *New Age*. Entertaining, laborious, unimportant. Am also plotting a book of essays for American publication. That's not of very breathless interest either. Really I feel as if I had writ an article a day for a month. Am trying to get "caught up."

The *Figaro* cutting was entertaining. Miss S. did not say it was from you. Probably never entered her head that anyone would suppose it to be her own, very own, unaided discovery.

Baker is worried about you. I do not think I picture your life as one of satin-coated ease. However, it is just as well to emphasise things. I have not read Barbusse, Dorothy did. Baker don't feel like reading it either.

I don't see what the hell any writer can add to one's imagination of things. However . . . that's no reason for not trying. And again neither Baker nor I can be taken as types of average imagination. All these books should ultimately be very useful [lacuna] . . . . has done one on the hospitals. "La vie des Mar . .[lacuna] . . s."

I on the contrary have been writing of Laforgue, Elizabethan classicists, etc. etc. Vildrac said "Ce serait bien plaisant, passer sa vie en belles études."

I believe my two cousins who certainly don't care a hang for European civilization have both been called up. Such is the irony of things.

There's an American employment something or other, which has told me to go away and be quiet, that in time our own troops will give us all the employment, etc.

None of which things will in the least temper the sounds of "The End of a Perfect Day" or kindred gramophone records or stay off crumps from your parapet.

I wish you would get a decent and convenient wound in some comparatively tactful part of your anatomy. Say the left buttock. But that makes lying in bed uncomfortable. Really it is difficult to choose a part suitable for mangling. Hell.

Such gossip as there is, it is NOT amusing. The *Strand* magazine for Sept. assures me the [lacuna] are effective. The *Morning Chronicle* assures me my compatriots are called "Teddies," which is one in the eye for Mr.

Woodie Wilson. However, transpontine politics may not amuse you. I have sent on the *Little Review*. I suppose the Aug. will arrive sometime, but it has nothing of yours. Etc.

132: TO HARRIET MONROE

London, 26 August

Dear H.M.: Here is the first of the French articles. Eliot is uncertain about his copy, undependable for anything at a given date. The work at the bank which at first seemed to leave him freer than teaching, now seems to use a deal of his energy. It is a great waste.

De Bosschère is busy with his illustrations. He says he will do Suares or Elskamp. But it is a bit hard to hurry him until his poem is printed.

Re what you said about the French articles accused of following in Amy's wake. I think you had better put this note in the notes:

"The Approach to Paris," Mr. Pound's first series of articles dealing with Jules Romains, Vildrac, De Régnier, Rémy de Gourmont, Laurent Tailhade, Corbière, Rimbaud, Klingsor, Jammes, and other contemporary French poets, appeared in *The New Age* in the late summer of 1913. (Vide a note on Romains, and one headed "Paris" in our issues for Aug. and Oct. of that year.)

I think that will stave off any suggestion of Amy's having led me. I met Romains and Vildrac in the spring of that year, and had read *La Vie Unanime* in 1912 or 1911.

Not that priority matters eternally. Amy had read a lot of French when I met her. I certainly did not initiate her into the mysteries of modern French, or she me.

The only thing, or at least THE thing one envies the rich is that they can order up fifty new books whenever the fancy takes them.

I did my reviews out of Fletcher's copies and, I think, cut the pages in several. He had a splendid lot of books. And *certainly* a lot of them had not undergone the paper-cutter.

My series of articles must have been running in the *N.A.* when Amy landed here on her first great political circuit.

Ah well, let us come to the present.

I went through a great pile of Margaret Postgate's poems. Found you had seen them and selected one. The rest seem to me to have a germ, but to be unready for publication.

The war seems to have stopped poetry here and in France. Undigested war is no better than undigested anything else. Now no one has time to digest.

SUNDAY

I am copying out and enclosing three poems by "P.T.R." I have come to no decision about them. They seem to me to "have come," i.e. the subject has made the poem. That is perhaps their only virtue, but it is in contrast to the flood of stuff wherein the author has so obviously been racking his head to find something to write about. At any rate they are not factitious.

I haven't the slightest conviction about the girl's ability (she is a friend of Miss Postgate's), nor do I expect, or not expect, anything about her future production.

If you don't want them, please send them back promptly. Most, or at least a lot, of my worry about *Poetry* has been due to delay in Chicago, and authors' fussing at this end.

Note, I am NOT in favour of using English stuff *unless* it is better than the local produce.

2. As the magazine has had practically no English support, I think it would be well after the war to use French stuff where possible, in place of English.

IF you are going to LEAD, that is about the only regular thing you can do now. We should have at least two pages of French poetry per month, if not four.

The time is not as opportune as when I first urged this five years ago; France will be more exhausted by the war than is England. Nevertheless, I hope to get to Paris when it is over. AND to distinguish ourselves from the Boston poetry this-that-and-the-others, a French section will be excellent. ONLY one must be able to be quite definite with the men when one meets them.

It will be a change, and the guarantors will want signs of life, AND you mustn't slip into the tone of *The Dial, The Seven Arts, The New Republic,* etc. . . . at least the magazine is done if you do, and its preeminence is departed.

All the other "new magazines" have found England by now.

On the practical side, I must be out to buy a certain amount of French verse before I can possibly get at what good there is. The actual putting this plan into effect is probably some time off, but one must prepare and agree about it.

I do NOT see anything new or alive coming here, and one might perfectly well give up the English pages to French. The format is now so big that four pages of French will leave plenty of room for all the decent American stuff (and space over).

I think also we should add a definite French correspondent IF I can find the right man. I think I have one who will do, i.e. who has some sense and who would take enough interest in the matter. There are several intelligent men who would NOT take an interest; they won't do.

The minimum offerable arrangement would be six articles a year at 10 dollars each. And someone would have to be paid 2 dollars or 2.50 each to translate them. That would possibly be me. I don't think it can be done any cheaper.

This ought to have been done long ago. But anyhow. A magazine can't stand still. It must grow or decay.

I suggest articles of 1500 to 2000 words. 2 pages of French poetry the month of the article and 4 pages the alternate months. And I should cut

out practically all London poetry save Yeats, Eliot, and stuff of really unusual interest. Also the weeds of U.S. vers libre which is getting to the state
the Celtic glamour had got to ten years ago.

Miss Tietjens' book had nice stuff in it, but was not tense enough.

I shall follow my essay on French satirists by one on The Hard and Soft
in French poetry. I have it in my head and think it will be a good one.

133: To Margaret C. Anderson

London, [? 30 August]

Dear M.C.A.: He "happens to know" I omitted a name because of personal dislike. He is a bloody and louse-eaten liar.

As a guide to tender feet, I suggest that my "personal dislike" of individual contemporaries has largely arisen from two causes (also that it has
arisen subjectively in the mind or boozum *of the disliked* and not in my
own).

Cause 1. a. My unwillingness to praise what seems to me unworthy of
praise.

b. My unwillingness, after having discerned a faint gleam of virtue in a young man's work, or even got some of his stuff
printed, then to be unable to note signs of progress in later
work, or even to be unable to retain my interest.

Cause 2. My interest (sudden or gradual) in the work of some other
artist or writer.

I think there is one slip in the number. "Help us to make the *L.R.* a
power." Bad wording. Nothing but our own blasted contents will do that.
Henley was a power, I have heard tell, with the *National Observer* when
its circulation had shrunk to 80 subscribers. I don't want to pursue domin-
ion to that extent, but it is a glorious precedent.

As for my "personal dislike" of poets. CRRRRHIST JHEEZUS when I think
of the hours of boredom I have put up with from people MERELY because
they have in an unguarded and irrecoverable and irresponsible moment
committed a good poem, or several!!!!!! Ah, that one might live to see the
expression on the face of a new poet, whom I had just been boosting, upon
seeing another still newer poet seated in an armchair.

And then there is Amy. Is there any life into which the personal Amy
would not bring rays of sunshine? Alas! and alas only, that the price, i.e.,
equal suffrage in a republic of poesy, a recognition of artistic equality,
should come between us.

I think, despite the difficulty of knowing what one will think in a year's
time, I think, credo che credessi, etc., that dear Amy Lowell's talents and
temperament will always be political rather than literary or artistic. She is
delightful. ONLY she wanted me to sell out lock stock and barrel, and I
said it didn't interest me. And still she would have it, so I named a price,
i.e., I said I would contribute to a democratized anthology IF she would
institute a yearly prize for poetry to be adjudged by Yeats, Hueffer, and

myself. (I even went so far as to name a committee including herself. I can't remember whether it was she, I and Yeats, or she, I and Hueffer, or all four.) But that touched the sacred springs of wrath.

I think she was a bloody fool, for we could have bust the British academic committee (called the British Academy) to smithereens, and she could have been somebody over here (which she wanted to be) rather than being driven back to the Hylo kennels.

134: To Amy Lowell

London, 30 August

My dear Amy: Are you going to get onto the Band Wagon?

You tried to stampede me into accepting as my artistic equals various people whom it would have been rank hypocrisy for me to accept in any such manner. There is no democracy in the arts.

And now what is this nonsense you write to Miss Anderson about "bitterest" enmities?

135: To Margaret C. Anderson

London, [September]

Chère M.: The Iris Barry and Rodker stuff is not a compromise but a bet. I stake my critical position, or some part of it, on a belief that both of them *will* do something. I am not risking much, because I have seen a lot of their mss. The Barry has done the draft of a novel, and it has the chance of being literature. Rodker has convinced me, at last, that he "has it in him." And one must have les jeunes. Rodker ought to be up to regulation in a few years' time.

He will go farther than Richard Aldington, though I don't expect anyone to believe that statement for some time. He has more invention, more guts. His father did not have a library full of classics, but he will learn.

They are neither of them STUPID, blockheaded as F—— and Lawrence are stupid and blockheaded. Lawrence had less showing above the waterline when Hueffer took him up than Rodker has now. And certainly Hueffer has been justified. Much as Lawrence annoys me, and inferior as he is to Joyce. — — — —

YES *The Seven Arts* is slop. YES. And *The New Republic* is dung dust, with an admixture of dung, also dust dry.

I must get out of the big stick habit, and begin to put my prose stuff into some sort of possibly permanent form, not merely into saying things which everybody will believe in three years' time and take as a matter of course in ten.

I.e. articles which can be reduced to "Joyce is a writer, GODDAMN your eyes, Joyce is a writer, I tell you Joyce etc. etc." Lewis can paint, Gaudier knows a stone from a milk-pudding. WIPE your feet!!!!!!

136: To EDGAR JEPSON

London, 7 September

Dear Jepson: I have the idea, scheme, plot, for THE spy-detective communication with the foe story. But I am too bleating green in the form.

Can you, or will you collaborate? And will you come in to tea, any day to say No or YES, or discuss the matter? I shall be in Saturday and Sunday at tea time. Or you can drop me a card if some day next week suits you better.

137: To WILLIAM CARLOS WILLIAMS

London, 10 November

— — — — My dear William: At what date did you join the ranks of the old ladies?

Among the male portion of the community one constantly uses fragments of letters, fragments of conversation (anonymously, quite anonymously, NOT referring to the emitter by name) for the purpose of sharpening a printed argument.

I note your invitation to return to my fatherland (pencil at the top of your letter sic g.t.h.); I shall probably accept it at the end of the war.

My knowledge of the ("stet") American heart is amply indicated in "L'Homme Moyen Sensuel."

I had no ulterior or hidden meaning in calling you or the imaginary correspondent an "American" author. Still, what the hell else are you? I mean apart from being a citizen, a good fellow (in your better moments), a grouch, a slightly hypersensitized animal, etc.?? Wot bloody kind of author are you save Amurkun (same as me)?

And whether, O Demosthenes, is one to be called a "damn fool" or a "person"?

Your sap is interrupted. Try De Gourmont's "Epilogue" ('95-'98). And don't expect the world to revolve about Rutherford.

If you had any confidence in America you wouldn't be so touchy about it.

I thought the — — — — millenium that we all idiotically look for and work for was to be the day when an American artist could stay at home without being dragged into civic campaigns, dilutations of controversy, etc., when he could stay in America without growing propagandist. God knows I have to work hard enough to escape, not propagande, but getting centered in propagande.

And America! What the hell do you a bloomin' foreigner know about the place? Your père only penetrated the edge, and you've never been west of Upper Darby, or the Maunchunk switchback. Would Harriet, with the swirl of the prairie wind in her underwear, or the virile Sandburg recognize you, an effete Easterner, as a REAL American? INCONCEIVABLE!!!!

My dear boy, you have never felt the whoop of the PEEraries. You have never seen the projecting and protuberant Mts. of the Sierra Nevada. WOT can you know of the counthry?

You have the naive credulity of a Co. Claire immigrant. But I (der grosse Ich) have the virus, the bacíllus of the land in my blood, for nearly three bleating centuries.

(Bloody snob. 'Eave a brick at 'im!!!!)

You (read your Freud) have a Vaterersatz, you have a paternal image at your fireside, and you call it John Bull.

Your statement about my wanting Paris to be like London is a figment of your own diseased imagination.

"I warn you that anything you say at this time may later be used against you." The Arts vs. Williams.

Or will you carry my head on a platter? Or would you like it brought over to be punched?? A votre service, M'sieu. I am coming to inspect you.

I of course like your Old Man, and I have drunk his Goldwasser.

I was very glad to see your wholly incoherent unAmerican poems in the *L.R.*

Of course Sandburg will tell you that you miss the "Big drifts," and Bodenheim will object to your not being sufficiently decadent.

(You thank your bloomin gawd you've got enough Spanish blood to muddy up your mind, and prevent the current American ideation from going through it like a blighted collander.)

The thing that saves your work is *opacity*, and don't you forget it. Opacity is NOT an American quality. Fizz, swish, gabble of verbiage, these are echt Amerikanisch.

And Alas, alas, poor old Masters. Look at Oct. *Poetry*.

But really this "old friend" hurt feeling business is too Skipwithcannéllish; it is *peu vous*. I demand of you more robustezza. Bigod sir, you show more robustezza, or I will come over to Rutherford and have at you, *coram*, in person.

And moreover you answer my questions, p. 38, before you go on to the p.s. p. 39 which does not concern you.

Let me indulge in the American habit of quotation:

"Si le cosmopolitisme littéraire gagnait encore et qu'il réussit â éteindre ce que les différences de care ont allumé de haine de sang parmi les hommes, j'y verrais un gain pour la civilisation et pour l'humanite tout entiere. . . .

"L'amour excessif et exclusif d'une patrie a pour immédiat corollaire l'horreur des patries étrangères. Non seulement on craint de quitter le jupe de sa maman, d'aller voir comment vivent les autres hommes, de se mêler à leurs luttes, de partager leurs travaux; non seulement on reste chez soi, mais on finit par fermer sa porte.

"Cette folie gagne certains littérateurs et le même professeur, en si tant d'expliquer le Cid ou Don Juan, rédige de gracieuse injures contre Ibsen

et l'influence, hélas, trop illusoire, de son oeuvre, pourtant toute de
lumiere et de beautè." Et cetera. Lie down and compose yourself.

P.S. It's also nonsense this wail that M.C.A. "dislikes" you.

138: To H. L. MENCKEN

London, 28 November

Dear Mencken: Mr. Hatteras hasn't sent me the leetle book he wrote of.
I suppose it is the same "Lives of Apostles" slated by Orage in *The New
Age,* on the same page with my "Fontenelle." You might jog his memory
when you see him.

I have enjoyed your *Book of Prefaces* (sent me by John Quinn). I was
doing a note on it for the L.R. but lost my temper over your remarks on
H. James on the page where you treat him and Howells together.

I see the idea *au fond,* and grant part of it, but your expression is very
careless, and you shouldn't treat a great man and a mutton-shank in one
page as if there were no gulph between 'em. I have taken my copy of the
book to *The N. Age* and asked Orage to give full notice to last essay. It is
worth it.

James was, I admit, touched with a sort of Puritanism but you will recall
that Goncourt in the preface either to *La Fille Elisa* or *Germanie Lacer-
teux* says "we have only been able to do crude types in our realism, but
realism will go on and manage to present more complex types, more complex psychology" (I quote from memory, but that is the gist of it). What
Henry calls "down town," or rather more than that, was done by the
Goncourts, and H.J. was, I think, more than justified in not trying to do it
again, especially as he was better fitted to cover a different terrain. Besides he HAS written the MOST obscene book of our time, puritan or no
puritan.

God save us from him when he gets off on connoisseurship.

I dare say you make Dreiser rather more interesting than his own books
are. Re Huneker I think you weaken your case a little by only having at
your disposal some very new artists NOT necessarily better than those
whom he "has got to." One may still prefer Debussy to Ornstein, even
though convinced that DeB. IS stuck at about 1910.

I think you have done a good, and much needed job, and have enjoyed
the book very much (with these few reservations).

Regards to Hatteras.

139: To HARRIET MONROE

London, 29 November

Dear H.M.: I wonder if you have seen H. L. Mencken's *Book of Prefaces,*
especially the last essay in it.

I think *Poetry*, with its intense, its almost oppressively respectable reputation for respectability, is in a good position to take up this matter of interference with the mails. (Not re war and pacifism, for I believe it is legal for a government to do almost anything in war time. That is, anything short of military law itself may be regarded as a palliative or substitute for military law.) BUT re the pre-war and coming post-war interference with the mails by Comstock's committee of blackguards, something certainly OUGHT to be done. And as *Poetry* has never printed anything that could bring the blush to the cheek of a deaf nun I think the magazine is in an excellent position to act.

Re the unGermanization of universities, which I have, as you may have forgotten, been yelling for some time, I now see that some professors have proclaimed it. NOT, of course, because they know what or why, but on "pathriotic" grounds.

However, that also should be encouraged. And the nature of philology, as a system of dehumanization, gone into.

140: TO MARGARET C. ANDERSON

London, [? December]

Dear M.C.A.: If London and particularly Mayfair, is going to take up the magazine, we must be more careful than ever NOT to have in too much Amy, and suburbs.

Re Amy: I don't want to hedge too much. I don't think we need bar her from the magazine, but she can't write for the mondaine London clientele. At least I can't see Lady Randolph Churchill (or May Sinclair, for example) reading her with any spirit of reverence. These people can take it just as strong as Lewis can pitch. Your own tone suits 'em O.K. (NOT that you'd care a damn if it didn't but you may as well know it.)

Hecht is an asset. Hard reading and a bit heavy, but he has the root of the matter in him. He is trying to come to grips also. When he recalls the fact that Maupassant does not exaggerate, he can write contes—i.e., can (future) will be able to.

1 9 1 8

141: TO HARRIET MONROE

London, 1 January

Dear H.M.: Nov. and Dec. numbers arrived last night and this A.M.

I enclose my harvest. I have made two series of it, one mediaeval. Before you blaspheme over it, do read the Canzon aloud. I have completely rewritten, or nearly finished completely rewriting all Arnaut Daniel. I use this translation among the adaptations in this series because it needs no explanatory notes, as do some of the other canzoni. The best one of the lot can perhaps appear only in the volume, where notes will be in place.

There has been no attention to sound for so long, save from Lindsay. And his is interesting only as Kipling's was. Believe me one can write it by the hour as fast as one scribbles. However you never will believe me in this matter, so passons. I don't in the least want to stop Lindsay, any more than I would have stopped *Barrack Room Ballads*.

The Provençal is to precede the "[Moeurs] Contemporaines." I think it will all go on about 11 pages. I have marked the first little alba to be put in small italics at top of right hand side of page, that will save space. As with the quatrain from Lope de Vega in "The Condolence."

I liked your comment p. 89, Nov. no. Naturally pleased to see the folk song idea smacked again. Even an eminent London musical critic has recently got on a platform and said "all folk songs have authors and the authors are individuals." The blessing of the "folk" song is solely in that the "folk" forget and leave out things. It is a fading and attrition not a creative process.

My lot should have two separate chief headings, as indicated. The Provençal are to have Roman numerals I. to V. I am not sure that numerals are necessary in the "Contemporaines."

I shall probably do some more work on sound. Anything really made to speak or sing is bound to lose on the page, unless the reader have some sense of sound. This I can not help. Simply the vers libre public are probably by now as stone blind to the vocal or oral properties of a poem as the "sonnet" public was five or seven years ago to the actual language, i.e. all that has made my stuff interesting since "Contemporania." This is simply to fore-say that the Canzon will set a lot of people grumbling. And that I don't care a damn. Not any more than I cared about the objections to vers libre. — — —

I am profoundly glad my earlier versions of Arnaut weren't published. It gives me a chance to do something with it.

The old man, and the harp, and Mr. Styrax will hold the balance. You won't have a wail about my having forsaken or forsworn the present. I dare say you are content to get ANYTHING rather than Canto IV.[1]

Knopf writes that he sold 323 copies *Lustra* in Oct. and 9 in Nov., and that nobody had offered any assistance. Sandburg has of course pretty well covered the ground, still perhaps there might be a brief notice of the existence of the American edition. It contains, as you have doubtless seen, earlier stuff than that which has appeared in *Poetry* and is fairly good value in pages. The note of acknowledgment is just before the Cantos. — — — —

---

[1] She wasn't. She accepted neither series, considering both "unprintable." Her notes on several of the poems are instructive. Of "Vergier": "lovely, but—frank!" Of "Mr. Styrax": "Impossibly frank—*virgo*." Of "Ritratto": "Amusing—about Lowell—but 'stomped into my bedroom.'"

142: To Margaret C. Anderson

London, [*? January*]

Dear M.C.A.: Do give me credit occasionally for at least a reason for my acts. Even if it isn't the sole and surviving reason left on the planet; and even if I occasionally do not hit a bull's-eye.

And do for god's sake realize that having graciously wasted a week explaining that I would accept K but could not pay for him; I cannot waste another saying that we will not print him. I have only a certain amount of energy; and that I have (a) to get my poetry written; (b) to pay my rent etc., (c) to assist in the promulgation of *The L.R.* (letters to be placed in any order you like).

There appears to be nothing in America between professors and Kreymborgs and Bodenheim. Platonic hemiandroi. Anemia of guts on one side and anemia of education on the other.

As yet since May of last year America has coughed up no "creative" stuff, i.e. no poetry or fiction to *The L.R.* apart from jh [1] on females with faces with noses level with ears which wasn't fiction. But apart from the editorial, the U.S. has given nothing to contents of *L.R.* save that treacle about Judas which affected me much more violently than K seems to have affected you.

Even so I think you were "right" to print it, on the principle that one must accept *something* now and again, if one is not utterly to choke off all inflow of mss. (a very dangerous principle, but pragmatic). And, as you say, I am ageing rapidly. Byron is described as very old, or at least gray and showing age at 36. I have but few years left me. I cannot be expected to keep up sufficient interest in the state of public imbecility to go on being "astringent" perpetually.

I wonder at what point a discussion of music would lead you and me into mutual assassination?????????? Gawd only know.

Joyce, by the way, approves of the clavichord. And he has also sung in opera. Lewis, I think, regards the instrument as a strange unaccountable sort of mouse-trap; the charwoman (after four months' service) spoke of it the other day as "the little black table" (observation the leading characteristic of the "lower orders").

Chère amie, I am, for the time being, bored to death with being any kind of an editor. I desire to go on with my long poem; and like the Duke of Chang, I desire to hear the music of a lost dynasty. (Have managed to hear it, in fact.) And I desire also to resurrect the art of the lyric, I mean words to be sung, for Yeats' only wail and submit to keening and chaunting (with a *u*) and Swinburne's only rhapsodify. And with a few exceptions (a few in Browning) there is scarcely anything since the time of Waller and Campion. AND a mere imitation of them won't do.

[1] Jane Heap.

143: To Wyndham Lewis

London, 13 January

Dear W.L.: —/—/

You will be grieved to know that *The Little Review* lost its case,[1] despite J.Q.'s noble defence "The man who wrote *that* story can *not* be a sensualist" etc. I have all the papers of the case, and some of them are rich and refreshing reading. I have been too busy with the XIIth Century to take any further steps in the matter. The job is now about done, and part of it decently.

I enclose more on Augustus, springing from the Castalian fount of the Chenil.

Virgin's Prayer

*Ezra Pound
And Augustus John
Bless the bed
That I lie on.*

(Authorship unrecognized, I first heard it in 1909.) It is emphatically NOT my own, I believe it to have come from an elder generation. However it is not pertinent to the subject. No one else ever coupled our names.

Orage hopes to get the Contemporary Mentality published as a book. It is not an important fandango. Enough of this.

144: To Margaret C. Anderson

London, [? January]

Dear Margaret: Right you are. Re Quinn, remember: Tis he who hath bought the pictures; tis he who both getteth me an American publisher and smacketh the same with rods; tis he who sendeth me the Spondos Oligos, which is by interpretation the small tribute or spondooliks wherewith I do pay my contributors, WHEREFORE is my heart softened toward the said J.Q., and he in mine eyes can commit nothing heinous.

Can you, on the other hand, see Mencken? He writes hoping the suppression won't drive you out of business; and if he chose to wail in his back pages re "Cantleman" (Lewis), it might do some good. After all he still has a circulation. AND his eyes discerned me years since.

Re Amy. I DON'T want her. But if she can be made to liquidate, to excoriate, to cash in, on a magazine, ESPECIALLY in a section over which I have no control, and for which I am not responsible, THEN would I be right glad to see her milked of her money, mashed into moonshine, at

---

[1] The October 1917 issue was suppressed in America because of Lewis' story "Cantleman's Spring Mate."

mercy of monitors. Especially as appearance in U.S. section does NOT commit me to any approval of her work.

Of course *if* (which is unlikely) she ever wanted to return to the true church and live like an honest woman, something might be arranged. *But* . . .

Is she yet weary of B——, and the mulattoism, mental and physical?

Do, or perhaps *do not*, regard the prospectus of *Contemporary Verse*. Of all the crapule that a reputed millionaire was ever responsible for. . . . I hope it *costs* Stork something.

(Also remember that I CAN'T possibly know from this side which of my damned suggestions are any good. Probably ANY suggestion I make re American policy is bad. However I may as well send 'em. You can reject 'em with perfect ease.)

Etc. I do have to stop and earn my board now and again. Malhaureusement.

145: To H. L. MENCKEN

London, 25 January

Dear Mencken: Thanks for *Pistols*. It has its moments. But it don't keep up the "Man of Sixty" tone, wherein Hatteras is at his best. It also does not appear to be the work of a man of "them years."

I sent off my notes on *Prefaces* to Miss A. I was too exhausted to recast them and told her to go ahead if she liked. Boyd has just proposed an article on the book, either for *Egoist* or *L.R.*, and I have asked him to send it on. I think the sketch of Nathan is better done than that of Mencken. It is a gay work. Orage is very stupid over it.

Can't find the bloody — — — — thing (i.e. his review) at the moment. As you never eat with authors, I hope you will drop in between meals on your way to the Tyrol. Unless you choose to regard me as, by brevet, an editor, or a human being.

There is great desolation in litterchure at the moment. Joyce's new novel has a corking 1st Chap. (which will get us suppressed), not such a good second one.

I think I have found a new writer of *contes*. At least he promises.

Hatteras *must* be sixty. I have been reading him for . . . well no, not forty years. Perhaps he need only be fifty.

146: To JOHN QUINN

London, 29 January

Dear Quinn: If my last cable has reached you it should answer your last two or three.

Maud Gonne was sent to a nursing home, which she left, apparently without opposition, at the end of about five days.

Home Office wrote me that the arrangement had been made for a week.

At any rate, she is now apparently free, living at Woburn Bldgs. and agitating for return to Ireland.

That country, so far as I know, has never been considered a health-resort for consumptives. As soon as she got to the nursing home she was interviewed for some Irish paper. Lansbury has since turned loose in the *Herald*. And M.G. is, I think, writing to other papers. I give it up.

She talks about there being no "German plot." Now, to the best of my knowledge, she was not accused of any complicity in German plots. Most of the arrests were, I believe, "preventive," the official position being that trouble was likely, and that it was better to lock up a certain number of people than to have a lot more shot and a few more in danger of hanging.

I enclose the rough draft of my letter to Lamar. It's no use, I haven't a typist, and can't do everything. I send you the draft merely for the sake of one or two points for your own consideration.

Orage is going to have a look at the papers of the case today. Thanks for booming me to him.

Re copying the Lamar letter. I have finished my Arnaut, and now Raymonde Collignon is really going to sing the old music, the reconstructions Rummel and I made six years ago. It means a new start on the whole thing (Provençal XII Century music), and probably the resurrection of as much of it as is worth while. We've been held up for lack of a singer WITH the right equipment, intelligence, etc.

Anyhow, it is more important than trying to save America from itself.

Fortunately, I've the reprods. of the Milan mss. and some copies we made of various mss. in Paris, so we'll be able to go ahead despite the Bibliotheque Nationale's being closed. Only inconvenience being that Rummel is in Paris, so some of the work will have to be by letter.

Re the rough draft for Lamar. I am glad it was not written *to* me.

Knopf wrote on Jan. 4 and on Jan. 7, before and AFTER Quinn. Contrast extremely amusing.

147: To Margaret C. Anderson

London, [? February]

Dear Margaret: Jan. number arrived. Feeling better. Number looks business-like, and "about to continue." Damn, damn, DAMN I must pull myself together and DO something.

I wish to Christ you would take an anaesthetic and print this cursed thing of Keary's; thereby saving me time to breathe and get something written.

Bill Wms. is *the* most bloody inarticulate animal that ever gargled. BUT it's better than Amy's bloody ten-cent repetitive gramophone, perfectly articulate (i.e. in the verbal section).

Whereas the bleating genius of the HOME product. Hecht might write good De Maupassant if he didn't try to crack jokes and ring bells; and if he would only realize that he DON'T need to exaggerate to be interesting.

SANGRE DI SAN PIETRO!!! WHY!!! do you recall that better to be forgotten libellule of Wilkinson's????? Raoul Root INDEED.[1] KHRRIST. Am I a pet pug to have blue ribbon curled in my tail?

Despite your wail, Lewis' description of the three American rescuers in the second half of "Sol[dier of] Humour" is excellent, Digit of the Moon, etc. Oh very good. I got him to rewrite some of it, but wot the hell can a man do in his present circumstances? It is, as he recognizes, a question of doing his stories somehow or other, or not doing them at all.

He will, if he don't get killed, revise later before book publication.

Dast it, the James and De Gourmont numbers are six months' work each. AND I do not want to sink wholly into criticism to the utter stoppage of creation. ETC.

148: To H. L. MENCKEN

London, 12 March

Mon Cher Henri Laureatus Laurentinus: No, I did not write it, Eliot wrote it,[2] but it would be extremely unwise for him, at this stage of his career, with the hope of sometime getting paid by elder reviews, and published by the godly, and in general of not utterly bitching his chances in various quarters, for him to have signed it.

This information is confidential. The proposition from N.Y. was to reprint the De Bosschère essay on me, but I thought it too high flown, too much about my noble soul and not sufficiently *documentè*.

I had just boomed Eliot, but he was the only person one could trust NOT to talk about the Rocky Mountains, the bold unfettered West, the Kawsmos etc.

The thing should have been signed with a nom-de-swank, but it got printed before that sane suggestion reached Knopf. —/—/

149: To JOHN QUINN

London, 3 April

Dear John Quinn: Thanks for yours of March 14th and the enclosure. It is awfully good of you to go on talking of getting more guarantors when you have so many causes to be displeased.

To the best of my recollection, my instructions were that my article was to be submitted to you.

---

[1] Pound's note on Mencken's *Book of Prefaces* appeared in *The Little Review* under this pseudonym.
[2] *Ezra Pound, His Metric and Poetry.*

I agree that the number [1] is too much on one note. The fault lies in Lewis' delay. The Joyce and Hueffer with something less pungent between them would have gone very well. Lewis' "Imaginary Letters" should have come out months ago. I had forgotten, or rather sending the mss. over so long ago I had not been able to plan the numbers very much. ~~Any other chapter of Hueffer would have~~ balanced with the Joyce or Lewis.

Miss A. was trying to get the Lewis out of the way to make room for my "Imaginary Letter," which couldn't precede Lewis' final one.

Also, with the change in size, which I couldn't calculate, either as to time or as to the effect on consuming mss., plus Miss A.'s elimination of all American contributions (possibly in deference to Kahn's remarks?), plus the uncertainty of Lewis' times and seasons, I have had to leave the order and grouping to Miss A.

I can't agree with you about Joyce's first chapter. I don't think the passages about his mother's death and the sea would come with such force if they weren't imbedded in squalor and disgusts.

I may say that I rec'd the fourth chapter some days ago, and deleted about twenty lines before sending it off to N.Y.; and also wrote Joyce my reasons for thinking the said lines excessive.

He does not disgust me as Wells does. — — — —

Hueffer's stuff was done five years ago. I think it was time somebody wiped up W——. Tho' I have never been interested enough in him to read him, I am glad to see him cleaned off and marked, "Not Necessary." Neither have I read Havelock Ellis. The "subject," as you say, does not particularly interest me.

My whole position is simply: "permettre à ceux qui en valent la peine, francement d'écrire leur pensée."

Jules Romains is ideologue, and undoubtedly mars his work by riding an idea to death. If he didn't he probably wouldn't give himself the opportunity of getting out the really good part of his stuff. He seems to me about the only "younger" man in France whose head works at all. There are interesting things in him. I don't think I have ever claimed more than that. Duhamel, Chennevière, Arcos, all less than Romains, and if they did anything good he would know it.

I don't believe in Rolland. Possibly prejudiced by Cannan, but still I don't believe in anybody Cannan would take up with.

I wish Romains was someone you believed in, but still—I can't see any way round that particular corner. I am not infatuated, I simply think him the best of the lot over there. One of the few who would be with *us*, rather than with the Poetry Book Shop and the Georgian Anthologies, Abercrombie, Eddie Marsh, etc.

There is *something* in his work. It is not the hebetude of a lignified cerebrum. And I think I did mention limitations in my note on the "Hard and Soft in Fr. Poetry."

I think also he is possibly an organizer. The other organizers in Paris

[1] The March 1918 number of *The Little Review*.

are either pure wind, like Mercereau and Parmentier, or else lunatics like Barzun (Lowells and Lindsays).

Romains has done at least as much creative work as talk about it. Which is more than one can say of most of his confreres, etc., etc. At any rate, it is the best that can be done. Hope Kahn won't think I am lying down on the job.

Poor Joyce is down again with his eyes. Lewis nearly dying of the attempt to paint something bad enough *in the right way*.

Eliot has emitted a few new and diverting verses. Sending 'em for Sept.

Thanks again for correcting *Pavannes*.

150: To Margaret Anderson

London, [? April]

Dear M.C.A.: I enclose another lost sheep. It has taken me months to recover it, samee Fenollosa.

It is not wildly exciting, and it is not news, but it is a small scrap of Voltaire's *Dictionaire Philosophique*, which considering its date might serve to show how far far far etc., how long long long etc., it takes for a light to travel across the darkness of Anglo-American literature.

I know it is too long, BUT it simply won't cut, and P. 17 with passage about Sarah is almost worth waiting for.

Also P. 3. "It seems probable that God was not attempting to educate the Jews in philosophy or cosmogony."

Etc., etc. The damned thing has bits, and they won't come out of the whole mass of it.

Frazer has of course done the whole job monumentally, BUT good god how slowly, in how many volumes. No reader of the *Golden Bough* is likely to relapse into bigotry, but it takes such a constitution to read it.

A reminder that "There once was a man called Voltaire" can do no harm. The measure in which he is unread, can I think be found by printing the fragments as "translated from an Eighteenth Century author" and see how many people place it.

Poetry has just come with a very asinine note on the Feb. number.[1]

Bad poetry being alike everywhere it is natural that Rimbaud should differ from Longfellow and Vaughn Moody, and Hen Van Dyke, and that Byron from Musset (both romantic and careless writers of same degree of relative goodness and badness) should be about even. Byron rather more snap, a good satirist and a loose writer.

[1] *Poetry*, April 1918, pp. 54-5.

151: To Edgar Jepson

London, [? May]

Dear E.J.: It would be very bad editing for me to devote ten pages to advertising the existence of Frost, Masters, Lindsay, all of whom are dead as mutton so far as the *L.R.* reader is concerned. The *L.R.* reader in America, anyhow, has had all he can stand of that lot. He knows what their stuff looks like etc. Masters we have said farewell to. Frost sinks of his own weight. Lindsay we have parodied.

Also the reference to me would have to come out. It would do anywhere save in a magazine where I had so much influence. Also we have just had a eùlogy of Eliot.

Also I don't think you have quite got the concentration of vitriol that you would have if you had lived IN IT, and suffered. If I sent the article as it stands Miss A. would merely send it back pointing out that Eliot "executes" with more certainty of fire in his *Egoist* articles.

What I should like would be to cut the thing to three or four pages, keeping all the sting. It is no use saying "this is prose": remark has been worn out on all sorts of vers libre good and bad. It is another matter to say "This is not only prose, but it is prose damn badly written."

It seems to me you get the gist of your criticism on p. 426.

A general statement that there is a Wild West school, that they write such lines as: then the specifically bad lines you have singled out. (No need long passages to illustrate. *I* simply skip 'em, and the American intelligent reader (where he exists), anyhow the reader of current Am. poetry would merely skip 'em.)

Then p. 426, and the allusion to Eliot, but no need to quote him at length. The thing was (obviously) aimed at *Poetry's* readers. The *L.R.* lot don't need it at the same length. *Eng. Rev.* readers need to be shown some of the rot. That's O.K. for *Engl. Rev.*

For us, it does too much honour to Frost, Masters and Lindsay to take 'em so seriously. Expression of *dislike* is no use. Illustration of rottenness by single punk lines DOES the job.

More than that is as much a waste of printer's bill as it would be for me suddenly to rediscover Masefield's diarrhoea, or Abercrombie's dessicated feces: and present 'em at length.

Four pages is perhaps too brief a space: you *have plucked some savorous blossoms.*

Don't know whether this will suit you. Have you a spare copy that I could try tentative cuts on, if it does. P. 426 does the job or most of it.

If you don't mind my messing about with it, I think I can leave *all* the sting, while casting less limelight on certain extremely dull and out of interest authors.

Mi credo, Masters, Frost, Lindsay are out of the Wild Young American gaze already. Williams, Loy, Moore, and the worser phenomena of *Others*, to say nothing of the highly autochthonous Amy (all over the bloody shop) are much more in the "news."

Also, mon ami, most of my stuff must upset you nearly as much as Masters, don't let's beat about the bush, not that bush at any rate. Nous ne sommes plus mioches à pleurer.

152: To Edgar Jepson

London, 23 May

Dear E.J.: That's the ticket. Thanks so much for bringing it down to the gist of the matter.

I didn't want the eulogy of Eliot removed, I only wanted to save the space required for quoting "La Figlia," and the other passage already known to "our readers."

I shall use it in the same number with four new poems of Eliot's. One entitled "Sweeney Among the Nightingales" which AUTOCHS to beat hell, and which should raize the haar on the fretful 'Arriet.

My thanks again for the cut-down and general compacting.

I think it has more punch in this form. Tante grazie.

153: To John Quinn

London, 4 June

Dear Quinn: More thanks for going through the proofs of *Pavannes*. You have got all the points I noted in the page-galleys, so I was right in not cabling about them. I enclose further documents re my attempted acceptance of your cabled suggestion, i.e. my attempt to cable you to call the appendices *Tergenda*, if that happened to please you.

Jules Romains writes his thanks for "ouvrir si largement votre revue. Je ne demande mieux que d'être 'french editor' comme vous me la proposez. Mais j'aimerais que vous me disiez en quoi au juste consisterait cette fonction, et de quoi j'aurait à m'occuper."

All of which ought to settle Orage's idiocies in this week's *New Age*.

I think I gave him a bad minute over his bluff. He hasn't been in Paris for years, and I don't know what poet he found scoffing at even Flint or Bithell.

However, his readers will swallow it. And as for the rest of his article, it is his old game. *Zarathustra* was intended to appear in an edition of 100 copies, afterwards countermanded to 40, and finally the author kept all but 8.

R.H.C.[1] is not in literature what his papa and corporeal or actual self is in Notes of the Week.

[1] A pen-name of A. R. Orage.

Romains (whatever one thinks of his "Mort de Quelqu'un") is, I think, the livest of the current French writers. He suffers less from mental paralysis. He couldn't have written *Tarr*, and he hasn't Eliot's discrimination, but he is not a matoid. At any rate, I have seen him in the flesh, and I have not heard any suggestions of any better possible collaboration, now that de Gourmont is dead. Vildrac is too naive to "edit."

~~Also, I think Romains will gather more people, more writers. Certainly~~ he will do more than Vildrac. I tried to get Vildrac to send me French mss. for *Poetry* some years ago. Of course, there wasn't much stimulus and Harriet wouldn't print anything without years of delay, and only a page or so, but still Vildrac didn't show much hustle.

Tailhade is over sixty, I daresay over 65. Anatole (beyond reach, and 90 or 120). Tailhade wouldn't have done *anyhow*, though I'd like some of his stuff.

I came on a volume which G. C. Cros sent me five years ago. Not enough mental activity *there*.

Spire is excellent in spots, BUT there is an AWFUL lot of rubbish in his books. De Bosschère is too queer, too utterly out of touch with everything. Besides, I can see his stuff here, what there is of it, and he'd be no use in getting a nucleus of French writers (besides, he is not utterly French).

If Griffin and Merrill hadn't been half American I don't think I should have mentioned them at all. Lord! How many *divargences* I am putting down in a lump! However, here goes. I don't think Yeats' *Silentia Lunae* hangs together. At least, I don't think it in the same street with his Memoirs as writing. And I find *Noh* unsatisfactory. I daresay it's all that could be done with the material. I don't believe anyone else will come along to do a better book on Noh, save for encyclopaedizing the subject. And I admit there are beautiful bits in it. But it's all too damn soft. Like Pater, Fiona Macleod and James Matthew Barrie, not good enough.

I think I am justified in having spent the time I did on it, but not much more than that.

In going thru James again, I find him at sea for years, between the first good stuff and the final achievement. Certainly the *American Scene* is of the best. The opening of *A Small Boy and Others* is disgusting. I think if one picked up James first with the beginning of that book one would be pardoned for never returning to him. It picks up at about page 30.

Hueffer on James spatters on for 45 pages of unnecessary writing before he gets started. I think there are good things in his book.

The notice of Joyce on the back of the February number says it is the continuation of "Stephen Daedalus." But it could just as well have been repeated in the March number in an editorial note. I didn't think of it.

I mustn't get to scribbling about Henry James here. I don't believe it will do any good to overlook his limitations. Nor that one's praise will be effective if one doesn't recognize the defects, or the great stretch between his best and his worst.

Meredith is, to me, chiefly a stink. I should never write on him as I detest him too much ever to trust myself as critic of him. The one phase of

James that one wants to *pass over* is, to me, James as contemporary of Meredith.

When he isn't being a great and magnificent author, he certainly can be a very fussy and tiresome one. I think the main function of my essay is to get the really good stuff disentangled from the inferior (if one ever can do that for an author).

He certainly has put America on the map. Given her a local habitation and a name.

Getting back to Joyce. It still seems to me that America will never look *anything*—animal, mineral, vegetable, political, social, international, religious, philosophical or ANYTHING else—in the face until she gets used to perfectly bald statements.

That's propaganda, if you like, but it seems to me something larger than the question of whether Joyce writes with a certain odeur-de-muskrat.

The present international situation seems to me in no small measure due to the English and American habit of keeping their ostrich heads carefully down their little silk-lined sand-holes.

I wrote an article on the "situation" a couple of months ago. I am told it is intelligent but unprintable. Orage simply said, "You mingle with people who are far too interesting. You should go to the National Liberal Club and learn how ONE intelligent remark can blast a man's whole career."

Oh well, one can't go back over all that. I don't care a hang for one matter more than another. It is the whole habit of verbally avoiding the issue that seems to be injurious. However, I mustn't get fanatical over it.

The kind of thing that drives one into this state is precisely the condition of other American publications. In my Swinburne article in *Poetry* I recounted Watts-Dunton's conduct at the funeral, and his preventing an officious vicar from saying the burial service. Harriet deletes these six lines. The American public must not hear that the burial service is not universally respected.

After years of this sort of puling imbecility one gets hot under the collar and is perhaps carried to an extreme. Even so, Harriet is much less an old maid than most American editors.

Other point, re centralization of power. Certainly, for execution of war measures, power ought to be centralized, and you know that I am as much opposed as anyone can be to any impediments to that. But this question of having the whole of a nation's reading held up by one man has NOTHING whatever to do with winning the war. It is a permanent state, for peace as much as for war. I don't think your argument holds.

I agree with you, on the other hand, that the March number was too "preoccupied."

On the other hand (the suppositious and possible third hand), who is there apart from the group of writers were are printing who is writing or can write?

Thanks again for the cheque rec'd, and for going on getting guarantors after you had made up your mind against it. I am more than sorry the annoyances have come during the very time of your illness. Hope by the time you get this that you will be again feeling fit.

Pardon the appalling length of this epistle. Also forgive its general gloom and cantankerousness. After all, it is something to get Joyce, Hueffer and Lewis into one number of one magazine. — — — —

Had a long letter from the father of all the Yeatsssssss a few weeks ago. Will answer him when I get time to breathe.

154: To John Quinn

London, 15 November

Dear John Quinn: Will you accept the dedication of *Pavannes and Divisions?* I had intended to wait until I had some more important book to bear this dedication, but delays are not much in the nature of either of us, and, moreover, you are more intimately connected and associated in the making of *Lustra* and this book than you will be in future books, after Knopf is trained, or after American publication of my stuff becomes more or less routine.

If you accept the dedication, just have

To
John Quinn

put on the page after the sub-title or title page, and add beneath, if the fancy takes you:

Americanus non moribus

unless you think the Americanus ought to be in the dative case. It is very hard to tell in case of mixing two languages whether to keep the Latin uninflected. On the whole, *Americano* is probably better.

Wrong. Have looked up Dante's epistle to Can Grande. It should be:

Americano natione non moribus

Have been misquoting it for eight years.

M[aude] G[onne] (statement from herself) did hold a meeting in Dublin to express sympathy with the Russian Bolsheviks. *If* there had been another rising I fail to see how she would have kept out of it, etc., etc.

She has no anti-German feelings, etc. She was released almost immediately (a day or two, or at most, I think, three, after the medical report was made). The fact that she could not go to Ireland until the British had shot MacBride had, of course, not entered her calculations.

Undoubtedly, Ireland tried to stab the Allies in the back, and was ready for another try during the spring offensive.

And I was ready to think Carson ought to be hung at the beginning of the war. But I'm hanged if I see how Ireland can demand self-determination for herself at the same time she utterly refuses all thought of self-determination for Ulster.

Etc., etc. Or why, being more or less of the party of the vanquished, she expects the Allies to feel toward her as they do toward their carefully constricted assistants in Czecho-Slovakia, Poland, etc.

Thank God, I don't have to settle it. Am afraid this letter does not arrange its statements into very coherent order.

However, there aren't any "details" to be cabled more than I sent in my last. M.G. was under "preventive arrest." She was released on grounds of ill health, not on grounds that she was a safe person to be at large or in Ireland.

Personally, I don't think the release was obtained by a policy of worrying officials. I think the health report did it on its merits, plus a little amiable influence.

The wholesale preventive arrests surely prevented another rising, and nothing else would have prevented it. Even now M.G. won't give any assurance of good behaviour IF permitted to return to Dublin.

Similar preventive arrests would have prevented the Easter rising.

I give it up. M.G. seems as able to ignore facts in politics as W.B.Y. does when it comes to evidence of psychic phenomena.

I certainly should not write her permit to return if I were responsible for order in Dublin. Though public order after a war is a very much less important thing than public order during a great campaign.

Seagan was quite intelligent when she brought him from France, but the months in Ireland have ruined his mind and left him, as might be expected at his age, doomed to political futilities. He is a walking giveaway of the real state of feeling there.

South Ireland certainly ought to be expelled from the Empire, but it is such an infernally inconvenient naval base that!!!!!!!!!!

So far as I can make out, M.G.'s only constructive political idea is that Ireland and the rest of the world should be free to be one large Donegal fair. She now favours a "republic," but she was Boulangerist in France, and I think they were once royalistic. Have *all* the Irish a monomania? M.G. is "reasonable" to a point, just as Yeats is on psychism, but then there comes the . . . I suppose "glamour."

I believe the Zulus or Oceanic tribes make war by marching out in companies and hurling invectives at each other by the hour.

As for the "revolution," we have had one here during the war; quite orderly, in the extension of franchise. Nobody much minds there being several more. But there remains the temperament that wants revolution *with violence;* no special aim or objective, but just pure and platonic love of a row.

Pacifists with lead-headed canes, etc.

The other point M.G. omits from her case is that she went to Ireland without permit and in disguise, in the first place, during war time.

"Conservatrice des traditions Milesienne," as de Gourmont calls them. There are people who have no sense of the value of "civilization" or public order.

She is still full of admiration for Lenin. (I, on the other hand, have talked with Russians.) The sum of it being that I am glad she is out of gaol, and that I hope no one will be ass enough to let her get to Ireland.

Thank God the war is mostly over. Am suffering from cold contracted on Monday, wandering about for hours, mostly in drizzle, to observe effect of armistice on the populace.

The Allies will have to sit on the head of each individual German for the next eighty years and take their indemnity a pfennig at a time.

P.S. I think the term "fanatic" in my cable was the just one. M. does not seem lunatic. But I notice with Yeats he will be quite sensible till some question of ghosts or occultism comes up, then he is subject to a curious excitement, twists everything to his theory, usual quality of mind goes. So with M.G. For example, she twists the burning of the posters on the Nelson column into an anti-monarchic demonstration. Says they were King's Fund posters. Now, I happened to see the kids tearing off strips of that canvas for the fun of burning something when their fireworks ran out. Same way they burnt gun carriages a few nights later.

M. wholly neglects the crowds cheering in front of Buckingham Palace, or the general enthusiasm for George on his drive through the drizzle in an open carriage, with no escort save a couple of cops. Poor devil was looking happy, I should think, for the first time in his life. I happened to be in Piccadilly about two feet from the carriage.

It is a great pity, with all her charm, that the mind twists everything that goes into it, on this particular subject (just like Yeats on his ghosts).

Heaven knows, I may have a touch of it myself re Xtianity, but I try to control it, and it is really a development of the belief that most of the tyrannies of modern life, or at least a lot of stupidities, are based on Xtn taboos, and can't really be got rid of radically until Xtianity is taken lightly and sceptically, until, that is, it drifts back into the realm of fairy-lore and picturesque superstition (mostly unpicturesque, at present).

I think the Theatre, Yeats, Synge and Company, had developed a wide sympathy for Ireland, which the revolutionaries have wiped utterly away.

155: To MARIANNE MOORE

London, 16 December

Dear Miss Moore: The confounded trouble is that I have come to the end of my funds, and can not pay for any more mss. for *The Little Review*.

I think the poems too good to print without paying for them: I know you have contributed to *The Egoist* unpaid. And I have myself done a deal of unpaid work: too much of it.

I hope to start a quarterly here before long (part of the funds are in hand); and to be able to pay contributors: at least to pay them something; and to give them the satisfaction of being in good company. I will either hold over your two poems for the quarterly and try to pay; or print them in *The L.R.* . . . as you choose or permit.

There are one or two details I should like to ask about. (Yeats and Eliot and various other people have had similar queeries leveled at them, and our friendships have weathered the strain, so don't take it ill of me.)

?Are you quite satisfied with the final cadence and graphic arrangement of same in "A Graveyard"? The ends of the first two strophes lead into the succeeding strophe, rightly. The ending

> "*it is*
> *neither with volition nor consciousness*"

closes the thing to my ear. Perhaps you will find a more drastic change suits you better. I do not offer an alternative as dogma or as a single and definite possibility. Very likely you are after a sound-effect which escapes me. But I don't quite see what it is, and I know that a critic often finds the wrong point in a verse when he can not say why it is wrong, and when his first proposals regarding it are useless.

Comme on est ridicule. I have copied your own order, instead of the thing that came into my head this P.M., namely: "Consciousness nor volition."

Hang'd if I now know which I thought better. But I think the eye catches either cadence rather better if you break the line at *is*.

I haven't analyzed the metric of the whole; but find it satisfactory.

I want to know, relatively, your age, and whether you are working on Greek quantitative measures or on René Ghil or simply by ear (if so a very good ear).

In "Old Tiger":

I am worried by "intentioned." It is "not English"; in French it is *intentionné*, and I have no objection to gallicisms if done with distinction, and obviously and intentionally gallicisms for a *purpose*. But "intentioned" is like a lot of words in bad American journalese, or like the jargon in philosophical text-books. It is like a needless file surface (to me—and will upset the natives here much more than it does me). You know, possibly, that I don't mind the natives' feelings, *but* I think when giving offence one should always be *dead* right, not merely defensible.

Pneumatic is le mot juste, but Eliot has just preempted it in Grishkin's "pneumatic bliss." This is not a final argument, but in so close a circle (you are in it willy-nilly, by the mere fact of writing verse for the members of the reading public capable of understanding). Also T.S.E. has jaguar'd— quite differently, but still . . . we *must* defend the camp against the outer-damnations.

T.S.E. first had his housemaids drooping like the boas in my "Millwins," and it was only after inquisition of this sort that he decided, to the improvement of his line, to have them sprout.

(Atque: I am rejecting imitators of T.S.E. who would be only too ready to rend anyone they might think at their preserve.) In the words of W.L. send us one to catch our fleas.

Do you want "its self" or "itself" at the end of 12 strophe? There *is* a slight, or rather a very considerable, difference. Whether the tail has a metaphorical ψυχη inside it.

And as for "peacock": is it the best word? It means peacock-green???

Or peacock-blue or p.b. green? Peacock has feet and other colours such as brown in its ensemble???

Also when you break words at end of line, DO you insist on caps. at beginning of next line? Greeks didn't, nor does Ghil. Not categorical inhibition, but . . .

Now, to be more amiable, have you a book of verse in print? And, if not, can I get one into print for you? My last and best work *Propertius* has just dodged two publishers, one of whom wants to print half the book, leaving out the best of it. Dopo tant' anni, I am not yet in the position of a Van Dyke or a Tennyson; but still, I have got Joyce, and Lewis, and Eliot and a few other comforting people into print, by page and by volume. At any rate, I will buy a copy of your book IF it is in print, and if not, I want to see a lot of it all together. You will never sell more than five hundred copies, as your work demands mental attention. I am inclined to think you would "go" better in bundles about the size of Eliot's *Prufrock and Observaions.*

For what it is worth, my ten or more years of practice, failure, success, etc. in arranging tables of contents, is à votre service. Or at any rate unless you have a definite scheme for a sequence, I would warn you of the very great importance of the actual order of poems in a booklet. (I have gone right and gone wrong in this at one time or another and know the results.)

Your stuff holds my eye. Most verse I merely slide off of (God I do ye thank for this automatic selfprotection), BUT my held eye goes forward very slowly, and I know how simple many things appear to me which people of supposed intelligence come to me to have explained. –/–/

Thank God, I think you can be trusted not to pour out flood (in the manner of dear Amy and poor Masters).

I wish I knew how far I am right in my conjecture of French influence; you are nearer to Ghil than to Laforgue, whose name I think I used in *The Future*. My note in the *L.R.* was possibly better. – – – –

O what about your age; how much more youngness is there to go into the work, and how much closening can be expected?

And what the deuce of your punctuation? I am puzzled at times: How much deliberate, and therefore to be taken (by me) with studious meticulousness?? How much the fine careless rapture and therefore to be potshotted at until it assumes an wholly demonstrable or more obvious rightness????

ANYHOW I will keep the poems for my quarterly unless you want to have them rushed into the *L.R. at once,* and unless you have something better for the Quarterly. No reason which they shouldn't appear simultaneously in both (only it will be the quarterly's proposed and hoped-for purse that will pay).

And are you a jet black Ethiopian Othello-hued, or was that line in one of your *Egoist* poems but part of your general elaboration and allegory and designed to differentiate your colour from that of the surrounding menageria?

I can't fit in the prose paragraph anywhere, so return it. Or rather, no. I will hold it and give it to the *Egoist,* if you so direct.

Do you see any signs of mental life about you in New York? I still retain curiosities and vestiges of early hopes, though I doubt if I will ever return to America, save perhaps as a circus.

How much of your verse *is* European? How much Paris is in it? This is, I think, legitimate curiosity on my part. IF I am to be your editor, and as I am still interested in the problem of how much America can do on her own. (Political divisions NOT mattering in the ultimate, but . . .)

I oughtn't to be too lazy to analyze your metric; but . . . I very often don't analyze my own until years after. . . . AND time, and one's energy. . . . At any rate, it is (yr. metric) a progress on something I (more or less, so far as English goes) began. . . . Whether my beginnings had anything to do with yr. metric is another matter. ONLY I am curious.

Syllabic, in stanzas, same shape per stanza.

1st work written A.D.???
1st work published????

Answers NOT for publication in small biographical note, as used in Tschaikago.

At any rate, the quarterly IF it comes off offers you a spiritual roof or habitation; question of its being domus, home, hearth, must be left to you.

DOES your stuff "appear" in America?

156: To Harriet Shaw Weaver

London, 17 December

Dear Miss Weaver: With the cost of printing soaring, and the *Egoist* having to retrench at all points, as I understand it is, I do not feel that the cost of keeping the type of this series standing, plus the probable cost of printing the booklet, would be justified, or that the interest in the series is likely to make the cash return sure enough to justify your reprinting it.

I mean to publish the stuff, without much revision, in my next prose volume, anyhow. AND if *The Egoist* has any money to spare I should much rather see it go to printing a book like Prufrock, by some new poet. I believe I have one in sight.

I don't mean "like" *Prufrock*, but simply an interesting book of poems of that size. And the printing of it would be of more literary interest than a reprint of these essays, which will ultimately be reprinted anyway.

They were hurriedly concluded during the week I thought I was to be rushed out to Persia; I don't say they were spoiled but . . . I don't on the other hand feel them quite final.

1 9 1 9

157: To William Carlos Williams

London, 28 January

My Dear Old Sawbukk von Grump: How are your adenoids? Am rejoicing in vacancy; prose collection [1] "finished," committed to the gaping maw of the post office; and I freed of its weight. Haven't heard from you since the pig died. —/—/

Lewis' new show opening Thursday, etc. Manning again in circulation.

All sorts of "projects" artoliteresque in the peaceconferentialbolshevikair. Switzerland bursting into Dadaique Manifestos re the nothingness of the All.

Fat Madox Hueffer in last evening; Aldington at "front," educating Tommies; Wadsworth and Lewis in town, more or less free.

I think it might be worth while for you to send me any mss. you have by you; there are several schemes in the air re quarterly and re a weekly; and something or other will probably start. There is the banked water of several years during which paper restrictions forbade starting of new periodicals; I think something will start. Can't yet say which or what; was offered a salary two days ago; but that is too wild a fantasy. At any rate shd. like to have some of your stuff by me in case of emergency. Mgr *said* the first number of a weekly wd. appear in March . . . but words of financiers . . .??

Am reprinting note on you from *Future* in next prose vol. which Knopf *says* he is bringing out this autumn.

Did a longer note for an American paper which cut down its size on receipt of article, which latter is still floating about in my progenitor's possession. Don't know that you will like it; but I did go so far as to say you weren't a matoid.

Are you capable of doing quarterly notes (1000 words say per three months) on American publications???? Or is there anybody in the great pure prohibition monarchy capable of writing brief summary criticism of contemporary abortions? — — —

158: To H. L. Mencken

London, [? January]

Dear Mencken: Thanks for your *Apologia pro Mulieribus.*[2] It is so good that even my belle-mère, a charming memorial of the XVIIIth Century, has read it with enjoyment.

---

[1] *Instigations.*   [2] *In Defense of Women.*

WHAT is wrong with it, and with your work in general is that you have drifted into writing for your inferiors. . . . Inevitable I think where one is in contact with a public.

WHEN you escape . . . and the time now seemeth not so far distant, I think you will begin your real work. (Damn'd cheek on my part to say so?) Still, on the island of Patmos with no early Christians to exhort, your style would solidify.

Am inclined to think the book the best of your stuff I have seen.

Have made my paragraph 2 fairly bald, but take it for what it is worth. No use my flapping about with amiable inanities. We have all sinned through trying to make the uneducated understand things. Certainly you will lose a great part of your public when you stop trying to civilize the waste places; and you will gain about fifteen readers.

"The first post bellum boat" ought to sail fairly soon now, and I hope to see you as soon as mines have passed away. (O roll dem mines ehway.)
— — — —

159: To Marianne Moore

London, 1 February

The female is a chaos,

the male

is a fixed point of stupidity, but only the female
can content itself with prolonged conversation
with but one sole other creature of its own sex
and of its own unavoidable species

the male

is more expansive
and demands other and varied contacts;

hence its combativeness,
hence its discredit for "taking up cudgels"
hence its utter failure to receive credit
for the ninety and nine unjust times
when it refrained from taking up cudgels
and was done in the eye
by the porcine and uncudgeled circumbelliferous;

hence,
the débâcle of its temper,
hence,
its slow recovery and recuperance from the yaller janders
hence also its more wide-spread insistencies,
hence its exposure to stings and mud-slings of the

ungodly and unco-decorous
                    etc. and ad infinitum

/−/−
Zagreus at the door of the parsonage,
Keeping a carbon copy. "We must not"
writes a contemporary Church of England theological author
"give up Parthenogenesis; it is the outpost of Incarnation."
((Custer's last fight for the Trinity!

Eight inch sans-serif on the posters
"O gawd deont dew bizniss thaat waye!"))
"St. Paul was a Gentleman"
                    no reflection
on the habits of your particular family
but they are not alone in their clerical functions. I have seen
Savanarola still swinging a crucifix,
down from Salò for the week-end of exhorting
the back-sliders of Venice; and the Reverend Cavaliere Dottore
     Alessandro
Robertson denouncing the Babylonian woman
and the Rrrroman releegion
with fervour::: O my Christ with fervour and sincerity
and conviction. I have seen

the inhibitions of seventeen sects
and the dangers of national internationalism, Eloi, Eloi.

(Also Voltaire on the Elohim)
and the wilderness will not be healed
either by fletcherizing or by a diet of locusts.
Splendours of vintages;
Guido in accented iambics.

     Chère Marianne: So much for the Muses (precedent).

     The rest of your statements are "satisfactory." No one could be "wholly
in sympathy" with *The Little Review* any more than I could be wholly in
sympathy with Lewis: my only contention is that genius ought to exist,
and that ALL publications should not exclude it.
     I also made early attempts at that dessication *The Atlantic*. Even *The
Egoist* would not have been there, i.e., attending to contemporary poetry
or printing your works save but for my cudgels. And I have got some
decent stuff into print: *The Portrait of the Artist*, and other things.
     As Richard said only six weeks ago (re *Poetry*): "It's that on the cover
that has beaten you. If you could have got that off (the silly question third-
truth from Whitman) you could have made something of it."
     Now, one buys leisure to work by selling one's stuff for what one can.
Harriet (Monroe) is too old to learn. Thank heaven I have conducted
some of her funds to a few authors who needed emolument.

I have repeatedly resigned. And it took a six months' struggle to get her to print Eliot's "Prufrock."

I have nothing but my name on the cover. And the prospects of a very mutilated piece of my Propertius appearing in her paper, because it would be criminal for me to refuse £10/10; and because it don't matter. It don't matter in the least what appears or does not appear in that magazine. The elect will see, ultimately, the English publication of the series.

(All of which is for your ear and no other. The woman is honest, and can not help her obfuscations.)

American painting and sculpture are proportionately no better than American writing, ONLY painters are comparatively unknown, i.e., all the creators of new expression. They have a chance to make almost fortunes, but they lead private and secret careers (you can't lead a career, but *passons*). Their works exist almost in secret.

You are probably right in so far as American imitators of earlier (1880) European painters are more thorough than American authors (don't know). Must let it alone (I must). Must return to the unconcern with U.S.A. that I had before 1911-12.

Private life, i.e. seclusion, "possible" in America; public, or printed, existence IMPOSSIBLE. Etc.

Shall probably want to print "Scalpels" here also. Pre-publication in *B.M. Lantern* no deterrent.

??Whether both it and predestined carrot haven't weak endings. Attention to strophic shape??? Kept your eye off main structure??? This merely a caution or instigation.

Statement possibly firmer than a question at end of "Scalpels."

Will not give hurried "judgment" about your revisions in other poems. Must think them over.

Definiteness of your delineations is delicious, in all the austerity of that much abused term. Can't have it lost. Must go on with it, you must. Thank God you don't tend to burble or to produce "FOUR epics" in one vol. as per last ad. of Amy.

(Was disappointed with the poem in *L.R.*; ergo relieved on receipt of your paragraph regarding it.) Etc.

160: To A. R. Orage [1]

London, [? April]

Dear A.R.O.: Here is the slam. The Chicago *Tribune* cut it somewhat but not in essentials. My points being:

That there was never any question of translation, let alone literal trans-

---

[1] This letter was first written to A. R. Orage, with the note "You might save this for me." At a later date the letter was redirected as follows: "Dear E.W. (?Ernest Walsh): Here is the attack, and here are some points I pointed at the time ere I reflected that it was scarcely suitable for me to do so."

lation. My job was to bring a dead man to life, to present a living figure.

As a Prof. of Latin and example of why Latin poets are not read, as example of why one would like to deliver poets of philologers, Hale should be impeccable and without error. He has NO claim to refrain from suicide if he errs in any point.

(Don't imagine this is any use.)

1. He ignores English.

"Their Punic faces dyed in the Gorgon's lake"

one of my best lines. Punic (*Punicus*) used for dark red, purple red by Ovid and Horace as well as Propertius. Audience familiar with Tyrrian for purple in English. To say nothing of augmented effect on imagination by using Punic (whether in translation or not) instead of "red."

2. Hale pretends to read Latin, but has apparently never *understood* anything but syntax and never seen the irony of Propertius, this from general tone of his note.

3. As for "trace of decadent meaning": he writes as if intending to convey meaning that it is not in Propertius.

Does the Drive to Lanuvium contain trace of gentle raillery to be found in my "distortion" of the "tacta puella"?

4. Precisely what I do not do is to translate the *in* as if it negatived the *solito*. IF I was translating, I [would] have translated *solito* (accustomed) by a commentary, giving "when they have got over the strangeness" as an equivalent, or rather emphasis of "accustomed." Absolutely the contrary of taking my phrase, as the ass Hale does, for the equivalent of *unaccustomed*. He can't read English.

5. Re the "punic" faces. It may instruct Hale to tell him that the Teubner text (printed 1898) uses Punica with a cap. P, especially emphasizing the Latin usage of proper name in place of a colour adjective. I.e., the Teubner editor is emphasizing a Latinism which I have brought over. He is not allowing the connection of the proper name with a particular dark red to drift into a uncapitalized adjective.

6. Mask of erudition is precisely what I have not assumed; it is precisely what I have thrown on the dust heap.

Re decadence: We all know Propertius went to mid-week prayer meeting.

AND as for accuracy, what are we to say to the bilge of rendering "puella" by the mid-Victorian pre-Raphaelite slush of romanticistic "my lady"?

What of Propertius' delicate use of "nostra," meaning "my" as well as "our," but in a stylist how delicately graduated against "mihi" by Propertius. Heine's poem ending, "Madame, ich liebe Sie" is clumsy in comparison.

Do him the justice to say that the bloody Marcian aquaduct is very very familiar, and that it was a thing I might very well have remembered. That is, confess to forgetting something as familiar to Romans as the Croton damm is to New Yorkers. But even the Croton damm may be forgotten in eternity.[1]

Also old brute only saw 1, 2, 3, and 6. BUT his plaidoyer for translation of letter and deathdealing to the spirit needs kicking.

Real poetry!!! Gosh. Look at that Bohn "Marcian flow." Exactly the phrase Propertius wd. have used if living today and writing English (not 'arf).

If possible I shd. even have wished to render a composite character, including something of Ovid, and making the portrayed figure not only Propertius but inclusive of the spirit of the young man of the Augustan Age, hating rhetoric and undeceived by imperial hog-wash.

P.S. On closer inspection of the full text as in *Poetry*, I find he is worse than in the *Tribune* which was all I had read before I began to write this for you.

I note that my translation "Devirginated young ladies" etc. is as literal, or rather more so than his. I admit to making the puella (singular) into plural "young ladies." It is a possible figure of speech as even the ass admits. Hale, however, not only makes the "girl" into "my lady," but he has to supply *something for her to be "touched* BY." Instead of allowing her to be simply *tacta* (as opposed to *virgo intacta*), he has to say that she is touched (not, oh my god, no not by the – – – – of the poet, but by "my words"). Vide his own blessed parentheses.

If I were, however, a professor of Latin in Chicago, I should probably have to resign on divulging the fact that Propertius occasionally copulavit, i.e. rogered the lady to whom he was not legally wedded.

161: To JAMES JOYCE

London, [? October]

Dear Joyce: I enclose letter from Quinn, which you need not of necessity read. Point is that "Nausikaa" has been pinched by the PO-lice. Only way to get *Ulysses* printed in book form, will be to agree not to print any more of it in the *L.R.*

I had already made this suggestion on other ground, namely that the expensive private edition planned by Quinn wd. have wider sale if it contained final chapters which had not already appeared in *L.R.*

Also in Paris I did, I think, explain to you that M.A. and jh had not spent any money on you. I got the original trifle that was sent you, and the printing deficits were paid by J.Q., and in general the editrices have merely messed and muddled, NEVER to their own loss.

The best thing to do, now that things have come to present pass is to turn the whole matter over to Quinn. He is on the spot and both will and can deal with local conditions better than we can from here.

[1] The Croton Reservoir occupied the site now occupied by the New York Public Library at 42nd Street and Fifth Avenue.

The excuse for parts of *Ulysses* is the WHOLE of *Ulysses;* the case for publication of bits of it serially is weak; the editrices having sent copy to someone who hadn't asked for it further weakens case.

ANYHOW, the only thing to be done now is to give Quinn an absolutely free hand. His cable address is QUINLEX, New York; and you will have to cable your full authorization to him at once if it is to arrive in time.

QUINLEX
New York

As you have said—"No country outside of Africa" wd. permit it.

162: TO JOHN QUINN

London, 25 October

Dear Quinn: *Quia Pauper Amavi* is at last out. Eliot has done a dull but, I think, valuable puff in the *Athenaeum;* granite wreaths, leaden laurels, no sign of exhilaration; but I daresy it is what is best in that quarter.

He has shown in earlier articles the "English Department" universitaire attitude: literature not something enjoyable, but something which your blasted New England conscience makes you feel you *ought* to enjoy.

— — — —

Have had two opulent weeks as dramatic critic on *The Outlook,* and have been fired in most caddish possible manner. Have had my work turned down by about every editor in England and America, but have never before felt a desire for vengeance. Circumstances too dull to narrate; but if you do see a chance for doing that rotten paper, its editor or owners, an ill turn I hope you will do so, in memoriam.

Orage is, of course, willing to do anything he can for me. I don't know whether there is any way of increasing his U.S.A. circulation. He is ready to give me two pages a week for myself. I had, as a matter of fact, three things in last issue; only he simply hasn't the funds to pay like the punk papers. And one simply can't afford to rewrite and properly compress stuff for his rates.

France is worse. The *Mercure* pays 4 francs per page for prose and nothing for verse.

Have just done an article, by request, for *France-Amérique;* pay better than the *Mercure,* at any rate.

Vanderpyl offers me space in *L'Arbitraire,* but it will cost him heavily to print English in Paris, and he has no funds for contributors. I can't see the thing as practical.

One Desfeuilles is very enthusiastic about *Noh* and wants to translate it; but I don't make out whether he has a publisher or whether the publisher "would like to publish but——."

Lewis' portrait of me was on the way to being excellent when I last saw it; have not see the final form of it yet, but hope to at the Goupil.

Nina Hamnett has greatly improved. Great persistence for a female.

Last ms. chapter of Joyce perhaps the best thing he has done. I don't

mean the last one to appear in *Little Review*, but the one I have just forwarded. Parody of styles, a trick borrowed from Rabelais, but never done
better, even in Rab.

Our James is a grrreat man. I hope to God there is a foundation of truth
in the yarn he wrote me about a windfall. Feel he may have done it just to
take himself off my mind.

1 9 2 0

163: To T. E. Lawrence

London, 20 April

My Dear Hadji ben Abt el Bakshish, Prince de Mecque, Two-Sworded
Samurai, Old Bird, Young Bird, Magister (?) Artium, etc. et quid tibi licet,
libet, decet, lubet, etc.: Thou hast in thee an exceeding hot, intemperate,
swift and precipitate manner of judging thy fellowe men, and in the present case mightest have weighed against six or eight pages of *BLAST* the
dozen or more volumes and thousand or more scattered pages of my other
labours and opusculi.

The Dial is an aged and staid publication which I hope, rather rashly,
to ginger up to something approaching the frenetic wildness of *The
Athenaeum*. They are much more afraid of me than you are.

Also I don't care a saffron . . . whether you use your own name or
not; only if you don't you will be under the shameful and ignominious
necessity of writing something which will interest the editor.

Can you "write"? Of course, having vortex'd a large section of Arabia
you are fed up with vortices; but why reprove me, who have merely
created a market for one or two artists and got a half dozen good books
into print despite John Murray, Sir G. Macmillan e questa puttazaia?

When you say you want to write for money, what do you mean
"money"? Lord Macaulay's rates or the fees I pick up by force of necessity
to pay my rent? The latter can't be called "money," but if you want to
sweat in an abysmally paid profession I think I can supply you with two
London editors who wouldn't insist on your using your cinema sign.

In sending copy to America, let me caution you to use an incognito as
well as a pseudonym. Thayer is, I think, quite decent (he is *The Dial*), but
I trust an American publication about as far as I wd. trust a British government; my bright compatriots are quite capable of printing an article by
Mr. Smith and then printing a leetle note at the end of the number saying
"The article by Mr. Smith is really written by the distinguished Sheik-
tamer and Tiger-baiter etc., who for reasons of modesty has concealed himself 'neath the ridiculous name of Smith-Yapper."

If you want to write about Arabia, I cd. simply write to N.Y. that I was
getting copy from the one man who knows, or you cd. get a written

promise from Thayer not to reveal your identity. I shd. prefer not to be instrumental in publishing anything likely to incite either Moslems or Xtns. to further massacres etc.

The songs of the desert might be safer. My notes on Elizabethan Classicists are considered "too technical" for the *Dial* readers.

I have just taken the job and can't, I'm afraid, give you much indication of what they *do* want, save that I am asked to provide 'em with Mrs. Meynell, Lowes Dickenson, Lytton Strachey, Yeats, Eliot, myself in homeopathic (very) doses, etc.

Hope to see you in August if not before. Shall be back here in Aug. Suppose you'll have spent your quarterly allowance and retired to Oxford by then.

164: To John Quinn

Paris, 19 June

Dear John Quinn: I came out of Italy on a tram-car, and reckon the next man will come out in a cab.

Joyce finally got to Sirmione; don't yet know whether he has got back to Trieste. Strike started half an hour after I got to Milan, and many trains stopped where they were at the stroke of 12.

Joyce—pleasing; after the first shell of cantankerous Irishman, I got the impression that the real man is the author of *Chamber Music*, the sensitive. The rest is the genius; the registration of realities on the temperament, the delicate temperament of the early poems. A concentration and absorption passing Yeats'—Yeats has never taken on anything requiring the condensation of *Ulysses*.

Also great exhaustion, but more constitution than I had expected, and apparently good recovery from eye operation.

He is coming up here later; long reasons, but justified in taking a rest from Trieste.

He is, of course, as stubborn as a mule or an Irishman, but I failed to find him at all *unreasonable*. Thank God, he has been stubborn enough to know his job and stick to it.

Re his personal arrangements, etc., all seems clear in light of conversation.

He is also dead right in refusing to interrupt his stuff by writing stray articles for cash. Better in the end, even from practical point of view. Also justified in sticking it out in Trieste, at least for the present. Both climate and other considerations.

In the stories of his early eccentricities in Dublin, I have always thought people neglected the poignant feature, i.e., that his "outrageous" remarks were usually *so*.

His next work will go to the *Dial*, but he should rest after *Ulysses*.

Linati, translator of Synge and Joyce, is to send Italian notes to *Dial* and beat up contributors. He seems sensible. Don't expect very much from Italy. Or from Spain. Have just written to Unamuno.

Here I suspect the war is still effective. Impression the people are being affable to each other (in literary circles) in hope of maintaining the illusion that Paris is still the hub of the universe. However, have only been here 3 days and may yet dig up something of mild interest.

After Gaudier, Lewis, Joyce, one wants something a bit meaty to excite one.

165: To Hugh Walpole

London, 30 June

But Bleeding Christ! Mr. Walpole: That is precisely what you shouldn't have done; and which if you didn't you shouldn't dash my hopes by professing to have accomplished.

The Dial for the past months has been too confounded dull to be born, it has been no better than the *London Mercury* or the *Athanaeum* or a dozen and one of these other mortuaries for the entombment of dead fecal mentality.

One hopes, with a flicker aroused by my past month in Paris (as witness the opposite column of names) to have in time a paper which an intelligent being can read.

And in the hope that your politeness has got the better of your candid opinion, I shall be very glad if you help in labour of making it so. Only do make it suitable to the 1920-21 *Dial*, not to last year's or last month's. With of course the damn'd postal censorship of the U.S. as a limit to vocabulary; I don't mean that sex is an asset either.

166: To James Joyce

London, [? July]

Dear James: News item or rather phrase of conversation from ex-govt. official: "The censorship was very much troubled by it (*Ulysses*) during the war. Thought it was all code."

167: To T. E. Lawrence

London, [? August]

Dear T.E.L.: Being neither a Christian, nor an Oxonian, nor even an Englishman, the idea that people "ought not to exist on one earth" merely because they differ one from the other is strange to me.

Doubtless you have *very* bad taste; not that I mind the romantic, or even the academic and idyllic, if they can be found free of mental paralysis.

Still . . . I have already sent over to N.Y. one hundred delicious pages of Manning, which I hope will in due course be printed; and Conrad has said he will probably send on something some day or other, but has too many unfilled promises hanging over him to make any more; and two stories (or somethings) by D. H. Lawrence have been accepted . . . through no particular fault of my own save that I asked Aldington to ask D.H.L. to send 'em in.

And Aldington gets steadily worse *because* he writes in the *Times* every week. What *can* be expected!!!!!!!!!!!!!!! (these by request, as you'd feel lonely if I didn't use 'em, in order that the skripture shd. be fillfulled).

I suppose I'd even print Hodgson (whom I like personally very much) . . . chief danger wd. be going to sleep between here and the pillarbox if I had a ms. of his in my hand. Tel est le pouvoir. . . .

Is Yeats any worse than the last volume of Conrad's?

As for idyllic and romantic—thought they were W.B.Y.'s particular line. Howsomever!

168: To James Joyce

London, 2 August

My dear Joyce: You are probably cursing me for not taking more direct action. I enclose both Huebsch and another epistle, i.e. from *Athenaeum* to myself, re what shd. have been my chief local asset, and which was (fu) my chief cash reason for return to this brass-bound clay-hummock.

Kindly return same. Modest mensuality amounting roughly to £120 per annum. Of course I shall welcome the leisure.

Equally of course I never had the faintest belief in Huebsch paying £ £ £ advance on mss. he hadn't seen; what*ever* he or anyone else might have written about it.

Re your letter before last. I shall take it as an extremely unfriendly act if you instruct your damn solicitors to do anything of the sort; which wd. be pure imbecility on the one hand, you being sure to need the cash three weeks later; and damn'd unpleasant of you on the other, as I should like to make at least that small contribution to the running expenses of *Ulysses*.

If you find your circle kantankerrrrous, you might also reflect upon the fact that Murray wrote me two letters while I was in Paris, and might conceivably have included in one of them the news so amiably conferred in his of 27th ult., as it wd. have only 'ave clouded the last Parisian hours.

I don't on the hole despair of hitting another couple of *small* bunches between now an' Sept. 25.

Rodker was delighted to see you, but his wife is in an interestin' condition and I suppose they are savin' for the layette. However, he offers to give an imprint to *Ulysses* if the *Egoist* will provide the £ for the actual printing somewhere else, which may possibly be a solution, though I think

American printing is the most economical way out of the difficulty. By printing near the sea-board the work can be legally exported.

Eliot leaves for France, via Paris, on about Aug. 15.

169: To James Joyce

London, 1 September

Dear Joyce: (You can forward this note to Dr. Ferrieri.) I strongly recommend that Rodker be asked to do the article on English literature. There are only a very few decent critics with "tendenze moderne." Neither Hueffer nor Eliot are to be had free, and both are very busy. I have recently said my say in *Instigations* besides doing articles on state of literature in England for French and Spanish magazines. Rodker will take more trouble, and be more interested in writing the article than any of the rest of us.

Dr. Ferrieri's article has been translated I think quite well, I will know when it comes back from the typist, as I can't be expected to read handwriting, life is too short. Am sending the article to New York as soon as it comes in from typist.

Regards to Sig. Ferrieri and Linati.

Hope your news is all good.

170: To William Carlos Williams

[The three letters following were written on receipt of Williams' *Kora in Hell: Improvisations,* in the "Prologue" to which Williams writes that Pound is "the best enemy United States verse has." Indeed, the entire prologue is an attack, through Williams, by the American school then as represented by himself, Sandburg, Bodenheim and Kreymborg on the international school, as represented by Pound and Eliot. It is, perhaps, the best American attack on "exoticism" in letters.]

London, 11 September

My dear old Hugger-scrunch: Un po' di giustizia!! Or rather: you're a liar. Precisely I am an "enemy of American verse."

That I sweated like a nigger to break up the clutch of the old — — — *Harper's,* etc. That I tried to enlighten — — — — Chicago, so as to make a place for the real thing. That I sent over French models, which have given six hundred people a means of telling something nearer the truth than they would have done senza. That I imported U.S. stuff here, to the prejudice of my own comfort (remember I have only what I get by my pen).

And on the contrary, some evidence that I have ever cursed anything but the *faults* of American verse. Produce it, you old village cut-up.

That Jep. is not a fountain of wisdom I admit, but he was a good bolus (or a bad bolus).[1] But at any rate there was no one else whose time wasn't too valuable to waste on trying to penetrate Harriet's crust. That silly old she-ass with her paeons for bilge . . . NOT, — — — —, that she matters, but every page of the magazine that goes to BAD stuff is just that much lost to ~~honest work.~~

~~You lay back, you let me have the whole stinking sweat of providing~~ the mechanical means for letting through the new movement, i.e. scrap for the mot juste, for honest clear statement in verse. Then you punk out, cursing me for not being in two places at once, and for "seeing no alternative to my own groove." [2] Which is bilge, just sloppy inaccurate bilge. And you can "take it back" when you get round to doing so.

You get various people who might be honest, who might do a bit of good work, flattered to hell like Masters, or pouring their stuff into leaky jars for want of someone to tell 'em to plug the leaks, and then when I do, you say I am a plugger, and that I plug, and that left to myself I would plug the mouth of the jar before the booze is put in, and vend the vacuous earthenware.

Not that I care a curse for ANY nation as such or that, so far as I know, I have ever suggested that I was trying to write U.S. poetry (any more than you are writing Alexandrine Greek bunk, to conform to the ideas of that refined, charming, and utterly narrow minded she-bard "H.D.").

Neither do I have the spinsterly aversion à la Marianne from tutto che non me piace.[3]

Can be, on the other hand, quite as stubborn as you are; if choose to write about decaying empire, will do so, and be damned to you. But can't see that it constitutes enmity to your work or to that of anyone else who writes honestly, whether in U.S. or Nigeria.

Amy Lowell's perfumed — — — — would be putrid even if it had been done by a pueblo Indian, or written on the highest pinnacle of Harriet's buggerin rocky mts.

It is curious, that with the relics of what I suppose was not [sic] scientific education you can't understand the spirit of research; even research into something so dead as a complicated aesthetic of sound . . . which

---

[1] Edgar Jepson (vide Letters No. 151 and 152, pp. 135-6) had written an attack on the Poetry (Chicago) prizes, especially those of 1916 and had used such terms as "cumbrous artificiality," "lumbering fakement," and "slip-shod, rank bad workmanship of a man who has shirked his job" in describing the work of Vachel Lindsay, Constance Lindsay Skinner and others. But his main argument was that such work was nothing new; Eliot's work, however, he saw as something new in American poetry. Williams then indicates that Eliot is only a rehash of Verlaine, Baudelaire and Maeterlinck and Pound of Provence and modern French: "Men content with the connotations of their masters."

[2] "I praise those who have the wit and courage, and the conventionality, to go direct toward their vision of perfection in an objective world where the signposts are already marked, viz., to London. But confine them in hell for their paretic assumption that there is no alternative but their own groove." Kora in Hell, p. 25.

[3] This refers to Marianne Moore's statement to Williams: "My work has come to have just one quality of value in it: I will not touch or have to do with those things which I detest." Kora in Hell, p. 12.

ain't dead in the least, though I dare say the canzone is too mummified to walk on its pins ever again.

Also whether I am better alive here, or dead, as I should have been from starvation if I hadn't had the remains of primitive animal instinct to "run" . . . is a problem which you can answer acc. cons.

Have I ever, on the other hand, tried to pass off Eng. punk on my compatriots? Have I sent you the dry dung of the Georgians, or the wet dung of the London Murkury?

Have you the adumbrations of intelligence enough to know that the critical faculty which can pick you and Bodenheim, and Loy, and Sandburg (and in earlier phases Frost) out of the muck of liars and shame IS of some use even to poetry in a country so utterly cursed by every – – – – god of the pantheon as to have Woody Wilson for its "choice," and individual liberty slowly growing illegal. If you weren't stupider than a mud-duck you would know that every kick to bad writing is by that much a help for the good.

When did I ever, in enmity, advise you to use vague words, to shun the welding of word and thing, to avoid hard statement, word close to the thing it means?

BUT I don't care a fried – – – – about nationality. Race is probably real. It is real.

And you might in fairness have elaborated my quotation on *virus*.[1] There is a blood poison in America; you can idealize the place (easier now that Europe is so damd shaky) all you like, but you haven't a drop of the cursed blood in you, and you don't need to fight the disease day and night; you never have had to. Eliot has it perhaps worse than I have—poor devil.

You have the advantage of arriving in the milieu with a fresh flood of Europe in your veins, Spanish, French, English, Danish. You had not the thin milk of New York and New England from the pap; and you can therefore keep the environment outside you, and decently objective.

With your slower mental processes, your later development, you are very likely, really of a younger generation; at least of a younger couche. – – – –

Different from my thin logical faculty. And, thank god, from Harriet's blow (really the gaseous American period of the generation or two before me . . . bluff . . . throwing the bull, town prospecting, etc.).

AND now that there is no longer any intellectual *life* in England save what centres in this eight by ten pentagonal room; now that Rémy and Henry are gone and Yeats faded, and NO literary publication whatever extant in England, save what "we" print (*Egoist* and Ovid Press), the question remains whether I have to give up every shred of comfort, every scrap of my personal life, and "gravitate" to a New York which wants me as little now as it did ten and fifteen years ago. Whether, from the medical point of view it is masochism for me even to stay here, instead of shifting to Paris. Whether self-inflicted torture ever has the slightest element of dignity in it?

[1] In his "Prologue" Williams had quoted a part of Pound's letter of 10 November 1917. See Letter No. 137, p. 123.

Or whether I am Omar.

Have I a country at all . . . now that Mouquin is no more, and that your father has no more goldwasser, and the goldwasser no obescent bon-homme to pour it out for me?

Or you who sees no alternative?

All of which is, as you have divined, in relation to your prologue. I will get on to the *Improvisations* (for which many thanks) later.

Have written to *Dial* that you are the best thing in the country. Can you keep up some push of American stuff—you, Bodenheim, Sandburg, Hecht, Sher. Anderson, etc.?

I really can't do the whole show. Besides I am not supposed to run the American end.

If you want to honour the country, à la your patriotism, you people who have some guts ought to crowd such whiffle as "Songs of the Pueblo Indians" by A.L. out of the international envoy ([*Dial*,] Sept. p. 247).

171: To William Carlos Williams

London, 11 September

Deer Bull: Got as far as p. 68. All that can be expected of middle-aged European in one day.

Inclined to think it best you have done. Don't know that it is more in-coherent than Rimbaud's *Saison en Enfer;* nor yet that it could be im-proved by being more intelligible. STILL, am inclined to think it is prob-ably most effective where most comprehensible.

The italics at any rate don't detract. Not that they, in many cases, much explain the matter either. Nor sure that you would lose much or anything by still further exposition. Not on other hand suggesting that clear Mau-passant modus would serve your every turn.

Re the dialog. with your old man,[1] which I don't bloody remember . . . remember we did talk about "Und Drang"[2] but there the sapphires cer-tainly are NOT anything but sapphires, perfectly definite visual imagina-tion. However, upshot (which you don't, certainly, imply) is that your old man was certainly dead right. And that whatever t'ell I said ten years ago, I certainly have since then endeavoured "to why in the hell or heaven"

---

[1] "My parent had been holding forth in downright sentences upon my own 'idle nonsense' when he turned and became equally vehement concerning something Ezra had written: what in heaven's name Ezra meant by 'jewels' in a verse that had come between them. These jewels—rubies, sapphires, amethysts and what not, Pound went on to explain with great determination and care, were the backs of books as they stood on a man's shelf. 'But why in heaven's name don't you say so then?' was my father's triumphant and crushing rejoinder." *Kora in Hell*, p. 13.

[2] This series appears in *Canzoni*. The reference here is to the seventh poem of the series, "The House of Splendour":

> *And I have seen her there within her house*
> *With six great sapphires hung along the wall . . .*

say it and NOT summat else . . . to the whatever t'ell improvement of my whatever t'ell style or modus.

Possibly lamentable that the two halves of what might have made a fairly decent poet should be sequestered and divided by the — — — — buttocks of the arse-wide Atlantic Ocean.

If I was as ornery in my clear verse as you are in yourn, I'd be up before the beak. . . . — — — — I wonder why Lamar lets you thru and pinches the innocent Joyce (non-conformist parson from Aberdeen) while you . . . ("ohe ma-ma" as ma chère Xelezine would remark under similar . . .) variant "Mum-my."

Will say that the cover design IS at any rate purr-fectly clear. Wholly definite indication of the spirit of the woik as a hole (Even there, the layman's ignorance. . . . Is there any occult significance in the black eggs?)

Not sure Gaudier oughtn't have dedicated the FIRST post-Xtn bust of the century to your rather than to my LIBERATOR. La gracieuse et souple rhythme de Properce fait croire à une flueve ou à une berge plutôt qu'à un chêne. (mummy)

If any one has patience enough to read I think the book does manage to convey general sense of what you are meaning . . . more one can not ask, perhaps. Problem (not five minute problem): would more 3rd person, objective statement . . . etc. . . . Oh hell . . . dare say it wouldn't.

Anyhow blaze away, and more power to your elbow. Don't listen to anyone else, and above all don't listen to me.

Should welcome your candid re both *Homage to S. Prop.* and *Mauberley* if you have the texts. Nobody tells me anything about 'em that I don't know already (and that they usually tell me à rebours) all except — who says . . . in confirmation of the remark on lunar ellipses, etc. that Callimachus is too much, and that the Rubaiyat is properly annotated. And when I think where I found her.

I must cross the proper names out of this, as you're such a devil for printin' one's private affairs.

172: To WILLIAM CARLOS WILLIAMS

London, 12 September

Voui, mon vieux coco: Another point re parodies, langue d'oc, etc.[1] To be "historic," the "Homage langue d'oc" was the first thing hit upon by *L'Intransigeant* as supposedly of popular interest to the populous French public. That's nothing, proves only that populous French are insular, like to think their country is noticed, etc. No importance.

But what the French real reader would say to your *Improvisations* is Voui, ç(h)a j(h)ai déjà (f)vu ç(h)a ç(h)a c'est de R(h)imb(h)aud!!

---

[1] "I do not overlook De Gourmont's plea for a meeting of the nations, but I do believe that when they meet Paris will be more than slightly abashed to find parodies of the middle ages, Dante and Langue d'Oc foisted upon it as the best in United States poetry." *Kora in Hell*, p. 28.

So much for your kawnscious or unkawnscious. I certainly never put up translations of Provençal as "American"; and Eliot is perfectly conscious of having imitated Laforgue, has worked to get away from it, and there is very little Laforgue in his Sweeney, or his Bleistein Burbank, or his "Gerontion," or his Bay State hymn book. And in fact you are talking through your hat when you suggest that I at any time was ever ass enough to have picked "La Figlia" for the fantastic occasion you hypothecate.[1]

Masters is not as good as Jammes' *Existences*. Your "representative American" verse will be that which can be translated in foreign languages without appearing ridiculous to us after it has been "accepted," and which will appear new to the French or Hun or whatever. Pas de bile.

P.S. Of course, for me to say "you're another" is no argument—it's only drawing attention to the vitreous nature of your facade on observing the bricks you heave at my conservatory.

173: To Agnes Bedford

London, October

Kattegorrikaly DAMN the woman. I refuse to spoil one of the best bits of Provençal by making a rush crib in twenty minutes to order. Meaning is all tied up with sound.

First strophe is about new leaves and flowers bring back fragrance to the heart.

Second—insomnia—due to natural cause usual at the season.

Then—where man's treasure is there will his heart be also.

Then—and if I see her not, no sight is worth the beauty of my thought —which is the trouvaille—can't spoil it by botched lead up.

There *is no literal* translation of a thing where the beauty is melted into the original phrase. Tell the brute to take a literal photo of the Venus de Milo.

[1] "Imagine an international congress of poets at Paris or Versailles, Rémy de Gourmont (now dead), presiding, poets all speaking five languages fluently. Ezra stands up to represent U.S. verse and De Gourmont sits down smiling. Ezra begins by reading 'La Figlia che Piange.' It would be a pretty pastime to gather with a mental basket the fruits of that reading from the minds of the ten Frenchmen present; their impressions of the sort of United States that very fine flower was picked from." *Kora in Hell*, p. 28.

PART TWO

PARIS

1921-1924

174: To William Carlos Williams

St. Raphael, 2 February

Deer Bull: Yours of Jan. 10 to hand. Dopo tan' anni (16), I can not *preciser* any address in Dock (?) St. or other. Any studio I was ever in was probably that of some friend or relative of Will Smith, who avoided a very unpleasant era of American life by dying of consumption to the intimate grief of his friends. How in Christ's name he came to be in Phila.—and to know what he did know at the age of 17-25—I don't know. At any rate, thirteen years are gone; I haven't replaced him and shan't and no longer hope to.

Apart from his friends', it might have been a studio of a middle-aged friend of Maturin Dondo's.

Re travel. I rather want to take a solid year in Paris. But if "they say" anything solid—i.e. expenses guaranteed and ??? (couple) of thousand (??? £) $ over, i.e. guarantee of leisure for a year after the whirlwind campaign—I will listen to the stern voice of duty and save as much of the country as is ready to be snatched from the yawning maw of gum shoes, Y.M.C.A., Chubb, e tutti quanti. — — — —

I had rather you came to Paris, but should be glad of "further information." I went to Newcastle year before last for one lecture—I suppose coming to U.S. would be like doing that for a year??? —/—/

175: To Marianne Moore
[postcard]

St. Raphael, 24 March

Good review. But are you sure the B. Jonson [1] doesn't bear a bit of confession that B.J.'s a dull subject and that it was very difficult to condone the fact through the whole of a *Times* article.

Probably the greatest tour de force of the book. Yes.

[1] T. S. Eliot's essay on Ben Jonson is referred to.

176: To Agnes Bedford
[postcard]

Paris, April

Find Cocteau and Picabia intelligent. Fools abound but are less in one's way here, or at least for the moment. Don't know that I have as yet done more than refrain from superfluous action and possibly talk too much. . . .

Joyce's new chapter is enormous—megaloscrumptious—mastodonic.

177: To Wyndham Lewis

Paris, 27 April

Dear W.L.: Can't see that *Tyro* is of interest outside Bloomsbury; and having long sought a place where

> *Sound of – – – – and – – – – well is forgot*
> *And . . . .r's visage overcast with snot*
> *Absent from the purlieus, and in fact*
> *A freedom from the whole arseblarsted lot.*

am not inclined to reenter.

Am taking up the *Little Review* again, as a quarterly, each number to have about twenty reprods of ONE artist, replacing Soirées de Paris.

Start off with twenty Brancusi's to get a new note.

You have had since 1917 to turn in some illustrations for *L.R.*, but perhaps the prospect of a full Lewis number will lure you.

Also, as I have never been able to get a publisher for a book on you, I have the idea of trying one on "Four Modern Artists" *if you* can collect sufficient illustrations. I know there is difficulty re S. Kens. stuff and re Quinn's stuff.

I however give you this chance for a communique to Quinn. Tell him I am contemplating the book. (He has just bought some Brancusi, by the way, and shown good sense in so doing.)

I should take you, Brancusi, Picasso, and, surprising as it will seem to you, Picabia, not exactly as a painter, but as a writer. He commences in *Pensées sans paroles* and lands in his last book. *J. C. Rastaquoère* and there is also more in his design stuff than comes up in reprod.

Also the four chapters wd. give me a chance to make certain contrasts, etc.

Format of *L.R.* will be larger and reprods therein as good as possible. It will also be on sale at strategic points here.

Yr. correspondent Marcoissis is an industrious and serious person who has "done som beeutiful graiynin' in 'is time," not a titanic intellect, but has German market. Very very much concerned with execution. Gleizes isn't. Bracque I have only seen for two minutes and am inclined to like.

You ought to get Eliot out of England somehow.

178: To Agnes Bedford

Paris, [? April]

Sat through the *Pelléas* the other evening and am encouraged—encouraged to tear up the whole bloomin' era of harmony and do the thing if necessary on two tins and wash-board. Anything rather than that mush of hysteria, Scandinavia strained through Belgium plus French Schwärmerei. Probably just as well I have to make this first swash without any instruments at hand. VERY much encouraged by the *Pelléas*, ignorance having no further terrors if that DAMN thing is the result of what is called musical knowledge.

Have you seen Cocteau's *Cock and Harlequin?* Pub. by Egoist 3/6. Considerable sense.

I haven't been able to exclude violins altogether; and I suppose there will eventually be a few chords in the damn thing. Fortunately Satie's *Socrate* is damn dull (and people endure it) and Auric, whatever he knows, is certainly out for even less system than I am. (I really having a damn definite system, which may bring up bang against Les Six.) They will hang me possibly as an academic but scarcely as a dynamitist.

179: To Marianne Moore

Paris, [? April]

Dear Marianne Moore: As a protest against the imbecile suppression of Joyce's *Ulysses* some of the best men here in Paris are joining me in filling a special number of *The Little Review* and propose to boost it in its new quarterly form.

I know perfectly well that I shall never get any adequate report of N.Y. from N.Y. editors of the *L.R.* I hope that you will join in the move; at any rate that you will write to me and let me know how things are in N.Y.

Could you, for example, see that the quarterly has a proper list of new books of LITERARY interest? I mean at least those which have some sort of significance in the development of poetic expression, or formal discovery. Books, in short, that you or I would read, or buy to keep, stuff of the sort that I have mentioned in *Instigations*.

Heaven knows I have done my share of this sort of thing, and if you haven't enough interest in the matter to do it yourself, you might at least find some one who can take the matter as serious.

It doesn't necessarily mean more than four lines to say a book has appeared. But a quarterly ought to have at least that.

One can trust M.C.A. to die on the bayonets, but not bring up the water and hard tack.

We start off with twenty illustrations of Brancusi, a complete trans. of Cocteau's *Cap de Bonne Ésperance*, and I hope stuff by Morand, Cros, Cendrars, Picabia—two of whom are out of Paris, and as I only got onto this job three days ago I haven't yet heard from them.

At any rate there is to be once more a review which doesn't consult the state of public stupidity or the dictates of prudence.

I thought I had at last got free of all Anglo-Saxon connections, am perhaps wrong to take this new plunge. However, you might let me know whether you can be counted on, or whether you also think I should allow the country to sink into its apparently ineluctable and fanatical gloom without the annoyance of transatlantic prods.

Most of your young fellow citizens appear to be heading for this side, judging from the literary appeals falling daily upon my desk.

The inducement to American contributors is that having the best of the French writers in the *L.R.* the thing will be seen here, as other Am. mags are not.

I have tried for a year to get Thayer to print—i.e., at least get—an article on younger American writers. No use. You might tell me if anything of interest has been written there.

(Have seen Bill's *Kora*.) Also *Contact* where he attacks me for having given, so far as I have been able, the autochthonous bard something like the same chance as those in London. This he interprets as an attack on the American pathriot (i.e., possibly his own dago-immigrant self). Pas de bile. I hope he will contribute to the new *L.R.* out of respect to his Hispano-French mother. (You might also tell him—or rather *forward him this letter* and save me the half hour of writing him—that Cocteau looks more like him than even his own brother Ed. Indeed much more; not full face but ¾; most amazin' resemblance—at least to Bill as he used to look in 1910.)

Also, entre nooz: is there anyone in America except you, Bill and Mina Loy who can write anything of interest in verse? And as for prose???

A quarterly must to some degree make as hard a selection as is compatible with admitting real experiment.

180: To Agnes Bedford

Paris, May

Continuing in desperation and despite the outrageous postal rates—

What in your exltd. opinion is the least amount of tarabiscotage the thing will stand? Ans. to be as technical as possible. After the *Pelléas*, as aforestated, I feel ready to make a *Partition pour deux Casseroles et une plance de buis*. Remembering that the accords, or rather identical note is

built up of several instruments forcement giving VERY different overtones,
how much bloody chord-harmony is necessary?

I said the other day—M. est-ce-qu'il y a de chose plus stupide qu'une
accorde?? Ça me donne l'effet d'un coussin de sofa. And got the answer
"Oui, on a toujours la sensation de s'assoir dessus."

Premier principe—RIEN that interferes with the words, or with the utmost possible clarity of impact of words on audience. . . .

Even an *instrumental* counterpoint developed ANYwhere near enough to
satisfy mere contrapuntalist would presumably bitch the words?????

Given the play for the eye, and the song, how much of actual orchestra-
tion DOES the audience hear???

181: To T. S. ELIOT

Paris, 24 Saturnus, An 1, [*24 December*]

Caro mio: MUCH improved. I think your instinct had led you to put the
remaining superfluities at the end. I think you had better leave 'em, abolish
'em altogether or for the present.

IF you MUST keep 'em, put 'em at the beginning before the "April
cruelest month." The POEM ends with the "Shantih, shantih, shantih."

One test is whether anything would be lacking if the last three were
omitted. I don't think it would.

The song has only two lines which you can use in the body of the poem.
The other two, at least the first, does not advance on earlier stuff. And
even the sovegna doesn't hold with the rest; which does hold.

(It also, to your horror probably, reads aloud very well. Mouthing out
his OOOOOOze.)

I doubt if Conrad is weighty enough to stand the citation.

The thing now runs from "April . . ." to "shantih" without a break.
That is 19 pages, and let us say the longest poem in the English langwidge.
Don't try to bust all records by prolonging it three pages further.

The bad nerves is O.K. as now led up to.

My squibs are now a bloody impertinence. I send 'em as requested; but
don't use 'em with *Waste Land*.

You can tack 'em onto a collected edtn, or use 'em somewhere where
they would be decently hidden and swamped by the bulk of accompanying
matter. They'd merely be an extra and wrong note with the 19 page
version.

Complimenti, you bitch. I am wracked by the seven jealousies, and cogitating an excuse for always exuding my deformative secretions in my own
stuff, and never getting an outline. I go into nacre and objets d'art. Some
day I shall lose my temper, blaspheme Flaubert, lie like a — — — — and say
"Art should embellish the umbelicus."

SAGE HOMME

These are the poems of Eliot
By the Uranian Muse begot;
A Man their Mother was,
A Muse their Sire.

How did the printed Infancies result
From Nuptials thus doubly difficult?

If you must needs enquire
Know diligent Reader
That on each Occasion
Ezra performed the Caesarean Operation.

Cauls and grave clothes he brings,
Fortune's outrageous stings,
About which odour clings,
      Of putrefaction,
Bleichstein's dank rotting clothes
Affect the dainty nose,
He speaks of common woes
      Deploring action.

He writes of A.B.C.s
And flaxseed poultices,
Observing fate's hard decrees
      Sans satisfaction;
Breeding of animals,
Humans and cannibals,
But above all else of smells
      Without attraction

Vates cum fistula

It is after all a grrrreat littttttterary period.
Thanks for the Aggymemnon.

1 9 2 2

[The following letter, which continues the discussion of *The Waste Land*, was
sent by Eliot to Pound. Pound's marginal notes are indicated in boldface.]

London, [? January]

Cher maître: Criticisms accepted so far as understood, with thanks.
    Glowed on the marble where the glass
    Sustained by standards wrought with fruited vines

Wherefrom . . . ??   **O.K.**
Footsteps shuffled on the stair . . .   **O.K.**
   A closed car. I can't use taxi more than once.   **O.K.**
   Departed, *have* left no addresses . . . ???   **O.K.**
What does THENCE mean (To luncheon at the Cannon St. Hotel)???
Would D's difficulty be solved by inverting to
   Drifting logs
   The barges wash . . . ???

1. Do you advise printing "Gerontion" as a prelude in book or pamphlet form?
2. Perhaps better omit Phlebas also???
3. Wish to use Caesarean Operation in italics in front.
4. Certainly omit miscellaneous pieces.   **Those at end.**
5. Do you mean not use the Conrad quote or simply not put Conrad's name to it? It is much the most appropriate I can find, and somewhat elucidative.

Complimenti appreciated, as have been excessively depressed. — — — —
I would have sent Aeschule before but have been in bed with flu, now out, but miserable.
Would you advise working sweats with tears etc. into nerves monologue; only place where it can go?
   Have writ to Thayer asking what he can offer for this.
   Trying to read Aristophane.]

182: To T. S. ELIOT

Paris, [? January]

Filio dilecto mihi: I merely queeried the dialect of "thence"; dare say it is O.K.
   D. was fussing about some natural phenomenon, but I thought I had crossed out her query. The wake of the barges washes etc., and the barges may perfectly well be said to wash. I should leave it as it is, and NOT invert.
   I do *not* advise printing "Gerontion" as preface. One don't miss it *at* all as the thing now stands. To be more lucid still, let me say that I advise you NOT to print "Gerontion" as prelude.
   I DO advise keeping Phlebas. In fact I more'n advise. Phlebas is an integral part of the poem; the card pack introduces him, the drowned phoen. sailor. And he is needed ABsolootly where he is. Must stay in.
   Do as you like about my obstetric effort.
   Ditto re Conrad; who am I to grudge him his laurel crown?
   Aeschylus not so good as I had hoped, but haven't had time to improve him, yet.
   I dare say the sweats with tears will wait. — — — —
   You can forward the "Bolo" to Joyce if you think it won't unhinge his somewhat sabbatarian mind. On the hole he might be saved the shock, shaved the sock.

You will remember (or if not remind me of) the occasion when the whole company arose as one man and burst out singing "Gawd save the Queen." The anti-lynch law (postlude of mediaeval right to scortum ante mortem) has I see been passed to the great glee of the negro spectators in the congressional art gallery.

Dere z also de stoory of the poker game, if you hab forgotten it.

183: To Amy Lowell

Paris, 10 March

Once more to the breach, My Dear Amy: The Syballine or however you spell 'em books are burning; once more, pas de bile, before it is yet too late, do you wish to repent and be saved?

Pas de bile, I have none. You have attributed to me malicious remarks that I have never made. I have heard that you pay for your advertising, but I have never *said* so to anyone.

But you haven't, and there it is, you simply haven't taken the turning that leads to your getting the most fun out of life, and in your better moments, you know it. It means a lot of wear and tear, and it ain't, no dearie, it AIN'T good for the nerves. The eye of the needle is narrow.

Further information if you want it.

184: To William Carlos Williams

Paris, 18 March

Deer Bullll: The point is that Eliot is at the last gasp. Has had one breakdown. We have got to do something at once.

I have been on the job, am dead tired with hammering this machine. Steps have been taken. Richard and I, pledged £10 per year. This merely to apologize for brevity. I enclose carbon outline.[1] Get to it.

[1] There is no organized or coordinated civilization left, only individual scattered survivors.

Aristocracy is gone, its function was to select.

Only those of us who know what civilization is, only those of us who want better literature, not more literature, better art, not more art, can be expected to pay for it. No use waiting for masses to develop a finer taste, they aren't moving that way.

All the rewards to men who do compromise works.

No hope for others.

Millionaires all tapped too frequently. Must be those of us who are. We are none of us able to act alone. Must cooperate.

Increase production of the best, by releasing the only energies that are capable of producing it.

"Bel Esprit" started in Paris. To release as many captives as possible.

Darkness and confusion as in Middle Ages; no chance of general order or justice; we can only release an individual here or there.

T. S. Eliot first name chosen. Must have thirty guarantors at £10 per year "for

Can you run to 50 dollars yourself???

I wd. try and make it good to you later. I mean the struggle is to get the first man released. "Release of energy for invention and design" acc best economic theories. AFTER Eliot is freed it will be much easier to get out the second, third and tenth prisoners.

I wd. back you for the second, if you wished. BUT I don't really believe you want to leave the U.S. permanently. I think you are suffering from nerve; that you are really afraid to leave Rutherford. I think you ought to have a year off or a six months' vacation in Europe. I think you are afraid to take it, for fear of destroying some illusions which you think necessary to your illusions. I don't think you ought to leave permanently, your job gives you too real a contact, too valuable to give up. BUT you ought to see a human being now and again.

One might, after freeing Eliot, run a yearly trip from America. Or at least you one summer, Marianne another, etc. when there was someone worth it. At present, although the necessary 30 for Eliot haven't been found, I can I think offer you a summer home. The "Bel Esprit" is definitely started. And the "pavilion" was offered me yesterday for suitable candidate. It is not the "sanctuaire" on card enclosed. – – – –

---

life or for as long as Eliot needs it" (anyone who don't like my choice is at liberty to choose some other imprisoned artist or writer, and start another "Bel Esprit" group).

Only thing we can give the artist is leisure to work in. Only way we can get work from him is to assure him this leisure.

As fast as his sales go up, amount of his subsidy will be decreased; this to insure quality: to prevent his being penalized for suppressing inferior work. Every writer is penalized as at present for not doing bad work, penalized for not printing EVERYTHING he can sell.

Wastage of literary prizes. Anatole France deserved the Nobel Prize, but no one will claim that giving it to him at age of 74 increases or betters his production.

Eliot, in bank, makes £500. Too tired to write, broke down; during convalescence in Switzerland did *Waste Land*, a masterpiece; one of most important 19 pages in English.

Returned to bank, and is again gone to pieces, physically.

Pound, Aldington, start with £10 guarantees, if they can afford it others can.

Must restart civilization; people who say they care, DON'T care unless they care to the extent of £5 in the spring and £5 in autumn, ridiculous to say they do, if they won't run to that, can't expect a civilization or grumble if they don't [lacuna].

NOT charity, NOT "pity the poor artist." Eliot wd. rather work in bank than do poor work. Has tried to live by pen and can't. (Poor health, invalid wife.)

NOT charity in his case nor in case of any other good artist which we may later choose.

It is for US who want good work to provide means of its being done. WE are the consumers and we demand something fit to consume.

In the arts quantity is nothing, quality everything.

Only certain men who can produce the grade of stuff we want. They must be in position to do so.

Only certain lands will produce copper, etc. Must go where the stuff is, no gathering figs of thistle bushes.

If not enough good will to release ONE proved writer, how do they expect to regenerate Europe?

Eliot first item on list. Anyone free to start group for their own choice.

It is a show down. Those who don't care 50 dollars a year for the arts, don't care for MUCH. It gags the sassiety muckers.

I want you to help. If you can't make the 50 dollars a year pledge, can you organize a group which will do so? I am writing to Bob McA.; I want you to work in America. It is the start that is the hardest. Once the nucleus formed. Once the Tom cat and the she-cat, the kittens will arrive without our worrying.

No use trying to unite people on critical basis, basis of common taste, or opinion, must unite on basis of common good will. Anyone don't like choice of Paris branch of "Bel Esprit" can start local branch, backing local fancy. If you don't approve sending American poet to Europe, you can invite European poet to U.S.A. I don't care.

First step is however necessary. MUST free the qualified energies if we are to get the stuff.

185: To H. L. MENCKEN

Paris, 22 March

My dear Henry: WHO is to pay my way to the "remains"? The Christian Era ended at midnight on Oct. 29-30 of last year. You are now in the year 1. p.s.U., if that is any comfort to you.

I thought you were coming over for a drink on the "first post bellum boat." Air' yeh waterlogged?

Will you come in on this "Bel Esprit" show? It will cost you fifty bones a year, but if I can afford it, you can. Nothing will get any better until some one does something decent.

Shaw now writes to me twice a week complaining of the high price of *Ulysses*.

Umbra, Instigations, why not the last vol. of my distinguished news.

Bad Stomackhk, I don't wonder. As the apostle says, take a little Pomeroy for thy belly's ache. –/–/

You better come away, Henry, before it is yet even too late.

186: To KATE BUSS

Paris, [?23] March

Dear K.B.: No, this circular is, as marked, for private circulation.[1] There can be *no* more publicity about ELIOT until his subsidy is fixed, as further talk might get him into a mess with the bank, before he is ready to quit.

This is important.

[1] The following circular was printed by John Rodker for "Bel Esprit":
"In order that T. S. Eliot may leave his work in Lloyd's Bank and devote his whole time to literature, we are raising a fund, to be £300 annually; this being in our

You can write about "Bel Esprit" (if you understand it). The present circular leaves only paragraph 1 on page 2 quotable.

I am going to write out a clear statement of "Bel Esprit" as soon as possible.

Main ideas:

1. That the reader is a consumer and that quality is a luxury; i.e. it can appeal only to a few people and they, if they want it, must pay for it.

2. As there is no aristocracy, one must form a combine of simple particulars to pay.

It is a risk. So is an oil well.

I will write in a few days.

---

opinion the minimum possible for this purpose. Method, £10, Fifty dollars . . . payable yearly by 30 subscribers.

"NOTE

"As three of the initial life members of Bel Esprit, Richard Aldington, May Sinclair and Ezra Pound are practising authors, having nothing but their writings to live on, we consider ourselves in a position to know, with some accuracy, conditions being what they are, about what Eliot can earn by his best work; and at what point hackwork, etc. would interfere with his good writing, i.e., interfere with it as much as or more than his present exhausting, but steady bank work (which brings him £600 a year).

"(*This notice for private circulation only*.)

"We are not a home for sick animals. We want the work of certain men. We want a better grade of work than present systems of publishing are willing to pay for. This is to our credit, and our choice of an artist should be an honour to *him*.

"Eliot's earlier poems are available. He tried some years ago to live by journalism, and found the bank preferable. Our aim is NOT to send him back into journalism.

"He certainly is not asking favours, our plan was concocted without his knowledge. The facts are that his bank work has diminished his output of poetry, and that his prose has grown tired. Last winter he broke down and was sent off for three months' rest. During that time he wrote *Waste Land*, a series of poems, possibly the finest that the modern movement in English has produced, at any rate as good as anything that has been done since 1900, and which certainly loses nothing by comparison with the best work of Keats, Browning or Shelley. As some of the subscribers approve primarily of Eliot, and some primarily of the aims of the society, Bel Esprit, the pledge forms are written so that the subscriber may make his donation either to Eliot direct, or to Bel Esprit *for* Eliot, in which latter case the treasurers of Bel Esprit (Mr. Aldington, England, Mr. Pound, France) stand personally responsible for the delivery of receipts to Mr. Eliot.

"I hereby pledge myself to contribute £.................yearly
$.................yearly
for.................years

to (*a*) T. S. Eliot

(*b*) To Bel Esprit for T. S. Eliot (in which case a treasurer of Bel Esprit, R. Aldington, Malthouse Cottage, Padworth, Reading, Berks, acting in England. Or—Ezra Pound, 70bis rue Notre Dame des Champs, Paris, acting in France, stands personally responsible for the transmission of funds to Mr. Eliot).

"This money is given on the understanding that Mr. Eliot shall devote his entire time to literary work. No restriction is placed on the nature of that work, and I, the present donor, will make no effort to influence either the subject-matter or the manner of his writing save by such literary criticism as any critic of literature might indulge in.

I will pay this money { annually } { semi-annually } ....date.
"

(Signature).................................."

187: To Wyndham Lewis

Siena, 5 April

Caro mio: There is no use my giving you advice re yr. own affairs. I have never known you to take any anyhow.

Don't see that "Bel Esprit" could ever do much more than provide you a studio.

Certainly can't start on you as you have to the public eye had nothing but leisure for years. Nothing to prevent or to have prevented you doing any damn thing you liked, save yr habit of fuss and of having a private life and allowing it to intrude on yr. attention. Try New York; I mean emigrate. England is under a curse.

Also re "Bel Esprit": Joyce worked for years as language teacher, and I have done all sorts of little jobs at £1/1 a shot.

I had left Paris before your writing re Schiff. I left on March 27th. Don't think wd. have done any good my meeting him as it wd. be esagg. to say I find him a kindred spirit.

Re "Bel Esprit": vide *New Age* for Mar. 30th.

Anyone who can afford to can buy annuities or place capital in Lloyds' (most of the subscribers can't).

T. bound to be sceptical until the actual sum is in hand. At present there is £120 a year. He wd. in time earn something by his pen. Annuities at £180 on T's life are obviously the preferable form.

Good will counts for something, also the possible spread of the society and there being a larger fund than T's £300 to fall back on.

The £120 is already flanked by several people willing to give £20, but who ought *not* to be allowed to do so. That margin acts as insurance.

If there aren't 30 or 50 people interested in literature, there is no civilization and we may as well regard our work as a private luxury, having no aims but our own pleasure. You can't expect people to pay you for enjoying yourself.

188: To William Carlos Williams

Venice, 4 May

See here ole son: If you hear a report of my death don't fer Xt's sake deny it. Say you expected as much. Suggest Xifiction or assification or any other —and xpress perlite regret.

Now as to the Pavilion: I wrote you from Paris that I hoped to be able to offer it to you. The matter re pavilion was broached at a tea fight 3 days before I left Paris and I was expected to come out and inspect it—hygienically etc. and pronounce it fit or unfit for literary habitation. On receipt of yrs. (containing Katz proceeds) I wrote to Paris to see if formality of my inspection, etc., were necessary. The Baronne de Clausel responds that it is fit for a European artist but that she shudders to think of effect it might have on an American. An American to her is evidently someone who wd. shrink from sharing his privvy with a chauffeur.

My studio won't hold three, but my spouse goes to Eng. about July 15th. I can therefore offer you a room for 6 weeks or 2 months during which you wd. have time to inspect the Pavilion and see if it is habitable—or worth bothering about for the rest of yr. vacation.

You wd., during the 6-8 weeks, have the inconvenience of my presence below you, balanced by the convenience of getting yr. breakfasts ready made and not having to struggle with charwomen. I need scarcely say that the incommodity of yr. presence wd. be but a greater delight to me—am not expecting to give birth to an infant. At least I have shown no symptoms of pregnancy and there is only 2 to four months in which you wd. be exposed to the dangers of a hurry call.

You can have a separate key to the back entrance, and put a couch in the work room if you want to receive female patients without my knowledge.

Thanks fer 5 bones recd.

I hope you'll come over.

Seriously, please don't contradict report of my demise if it has the luck to spread. I want a little quiet.

And let me know probable date of yr. arrival and length of yr. time off. ?You don't want to take a boat to Genoa and come to Lago di Garda for a week first? Probably not worth bore of extra visas, of train trip up to Paris. I shan't be back in Paris before about 7th July. (Not trying to nurse you or personally conduct you thru Europe—only you can't get into the studio in my absence as the key is here in my pocket and the lease forbids loan or sublet. Hence the meticulous necessity of my being there to open the door if you deign to enter.)

There's also the very faint possibility that I might have to form a junction with X. here in Italy which might (tho' unlikely) delay my return a week or so. Will let you know as soon as pos. but in any case, in anny kase, so far foresight permits nothing visible at the moment, menaces your having 6 weeks or two months free shelter at 70bis. and more in Baronne's back garden IF her shack is good enough.

As you have been so explicit in yr. optation of undisturbed solitude I hesitate to offer to prolong my sojourn in Italy—if you shd. care to shed the lustre of yr. medical knowledge on this land already flavoured with sunlight—possibly cd. offer you at least four nerve cases, if that's any inducement.

As to Paris. If you take the room off my studio, don't fer Christ's sake think you need see me except at breakfast or that your quiet need be infected. I've got (or suppose I have) loan to use a room and garden elsewhere so that we shdn't be cramped.

189: To Felix E. Schelling

Paris, 8 July

Dear Dr. Schelling: The length of the enclosed is an outrage. But having written it, I may as well send it. I intended only three or four pages.

Dear Dr. Schelling: May I thank you for the grave tone of your review which has just reached me; and also since there is so little tempered criticism; and since there can be no sort of literary life in America unless at least two or three people talk about the same subject once and a while, may I take up one or two points?

(I mean in the *Dial*, for example, with Brooks, etc. etc. all talking at tangents, and never once *discussing* any point, never answering anything, never trying to give a more precise contour to *any* idea advanced by *any* other writer in the magazine, one gets no centre, no live litteraire properly so-called or callable.)

Criticism, I take it, is written in the hope of better things. With all my legendary cantankerousness, I think I have tried to learn from critics. . . . Sum total of debts to date:

One caution against homopnones, recd. from Robt. Bridges.

Considerable encouragement to tell people to go to hell, and to maintain absolute intransigeance, recd. from Mr. W. B. Yeats.

Any amount of good criticism, chiefly in form of attacks on dead language, dialects of books, dialects of Lionel Johnson, etc., recd. from F. Madox Hueffer.

One impractical and infinitely valuable suggestion recd. from Thomas Hardy.

(This latter a suggestion re change of title of *Homage to Propertius*. Don't know that T.H. realized how much he was revealing of the gap between himself and the '90s. But he woke one to the extent of his own absorption in *subject* as contrasted with aesthetes' preoccupation with "treatment.")

In your review there are the following:

1. No, I have not done a translation of Propertius. That fool in Chicago took the *Homage* for a translation, despite the mention of Wordsworth and the parodied line from Yeats. (As if, had one wanted to pretend to more Latin than one knew, it wdn't have been perfectly easy to correct one's divergencies from a Bohn crib. Price 5 shillings.)

I do think, however, that the homage has scholastic value. MacKail (accepted as "right" opinion on the Latin poets) hasn't, apparently, *any* inkling of the *way* in which Propertius is using Latin. Doesn't see that S.P. is tying blue ribbon in the tails of Virgil and Horace, or that sometime after his first "book" S.P. ceased to be the dupe of magniloquence and began to touch words somewhat as Laforgue did.

2. About Provence. The Wm. Morris tapestry treatment of the Middle

Ages is unsatisfactory. The originals are more vital, more realist. De Born writes songs to provoke real war, and they were effective. This is very different from Romantic or Macaulay-Tennyson praise of past battles.

— — — —

(Interruptions. Got back from Italy last Sunday and am having a show of Koumé's paintings in this studio on Tuesday . . . large canvases, some of them . . . etc. However will try to keep to thread of my discourse.)

9 July

My assaults on Provence: 1st: using it as subject matter, trying to do as R.B. had with Renaissance Italy. 2, Diagrammatic translations (those of Arnaut, now printed in *Instigations*); all part of study of verse-form (as trans. of Cavalcanti). Note that the English "poet" en masse had simply said: "these forms are *impossible* in English, they are too complicated, we haven't the rhymes." That was bunkum, usual laziness of English, and hatred of craft. (I suppose I have by now a right to be serious about this matter, having been plugging at it for twenty years.) Eh bien. 1. I have proved that the Provençal rhyme schemes are not *impossible* in English. They are probably *inadvisable*. The troubadour was not worried by our sense of style, our "literary values," he could shovel in words in any order he liked. Milton ruined his work by not understanding that the genius of English is not the genius of Latin, and that one can NOT write an uninflected language in the same way, using the same word-order that serves in an inflected language. The troubadour, fortunately perhaps, was not worried about English order; he got certain musical effects because he cd. concentrate on music without bothering about literary values. He had a kind of freedom which we no longer have.

There is, however, a beauty in the troubadour work which I have tried to convey. I have failed almost without exception; I can't count six people whom I have succeeded in interesting in XIIth Century Provence. Perhaps the best thing I have done is with the music. Note *Five Troubadour Songs*, Provençal, with Chaucer's words set to the music. (Pub. London two years ago.)

In the *Quai Pauper Amavi* vol. and Liveright's *Poems* 1921: The point of the archaic language in the Prov. trans. is that the Latin is really "modern." We are just getting back to a Roman state of civilization, or in reach of it; whereas the Provençal feeling is archaic, we are ages away from it. (Whether I have managed to convey this or not I can't say; but it is the reason for the archaic dialect.) (Anecdote: Years ago when I was just trying to find and use modern speech, old Bridges carefully went through *Personae* and *Exultations* and commended every archaism (to my horror), exclaiming "We'll git 'em all back; we'll git 'em *all* back." Eheu fugaces!)

Next: There's plenty of "premeditated thrust" in Provençal satire. I don't think one ought to hurt unless one means to.

As to the free verse translation and adaptations of "Langue d'Oc" in the last volume. The charm and lyricism may be gone, but I think you were wrong about the "music and ease" (try 'em aloud). The "clamour" and "charmer" are not intended to be an impression of rhyme, but of syzogy such as one finds in Arnaut's stanzas without internal rhyme: "comba," "trembla," "pona" followed in that strophe by rhyme in "oigna." Or the "-iers" "-ors" sequence.

However, you are right in not finding the "Langue d'Oc" satisfactory. (Save perhaps the "Descant"? On Cerclamon.)

Years ago Yeats was struggling with my rhythms and saying they wouldn't do. I got him to read a little Burns aloud, telling him he cd. read no cadence but his own, or some verse like Sturge Moore's that had not any real characteristics strong enough to prohibit W.B.Y. reading it to his own rhythm. I had a half hour of unmitigated glee in hearing "Say ye bonnie Alexander" and "The Birks o Averfeldy" *keened*, wailed with infinite difficulty and many pauses and restarts to *The Wind Among the Reeds*.

Sennin are the Chinese spirits of nature or of the air. I don't see that they are any worse than Celtic Sidhe.

Rokku is a mountain. I can perhaps emend the line and make that clearer, though "on" limits it to either a mountain or an island (an ambiguity which don't much matter at that point). The name and title indicate a French priest (as a matter of fact he is a Jesuit).

Perhaps as the poem goes on I shall be able to make various things clearer. Having the crust to attempt a poem in 100 or 120 cantos long after all mankind has been commanded never again to attempt a poem of any length, I have to stagger as I can.

The first 11 cantos are preparation of the palette. I *have to* get down all the colours or elements I want for the poem. Some perhaps too enigmatically and abbreviatedly. I hope, heaven help me, to bring them into some sort of design and architecture later.

Next point: This being buoyed by wit. No. *Punch* and the rest of them have too long gone on treating the foetor of England as if it were something to be joked about. There is an evil without dignity and without tragedy, and it is dishonest art to treat it as if it were funny. It is perhaps difficult to treat it at all; the Brit. Empire is rotting because no one in England tries to treat it. Juvenal isn't witty. Joyce's isn't harsh enough. One hasn't any theology to fall back on.

I am perhaps didactic; so in a sense, or in different senses are Homer, Dante, Villon, and Omar, and Fitzgerald's trans. of Omar is the only good poem of Vict. era that has got beyond a fame de cénacle. It's all rubbish to pretend that art isn't didactic. A revelation is always didactic. Only the aesthetes since 1880 have pretended the contrary, and they aren't a very sturdy lot.

Art can't offer a patent medicine. A failure to dissociate that from a profounder didacticism has led to the errors of "aesthete's" critique.

(Of course, I'm no more Mauberley than Eliot is Prufrock. Mais passons.) Mauberley is a mere surface. Again a study in form, an attempt to condense the James novel. Meliora speramus.

Eliot's *Waste Land* is I think the justification of the "movement," of our modern experiment, since 1900. It shd. be published this year.

P.S. If I ever plagued you about Shaw in the old days, I apologize. He is fundamentally trivial.

Minor quibbles: "confirmed devotee of vers libre"; search for quantitative element in English, for liberty of the musician.

Provençal "poetry romantic." That doesn't so much interest me. The fact that Arnaut and Guido were psychological, almost physiological, diagnosticians does interest me. It also interested the late T. E. Hulme (mei gratia).

Cerclamon was insouciant in cadence; Guillaume de Poictiers satyric (the "leer" can be his, quite correctly).

In the cantos, as yet?? I have managed to make certain passages intelligible in themselves, even though the whole is still unintelligible???? Or perhaps I haven't.

Also if I am unlike other people, how is it a pose? Isn't it merely common honesty? There are twelve or more vols. to prove some slight biological variant between me and the other ex-Penn '05 or ex-seminarists. Isn't it nearly time that one allowed me the honesty of never having pretended the contrary?

And "original"??? when I can so snugly fit into the words of Propertius almost thirty pages with nothing that isn't S.P., or with no distortion of his phrases that isn't justifiable by some other phrase of his elsewhere?

"Affectation of fine phrase": I don't know. I thought it was onomatopoeia. For fifteen years "di lontano connobi il temmolar della marina" and for eight or perhaps six years "para thina poluphloisboio thalasses." And perhaps even now one has to over-stress the *au* in *au*dition before one gets the effect I was after.

The metre in *Mauberley* is Gautier and Bion's "Adonis"; or at least those are the two grafts I was trying to flavour it with. Syncopation from the Greek; and a general distaste for the slushiness and swishiness of the post-Swinburnian British line. (Cf. Dante's remarks in the *D.V.E.*)

Shock troops. All right. There are things I quite definitely want to destroy, and which I think will have to [be] annihilated before civilization can exist, i.e. anything I shd. dignify with the title civilization, lest vestiges of which probably went by the board in the counterreformation. I mean all that is left is exiled, driven in catacombs, exists in the isolated individual, who occasionally meets one other with a scrap of it concealed in his person or his study.

My main objection is to your phrase about being buoyed by wit. If the poets don't make certain horrors appear horrible who will? All values ultimately come from our judicial sentences. (This arrogance is not mine but Shelley's, and it is absolutely true. Humanity is malleable mud, and the arts set the moulds it is later cast into. Until the cells of humanity recognize certain things as excrement, they will stay in [the] human colon and poison it. Victoria was an excrement, Curtis, Lorrimer, *all* British journalism are excrement. Bottomley has been jailed and Northcliffe gone off his head to prove this.)

It isn't enough to give the Rabelaisian guffaw. Aristotle has used the word, cascarets. Honestly I think *Lustra* has done a work of purgation of minds, meritorious as the physical products of Beecham. Being intemperate, at moments, I shd. prefer dynamite, but in measured moments I know that all violence is useless (even the violence of language. . . . However, one must know an infinite amount before one can decide on the position of the border line between strong language and violent language). The governed explosion of dynamite in a quarry, useful, O.K.; and the calamitous useless explosion.

La la. I run on too long.

190: To Harriet Monroe

Paris, 16 July

Dear H.M.: Yours of April 13 to hand. Got back from Italy a fortnight ago.

Yes, there is, as per enclosed "Bel Esprit" private notices, a very definite scheme not only for Eliot, but for literchure and the ahts in general.

Eliot is the first stone. 22 of the 30 subscriptions are in; and with two lump gifts, the £300 for the first year is either in hand or promised. Some of the pledges are not very well secured. I still want another ten. They are mostly "life" pledges, but there are three that are for only three or five years.

I shall hang out myself until the U.S. is ready to start a ministry of Beaux Arts, and put me in charge. They won't do that until nearly the end of the hecker era, and the crepuscule of the boobs. Also they will have to digest one or two facts, stated in the elementary geography books, but never digested by the pupils.

As Bill Williams needs time rather than cash, I think the next "B. Espr." move may be a yearly travel fellowship. Possibly 1000 bones wd. cover it. My first nomination wd. be, I think, Marianne Moore . . . though I am open to suggestion. — — — —

Re the Anthology: I have had to stop all permissions to anthologists. I can only promise you that if you print the poem, no steps will be taken, and no protest uttered. Perhaps you had better use it, to give a fuller synopsis.

As to anthologies in general (except those that are a sort of group manifesto) the collectors seem generally to want to prove that one agrees with their particular form of idiocy. Your anth. is rather better. You do give a sort of outline of the earlier part of my work. BUT you *never* have permitted minority reports. Damn remnants in you of Jew religion, that bitch Moses and the rest of the tribal barbarians. Even you do still try at least to leave the reader in ignorance of the fact that I do NOT accept the current dung, and official opinions about the dregs of the Xtn superstition, the infamy of American laws, etc. Bulbous taboos, and so forth.

You might at least print a footnote saying that I consider many American laws infamous, and that I do not accept many beliefs which it is not at present permitted people to contradict in print or in school textbooks in the U.S.

That wd. give better equilibrium to your ladylike selection of my verse.

Say that I consider the Writings of Confucius, and Ovid's *Metamorphoses* the only safe guides in religion. This doesn't repudiate "The G[oodly] F[ere]." Christ can very well stand as an heroic figure. The hero need not be of wisdom all compounded. Also he is not wholly to blame for the religion that's been foisted on to him. As well blame me for . . . for all the bunk in vers libre.

Christianity as practised resumes itself into one commandment dear to all officials, American Y.M.C.A., burocrats, etc., "Thou shalt attend to thy neighbor's business before attending to thine own."

In your footnote you ought to point out that I refuse to accept ANY monotheistic taboos whatsoever. That I consider the *Metamorphoses* a sacred book, and the Hebrew scriptures the record of a barbarian tribe, full of evil. You have no decent right to palm me off for what I am not, even if it does happen to suit your convenience. — — — —

191: To AMY LOWELL

Paris, 19 July

Dear Amy: Letter from Richard this A.M. repenting of his outburst in N.Y. *Post*, and containing the Caesarean Jesus Wept, in the words "Amy refuses."

Auw shucks! dearie, aint you the hell-roarer, aint you the kuss.

P.S. The first year's £300 is in hand or promised, and 22 subscriptions recd.

192: To WILLIAM CARLOS WILLIAMS

Paris, [1 August]

Cher Bull: There's a printer here wants me to supervise a series of booklets, prose (in your case perhaps verse, or whatever form your new stuff is in). Gen. size about 50 pages (??? too short for you). Limited private edtn. of 350 copies. 50 dollars down to author, and another 50 later.

Is this any use to you for anything? Appearance in this series wdnt. interfere with later reprint in pub. edtn. or inclusion of the 50 pages in some later longer book. It is a means of getting in 100 dollars extra before one goes to publisher.

Yeats' sisters' press in Ireland has brought him a good deal in this way. I got nearly as much from my little book with them as from the big Macmillan edtn. of *Noh*.

I shall keep the series strictly modern. One can be more intimate. The private limited edtn. don't imply that one is talking to the public, but simply to one's friends.

Anyhow. Explode: let's hear what you have and what you think.

I think it is probably better, at point where we have now arrived, than stray contributions to stray magazines. On peut bien être soi, et chez soi. Also the printing will be good, as the chap is doing it himself. (His name is Willyum Bird.)

Also what tips can you give the press re American book shops *if* any? And how many *Contact* subscribers wd. be likely to want your stuff?

It's hell the way I always seem to get sucked into editing something or other.

I suppose the people included in the series wd. more or less pool their lists of likely addresses.

I shall probably use the series for an annual outburst: and only send enough stuff to magazines to pay my rent. I haven't exactly flooded the world with muck during the last two years, anyhow.

The series is OPEN: Though I don't at the moment see much more than half a dozen names: Hueffer, you, Eliot, Lewis, Windeler, Hemingway, et moi même. (That's seven.)

I take it Marianne never has anything but verse???

This is a prose series. General success or point of the thing wd. lie in its being really interesting.

As Bird says, he can make money issuing bibliographies, that is NOT what he wants.

1 9 2 3

193: To JAMES JOYCE

Rapallo, 16 January

Ballade of the most gallant Mulligan, Senator in ordinary
and the frivolous milkwench of Hogan

afftl. dedicated to
S. Daedalus
Tenor
by his friend
Simm McNulty

Ohe, ohe, Jock Hielandman,
The strong and brawny Mulligan
Took off his overcoat and ran
Unto the river Liffey,

Peeled off his breeches and jumped in,
Humecting thus his hairy skin;
All heedless of pursuers' din
He struck out like a porpoise.

"Who goes there, where the waters pour
"Across the mill-dam, say, koind sir?"
"I am a celtic senator,"
                    To her replied Buck Mulligan.

"Put on your breeches, sir, again,"
To him replied the milk-maiden,
"before you land by our hog-pen,
                    on this side of the Liffey."

"Ach, darlint, do not but lend me yours,
"Oi left moine wid them rebel boors
"whom you see fearin' wather-cures
                    on to'ther side the Liffey."

"Oi will, sir," says she, as cute a cheeze,
"To shield you from the gaelic breeze,
"Bedad, oi think they'll reach your knees,
                    "Kind, kindly kind, sir senator,

"And I but one condition make
"Before I doff now for your sake
"—think—Jaysus! think what oi've at stake,
                    "O kindly kind, sir senator,

"If you will wear them and go down
"To the senate hall in Dublin Town
"In that attire,—do not frown,
"Promise me, dear; or, damn you, drown."

194: To William Carlos Williams

Rapallo, 9 February

Deer Bull: The 3 Mts. printing is beautiful as the feet of young damsels
on the hills (or rather better).

Hope the Kittens are A-1.

The Dial has kindly sent me the enclosed for "Ed." *Dew* send it to him
with my compliments.

I do NOT advise you to pay for having vol. of poems printed. You *can't*
sell a vol. You can get it published on royalty basis—that's all anyone can
do except possibly Kipling.

S'Oiseau is putting so much energy and cash into making 3 Mts. printing the A-1 double X, that I don't know how the press will survive the
prose series. IF it does go on and if your *Gt. Am. Nov.* sells 200 copies, I
think he might do the poems (yours). At least I shd. like to see the mss.
and consider it if the press continues. (This is *private*. Officially the press
is to last forever and rival Aldus, Froben, Gypsum etc.) Bill Bird he is
sparin' no pains (save on proof correcting).

Hem and his missus and me and my missus start south on Monday. Hear Robt. McA. is in Florence.

P.S. Re the Gt. Novel—all that need be done re that Ladies' Home Urinal is to put woppin gt. double sized quote marks before and after the quote —say a line space and then the quotes. Sic.

Please write to Bird and tell him where to put 'em. I.e. where the L.H.J. begins and ends.

195: TO KATE BUSS

Paris, 12 May

Dear K.B.: I don't know anything about literary agents. How should I, being completely unsaleable? Have you tried Liveright?

The Four Seas publish Bill Williams. That's all I know about U.S. publicators.

Re Three Mts. Press: Your friend can get, or shd. be able to get copies in a hurry from the trade agents in N.Y., Gottschalk, as per enclosed. Hueffer's book is just out, and the next two at the binders. For further arrangements Vinal had better write direct to the Press, – – – – I have nothing to do with the business arrangements.

The Dial has sacked me; so there will be no more Paris letters. Public laments over this might be useful. I don't expect there will be any unless they are engineer'd or faked by my friends. *The Dial* reader, biologically speaking, the "*Dial* reader," will probably be glad to have me eliminated. I don't know where to go next. As far as I can see, my communication with America is over. I.e., public communication. The last link severed.

That utter skunk ....d has invited me to contribute to Vanity Puke; but he wants me to emit the kind of assininity used in Vanity Puke; and that can't be did. Besides it wdn't. constitute communicating. To communicate one must say something one means, not merely dress up as a Bostonese jack-ass.

Waal, there it be. If any of you people exiled in America wants news from the front you'll have to organize a demand. Or find some editor who will stand for it.

I haven't seen any of the other once-high-brow magazines. Do they still exist? Are they still glued to 1876?

The Criterion wants me to send in stuff; i.e., that is in London; *The Criterion* has to be so heavily camouflaged as Westminster Abbey, that the living visitor is not very visible. On the other hand, imperfect Paris is still breathing, respiring.

The Three Mts. is following this prose series by a dee looks edtn of my Cantos (about 16 of 'em, I think) of UNRIVALLED magnificence. Price 25 dollars per copy, and 50 and 100 bones for Vellum and illuminateds.

It is to be one of the real bits of printing; modern book to be jacked up to somewhere near level of mediaeval mss. No Kelmscott mess of illegibility. Large clear type, but also large pages, and specially made capitals. Marse Henry [Strater] doing these; and the sketches already done are A-1.

Not for the Vulgus. There'll only be about 60 copies for sale; and about 15 more for the producers.

AND so on.

196: TO WILLIAM BIRD

Paris, [? December]

Further developments.
                    M.P., accompanied by a beautiful and
distinguished American authoress, visited M. le
Commissaire de p'lice, dans son bureau, as invited.
He discussed the sins of Scandinavians at length,
also their propensities to dance above his head at three
A.M.
   he pointed out that the Scandinavians also had a
piano, ils ne sont pas des musiciens mais ils
jouent au piano.
After some discussing M. le Commissaire wrote:
Monsieur (Pound) repond qu'il est compositeur de musique
et qu'il est necessaire qu'il fasse du bruit.
that he makes no more noise than habitually.
No further developments save that M. Antheil has
continued the composition of his second violin sonata,
and broken the — b flat base hammer of his Steinway
("a good tough" piano).

1924

197: To WILLIAM BIRD

Florence, 17 April

Deer Bull: 1. I had no intention of *giving away* 20 copies. I wanted 'em to be sold to people who won't stand Mike's illustrations and who will sit on my chest and bellyache about 'em tomorrow an' tomorrow an' tomorrow.

I enclose Mike's letter which might be taken as licence to eliminate superfluous muck—such as the love knot in lower right hand corner. Also if we can't—for technical reasons have a few clean copies, it seems to me ALL the more reason for cutting away offending parts: i.e. 1) the love knot; 2) the tail of "P"; and 3) the extra scene across top of page: P————.

It will be perfectly easy to do this, though I see (and saw) that it wd. probably be too difficult to effect composition of lines inside the loop of the "P." —/—/

Oh yes. *Point* was to restrict Strater to *design*. Instead of staying in the design, he has wandered all over the page. I know that he started in correct ambition to make the page good as a whole. *But* it has in this case bitched the original idea. He said in his letter that the stuff had got "*sophisticated*" i.e., apparently lost all quality.

Re yr. last: the only course now open is to cut away superfluous rubbish. *Ci inclus:* the tail of "P" and the scene across the top of the page. And other such delenda in other caps. Such operations as can be performed by simple scission and omission. Considering the *amt.* of work you have put into the matter, I don't see why you want the edtn. damaged by retention of same. As to the quality of line in the "P," it is equal to any 1890, Walter Crane hammered brass. —/—/

As to work: I have had to scrap a full year's work more than once. That is what art is and why it is so damn rare. Mike may think he has spent a year on this job, but most of the year he spent on his private life.

Certainly the edtn is to stay within the 100. The 20 copies I mentioned were intended to come out of the 100 (careful reading of my last effusion shd. [?corroborate] this), and to be for sale.

However, as you point out so Konclusively that the block has to be the same in all copies, that is washed off. And we concentrate on *elimination*—economical, but severe. And you leave Mike to me.

Do you want me to write him? I can't until I see the whole set of letters anyhow. And *had* come to conclusion that it wd. be waste effort and there wasn't enough likelihood of his ever learning anything to make it worth the postage and expenditure of time.

As to how *much time* you are putting into the job, I think I can guess. As anybody who has ever made a good job of anything knows the last 2% of excellence takes more time than the other 98%. That's why art and commerce never savvy one another. — — — —

198: To WILLIAM BIRD

Assisi, 7 May

D.B.: Do recall that the title of that book is "*A DRAFT* of 16 Cantos for a poem of some length." If you will stick to that you will produce something of gtr. val. to collectors. Also it ain't an epic. It's part of a long poem. Yr. best ad is the quiet statement that at auction recently a copy of Mr. P's *A Lume Spento* published in 1908 at $1.00 (one dollar) was sold for $52.50.

No use selling people things on false pretenses. The collector will prefer this half-time report on the poem to a pretended complete edition. — — — —

199: To WILLIAM BIRD

Rapallo, [? November]

Dear Bill: Better put it *nemo obstabat*.

Re Studio. If Hem don't want it, can yr. friends find 2000 fr. recompense for beds, cookstoves, electric wiring? Or how much *can* they find?

I don't suppose the landlord (lady) will accept the same franc rent again, but equivalent in $'s. It is now only $15 a month; it *was* $30 when we took it. ALso do yr. friends want the *cat*? And will they let me leave Koumé's big picture until further notice? If they dislike it, they can put it face to wall on gallery.

Now to something serious. I am leaving this address for parts unknown and they've got to *damn well stay unknown*. Mail from friends will reach me with 48 hour delay. As this wd. be inconvenient for 3 Mts. Press, I confide to you that my address is now: *Albergo Monte Allegro, Rapallo*.

But keep it to yourself. Stuff sent to the [Hotel] Mignon and callers arriving there will reach me soon enough.

I suppose *nemo* is declinable and *nil* isn't. Error by bhloody analogy. Anyhow, I haven't any works of ref. to hand.

No. The Studio is not viewable till I get back.

I am not yet working full six cylinders, but am considerably nearer alive than when you last saw me. — — — —

200: To R. P. BLACKMUR

Rapallo, 30 November

Dear Mr. Blackmur: Adagio! Give me a little time, perhaps I may even manage a little cosmogony. The first impression of life is somewhat chaotic. Mind you, I can't at this stage guarantee to indicate the curvatures of Euc- or non-Euclidean space with a precision that will satisfy the Ecole

Polytechnique. And we agree, je crois, that one can no longer put Mt. Purgatory forty miles high in the midst of Australian sheep land.

Why the 100 readers? There were only five men hanged with Villon, or rather without him. Nobody can pay 25 dollars for a book. I know that. I didn't make the present economic system. The book, of course, can't be made for 25 bucks. Not if Strater and Bird and I were to be paid. That is not the point.

Neither is it my fault if America is so mentally and spiritually rotten as to permit filth like Article 211 of the U.S. Penal Code to lie around empesting the atmosphere.

My American publishers do not exist. It becomes more and more evident that the American publisher must be left out of one's calculations. Likewise English and henglish publishers. There may some day be a cheaper continental edition. One hopes that the Three Mts. and McAlmon's press in Paris will lead to some more general system of printing over here. At least I have suggested the matter. I do not, personally, intend to devote much energy to it; and as I see things at present, I shall never again take any steps whatever to arrange publication of any of my work in either England or America. *Tant pis pour les indigènes.* They will have to cure their own sores and spew out their idols.

There will be a public copy of the XVI in the Malatestiana at Cesena, if Dazzi consents to house it for me. Dad has typescript of XVIII and XIX, but I do *not* want them commented on, *yet.* ETC.

201: To WYNDHAM LEWIS

Rapallo, 3 December

Wall, ole Koksum Buggle: I have just, ten years an a bit after its appearance and in this far distant locus, taken out a copy of the great MAGENTA cover'd opusculus [*BLAST*]. We were hefty guys in them days; an' of what has come after us, we seem to have survived without a great mass of successors, save possibly the young Robert (NOT with the terminal -s) and in another line the young Gawge [Antheil]. (I think I asked A.B. to deliver you a copy of my leetle Blarst on that subjek.)

I have never been converted to your permanenza or delayed dalliance in the hyperborean fogs, ma!! Having rejuvenated by 15 years in going to Paris and added another ten of life by quitting same, somewhat arid, but necessary milieu, etc. . . .

Am also letting out another reef in my long job. Installment of which should soon be inspectable. XVI have gone on, I think with more kick, since arrival here.

Question being (now that we have emerged, or if you like, now that I have emerged) from VARIA, that you found alien: Can we kick up any more or any new devilment??

I am going down to Etna, d.v. in a fortnight. Have you any suggestions?? I don't know what the – – – – you are doing. It strikes me that ten or a dozen BLACK designs about the size of this type sheet wd. be serviceable.

(Can't remember whether I have ever discussed Strater's initials with you. Need something for press, etc. etc. etc. proportion of design lines to type. Lot of boring detail—had to be . . . between printer and orantor.)

Neither here nor there, but perhaps ten or a dozen designs for the two cantos dealing with Hell might be circulatable. As that section of the poem can NOT be circulated freely.

You did years ago in Kens. Gds. discuss a book of verse and designs. In this case it wd. be designs only but with cantos as reference.

You will readily see that the "hell" is a portrait of contemporary England, or at least Eng. as she wuz when I left her.

I don't know that the designs need have much to do with the text, or anything. Merely that I have failed on various occasions in attempts to RAM unrelated designs of yours into the continental maw; and shd. like a try at ramming designs related, or supposed to be related to something that had already gone in.

The de luxe had more than paid for itself some time ago. 2 of 100 buck copies had gone when I last heard, and requisite number of the 25, also some of the 50.

Anyhow, wait till you see the text, and if you approve, or if it starts you, I shd. be glad to try either to make Bird print 'em, or to get some other sort of ballyhoo in action on the matter.

Have also iron in fire for some more general sort of publishing that the 3 Mts. offers and more satisfac. than afforded in Eng. or Am. pub. circles.

(In parenthesis, I aimed a kick at that – – – – D.B. this morning. This purely en passant. Of no importance. Really a country that will tolerate that pyper for any purpose, even that of wiping pigs' arses, is beneath the jo level.)

It rained yesterday, the feast of St. Bibiana. That is said to mean rain for forty days. So that I shd. have leisure to attend to your correspondence if there were any. . . . Benedictions.

P.S. You understand this suggestion of designs *for the hell* is merely an idea that came to me as I was writing this note. If you can think of something better, blaze away. Only I think the idea of ten or twelve BLACKS of size that cd. go by post, and that cd. be done in line block, might be useful. No use trying to drag J.J.A. or W. Robs. or anything or anyone else into it. The rest of our companions presumably HAVE belonged to the decade just past. Apart from Robert and young George I think the rest of the buds have disappeared in unblossomed fragrance.

Whether we can produce further and larger detonation by a new combination I leave to yr. wisdom to konsider.

I can't and don't believe in Mr. Ingres. In-gress. NOR Seurat, nor Greco, nor . . . oh damn it all. . . .

I am not very sure about Cézanne. But I like Rousseau's Baboons, and the warts on Feddy Urbino's nose.

And I think . . . some of the chunks of Manet's execution picture . . . ??? The Timon, on Plate V of *BLAST*, still looks O.K. etc. – – – –

202: To William Bird

Taormina, 26 December

On further consideration, better NOT send copy *Cantos* to Hardy. He may drop off at any moment. Don't want the hell to fall into the wrong hands until there are enough later chants to bring it into proportion with the hole.

Lov to Sally. An a 'appy New Year.

PART THREE

RAPALLO

1 9 2 5

203: To James Joyce

Siracusa, 21 January

Can't make out whether Jean de Gourmont wants to translate it or wants
ME (porca santa) to trad. In any case as he is a gentleman, send him a line.
His firm ought to do *Dubliners*. Also *you* might smoke 'em up to start the
series of continental editions of contemporary English books—before Ber-
lin does.

P.S. J. d. G.'s address is 71 rue des Sts. Péres, in case his handschrift is
more illegible than mine.

204: To William Bird

Palermo, 25 January

Dear Bill: Bozze recd. COMPLIMENTI. *Much* finer than I had expected.
Also various things of Henry's look O.K. in double page [drawing] that
I had disliked in single [drawing].

He has the larffff on us for p. 16 [drawing] because it wd' have goed
better the way he meant, only we fergotttt abaht the "C" on the next page.

Vurry noble work. And up to date *no* misprint of any importance—only
an *i* for an *o* at the end of Piccinini, where it don't matter a cuss. Mos'
remarkable. Even the subject matter don't seem so objectionable.

II. Have you a spare page 31 (Canto IX)? Preferably with red. It don't
matter about the type. I shd. like to send that sheet to the ole archivista at
Ravenna who made me the sketch of the ox-carts. Don't think he reads
English. Want enough of page to show him it is part of a book, not a
detached picture. Can be sent folded once from top to bottom, but not up
the perpendicular middle of page. Not matter of life and death. But if there
is a spare slip of that page, on the top arf, can you send it?

III. —/—/ Am *much* more pleased than I Xpected to be. And satisfied
with Strater where I had before been worried abaht his effex.

Engkore mes compleemengs.

Also size of bok. is pleasant. Can be held on lap, not too heavy, and type
read at that distance. A bhloody ghood job. After awl yr. night sweats.

Placuit occulis.

205: To Simon Guggenheim

Rapallo, 24 February

Dear Sir: Permit me to congratulate you on the terms in which your Memorial Foundation is announced. For the first time I see an endowment that seems to have a chance of being effective. That is to say, the terms of the announcement do not of necessity imply defeat of the announced object.

Are you going to pick the men who can do the work? I mean to say, an American college picks a football team or a rowing crew intelligently; they take men who have the capacity for the job.

Every other educational endowment, at present, tends to produce mediocre students and to stop the good man just as soon as he starts. Thousands of music *students* paid, and hardly one composer, possibly *no* composer of merit. In literature, situation worse.

The most damnable and idiotic reply I ever received in my life was from my old professor, Schelling, when I was trying to persuade him to admit some men of literary ability (proved ability) to the benefits of the literary scholarships of his dept. He wrote me: "The University is not here for the unusual man."

This reply is beyond imagination if you consider what civilization is and what the Renaissance was. And that you can no more get results in art, literature, the amenities, from mediocre minds than you can get athletic records from mediocre bodies.

I am not writing thus hotly, and thus without form and due introduction, on theory. I have in my eye and have had for some time, flagrant cases of men of unusual ability hampered, infamously hampered, by financial stress, while hundreds of mediocrities swallowed up America's heavy endowments.

In the case of T. S. Eliot it may be too late to intervene. I don't know that the man's mind has been killed; he is fairly tough; but for ten years he has been entirely held off from research (that after full academic equipment and post grad. work). And his literary production has been reduced to a minimum, and that not of his best potentiality, from fatigue.

I will go into details if you answer my letter. I have written unceasingly for fifteen years on this and kindred subjects. Literature and the arts are the best means of inter-communication; the most condensed, the least likely to be vain argument.

The whole of our literature suffers from ignorance; and the American parody of German philology is often, most often, *not* a system of enlightenment but a conspiracy to prevent the student from learning more than his teacher.

The second case is George Antheil. I send you, separate, book on him. He don't need to be advertised, but as I have no money I can only take the indirect means. There are plenty of stage pianists; one has in the case of

Antheil a man capable of *making* something; he ought to live in sanitary conditions, with piano and necessary instruments for experiment. I have given him what money I can spare (which amounts to nothing, a month's rent or so) but he ought to be kept a composer, not diluted into an executant.

I take it Marianne Moore of New York is another case where subsidy would be repaid. All these three people are known to be steadily industrious and capable of producing results.

I don't know whether Wyndham Lewis comes within the scope of your endowment.

Gaudier went to his death in the war, but John Quinn would have kept him if he had lived.

I have a sort of right to ask these questions; I have my fifteen years of steady production and research (at my own charge and cost and with opposition rather than help) behind me; and the proof of this is in my published works. I want to know whether your endowment will consider the claims of exceptional men or whether it is to be limited by red tape and examination records.

I will take any trouble you see fit to impose to present the claims of a few men whose work seems to be worthy of support. In each case the nominee is capable both of research, investigation, and execution.

I know how these things go; I remember Harrison's scholarships for the "extension of knowledge," I think the phrase is. I tried to discuss the matter with him (I had held a fellowship under the trust). All I could get out of him was that he "knew nothing about the matter, he wished to erect a monument to his father."

As nearly as I can judge from the terms of your announcement, your endowment represents a new phase. You really want the goods delivered.

The only way to make a civilization is to exploit to the full those individuals who happen to be given by nature the aptitudes, exceptional aptitudes, for particular jobs. By exploit I mean that they must be allowed to do the few things which they and no one else can.

If this note is harsh, set it down to my desire for clarity; if disjointed, to a desire for brevity. (I can explain in a later letter any point that may arouse your attention.) And in conclusion: if there ever was a man who worked constantly and without reward for fifteen years for the very objects your endowment professes to further, I am that man. And as such might perhaps be allowed to help prevent wastage of ability.

206: To H. L. Mencken

Rapallo, February

Dear Mencken: I might have written to you on this matter some time ago, except that one tried to get things done without bothering others. However I seem to be so far out of touch with . . . etc. . . . to such a degree, etc. . . .

Will you have a look at Cheever Dunning's *The Four Winds*, clearing your mind of any impression you may have of his stuff written before this vol.

I sent it to Liveright with hope of getting it published, but L's advisors, whom I have always thought a set of goddamd idiots, seem to have carried the contrary.

I am as aware as you will be that the opus is more or less in the dialect of Swinburne, Rubaiyat, Dowson, etc. . . . but I don't see that it matters (i.e. in this case).

You are in better position than I am for placing the book, as you are less tied up with free verse affiliations (not that I have ever been fanatic on the subject of line length, but nearly everyone who has flocked about me is).

I suppose the day labourers in the—vineyard no longer: hayfield—can see only one thing at a time.

ANNYHOWE: I wish you would have a look at the mss. — — — —

Dunning is 47, first case I have met where a chap has done mediocre and submediocre stuff up to such an age, and then pulled the real thing. (Mr. Eliot don't like it, but then he don't see either Yeats or Hardy); possibly Dunning is of our generation and concealed from the young.

207: To R. P. BLACKMUR

Rapallo, 26 March

Dear Mr. Blackmoor: Stray bits of curiosity re unfinished work have no general utility. Or at least very slight utility.

The question remains whether you are amusing yourself or whether you want to collaborate in a la vie littéraire, a vie rather more potential than actual, but still . . . one has a shot at trying to maintain it, now and again.

I have, as you may know, spent a good deal of time trying to establish or maintain communication between the two sides of the Atlantic, to circulate the better works of the day, etc. . . .

McAlmon, who is possibly the most fertile of your contemporaries, is also the one who is now working harder than anyone else for the general utility, and distribution of interesting contemporary work.

1. Why shouldn't you collaborate with a chap called Edwin Seaver, who writes to me from Woodstock, Ulster Co., N.Y.?

2. With the Three Mountains Press, 19 rue d'Antin, Paris, 1re.

3. As to being of use to me?? You can't be any use re *Cantos*. The Three Mts. can look after them.

There is, however, a certain amount of uncollected prose that ought, perhaps, to appear as a volume. Not on your private press, but from a publisher.

There is the question of whether the eight *Dial* letters, which I happen to have reread this A.M. are more useful than Paulito's recollection of having sat on Sarah's lap.

There is also a point that has not been raised: i.e., whether I haven't outlined a new criticism or critical system. I don't propose to go back over my printed stuff, volumes, etc. and detach this. But there is material for an essay, or a Ph.D. thesis, or a volume.

Even if I had the time I shd. run against copyright and publishers' agreements if I tried to plunder several of my own volumes to make a new short book about the length of my *Antheil*.

As to establishing any sort of milieu in America: it is not my job, and I can't be expected to see from this distance who *could* compose such a bearable milieu.

Both Seaver and H. S. Gorman have written me letters which show traces of intelligence.

At the start a man must work in a group; at least that seems to be the effective modus; later in life he becomes gradually incapable of working in a group. But in any case no one man can do everything, or be the whole of a milieu.

A man, at the start, before he is committed to 78 separate and interlocking feuds, can often establish a communication between various camps, which an older man could not.

I don't know, from here, why various people in America seem to exist to total oblivion of each other: 50, 50, sometimes good reasons, sometimes none.

Seaver seems to be the only person who WANTS to run something to take the place *The Little Review* HAD in 1917. After eight or ten years one might suppose there was room for a little liveliness. Possibly in Paris? and not in the U.S.?? Of course, you may feel that you are isolated and without influence etc., but I doubt if you are any worse off than I have been at various periods, as before starting of *Egoist*, or in case of *L.R.*, etc., or when I was trying to get *Dubliners* into print or in minor cases unrecorded and not worth digging up.

But whatever you want to do, you will I think find the following mode or procedure almost necessary.

1. Make up your mind what you want.

2. Find two or three men of your own generation.

3. Conspire, and incidentally find out what points you agree on, and what you consider essential, and what most important.

4. Invoke the nearest power, not necessarily a very large one. Say in your case, a chap like Gorman who has some access to print.

5. Remember that you can only put across one or two things, or authors, at a time. (Imagism had three specifications, but the 2nd., i.e., the important one, was omitted by the time the noise reached the boobs.)

208: To William Bird

Rapallo, 18 August

Dear Bill: Hemingway has been killed by a bull in Saragossa.

Antheil on way to fighting in the Riff where he hoped to get a little experience and conduct an airplane attack, has been CRUSHED BY A CITROEN auto-caterpillar.

McAlmon is standing for Parliament for division of Bermondsey and Scrope, on conservative ticket, by-election to unseat Johnson Hicks. Good chance of winning.

Mr. Ford Madox Ford is personally supervising the erection of a ceno-taphary sarcophagus in his honour being erected by the Legion of Honour at Chantilly.

Bill Bullitt has been copped by the high-jackers in Texas, but it is hoped he will recover.

Stef has given birth to a son, at Lausanne.

Thought you might like to know, but don't see that you can do any-thing about it. Mr. Joyce has gone on a yachting cruise in his son's steam yacht with sails called the *Daisy Claire*. It is rumored that there are no women among the party. Yrs ever contritely.

209: To William Bird

Rapallo, 24 August

Deer Bull: If you will go thru the archives of the late Mme Rosen, o.b.e., I think you will find a Xtrak from the fascist organ of Rimini stating that the opus is a CAPOLAVORO magnifico.

It was carried thru the village, not on a triumphant ox-cart draped with scarlet, but at any rate with due order by il Commandante. (I declined to see the sindaco, but expressed no unwillingness that he shd. gaze on the edition.)

Marchetti stated that he had shown my poem "anche a Domini Deo."

The copy was placed in the Malatestiana at Cesena by my own honour-able hands with fitting inscription, and various of the studiosi were later assembled (in my absence) and those who cdn't stumble thru English 'ad it hexplained. Dazzi very much surprised when I said Hell cantos wd. not travel thru American post. (That shows what a proper Dantescan educa-tion will do for a man. He said no modern Eyetalian wd. have the guts to do 'em. That they were of a vigore propriamente Americano.)

They really need the GERYON to elucidate 'em. I read Dazzi the Sidg., the Hell and the new typescript (Geryon) XVIII and XIX (which you may sho'tly see).

The copy was *not* sent from yr. office to Cesena; that is prob. why you have no official record. Copy sent here, and I toted it over.

Thanks for the Malatesta Roma and Japan sheets recd. Am sending the Roma to il Commandante; and ascertaining whether the museum is ready to frame and hang the vellum. If it ain't, they will do very nicely here. Am glad to see the vellum, with space enough to see the proportion; couldn't get full effect in print shop. I see some reason for the vellum edtn. I also see that the Whatman takes a better imprint than the Roma, *but* the stink!!!!!!!

and the transparency of the paper seem to me to make it *most* ondesirable sort of paper to print anything but obstetric woiks on. −/−/

210: To William Bird

Rapallo, 11 November

Deer Bill: −/−/ Do you want story of my meeting with Carson the Desert Rat, in 1910, before he made 20 millions? I can't have it spoofed, or Frank Harris'd or presented as a search for Irriwaddi basketwork patterns by an intrepid searcher of the Afrikan sands. I think it might save you thinkin up a weekly article, but decline to supply the data unless you agree to use it soberly or *not at all.* Supposing Carson is the inventer feller I knew, I do, however, appear to have picked a winner, the one and only time I ever tried to pick one outside the purleius of aht and letters. Alas for art and letters that thru no fault of mine or the inventor's the deal did not go thru in 1910. Acc. to last reports C.G.C. is now sittin in a sailor's boardin house in Frisco, with 20 millions and not a gawddamn idea what to do with same (but firmly and rightly determined not to be diddled). I don't know whether it is a case for Wm. Ivy or for the late H. James.

However, you can let your fancy play as to the course of modern art if I had had an income, esp. during the 1912-14 period, Epstein, Gaudier, Lewis, and also to lesser extent, litterchure, with printing and distrib. facilities. And, later, Brancusi's temple etc. Mewsikal seasons, etc.

And in lit. we suppose the moral effect of all the − − − − and demi- − − − − standin' round, hopin' and trying to do right.

Of course, I shd. by now have been puffikly insufferable . . . ma . . . that don't hinder the play of fawncy. Besides it is *not* good publicity at the present stage of our campaign (if you call it that), the point being to inflame in public mind with the idea of lettin us spend its money in a intelligent manner. *And therefore not* a matter to play the ass about.

1926

211: To E. E. Cummings

Rapallo, 10 November

Dear Cummings: Three weeks of bad weather, driving one off the tennis court and the general spread of Vinalism thru the "field of murkn licherture," possibly resurgence of early and perneecious habit, have driven me to consider a infinitesimal review as "outlet."

I suppose you ought to be consulted about it. I shd. like to have you at hand to parody my editorials before they get into print; the difficulty of getting any simple fact or idea into terms simple enough for transmission even to the smallest conceivable number of subscribers . . . etc. . . .

It will not, need we say, pay. I shall probably offer head money, but no rates. Spectamur agendo; or rather, not by the act but the effect shd., etc., the value be judged.

In your case I shd. incline to overlook your early misfortunes.

I wonder if Bishop and his scholastic friends have done any more Provençal philology (a little of it might be useful to annoy my more modern collaborators . . . if I get any). In fact, any measures that wd. save the proposed affair from the monumental pomposity of both our generations. (Parenthesis: can't afford suppression or stoppage by Customs House, at the outset.) However, the natural functions are probably known by now to the majority of our possible readers.

Is there anyone whom one ought to have, that all of our honoured, perhaps too highly, contemporaries absolootly refuse to print at any price?

I don't want anything people can sell, or that they wd. find useful to them in keeping the wolverine from the portals. (Neither do I want slabs of "work in progress" unless there is some vurry speshul reason for it.)

Can't announce publication till I get at least three items of interest.

P.S. No objection to perfectly serious articles IF the authors thereof have anything to say.

In yr. own case, you needn't feel obliged to keep up to your godawful reputation for cleverness (perhaps you find it rather constricting at moments . . . like, let us say, Possum's rep. for decorum and subtlety). There were bits of *The E. Room* that were good and not in the least bit clever.

212: To James Joyce

Rapallo, 15 November

Dear Jim: Ms. arrived this A.M. All I can do is to wish you every possible success.

I will have another go at it, but up to present I make nothing of it whatever. Nothing so far as I make out, nothing short of divine vision or a new cure for the clapp can possibly be worth all the circumambient peripherization.

Doubtless there are patient souls, who will wade through anything for the sake of the possible joke . . . but . . .
having no inkling whether the purpose of the author is to amuse or to instruct . . . in somma. . . .

Up to the present I have found diversion in the Tristan and Iseult paragraphs that you read years ago . . . mais apart ça. . . . And in any case I don't see what which has to do with where. . . . Undsoweiter.

213: To Harriet Monroe

Rapallo, 15 November

Dear Harriet: Have been looking through your last 18 or more numbers, find many of 'em uncut.

My impression is that you have tried ladies' numbers, children's numbers, in fact everything but a man's number. And that you tend to become more and more a tea party, all mères de famille, only one fallen woman among them (and 'er with the sob of repentance).

You might as well admit that trying as you may to be catholic, you miss being any kind of arena for *combat;* you get a general air of mildness. One rich barrytone (Mr. Cullen) in all that soprano . . . and the rest, requested to lower their voices as it might wake popper if they was to sing out.

Fraid I will hav to take the bad boys off your hands and once again take up the hickory.

214: To James Joyce

Rapallo, 19 November

Cher. J.: Sorry, I dunno no lawyer. I cabled my father to start proceedings against Roth last winter; but he didn't as he found it wd. be expensive. However I did succeed in getting my name off the cover. (In return for which recd. several obscene and abusive missives from the impeccable Roth.)

You are in worse shape than I was as you have taken money from him . . . and you have known for some time that he was a crook. All I can suggest is that you write to as many papers as possible, denouncing Roth, and stating that text is garbled and unauthorized. There is no known way of getting at R. as he has only "desk room," i.e. comes in now and again to get his mail in an office containing forty other desks (probably of various flavours and integrities).

I mean if you go to law you have nothing to get damages FROM.

Are you in communication with Collins?? If so, can you get any information from him about the art collector, Barnes. Don't say it is for me.

Re your own affair: certainly write (typed letter? they won't read your script) and SIGN your letter to N.Y. *Post.* That is your best way of annoying R.

Also you better stir up JANE HEAP. It is to interest of *Little Review* as well as yours to stop Roth. I have no friends in America. I don't know whether McAlmon is in N.Y.; you can organize a gang of gunmen to scare Roth out of his pants. I don't imagine anything but physical terror works in a case of this sort (with a strong pull of avarice, bidding him to be BOLD).

He had nothing to make out of me, so consented to remove my name from his title page, after I had written to various offices protesting against his use of my name in his ad. That however was not fear of the law, he merely saw he had more to lose by having me on the war path than to gain by having my name on his sheet.

The man is quite clever. He has more interest in the matter than your lawyer wd. have.

Your only weapon is firmly abusive campaign in the press.

Also you can write to Roth, threatening action. You will get a good deal of impertinence in reply but still. . . .

You can also state in your letters to press that *Parts of* Ulysses *that were printed before suppression are copyright*, and that you are proceeding against Roth. (That may make his subscribers nervous about receiving future numbers.)

However, you have a skunk to deal with and the perfume will possibly fly.

215: To Harriet Monroe

Rapallo, 30 November

Dear Harriet: I have not, at the moment, any strong objection to visiting America. I shall probably be HORRIFIED if or when I do get there. It is probably infinitely worse than anything I am prepared for, despite my being prepared for ANYTHING within the range of my imagination. . . . But still . . . the risk is not a particular deterrent. — — — —

As to lecture tour: the question is simply: what wd. it pay? I can not afford to do it on the cheap. If I blow all that energy, I have got to have a few years free from worry AFTER it.

Poverty here is decent and honourable. In America it lays one open to continuous insult on all sides, from the putridity in the White House down to the expressman who handles one's trunk.

I don't care to place my head under the guillotine or my feet under the trolley wheels. —/—/

Poor Walsh; carried his desire of expression perhaps . . . however . . . (not having seen the poem in question, I can't judge as to the aptitude of his objection). After all he came down on my head in *Poetry* (as also did Carnevali, years ago), and he more recently annoyed Mr. Hemingway, etc. . . . I can't take it very seriously. He had his merits and probably knew his time was short. Also in the midst of his farragos he occasionally said something amusing. Tout ça a une valeur. I don't think Walsh's cursing did anyone any harm. (For example, Thos. Hardy survives.) I never noticed the ref. to the anonymous "D." until your letter called it (this instant) to my attention.

W. was impulsive; the impulse more often generous than not; and nearly always at least grandiose. Better than Coolidgism. Though more obviously open to attack.

Dunning was in Paris last summer. I was very busy with trying out bits of my opera, and saw very little of anyone. Dunning in good enough form to beat me two games of chess and draw one, I think, on the one occasion we had a little spare time.

Yes, I saw your article, if you mean the one that says what a delightful writer I used to be, and what a shame I have probably petered out. Also you blame Wabash for doing in 1907 very much what you did in 1917, ne c'est pas?

Miss Moorhead says she is bringing out another number of T[his] Q[uarter]; I don't know whether she means to use the machine supplement I did for them or NOT. Will prob. be in better shape to discuss matter with yr. brother after it has come out. If she don't issue it, I am on the way (more or less) toward a book on "Art and Machines," both plastic and acoustic phase. Perhaps your brother cd. help me on one or two matters when or if the said book materializes.

Have never met Westcott. Thought he was one of The Dial's "young men."

Carnevali's address is Il Cavalletto, Bazzano, Bologna, Italy.

I don't honestly know anything more. His letters SEEM active enough. Last one was to thank me for a pile of books and old magazines, which were what he had asked for. (Last year he asked for clothes . . . I don't know whether the difference in the request indicates a difference in degree of need, or only in quality.)

I personally think extremely well of Mussolini. If one compares him to American presidents (the last three) or British premiers, etc., in fact one can NOT without insulting him. If the intelligentsia don't think well of him, it is because they know nothing about "the state," and government, and have no particularly large sense of values. Anyhow, WHAT intelligentsia?

What do the intelligentsia think of Henry Ford? He has given people a five day week, without tying it up in a lot of theoretical bunk. I can't imagine ANY labour party consenting to the results; it puts such a lot of "secretaries" out of a job.

Re your question is it any better abroad for authors: England gives small pensions; France provides jobs. A ninth rate slob like Claudel gets a job as ambassador. Giraudoux, Morand, Cros, etc., etc., get quite comfortable posts. Italy is full of ancient libraries; the jobs are quite comfortable, not very highly paid, but are respectable, and can't much interfere with the librarians' time.

As to "betterness," if I were a citizen of any of these countries I wd. have some sort of appui, which is unthinkable in America. As for professorships??? I have not been overwhelmed with offers . . . I reckon the danger is not imminent.

You might devote a special number, poesy contest for best estimate of psychology of the man who paid 20,000 bucks for copy of Poe's Tammammwhatever it is. Interest on 20,000 bucks wd. keep a live writer for life. Wot these dastards lack is a little intelligence. Also I spose they want a quick turn over. 20,000 invested in Poe in 1850???? what price now? Try it on yr. financial edtr.

P.S. What has become of A.C.H.?

216: To James Joyce

Rapallo, 25 December

Dear Jim: I answered S[ylvia] B[each]'s letter explaining why I do not care to sign your protest. I.e. I consider it a miss-fire, that omits the essential point and drags in an irrelevancy.

I am glad SOME use has at last been found for Claudel.

I enclose a note that you can use as p.s. to the general protest.

Merry Xmas and greetings to the family.

217: To James Joyce

Rapallo, 25 December

My Dear Joyce: My only reason for not signing your protest is that I consider it misdirected. To my mind the fault lies not with Mr. Roth, who is after all giving his public a number of interesting items that they would not otherwise get; but with the infamous state of the American law which not only tolerates robbery but encourages unscrupulous adventurers to rob authors living outside the American borders, and with the whole American people which sanction the state of the laws. The minor peccadillo of Mr. Roth is dwarfed by the major infamy of the law.

You are perfectly at libirty to publish this statement or to make any use of it you think fit. Parts of *Ulysses are* protected, as they appeared in an American periodical, were copyright, and were not suppressed. I understand that Roth has reprinted these parts, in which case he is liable to due penalty.

1 9 2 7

218: To James Joyce

Rapallo, 2 January

Dear J.: First number of my new periodical designed to deal with various matters not adequately handled elsewhere has gone to press. I don't see that it can be much direct and immediate use to you. It comes out 3 times a year, so that serialization is out of the question.

I think, and always have thought, that the "sample of woik in prog" stunt was bad. *The transat.* did it because there simply wasn't enough copy to fill the so large review.

If I had an encyclopedicly large monthly, the kewestion wd. be different. Present view is that your daruk pool shd. be sold whole on *Ulysses* and that further distribution of bits wd. do final sales more harrum than good. However, I may be wrong. The law-court bit, livens up.

Wot I nevurtheles suggess re the oncoming review is that it will do no harm to have it circulate freely to such as will pay for it. There are plenty of seguidores after the act; but it can do no harm to establish a means of communication that in case of emergency will not have to stop, to hem, to haw, to whit, to whom, etc.

Notice of forthcoming novels, romans, etc., can be conveyed and at any rate, the air of ambiguity so . . . shall we say . . . widely ambient . . . etc. . . . vb sap.

219: To Sisley Huddleston

Rapallo, 13 February

Dear Sisley Huddleston: Trust you noticed that 250 socialists were arrested after the Antheil concert in Budapesth. Tis, we ween, such stuff as nooz are made of.

The young rip is now loose somewhere in Italy with cat, rucksack, no proper clothing and nothing deeply resembling an address. O[lga] R[udge] stood (as the Eyetalians say) to give a Mozart concert in Rome; but judging from telegrams, mainly indefinite and illegible, the young Antheil will prob. arrive in time to stop it. Also with Casella out of Rome, as O.R. has long been trying to ram Antheil down C's thorax or into his concerts, it is to be presumed that they will thrust his music incontinent upon the Romans.

As G.A. is due to sail to N.Y. on the 24th for orchestral show and as his American manager is worrying him for publicity and as he passes it on to me, I also, leaning toward your vaster bulk, offer the facts to your clemency.

I am telling ces jeunes gens to send you their photos and program (if you don't want same, chuck 'em into the scrap and blame it on me).

Possibly the vision of G.A. arriving on platform in walking togs, with cat and rucksack, to somewhat annoyance of the blondine young gent. engaged to play Mozart piano parts, etc., perhaps all this is too picturesque for your high-class and uplifting journals. (And I am not sure you didn't tell me you do not descend to illustration by photo . . . but I am taking the chance.)

If you want any more definite data, I will try to have any sent you after the fact, by post or wire.

The show takes place on the 19th at the Sala Capuzucchi, Rome. Antheil or no Antheil. Saturday afternoon.

It is all very bouleversant, as A. was expected to go from Buda to Paris in an orderly fashion. *Not,* of course, that I ought to feel paternal responsibility in such cases. . . .

Part of the beauty of my anticipation is the vision of the young pyanist already, I believe, engaged for the show. He is tall, trés blond, trés beau, composes a bit on his own and fawncies himself a good deal. He has a name like Circus Maximus. Of course, he may refuse to walk on. It all offers "colour," perhaps lit. val. rather than news val.

The Roman pianist, for one so young, is very classic in his taste; the Italians only discovered Strawinsky last year. . . .

One shouldn't be nasty about it. Respighi is personally charming. Strawinsky I suppose is *not* (judging from looks, tho I have never met him). Etc. –/–/

220: To WILLIAM BIRD

Rapallo, 4 March

Dear Zsoiseau: Yrs. with the camels to hand.

Wot can you do with Olga's Mussolini business? Have now more details.

Do you want to syndicate Miss Gibson's full article? The *Herald* has been goddam silly. Miss G. sent 'em the stuff last Friday, with a lot of highlights.

Olga pulled it off on her own (no Embassy or Murkn Academy strings) *after* young Gawge's departure. Muss prefers classics, but O. did what she cd. to pave way for Antheil audition later, bringing talk round to modern music and machines. The lowdown Greek Rhooshian Amphitheatre tried to crab Gawge and spake contempshus of people who take piano for "percussion instrument." "So it *is*," sez Muss, taking the wind out of Mons. Circus Minimus. – – – –

221: To HARRIET MONROE

Rapallo, 23 March

Note the underlined from "Wings," advertisement of Licherary Guild.

That is, the selections for one year will probably contain six books of fiction (novels and short stories) *and six selected from history, biography, travel, essays, science, and public affairs.*
Van Doren, Glenn Frank, Z. Gale, J. W. Krutch, Henrik van Loon, Elinor Wylie.

I dare say it is the best they can do; but they all (??) represent . . . 2nd-rate aspiration. No need of raising that point. Point for you is that they exclude poetry. Point for me is that they represent the parochial standard; but pass that. They are the present equivalent of "Concord" group of the last century. At least I bet halluf a dollah on it. — — — —

Question is: can *Poetry* organize a similar scheme; not of course printing the books, but selecting 6 vols. of poetry a year (prob. better begin on six) and getting combination price from the publishers in return for distributing a (few) thousand copies of each?

And get a jury with at least one member who has heard of an international standard of values, who don't think patriotism consists in protecting the inferior product but in bringing it up to top level and making it bite on the nail.

How many subscribers have you?? What percent of 'em would agree beforehand to say 10 bucks a year for 6 vols. of selected poesy? If there were a thousand, even expensive books like *Personae* could be supplied in paper or cardboard back at that rate. I mean books that came inside price would be uniform with general edition and expensive books cd. be done in cheaper paper and binding from the same plates.

This might take a little time. The immediate thing is to cry "HARO!!" in about two lines and quote the Lit. Guild exclusion. Or even better (don't say the idea comes from me) print the Lit. Guild exclusion and a query:

Are there as a start 1000 readers of *Poetry* who want to combine in co-operative buying of the best poetry published?

The scheme presents difficulties and suggestions are in order as to how it can best be managed.

Please say whether you are for it unconditionally; whether you want only new books; or whether you want us to start with a group of six of the best vols. already published. No harm in doing both.

Census: Eliot, Sandburg, Bodenheim, H.D., Carlos Williams, Pound. Go on, fill out list. I spose everybody has *Spoon River*.

1st, you've got to see how many will subscribe. 2nd, *if* the publishers will issue special edtn. for the co-opters—extra 1000—at special price.

An offer on six good names for delivery in 4 months' time might lead to possibility of a second list of newer people. Rorty, Cullen, whoever they are.

I dunno who is going to be bloody well bored by being *jury*. I spose Bill Williams has the necessary patriotism. I spose I'm the goat, having proposed it. I suggest Bodenheim or some irreconcilable to keep it from getting dead and academic and ladylike.

At any rate *if* I am roped in I've got to have ONE other live member on a committee of not more than six. I spose there'll have to be one soft-shelled weeping rube to keep in touch with the great heart of the republic. You get roped in as the only person who reads all the rot pubd, not as jury but as executant. If you're too weary of combat, you might let M. Strobel or Dillon branch off and take charge of the show (not Hen. Fuller, too old; the thing wants someone active). —/—/

222: To Homer L. Pound

Rapallo, 11 April

Dear Dad: —/—/ Afraid the whole damn poem is rather obscure, especially in fragments. Have I ever given you outline of main scheme ::: or whatever it is?

1. Rather like, or unlike subject and response and counter subject in fugue.

A. A. Live man goes down into world of Dead
C. B. The "repeat in history"
B. C. The "magic moment" or moment of metamorphosis, bust thru from quotidien into "divine or permanent world." Gods, etc.

In Canto XX, fragment in *Exile*. Nicolo d'Este in sort of delirium after execution of Parisina and Ugo. (For facts vide, I spose, the *Encyclopedia Britan*.)

"'And the Marchese
was nearly off his head
after it all.'"

Various things keep cropping up in the poem. The original world of gods; the Trojan War, Helen on the wall of Troy with the old men fed up with the whole show and suggesting she be sent back to Greece.

Rome founded by survivors of Troy. Here ref. to legendary founding of Este (condit (founded) A*testen*, Este).

Then in the delirium, Nicolo remembers or thinks he is watching death of Roland. Elvira on wall or Toro (subject-rhyme with Helen on Wall). Epi purgos (on wall); peur de la hasle (afraid of sunburn); Neestho (translated in text: let her go back); ho bios (life); cosi Elena vivi (thus I saw Helen, misquote of Dante).

The whole reminiscence jumbled or "candied" in Nicolo's delirium. Take that as a sort of bounding surface from which one gives the main subject of the Canto, the lotophagoi: lotus eaters, or respectable dope smokers; and general paradiso. You have had a hell in Canti XIV, XV; purgatorio in XVI etc.

The "nel fuoco" is from St. Francis' "cantico": "My new spouse placeth me in the flame of love." Then the remarks of the opium smoker about the men who sailed under Ulysses.

"Voce profondo": with deep voice.

And then resumé of Odyssey, or rather of the main parts of Ulysses' voyage up to death of all his crew.

For Elpenor, vide Canto I.

Ear wax, ears plugged so they couldn't hear the sirens.

Neson amumona, literally the narrow island: bull-field where Apollo's cattle were kept.

Ligur aoide: keen or sharp singing (sirens), song with an edge on it.

That gets most of the foreign quotations.

Tan mare fustes: is Roland's remark to moor who comes up to finish him off, as nearly as I can remember his sword is broken, but he smashes the moor over the head with his horn (olifans: elephant: olifant tusk) and then dies grumbling because he has damaged the ornaments on the horn and broken it. Tan mare fustes, colloquial: you came at a bad moment. Current cabaret song now: J'en ai marre: I'm fed up.

Any more ke-weschuns???

As to the Rodker: I rather think he gets more into the 90 pages (that makes the complete nouvelle) than most novelists get into 300. However. . . . —/—/

223: To H. L. Mencken

Rapallo, 27 April

Dear Henry: Something ought to be done about this scoundrel Roth. Damn his impertinence. Bloody crook; and the American copyright law is a worse crook than he is.

Strikes me that you people who pay your authors are as likely to lose by this impertinent piracy as any one else. If he merely swipes everything that isn't copyright, he can obviously undersell "honest enterprise."

A man named Vestal has put up a decent bill that wd. stop Rothism. Somebody ought to get out and root for it.

Also *you*, confound you, with your columns on asinine legislation ought to dig out Article 211, U.S. Penal Code. You can find it in my *Instigations* if you haven't it elsewhere.

224: To Harriet Monroe

Rapallo, 24 September

Dear H.M.: Re your last private communication on the subject of pipe dreams. I have never said you could make poesy out of dollars. I have—any time these past twenty years—said that certain methods could be used advantageously for the amelioration and increase of works of art. The effect shows more in arts other than poetry, where the artist is bound by material need in his actual production. I mean he has to have expensive raw material, paint, stone, a good fiddle, or he has to hire or have hired expensive executants for musical or dramatic representation.

A few kicks are probably good for the poet, but it is not proved that he should receive a steady stream of them from cradle to monument. Maecenas did not pick the two best poets of his time, but it has taken 2000 years to start a reaction in favour of the fellow he missed.

Dante was better than Petrarch, but the fact can not be blamed on the gents who asked Petrarch to dinner.

From the patron's angle, Giusto de Conti and Bassinio were the best poets of their day. There will be no celebrations on their cinquecentennials, but neither will there be celebrations on the cinquecentennials of any of their contemporaries; they stretched their legs under the same table that had received Pier della Francesca, Pisanello, Giovan Bellini, Battista Alberti, Mino da Fiesole; and the young Bassinio, at least, profited, presumably in head as well as in stomach.

I have never contended that the American millionaire or "ploot" was an idiot. It have said and still maintain that he is an uncivilized barbarian usually unpleasant and never interested in the arts. He will endow any number of "institutions" employing any number of boneheaded dullards with "degrees," in order that they may still further befuddle the young. He will, in rarer cases, express his dislike of the arts by committees.

If he or she be that curse of god, the "amateur," he or she will express his or her dislike of the arts by trying to present his or her dablets in lieu of the better contemporary work.

And in proof of bluff we have but to observe the "hard-headed" American business man when really interested in something and wishing to improve the quality of creation. Thus *Time* for Aug. 8 re Col. E. H. R. Green (son of Hetty) who is interested in aviation. Sic loquitur Green: "I want young fellows with good ideas and no money . . . to feel that there is a place where they can come. I will grub-stake them when their ideas appear sound and let them perfect and experiment. If they develop anything marketable, they can take it out and it is theirs."

That is to say he knows what he wants, he expects to be interested in seeing it happen *now* and not in A.D. 2547 under the auspices of a committee appointed by the trustees. He is not making a collection of the extant fragments of the war-machinery found in Byzantium or of models of Leonardo's project for a monoplane. Neither does he expect to have apoplectic stroke when some fellow invents something he hadn't thought of. Q.E.D.

225: To GLENN HUGHES

Rapallo, 26 September

Dear Dr. Hughes: Your letter (7th inst) has crossed mine.

It wd. not interest me in the least to write my literary autobiography. You might put one of your students onto the job; wd. probably educate *him* a good deal, but I don't see how that form of retrospection cd. be expected to count as part of my own mental life, and I have no inclination to start dying before it is necessary.

As to contemporaries, since you ask it, I will, privately, go so far as to say that Lawrence was never an Imagist. He was an *Amy*gist. Ford dug him up and boomed him in *Eng. Rev.* before Imagism was launched. Neither he nor Fletcher accepted the Imagist program. When the prospect of Amy's yearly outcroppings was by her assured, they agreed to something different. This is not an attack on L's ability as a writer but merely to emend the statement in yr. circular.

The name was invented to launch H.D. and Aldington before either had enough stuff for a volume. Also to establish a critical demarcation long since knocked to hell.

T. E. Hulme was an original or pre-.

Bill Williams was as "original" as cd. be managed by writing from London to N.J. Flint was the next acquisition, tho really impressionist. He and Ford and one or two others shd. by careful cataloguing have been in another group, but in those far days there weren't enough non-symmetricals to have each a farm to themselves. Several others have since faded. Lawrence wasn't asked, and Fletcher declined.

The test is in the second of the three clauses of the first manifesto.

Even this amount of reminiscence bores me exceedingly.

226: To James S. Watson, Jr.

Rapallo, 20 October

Dear Watson: It is impossible for me to accept an award except on Cantos or on my verse as a whole.

It would also be foolish, I think, to send in a prose squib for a criticism of some Whifflepink like friend Morand. There has been no definite request for Cantos, but there is no other verse available, and will be none. The available detachable sections are Canto 22 and the part of 27. XXII is probably too frivolous for your purpose. I suggest that you use the XXVII by itself; it will take less room and probably cause less friction. It is also possible to take the Gibraltar fragment, by itself, from point beginning "And a voice behind me in the street" on page 17 (or red 3).

As the immediate appearance in the *Dial* is largely a formality perhaps the XXVII will serve.

It wd. be stupid to make the award on prose-basis as my prose is mostly stop-gap; attempts to deal with transient states of Murkn imbecility or ignorance.

227: To Glenn Hughes

Rapallo, 9 November

Dear Hughes: On reading over my translation of *Ta Hio*, it strikes me that the acrid and querulous preface I had sketched is a bloody impertinence and that any attempt to force local application, talk about need of present America, etc., bloody bureaucracy, etc. etc., would be a damned impertinence. I mean tacking my bloomink preface onto the work itself. Hope you'll agree.

Seems to me it will be introd. enough if you say in the prospectus:

In this brochure (or chapbook) Mr. Pound does for the first of the Confucian classics what he did, in *Cathay*, for Rihaku.

Any question of method or interpretation of ideograph can wait for or be referred to Fenollosa's "Essay on the Chinese Written Character."

Thanks for the Japanese poets. I like it. In fact the first clean translation from Japanese I have seen since I did my own job with Fenollosa's remains.

I wonder if Iwasaki is trained in No or if you and he want to undertake revision of my redaction of Fenollosa's paper on the Noh (or No; better I think spelled with the "h" to avoid homograph with simple Murkn negative).

Don't know whether you know the work (pub. by Macmillan, now out of print). I think Fenollosa did a lot that ought not to be lost. I had not the philological competence necessary for an ultimate version, but at the same time Mrs. F's conviction was that Fen. wanted it transd *as* literature not as philology.

Whether it wd. be more bother than worth to go over it and correct errors, I know not. I might want to look over result and possibly re-revise, though judging by 3 Jap lady-poets, not to any gt. extent. General principle of not putting in mere words that occur in original when they contribute nothing to the SENSE of the translation.

One wants a Jap on the job, and one wants a Jap who knows Noh. I shd. like to protect Fenollosa from sonzovbitches like —— and in general from the philologs who were impotent till Fen. showed the way (via y.v.t.) and who then swarmed in with inferior understandings.

I am perfectly willing to split the proceeds with you and Iwasaki, 50/50. Mainly depends on how much revise and correction Iwa. thinks the work needs.

If the work were copper-bottomed and guaranteed correct in every detail, I don't think there ought to be difficulty in getting a good publisher or in making it a "standard work on the subject." I take it you don't pub. large vols. Would try this on Harper or Scribners' I think.

At present it is the scattered fragments left by a dead man, edited by a man ignorant of Japanese. Naturally any sonvbitch who knows a little Nipponese can jump on it or say his flatfooted renderings are a safer guide to the style of that country.

This offer is intended as a compliment.

Re the preface to *Ta Hio*: I don't think I ought to use Kung as a shoehorn for a curse on American State Dept. and the Wilson-Harding Administrations, etc. At least thass the way I feel this A.M.

Re printing: I think text of *Ta Hio* shd. be one size type and commentators' remarks (including my own) another, or possibly better italic. I had thought of having three sizes: 1) Text; 2) Comment; and 3) transtr's notes; but think it would prob. make ugly page.

Re preface: Wot's use telling 'em they are damn sick? I mean I prefer trying giving 'em the medicine; if they don't feel better after it or don't feel they needed it, woss use telling 'em?

Re the "Written Character": Will enclose it, or better send it on in a day or two. I have permission from Liveright to use it in any way we like.

I think it ought to have separate printing apart from huge bulk of *Instigations*.

Re *Ta Hio*: Everything one tends to put into a preface merely tends to draw red herrings across trail. Most of what I had written wd. merely raise irrelevant issues re state of America, damnd perversion of Constitution, sonsovbitches in office, of collapse of Xtianity, goddamnability of all monotheistic Jew, Mohammed, Xtn. buncomb, etc.

So I

Cut it aht. If they can't see from the text, they won't see any better from being irritated by my irritability beforehand. — — — —

228: TO HARRIET MONROE

Rapallo, 29 December

Dear H.M.: Orl rit, you put in your bloomink feetnotes, you follow up and stick in this answer:

Madame: The point of view taken in your footnote to my article in yr. December number is precisely the point of view that I do not take. It appears to me to be the "remains of bourgeois mentality." I mean that I do not consider the practice of poetry any more degrading than the practice of chemical research, and I consider original composition rather more important than the writing of semi-ignorant theses about the work or laundry-lists of deceased authors.

In our several thousand of nearly useless institutions of learning no student has ever been known to reject a scholarship or fellowship or any form of endowed sop. In fact, budding millionaires often grab them with great joy in order to slew off an inferiority complex and show that they are just as good as the sons of the proletariat.

If you wd. once divest yourself of the notion of the author as an object of charity or of the feeding of authors as a form of preservation of the unfit and arrive, even if slowly, at the idea of "aiding production." Confound it: PRODUCTION!

Am I expected to respect either myself or anyone else because some graduated ribbon-clerk offers me 75 bucks for writing blah in a false-pearl and undies monthly?

Did any 100% Ohioan ever offer Burbank a large salary to interrupt his work and write ads for the local florist?

There is one source of confusion, namely that a man can get more for doing rotten writing than he can for doing rotten chemistry. The standards in science are easier for examiners to get at: or at least they are supposed to be. The confusion between the scientist and the fake is less likely to occur. But this should not be allowed to obscure the whole and main difference between stimulating *production* and pampering the producer.

Between definite individual desire to stimulate the arts (which means Maecenism) and pure communism there is only a middle ground of muddle, blah, sentimentality. Pure communism seems unlikely to affect the U.S. in our time, pending which I suggest emergency measures on a line known to be quite efficient. But for gawdzake cut out the idea of the highschool boy and his gilded medal.

1 9 2 8

229: To René Taupin

Vienna, May

Cher Monsieur: Naturellement, si vous accordez une inversion du temps, dans une relativité Einsteinienne, il vous semblera probable que j'ai réçu l'idée de l'image par des poèmes d'H.D. écrit *après* que cette idée etait réçue. Voir les *dates* des livres divers.

J'ai tant écrit et publié à ce sujet—et je ne peux pas écrire sans machine à écrire.

En 1908-9 à Londres (avant le début de H.D.): cénacle T. E. Hulme, Flint, D. Fitzgerald, moi, etc. Flint, beaucoup français-ifié, jamais arrivé à condensation. { concentration / avoir centre } Symbolistes français > les "90's" à Londres.

contemporaine
veut dire ⊃ equivalence

Technique de T. Gautier in "Albertus."

Mais tout ça, j'ai imprimé. Voir *Pavannes et Divisions* et *Instigations*. Est-ce-que on peut causer?—ici maintenant ou à Rapallo en Juillet? Poésie anglaise (la langue même < à racines fr. consider elements de la langue:
"Anglo-saxon"
latin (église – loi)   prin.
                            2nd
français 1400
latin scientifique
greek. .   "

Influence fr. sur moi—relativement tard.

Rapports fr.>eng. via Arthur Symons etc. 1980. Baudelaire, Verlaine, etc.

F. S. Flint special number *Poetry Review*, Londres 1911 ou 1912. Fort difference entre Flint: (*tolerance* pour *tous* les fautes et imbécillités des poètes français.) Moi—examen très sévère—et intolérance.

Soi-disant "imagists"—"bunch of goups" trop paresseux pour supporter sévérité de mes premiers "Don'ts" et du clause 2me du manifest: "Use no *superfluous* word."

Certes progrès du *technique* poétique.—Fr. en avant. Gautier "Albertus," England 1890-1908. Ce que Rimbaud atteint par intuition (génie) dans certaines poèmes, érigé en esthétique conscient (??peut-être)—je ne veux pas prendre une gloire injuste—mais pour tant que je sais. J'en ai fais une esthétique plus ou moins systématique—et j'ai pu citer certaines poèmes de R. comme example. (*Mais* aussi certaines poèmes de Catulle.)

Et c'est certain que apart certains procédés d'expression—R. et moi n'avons point de rassamblance. Mais presque *toute* l'expérimentation, technique en poésie de 1830—jusqu'à moi—était faite en France.

En fait de "poètes," c'est une autre affaire. Il y avait Browning (même Swinburne), Rosetti, E. Fitzgerald, qui s'interessaient plus qu'aux sujets à la matière à exprimer nouveaux qu'aux procédés d'expression.

Vous avez en *Poetry*, Chicago, (1912, je crois) mon premier citation des Fr. contemporaines. Temps des unanimistes.

Avec toute modestie, je crois que j'étais orienté avant de connaître les poètes français modernes. Que j'ai profité de leurs inventions techniques (comme Edison ou aucun autre homme de science profite des découvertes). Y'a, aussi, les anciens: Villon, les Troubadours.

Vous trouverez en mon *The Spirit of Romance*, publié 1910, ce que je savais-avant d'aborder les Fr. moderns.

C'est probable que la France a appris de l'Italie et de l'Espagne. L'Angleterre de la France et que la France ne peut rien absorber ou apprendre de l'anglais. (?Problème—pas dogme.)

Autre dissociation à faire: quelque fois on apprend, ou subit "influence" d'une idée—quelque fois en lutte contre barbarisme, on cherche un appui —on s'arme du prestige d'un homme civilizé et reconnu pour combattre l'imbécillité américaine.

J'ai cité Gourmont, et je viens de donner un nouveau version du *Ta Hio* de Confucius, parce que j'y trouve des formulations d'idées qui me paraissent utile pour civiliser l'Amérique (tentatif). Je révère plutôt le bon sens que l'originalité (soit de Rémy de G., soit de Confucius).

Pour y revant: Je crois que la poésie français soit *trés difficilement* raciné de un bon poésie anglaise ou américaine, *mais* que la *technique* des poètes français était *certainement* en état de servir d'*education* aux poétes de ma langue—de temps de Gautier, jusqu'à 1912.

Que les poétes *essentials*, a cette étude, se reduissent à Gautier, Corbière, Laforgue, Rimbaud. Que depuis Rimbaud, aucun poète en France n'a inventé rien de fondamentale. Y avait des modifications interessants, des presque-inventions, des applications. (Voir *Instigations* ou mon numéro de *Little Review* sur Poètes Français.)

Je crois que Cocteau, que vous glorifiez comme metteur-en-scène et negligez comme fort bon poète mineur, a fait quelque chose pour libérer la langue fr. des ses manchettes (*Poésies* 1920). C'est pour la *langue* française—parfaitement inutile pour nous autres qui écrivons en américain —veut dire: invention d'utilité locale.

Peut être vous aurez un instrument de pensée. Si vous vous proposez la question.

Est-ce-que il existe *une* langue anglais pour exprimer les lignes de Rimbaud? Je ne *dis pas* un traducteur capable de le faire, mais est-ce-que cette langue existe? (comme moyen)—et depuis quand?

De cette balance, vous devez trouver les relations justes—au moins du côté technique.

Si vous voulez, vous pouvez m'envoyer votre étude avant de l'imprimer et alors je pourrais indiquer les differences de vue, ou les erreurs (si y en aurait) de fait, de chronologie mineur, etc.

P.S. Je crois que ma sévérité soit mieux la reputation de la lit. fr. que lés épanchements des francophiles ou parasites qui cherchent à faire passer les mauvais poètes fr. au premier rang. Qu'on bâtit une gloire plus sûre, en voulant présenter les auteurs solides (même si de nombre rostreint, qu'en y ajoutante les flaques, les gonflés, etc.)

Je crois que Eliot, dont les premiers poésies ont montré influence de Laforgue, a moins de respect pour Laf. que le respect que j'ai pour Laf.

Gautier j'ai étudié et je le révère. Ce que vous prenez pour influence de Corbière est probablement influence direct de Villon.

"   de Tailhade, superficielle
"   " Jammes !!j'espère que non.

Quant aux sonnets? Catulle, Villon, Guido, Cavalcanti, des grecs qui n'etaient pas Pindar, des Chinois.

Und überhaupt ich stamm aus Browning. Pourquoi nier son père?

Symbole?? Je n'ai jamais lu "les idées des symbolistes" sur ce sujet.

Dans ma jeunesse j'avais peut être quelqu'idée reçue du moyen âge. Dante, St. Victor, dieu sais qui, des modifications via Yeats (ce dernier plein de symbolisme méconnu—via Boète, symbolisme français, etc.)— mais je ne sais pas dénuder les traces.

Je ne me rappelle rien de Gourmont au sujet de "symbole."

Ma *reforme:*

1. Browning—denué des paroles superflus
2. Flaubert—mot juste, présentation ou constatation

Reforme metrique plus profonde—date de 1905 on commence avant de connaître Fr. modernes.

J'ai "lancé" les Imagistes (anthologie *Des Imagistes;* mais on doit me dissocier de la décadence des Imagistes, qui commence avec leurs anthologies postérieures (même le première de ces anthologies)).

Mais "voui": l'idée de l'image doit "quelque chose" aux symbolistes français via T. E. Hulme, via Yeat<Symons<Mallarmé. Come le pain doit quelque chose au vanneur de blé, etc.

Tant d'operations intermédiaires.

Mais aussi à Catulle (pas mendès)—Q. V. Catullus—qui avait une conception fort nette à plusieurs mille ans.

Mais ma connaissance des poètes fr. mod. et ma propagande pour ces poètes en Amérique (1912-17-23) venait en sens genérale *après* l'inception de l'Imagisme à Londres (1908-13-14).

Je crois que l'influence soit de Laforgue (par Eliot) soit de Maupassant sur l'Amérique est souvent assez de 2me, 3me, 15me main.

230: To H. L. MENCKEN

Rapallo, 3 September

Respected Mencken: Thanks fr. yr. brotherly words. You "advocate" the severance of Maryland, but do I not set example by action? At any rate the State of Pound did very largely sever 20 years ago. It is the only state in which I have any preponderant authority or even influence. My weight with Vare wd. be less than a milligram. And with the Borah of my native mountainy fastnesses!!! Even my mild arguments with natives still there resident have failed to rouse up an assassin.

I spose my murkn correspondents reveal to me things they wdnt. tell to the local Y.M.C.A. secs. or to the alderman of their villages, i.e., that I am prob. as well informed as to the events in our vaterland as I wd. be if in residence there.

I dunno wot I cd. shoot on publicke questions, more'n what you do yourself. I believe I have introduced the word bureaucrat into the nashunul langwidge. At least an editor I met in Vienner hadn't heard of there being any govt officials until I told him. Yaas, I told him there wuz. He said they caused no discontent in his N.Y. circle.

I'm puffickly willing to fire depth-charge at any time if anyone wants to read the sound of my syllables. Mr. Villard still thinks I'm a lily-carrying aeeesthete with green hair and blue whiskers. He only let me in on Sundays and holidays. I do what I can to keep the Bill of Rights waving above the Paris office of the Chicago *Trib.* (heaven knows what they print on the Lake front).

I go for days, at times even weeks (not probably very plural) without likker; but shd. hate to feel I had to square the cop or the local J.P. every time I wanted to buy a box of Lowney's chocolates or have a little rosso with my spaghetti.

Besides all this bloody business must cut into one's TIME. HELL!!!!!

States Rights, surtunly, sah. But if not them, at least our own.

231: TO JAMES VOGEL

Rapallo, 21 November

My dear Vogel: Were any of the things mentioned in yrs. of 8th and 9th inst. otherwise, I shd. not have bothered to give yr. name to Zuk.

The science of GROUPS is as follows: at the start you must find the 10% of matters that you agree on and the 10% plus value in each other's work.

You "all" presumably want some sort of intelligent life *not* dependent on cash, and salesmanship.

Take our groups in London. The group of 1909 has disappeared with-

out the world being much the wiser. Perhaps a first group can only prepare way for a group that will break through.

The one or two determined characters will pass thru 1st to 2nd or third
groups.

I mistrust ....n, not from fault of heart, but that he is sterile. All his
groups have had sterilizing effect on themselves. A critical ideal. *No* use
starting to crit. each other at start. *Anyhow* it requires more crit. faculty
to discover the hidden 10% positive, than to fuss about 90% obvious im-
perfection. You talk about style, and mistrusting lit. socs. etc. Nacherly.
Mistrust people who fuss about paint and finish before they consider
girders and structure.

Recently recd. book from Milan with dedicace: from Scheiwiller, em-
ployee, publisher and messenger boy. He at least hasn't waited to make
his pile, he is a clerk in Hoepli's, but he is also publisher of "Chirico,
Prampolini, and I don't know who else."

Also if you yell loud enough, if you get Mrs. S—— to weep loud enough
over copyright infamy, you can have yr. books printed here. *Or* cave in
the U.S. printing prices. *You have got to damm and dynamite the American
censorship and customs interference.* It all hangs together. As for rich fat
ladies, *don't* try their intelligence. Tell 'em the arts are being murdered
by copyright infamy, printing costs, customs barriers, copyright lack of
law. *If they try to act and fail*, the sheckels may flow. In any case effort
wd. educate 'em.

Money won't do a damn thing in the arts *by itself*. It can't. The essential is inside the artist. Don't fergit that. He really has the whip hand.

As you say, the murkn intelligentsia is soft. It is not organized, and
hasn't the ghost of a suspicion of how much power (latent) it has.

However, I ought not to have to tell 'em the first, second, third, fourth
and fifth times. Someone on the spot ought to *start* telling 'em, and when
they get to wavering point, let me come in as authority or reserve troops.

It will economize some energy if what I write to you can be passed on
to Zuk. etc. I oughtn't to have to write the same thing twice when once
wd. serve.

I have never heard of yr. Mrs. S. but if she is a banker's wife it wd. prob.
be hopeless to tell her anything about literature, i.e. to educate her to know
good from bad. These marginal people shd. be put to fighting *general conditions:* the gen. conditions are: copyright, custom, art. 211 of Penal Code,
and cost of printing.

The first three to be fought openly. The fourth to be attacked via subsidized plant. I.e., one that needn't pay rent, that hasn't sunk capital in its
machinery, that is manned at least in part by volunteer staff, or amateur
staff, or people who write and can take some of their exercise on working
the press. They won't be scabbing the printers, as they wd. be doing work
not done by printers, i.e. not taking work from them.

The worse a book is the more it ought to cost to print.

Don't worry about some 2nd rate bloke getting praised. What if I had
sat down and wept over the booms of Abercrumbie and Fuggis!!

Ole Hen Ford has seen several points that wd. be useful in la vie littéraire. I.e., anteriority of production to blurb.

There were 16 millions that did *not* elect Hoover. It takes about 600
people to make a civilization. There were umpteen billions of unbreached
barbarians in the north woods when Athens etc. . . .

If the 243 Americans who ever heard of civilization wd. quit crabbing
each other and organize, it wd. be a start. To hell with what somebody
else *isn't* doing.

As Yeats has said: "Fortunately they don't know we are here, otherwise
they wd. abolish us all."

Re p. 2 yrs. Nov. 9.

What a good man gets from another man's work is: precisely the knowledge that the other man has done a job, and that he, the first man, *need not*
do that same job or an imitation of it, but is free to do his own job.

The utility of education or of knowing the subject is mainly to know
what one *needn't* bother to do. *The pt. from which* one can start to do
one's own bloody bizniz.

The ones with nothing to say get scared, are afraid to recognize the
qualities of others for fear there won't be a place on the bandwagon for
themselves, etc. NO GOOD WORK EVER KNOCKED OUT ANY OTHER GOOD WORK.
It is the pikers who get knocked off and who get uneasy when a good job
is done. Etc.

Point of group is precisely to have somewhere to go when you don't
want to be bothered about salesmanship. (Paradox?? No.)

When you get five men who trust each other you are a long way to a
start. If your stuff won't hold the interest of the other four or of someone
in the four, it may not be ready to print.

Also at 24?? I came thru, if you like, at 23, but I had already known
what I was at, for eight years.

Etc. Got a pile of work on my head.

232: To James Joyce

Rapallo, 23 December

Dear James: With respected greetings of the alledgedly happy but in
reality rather frigid season.

As a philological note: The Yeats alledges that in time past (80 or 90
years ago) thou madest some traductions of the plays of G. Hauptmann.

2ndly that these cd. not be used at the Abbey because it was then con-
stitooted or red taped to do nowt but 100% green or Erse plays.

If these juvenile indiscretions still exist the time may now have come to
cash in on 'em.

The noble Gerhardt [*Hauptmann*] is struggling both with *Ulysses* (im
Deutsch) and with the germanly traduced works Wm. He sez *Ulysses* in
choimun is like looking at a coin through his microscope, can't see it cause
it's aggrandized to such etc. . . .

Seems quite as likely that it was Grillparzer or Ibsen that you'd traduced, *but* you might lemme have the reel dope on the sichooatshun. — — — —

233: To HARRIET MONROE

Rapallo, 30 December

Dear Harriet: Carnevali's minimum expenses are 40 dollars a month. His assets (including your 5) are 15 a month. McAlmon has paid his bills for, I think, four years, but can not continue.

I am trying to get something from the Authors' League — — — —, and hope you will back me up. They can only give sporadic grants; not allowances.

The case is so clear that I think someone like Mrs. Moody, etc., on basis of charity ought to be put onto it.

As he never stops shaking, save immediately after his medicine, he obviously can *not* do any great amount of work. I don't know how much longer he can last. They told me in Bologna three years ago that the disease is incurable. With America reeking with money, some one ought to be found to deal with the matter.

More cheering news items are that Aldington seems to have awakened from his slumbers. I may be sending you something of his, before long. Or he may be induced to take direct action. 2ndly, there is a new chap called T. McGreevy whose work Yeats admires. I think W.B.Y. intends giving him an introduction to you. I have myself seen a good poem by him in an Irish anthology.

1 9 2 9

234: To JAMES VOGEL

Rapallo, 23 January

Dear Vogel: Yr. painfully evangelical epistle recd. *If* you are looking for people who agree with you!!!! How the hell many points of agreement do you suppose there were between Joyce, W. Lewis, Eliot and yrs. truly in 1917; or between Gaudier and Lewis in 1913; or between me and Yeats, etc.?

If you agree that there ought to be decent writing, something expressing the man's ideas, not prune juice to suit the pub. taste or *your* taste, you will have got as far as any "circle" or "world" ever has.

If another man has ideas of *any* kind (not borrowed clichés) that irritate you enough to make you think or take out your own ideas and look at 'em, that is all one can expect.

Not that you or anyone else can work beside a chap that gives you the creeps.

If it is any use, I shd. be inclined not to make an effort to bring out another *Xile* until one has seen whether *Blues* can do the job. Or do you consider this excessive on my part?

I don't see that there is room or need for two mags doing experimental stuff . . . at present moment. If *Blues* can bring out a good wad of Joe Gould it seems to me it wd. about cover the ground.

The other "find" was Howard Weeks; it don't show in *Xile*. His stuff looked as if it wd. be such a damn sight better in a few months, during which time he died.

Blues had better take on McAlmon. Haven't seen anything new of Rodker's up to level of *Adolphe*. Besides it is not your job to print foreign authors. That can be done here.

I personally don't want to write any prose for the next year or two or three. If you get Bill Wms., McAlmon, Joe Gould and the authors you've got, there ought to be enough solid core to carry the thing.

Cummings and Hemingway and Callaghan are all doing the dollar a word or something of that sort.

Seems to me a chance for the best thing since *The Little Review* and certainly the best thing done in America without European help. McA. is in Europe but the only reason he isn't printed in the U.S. is that he is so gol darned American they can't stand it.

Gould, I believe, ought to be paid. I believe *Blues* has a little money in the chest? There are times when the difference between 5 dollars and zero is *all* the difference. –/–/

235: To Charles Henri Ford

Rapallo, 1 February

Dear C.H.F.: Every generation or group must write its own literary program. The way to do it is by circular letter to your ten chief allies. Find out the two or three points you agree on (if *any*) and issue them as program. If you merely want to endorse something in my original Imagist manifesto or the accompanying "Don'ts" or in my *How to Read* that has just appeared in the N.Y. *Herald* "Books," simply say so. Or list the revered and unreverend authors you approve or disapprove of.

Re my "Program" [1] enclosed: A man's opinions are his own affair. When

---

[1] PROGRAM 1929.

1. Government for utility only.

2. Article 211 of the Penal Code to be amended by the 12 words: *This statute does not apply to works of literary and scientific merit.*

3. Vestal's bill or some other decent and civilized copyright act to be passed. Footnote: instead of *everybody's* going to New York, ten or a dozen bright lads ought to look in on the national capital. We need several novels in the vein of Hemingway's *The Torrents of Spring* dealing not with helpless rural morons but with "our rulers" and the "representatives of the people."

writing a poem he shd. think only of doing a good job. But a *magazine* is a public matter. It is there as mediator between the writer and the public. A magazine shd. think of the welfare of literature as a whole and of conditions in which it is possible to produce it. I shd. like you to print my "Program." Note that it is civic NOT political. Not a question of messing into politics but of the writers or intelligentsia raising hell all day and every day about abuses that *interfere with their existence* AS WRITERS and that represent an oppression of literature by the stinking sons-of-bitches who rot the country.

As to magazine policy: Most "young" magazines play ostrich. They neither recognize the outer world nor do they keep an eye on contemporary affairs of strictly literary nature.

You shd. *look at* all the other poetry reviews and attack idiocy when it appears in them. The simplest and briefest form of attack is by a sottisier. As has been done by *Mercure de France, New Age, Egoist* and *Am. Mercury*. The only thing is that instead of Mencken's "Americana" you shd. run sottisier confined to literary criticism. It is no longer my place to point out the idiocies that appear in *Poetry*, for example. The older boy shd. not stick pins into the younger. It is courageous of the young to stick pins into the pompous.

Make your sottisier from *Poetry* and the main literary reviews, Sunday supplements, etc.

These sottisiers are often the first parts of a live mag that people read. Let everyone collect 'em.

As you don't live in same town with yr. start contribs, you can not have fortnightly meeting and rag each other. Best substitute is to use circular letters. For example write something (or use this note of mine), add your comments, send it on to Vogel, have him show it to Spector, and then send it to Bill Wms. each adding his blasts and blesses or comment of whatever-damn natr. Etc. When it has gone the rounds, you can send it back here.

I don't see any Philadelphia group listed in yr. announcement. You might drop a line to Frank Audenbrand, c/o my father. — — — —

You shd. look into Art. 211 and the copyright mess. If you don't want to attend to that part of the mag, get Vogel or Spector or some of the huskier and more publicke minded members to do the blasting.

There is no sense in living in a country covered with — — — —. It distracts the mind from more interesting matters. Simplest method, discovered by the Romans or some earlier people, is to dig a good sewer at the start; and then turn your attention to architecture. —/—/

236: To the Alumni Secretary
of the University of Pennsylvania

Rapallo, 20 April

Sir: Your circular letter of April 8 is probably excusable as a circular letter. If it were a personal letter I shd. be obliged to correct it.

Any news that the grad. school or any other "arts" segment of the U. of P. had started to take an interest in civilization or "the advancement of knowledge" or any other matter of interest wd. be of interest.

The matter of keeping up one more otiose institution in a retrograde country seems to me to be the affair of those still bamboozled by mendicancy, rhetoric, and circular letters.

In other words what the HELL is the grad. school doing and what the HELL does it think it is there for and when the hell did it do anything but try to perpetuate the routine and stupidity that it was already perpetuating in 1873?

P.S. All the U. of P. or your god damn college or any other god damn American college does or will do for a man of letters is to ask him to go away without breaking the silence.

237: To JOHN SCHEIWILLER

Rapallo, 26 November

Dear Scheiwiller: The trouble is that I have never seen any of Modigliani's work. He died in Paris while I was living in London. I know of his position and I know the work by reproduction, and I know how good artists respected him; but my respect for artistic criticism as such prevents me for having or printing opinions on what I don't know.

I don't know what I can say.

"Premature death of Modigliani removed a definite, valuable and emotive force from the contemporary art world."

If that is any use to you. ?

238: To WILLIAM CARLOS WILLIAMS

Rapallo, 2 December

And now to speak of something conskruktive: Since my progenitors cum over here, I don't see any god damn American magazines cos nobody sends 'em. *And* I shd. like to see the advertisement of one of those latest smallest lightest printing presses again. The kind advertised fer bizniz houses: "Do your own printing."

Old fashioned 'and press for marrvelous fine printing is no use az far as I'm concerned. To damn much work, technical skill, etc.

Damn it, I oughtn't to have to bother with the thing at all; but the rest of the world is so lousy lazy that I may as well look into the matter. Self-inking, self-feeding, etc. Something that wd. give a decent imprint (say as good as *Exile* or the French edtn. of my *Antheil*). Roller cylinder, of course. I.e., main want is to know *if* there is anything that can be worked with little enough bother to make it possible. Shd. also want to see a sample of work actually done by one of the b....y things. Couldn't cost too much as it wd. certainly be idle most of the time; and *no* chance of "merchant-ing" the products in any conceivable case. Some general idea of shipping costs etc. And whether agency exists in Europe or Italy wd. help, etc.

Easiest thing for you wd. be to sight one of the ads. and drop note to the makers telling 'em to send me FULL an bloated particulars. — — — —

Drawback mainly the feeling that *if* I buy the damn thing there will for eight years be nothing to print on it.

239: To Agnes Bedford

Rapallo, December

I have done a great deal of work of plodding keraktur. If the G[uido] C[avalcanti] ever gets out of press, it should be a "standard woik," etc. Only great emptiness can produce profound scholarship. Und so weiter.

1 9 3 0

240: To William Carlos Williams

Rapallo, 16 January

Dear WillYam: Zuk tells me that Reznikof has a printin press. In any kuntry but Murka this wd. solve a lot of problems.

2. Untermeyer (and wife) is (are) here. He seems a man of good will and without hamstringing prejudice. Mrs. U. let off some sentiments the other evenin that might have fell from yr. own hnrd. lips. In fact I believe they in a dif. form have. I gather McA. handed him some rough stuff on first meetin, but he don't bear no mangy.

Nancy [Cunard] has agreed to print Zuk's "The." Also wants some-thing of yours, as I indicated when writin to Z. so'z to save a week's time.

In return for which virchoos aks peeraps you can shoulder the follerin.

I invented the Poetry Clan.[1] Harriet and Co. hung crêpe until they found it wd. work. I have never asked 'em anything and they have never asked my advice. Have you any infloonz with 'em?

It so happens that a chap named Macleod (*not* Fiona) has writ a good poem 70 pages long, i.e., too long fer Nancy and too long to print in *Criterion* or any review. I want the bloody Clan to do it. Naturally they'll have to see the ms., etc., but I have no reason to spose that any of their anonymous (god damn it, why anonymous?) committee will be able to see why it is good.

Have yeow any snug-gestions?

[1] See Letter No. 221.

As fer yr. guesses re Zuk and Mac: Z seems to be lookin fer more punishment.

241: To E. E. CUMMINGS

Rapallo, 17 February

Dear Cummings: Van Hecke is asking me to help him make up an American number of *Variétés*. I don't know whether you know the review. It has weak numbers; but four or five together keep up a more lively average with less chapelle than anything else I see hereabouts. He seems to take my word for certain lit. values.

I am expecting a set of yr. books that I ordered some weeks ago. I hope (praps vain optimism) to find an intelligent translator. In the meantime, I want your photo and any suggestions you have to offer re what bits of yr. work you would prefer to have translated into French; i.e., is there anything you think more representative than anything else or wd. prefer to see transd. before anything else? Or inédit that won't pass censor in N.Y. and that needs European imprint (mag is pubd. Bruxelles)?

You might mention any one (or thing) you think ought to go in and whom or which I am likely to omit *and* a bibliography of yr. woiks.

Photos illustrating the number to be mainly machinery, etc., plus the noble and rep. viri murkhani. Of course, if you have any really funny photos representing the habits of the American peepul, they cd. be used with advantage. I shd. like the number to be as good as my French number of *The Lit. Rev.* (1918), but the photos need not maintain the level of high seriousness demanded by our late friend *The Dial*.

Van H. has already printed photos of Voronoff operation, the streets of Marseilles, etc. Bandagistes' windows also a favorite subject.

If you have a photo of a Cigar Store Indian or can get one, it wd. be deeply appreciated. Our autocthonous sculpture is comparatively unknown in Yourup, though I suspect the c. (or segar) s.i. was possibly of Brit. or colonial origin. Van H. has got a lot of Berenice [Abbott]'s photos of N.Y. I don't know just what. Still he hasn't mentioned an Indian and B's prob. too young to remember 'em.

242: To E. E. CUMMINGS

Rapallo, 25 March

Yr Eimminence: One piece nicotine refined woodlady, 2 views, recd. Re "regress": priority claimed. Expressed thanks già Sacher Zorach. Ever a pleasure to have something to decipher that *ain't* dear Jim or oedipus Gertie. Bibliography duly registered. Competition of Soviet number *Variétiés* demanding all poss. pathriotic zeal. Mr. Rus. Wright appreciated.

HELLass have llost the llovelly pixture (helas only nzp cut) of nat. com. of largeladies visiting blanchhouse.

Wot's the Belgium for "Yale"?

Tears of nostalgi inwit welling at name of Patchin. Youth returns aged thorax. Cd. use yet again more seegar Injuns. N.Y. *Herald* Paris has beat us on Coolidge: one of Cal. with parrot that in onconscious humour defies concurrence. Besides one might find something of more topical interest.

P.S. Does a venerable figure called Dahler still live at No. 7 Pat. Pl.?

243: To Harriet Monroe

Rapallo, 24 October

Cheers, my dear Harriet, CheeUHHS!!! In a few days it wd. have been a birfday present.

And now proceeding in order. No, I did NOT mean Norman Macleod when I wrote J.G. meaning Joseph Gordon (purrrnounced I prezoom Garrrdun) Macleod (perrnounced Mclwd) whose *The Ecliptic* has just been pubd. in vol. by Faber and Faber of Lunnon.

Secondly as you rashly ask for further hint. Did I or did I not suggest tempering Zukofsky with McKenzie? Zuk to provide the good sense and McKenzie the conviction of the value of the new group. I dunno what can be done now to make up for that bit of motive power. I may have said "or" instead of "and."

Anyhow I shall urge Zuk to take the March or May in order to have time to get the most dynamite into it. — — — —

As to N? Yok. you know that I have always played Chicago (or ANY western township against N.Y.) whenever I cd. get standing room west of the Alleghanies. The trouble is that they won't *stay* west of the Alleghanies. Margaret, Covici, Putnam, etc. . . . *Morada* is my last stab at this and before I can get an answer they are in Munich (having excema and asking my advice about health resorts . . . vivaHHH the he-man of the wilds!!). I got a ten gallon hat last week and still got more hair on meh chest than any of 'em, me, the etiolated European!!

By the way met a frien' of yours in Rrome. You might get her to release another ten bucks a month for the lily-souled Emanuel. Pleasant woman, Mc something.

Waal, waal, my deah Harriet, I sho iz glad you let these young scrubs have the show to their selves, an ah does hope they dust out your office. My only fear is that Mr. Zukofsky will be just too Goddam prewdent.

No, I haven't seen dear Margaret's outburst. When she and Jane got to sequestering my mss. on the ground that what I had writ wd. do me "so much harm in America," I sought younger companions.

It ain't *my* idea of Pegasus, it's Mr. Gill's. Mebbe Pegasus looks like that in England. I'd rather have one from Kentucky even if he hadn't wings and wisp of spinach for a tail. I never did think much of Mr. Gill or of Henglish Hawt anyway. (Wyndham Lewis's dad was a West Pointer of

Murkn nashunality, so he ain't under the Bris'h nachunul coise.) That Damn hoss wd. be perfectly at home on the Georgian anthology. However, there he is, you gotter keep him for a year. He ain't 'et fer some time and he is powerful curious about that carrot (no room fer carrot on the cover).

If you'd read Pisanello's letter (vide Canto XXVI) and then look at some Pisanello medals or frescoes you wd. be able to work out my opinion of Mr. Gill on the subjekk of hosses.

244: To WILLIAM CARLOS WILLIAMS

Rapallo, 22 November

Deer Willyum the Wumpus: How badly does Zuk want to git to Yourup? And how badly OUGHT he?

Until his last letter (in which the question is not mentioned) I had held the view that he ought to git some sort of root in N.Y. before wandering. *And* I have allus held that sometime somehow *god damn* etc. something ought to git started ON THE BLOODY spot (especially as ole Europe ain't what she wuz).

However, if it merely means killing off yet another generation. . . .

Secondly *if* in yr. judgment he ought to have a breathing spell, can we in any way manage it? Has he *any* resources (fiscal)? Question of whether it wd. weaken his fibre etc. to be helped, whether to add yet another to an unpaid perfession in which even the old stagers are havin hell's own helluva to pay for their beer and sandwiches . . . etc. . . .

What sort of degradation is he willing to undergo?

Etc. First question is whether you think it wd. be a good thing for him to be exported TEMPORARILY, or if he once gets his nose out whether he cd. ever stand repatriation?????? Etc. etc.

God damn it, who are the just men in yr. transpontine sodom ennyhow????

1931

245: To HARRIET MONROE

Rapallo, January

Dear Harriet: Am forwarding yrs. to Yeats.

Re yrs. in *Eng. Journal:* have you never answered a straight question re my Propertius: Did either you or Hale suppose that my reference to Wordsworth in my *Homage* was a mistranslation from the Latin?

Hale was a god damn fool, I don't know whether that demands "forgiveness" or not. At any rate I leave both vendetta and pardon to the forces of nature. I was not in the habit of answering criticisms of my own work. The irritation was caused by its being impossible to conduct an argument on the basis of Hale's being fool enough to have based his crit. on the whole poem as only a fragment of it had been printed.

As to "whole" numbers. If it was possible for Neihardt it was "possible," however antipathetic it may have been to you personally, to have extended the same amt. of space to "other writers."

Hale's one "discovery of error" reduces itself to the passage about the aquaduct which he got not from his own intelligence or from a knowledge of Latin but from using an annotated edtn.

If you think the trade gains by putting poetic quality below pedantry or even below scholastic distinction, this is the one case in 18 years in which you have ever shown signs of that attitude.

There is an unimportant error or vagueness in yr. remarks re my fatigue. Not weariness but indignation (beginning with the 2nd number) and overcome time after time, divorced me from *Poetry*. No elephant has my patience.

The Lit. Rev. ejected me. *BLAST* ceased through no act of mine. *The Dial* was always hell, or nearly always, endured on the principle "faim saillir le loup du bois."

Exile was undertaken to print what no other mag. wd. print. As soon as there were other mags in existence that cd. carry on I desisted.

As for the joke about *when* various revs. were useful: All right. Make out another list of what those reviews and any other li'l reviews published when they were trying to prove me an imbecile.

You've got the spectacle of the Georgians in Britain, Stork and heaven knows wottell . . . in U.S.A. Cf. *Little Review* itself under Ficke's effulgent aegis.

Re Zuk: gord knows wot he has done to yr. respected pubctn. At least it will be a different point of view. Let us hope a younger pt. v. than mine.

You might also concede the constructive value of my kicking about mutilations. *Propertius* and *Mauberley* were cut, but on the strength of my howling to high heaven that this was an outrage, Eliot's *Waste Land* was printed whole. In which action I also participated. Dragging my own corpse by the heels to arouse the blasted spectators.

246: To the Editor of the *English Journal*

Rapallo, 24 January

Sir: It is fatiguing to argue about one's own work but Miss Monroe's persistent errors seem to demand a reply.

1. Four sections of a poem written in 12 sections do not constitute the whole poem.

2. My *Homage to Sextus Propertius* is *not* a translation of Propertius.

3. I am unable to imagine a depth of stupidity so great as to lead either

Miss Monroe or the late Hale into believing that I supposed I had found an allusion to Wordsworth or a parody of Yeats Propertius.

4. I did not at the time reply to Hale because I could not assume that he had seen the entire poem.

5. Hale's "criticism" displayed not only ignorance of Latin but ignorance of English.

6. If Miss Monroe is unable to discover proof of Hale's ignorance I will (if any interest be now supposed to inhere in the subject) on receipt of a copy of Hale's "criticism" indicate his errors. Miss Monroe appears to preserve the superstition that a man is learned, or, *me hercule*, infallible *because* he is a professor.

P.S. As Miss Monroe has never yet discovered what the aforementioned poem is, I may perhaps avoid charges of further mystification and wilful obscurity by saying that it presents certain emotions as vital to me in 1917, faced with the infinite and ineffable imbecility of the British Empire, as they were to Propertius some centuries earlier, when faced with the infinite and ineffable imbecility of the Roman Empire. These emotions are defined largely, but not entirely, in Propertius' own terms. If the reader does not find relation to life defined in the poem, he may conclude that I have been unsuccessful in my endeavour. I certainly omitted no means of definition that I saw open to me, including shortenings, cross cuts, implications derivable from other writings of Propertius, as for example the "Ride to Lanuvium" from which I have taken a colour or tone but no direct or entire *expression*.

247: To Harriet Monroe

Rapallo, 27 March

Dear H.M.: Agree that *transition* was mainly slop, *but* the review was useful.

As to Feb. *Poetry.* . . . The point is that although most of the contents was average, the *mode* of presentation was good editing. The zoning of different states of mind, so that one can see what they are, is good editing.

This gang is not the *same* mess as the Neihardt stuff you used to include. Vide infra.

Zuk's own poem is part of a whole poem and therefore loses 9/10ths of its intelligibility, cut off as a fragment.

But there has been a development in American verse during 20 years; and the messy britons have not kept up with it.

Have done a brief note on Feb. *Poetry* for Putnam's *New Rev.*

An editor is not there to represent him- or herself save as a PART of the period. Different facets shd. be presented with as much separation as possible, so as to show what they are, not merely partly boiled legumes in the soup. Only a small part of any epoch or decade survives. Service of Feb. number perhaps not so much re what is to survive of present infants as in strong indication of what *will not* survive from former mediocrity and faintly-above-medioc. A pruning of the tree.

There *always* is "mighty little" being done.

If you want to insult yourself by taking *transition* as criterion of comparison, do so: but I didn't. Neither do I see why a magazine shd. stop with the stoppage of its initial editor.

I don't in the least mind opposition. I regard it as being there to be eliminated. I.e., resistance to develop the force of action. Very useful in lit. discussion as it gives opportunity to elucidate fully points left obscure (unconsciously) by the first expressor.

But anybody being a friend of anybody has nothing to do with literary criticism. I hope to maintain at least that point, even if no sonzofbitches ever come to my funeral and if no stinking Judge Thayer of Massachusetts ever places wreathes on my unknown tomb.

Re Bunting: there aren't a whole plateful of Eng. extremists. B's in correspondence with J. G. Macleod. I personally do *not* share the Auden craze, it isn't as much as a craze anyhow; it is merely that Auden is so large a part of what little they've got. Mutatis mutandis, another J. E. Flecker, I mean about that general mule-power.

Re yr. last page. If you had ever told me you repented of Neihardt I wd. have looked up some other more recent instance (even though by such doing I might have obscured my general idea).

My idea of Brit. number was that it shd. give 'em the best show possible, but that it was bound to be American chauvinism, because the best Brit. show wd. be very much inferior to Zuk's number.

Good editing, as I see it, means the most effective presentation of the best of *whatever* is on hand.

An English number ought to show Eng. different from America, but no longer, as in 1892, better in re the art of poesy.

Obviously in the last analysis the grade of any period depends on one, two or a few of the best writers. The Greek anthology is not a contradiction; it does not represent the mediocrity of one decade but the florilegium of a long series of decades.

It is time there was another such report on France as I made in 1918 in *Little Rev.*

In 1911 France led. I doubt if she does today. But that question does not take ref. to two hundred writers. It is a question of the state of awareness of Ford, Joyce, Eliot, Bill Wms., E.P. to Gide, Claudel, smut nut etc. Cocteau, Aragon, Peret.

Italy gets into internat. locale by reason of Tozzi (prose).

Re opposition: if one aims at 100%, the opposition is there either to affect one, *i.e.*, rectify one's direction or to be rectified *by* one's direction. Difficulty generally is to get ANY opposition that will define a position at all: or stick to a point of discussion until, between the disputants, one gets the right answer (in cases where there is one).

Re *Poetry* stopping: Having performed the great feat of manipulating the god damned borzoi into spending a little money on the best poetry at

yr. disposal (given yr. lights) it wd. be a crime to plug the hole. You ought
to leave as durable and continuing a monument as possible to the fact that
you extracted from among the porkpackers a few less constipated and
made them PAY money for the upkeep of poesy. The five just men in
Sodom were as nothing by comparison. I forget; I dare say they weren't
to be found, and the angels' morals had to be kept in the family.

I don't care *how* they are made to do it. If love availeth not, tell 'em *all*
the young writers will go communist the moment they stop. That's *not* so
far out, anyhow. Bourgeois litcherchoor is pretty well on the blink. Am
a democrat myself . . . but one must observe the general current of things.

When it comes to the yearn after vanishing kulchuh I suspect that Mr.
McAlmon's feelings toward Mr. Farrell (who writes of American *low* life)
are almost as H.J.'s might have been toward Mr. McA. —/—/

P.S. Yet again: say the Feb. number doesn't "record a triumph" for that
group. GET some other damn group and see what it can do. What about
the neo-Elinor-Wylites? Have they got any further than the neo-Vance-
Cheneyites of 1904?

Zone the barstuds.

Or the neo-hogbutchererbigdriftities? They all gone Rootabaga?

Tyler prob. has something. C. H. Ford prob. not.

You may have kept at it more persistently than *Exile:* but what about
Exile's editor? What earthly dif. does it make whether *Exile* appears sep-
arately or in the pages of some other review. The next time there is no
Lit. Rev., Dial, BLAST, H and H, Symposium or other review to print
something I think needs printing you may have the sweet torture of seeing
a No. 5.

Anyhow the damn porkpackers ought to *pay my* rent. Expect me to be
the leading Xponent, patron of arts, committee of information. Wotter-
hell!!!!!! Tell your damn guarantors I consider 'em as holy lights amid a
great flock of cattle (millionaire illiterates, dumb and speechless tribes of
unconscious pawnbrokers).

> *The hayseed walked across the road at night*
> *He said to his old woman, Now say, I say*
> *Maggie, don't yew think it's about time I started hoeing?*

What about the ole bucolic school? Have they got any agricultural
epigons?

Here, I'm exceeding myself.

P.P.S. Tenny rate, whooz down-hearted?

248: To Lincoln Kirstein

Rapallo, [? May]

Dear L.K.: –/–/

Costa più della *Divinia Commedia*

1. In reply to your earlier letter. Your statement about live types etc. amounts to saying that there is good low life in America. There is good low life anywhere. The lower it is the less it is national and the less it reflects any credit or interest on the *particular* place in which it exists.

I can only repeat my malediction: God eternally damblast a country that spends billions interfering with peoples' diet and that can not support a single printing press which will print stuff that people like me want to read, *i.e.*, regardless of immediate fiscal profit.

The endowments are sabotaged. Even when some vague and good-natured millionaire "founds" something with allegedly cultural or creative intent, the endowment is handed over to academic eminences who are as incapable of picking a first class painter or writer as I shd. be of making a sound report on a copper mine. The one thing they are sure to hate is the germ of original capacity. They will go on backing the Howells, the Tarkingtons and the W. Churchills to the end of their ignominious history.

– – – –

My heading was found in the local pharmacy. I asked for a certain brand of excellent American toilet paper and the pharmacien replied with this epitaph on Anglo-Saxon civilization: "È essagerata. Costa più della *Divina Commedia*." Yes, he wd. sell it to me, but really it cost too much. It cost more than the *Divina Commedia*.

Our race still maintains this proportion in estimate. It is the reversal of the old epigram about hyacinths.

2. Re style in America: Yes. And it is worth irritating people and sticking to that somewhat Toryish (tho' not fundamentally Tory) position however unpopular.

But it is dangerous internally and ex–. Danger of Concord school omitting to notice Whitman. Historically, people in rough environment, if they have any sensibility or perception, want "culture an' refinement." Whitman embodying nearly everything one disliked, etc. Failure to see the wood for the trees.

Secondly or thirdly: Danger of confusing your (for example) lyric impulse and yr. editorial function. As lyricist you can WANT (and shd. want) whatever you damn please. Editorial function something very different. In that function one has to (at least) observe, admit the capacities of people who like what one does NOT like.

Life wd. have been (in my case) much less interesting if I had waited till Joyce, Lewis, Eliot, D. H. Lawrence, etc. complied with what my taste was in 1908.

O HELL, how shall I put it. My son, elucidate thine own bloody damn point of view by its contrast to others, not by trying to make the others conform.

All right. You want a STYLE out of America. Stick at it. But when it comes it mayn't be where you are lookin' fer it. As editor all you can do is to get the best of what is done

    A. from those you more or less agree with

    B. from those you DON'T

and in latter case you can editorially profess to be conscious of an energy, which you believe to be wrongly directed.

249: TO HARRIET MONROE

Rapallo, 6 October

Dear Harriet: Not being given to gloom or to worrying about calamity I had not given much thought to *Poetry* a mag for 1951. I forget how old you think you are, but you are good for another ten or fifteen years anyhow. However, if you insist on making a will, the coincidence etc. incites me to the obvious idea that the only person in Amurikuh who cd. continue your periodical is Marianne. The necessary irreproachable respectability, the that against which no lousy ploot can object on the grounds of her not bein' a lady or bein' likely to pervert the growing school child, etc.

It shd. also be possible to get a certain amount of backing for Marianne that wd. *not* be available for the wild and boisterous or cerebral younger males.

Taking yr. editorial as basis, the essential in a continuator wd. be, now or any time, in the next two decades, someone who could command a certain amount of financial support. And someone not merely brought up by you in yr. office. Question of changing name of magazine seems to me immaterial. Seems to me a continuation of *Poetry* wd. be the best memorial you cd. wish IF it can be arranged that it shd. be a creditable continuation. You can at any rate finish the quarter century and then retire if you like. I don't see exactly why you shd. retire, but still if you are making wills, one may as well discuss will-making.

I will not mention the contents of this note until I hear from you. I am perfectly willing to undertake solicitation IF the idea strikes you favourably. It wd. be better I think for you to consult your firmest guarantors or even all the guarantors. It wd. then be time to find out if Marianne wd. entertain the proposition and 3dly, to see what extra support cd. be gained for her to replace those of your circle who wd. naturally cease to support *Poetry* under *any* change of management.

Let us take it you must have a Christianity-addict: I cede on that point.

Marianne has experience—quality dear to the cautious ploot. Kulchuh—more than enough. Conservatism but not absolute plantedness. At any rate I see no other successor who wd. do you honour and who is a practical proposition.

In reply to yr. last: I am not interested in roach-powder but if the janitors and swabbers can't keep the place clean, I take it *somebody* has got to provide insecticide or even squash the individual cockroach. In the general cause of health. "Modern cities are impossible without preventive medicine and modern sanitation."

At present I shd. say (to return to constructivity) that Marianne's talents (discretion, etc.) were not being used by her god damned country.

I don't know how much she makes at whatever she is doing; someday or other she will presumably need less and have less weight to carry . . . etc. . . .

I dunno 'bout the Chicago pt. of view. Nothing but a definite position wd. I suppose take M.M. to Chicago or move her from one side of 4th Ave. to the other. But Chicago might be inspirationated to BRING one of the best contemporary Amurkun minds into Chicago. After all Marianne wuz born in St. Louis, and can be claimed by the West in general.

The decision seems to rest more with you personally than with the outer circumjacence.

Anyhow, lemme know if it's worth a try.

P.S. Nacherly I can't tell anything about your local factional fights. Utterly unable to SEE that your advisory committee have ever contributed either brains, knowledge or energy.

M.M. ideal presiding officer; IF you think there is a local faction that wants or insists on a representative of vagueness and slush and glad-handing, I suppose vice-presidencies were invented for conciliating such. . . .

250: To H. B. LATHROP

Rapallo, 16 December

Dear Professor Lathrop: I have just written to Hatfield re a matter that might have been dealt with more directly.

I strongly suspect that a few hundred, perhaps a few dozen swine in editorial offices do more harm to contemporary letters in America than all the pubk bad taste and ignorance put together.

AN ANTIDOTE. A Who's Who of editors stating the four cardinal points.

1. Whom did they (do they) print?
2. Whom did they print before anyone else, or before the author had a reputation?
3. Whom did they refuse?
4. Whom did they fail to invite (in a suitable manner, for and in regard to resources at their disposal)?

Book shd. be compiled by impartial patient students, having no personal ax to grind in any particular case. It would be of gt. national service, as well as being thesis for Ph.D. or several theses.

Our young friend Z nicely fixed as edtr. for new publishing house. Question of cheap book of first quality seems much nearer solution.

Crosby, TO (Oppen), Rexroth all promising to deal with it, and the first two have work in press. Carlos Williams, Hemingway (unpopular item) and my collected prose among things being handled by the three producers.

My Cavalcanti nearly ready. I don't know whether you can put me through to yr. Romance dept. or in fact any part of Univ. dealing with polyglot letters. The edtn. ought to serve as START for a new method of handling international texts. I want names both of men who can do the work, and of "powers" capable of assisting. Having (that is to say all but 4 pages) got through with the Cavalcanti in spite of all the devils in Eng. or Am., I am in stronger position than when merely having something of my own that "wanted doing."

251: To Harriet Monroe

Rapallo, 27 December

Dear Harriet: The intelligence of the nation more important than the comfort or life of any one individual or the bodily life of a whole generation.

It is difficult enough to give the god damn amoeba a nervous system.

Having done your bit to provide a scrap of rudimentary ganglia amid the wholly bestial suet and pig fat, you can stop; but I as a responsible intellect do not propose (and have no right) to allow that bit of nerve tissue (or battery wire) to be wrecked merely because you have a sister in Cheefoo or because there are a few of your friends whom it would be pleasanter to feed or spare than to shoot.

If that indescribably vile town Chicago don't treat you right, I shall also have something to say about *that*.

Of course there are several things I have been tryin to teach you for the past 20 yrs. I don't lay as much stock by teachin the elder generation as by teachin' the risin', and if one gang dies without learnin' there is always the next. Keep on remindin 'em that we ain't bolcheviks, but only the terri-fyin' voice of civilization, kulchuh, refinement, aesthetic perception.

If you want to mark the *end* of anything, all right. The continuation can be called Poetry, Second Series, or new series, if that hackneyed term is still heap big mumbo on the lake shore (New Buildings, Blunt's, built in 1467 etc.).

Secondly, entirely apart from the above, can you tell me which, if any, of the guarantors is not violently hostile to *me* personally?

Note that from your 20 years' correspondence to me one wd. have gathered that the guarantors are mostly a set of swinish savages, with a few rare wooden-headed pedants among them, all hating me like the devil and rigidly hostile to any and every development in art and letters. If this im-pression is incorrect, it shd. be easy for you to correct it?

What can you tell me of Breasted?

Now, lie right down and git a bit of rest. I am not going to essplode any dynamite till I get an answer.

It is up to you to provide me with a committee that can at least *look* as if it wuz galvanized.

With Possum Eliot apptd. to Hawvud, he won't bring the glad polyanna yawp, but the ignorance of the Stork-Auslander-Mabie-Canby period can't continue.

You jess set down on the sofa. The dentist isn't goin to hurt.

You send me a list of the ten best people. I promise not to call Chicago a pig-stye or hog-butchery, or say anything narsty.

I spose Alice is still vigorously tubercular. A doc last night wuz tellin of a tub. family, all the sons died of tubercules at from 70 to 74, whereas the ole tubercular father died of it at 97. Still I spose she wd. have to give Chi. absent treatment.

Why ain't the list of guarantors published more often? The bastuds sometimes like pubcty.

In the meantime, let Zab use his ingenuity livenin up the maggerzeen. Experiment to see which way it can [*lacuna*] not and should not include the least taint of pity for your errors and limitations. The latter can be pardoned *to you*, but not tolerated in themselves, or for themselves.

Not only shd. the nation have an intelligence but it shd. have a bloody sight better intelligence than it now shows any protuberant signs of. It shd. be so intelligent that things like C—— and S—— wd. die pumb bang of the shock. Health kills no end of bacillae.

You are good for at least another ten years. Pass on yr. local job, and come abroad an git edderkated.

Your past correspondence wd. lead me to believe that Zabel is the only thing you have ever had in the office that wuz worth a damn or able to putt on a postage stamp. *And* that Zab is not the pussonality required to get cash out of the pig-packers. All right . . . got to work with what there is.

Marianne has got the brains to edit (all sewed up in a bag).

What about Genevieve Tagrt as a magnifique facade for the [*lacuna*]

A factory is a better muniment than a crematorium. Cemeteries interest me very little.

Chicago has had the energy to run *Poetry* for 20 years with you jabbin' the blighters in the small of the back. Quinn reported that it was the only thing going on in Chi. (That was an error; or rather, years after, they got an oriental institoot.)

I suggest that you take 5 months in Cheefoo and one month in Rapallo. I dare say my ancestors cd. give you a bed and breakfast; and you cd. catch yr. lunch in the gulph. They got a octopus rather biggern you are only 2 days ago.

I also suggest that you find someone (polite if necessary) to take on the sweaty work. I don't care whether Chi. pays its guarantee to *Poetry* via politeness or at the point of a gun. You got it by bein' more civilized than the hog-packers. Savage tribute to the beau monde.

What *ought* to be iz that Marianne or someone ought to take on the work, an you ought to git either a pension or you ought to git a small salary and write your little piece about 'ope, charity, and the Xmas sperrit when you so feel inclined.

1 9 3 2

252: To John Drummond

Rapallo, 18 February

Dear Mr. Drummond: It might almost be worth while to correct (publicly) the error of yr. opening sentence. It is NOT expensive editions that discourage circulation. The sacks of pus which got control of Brit. pubctn. in or about 1912 or '14 and increased strangle hold on it till at least 1932 have done their utmost to keep anything worth reading out of print and out of ordinary distribution via commerce (booksellers).

You have only to note that the best work of Joyce, Eliot, Wyndham Lewis (not Beachcomber) have only got into print *via* specially started publishing ventures, outside the control of the Fleet St. ring.

There is no reason why young England shd. pardon the ineffable polluters and saboteurs. What they have done to stifle literature in Eng., tho not so important as the press-bosses' stifling of economic discussion, is all of piece.

The hell cantos are specifically LONDON, the state of English mind in 1919 and 1920.

Dear J.D.: The foregoing sheet you can cite publicly; the rest of this is private.

1. Don't knock Mussolini, at least not until you have weighed up the obstacles and necessities of the time. He will end with Sigismondo and the men of order, not with the pus-sacks and destroyers. I believe that anything human will and understanding of contemporary Italy cd. accomplish, he has done and will continue to do. Details later. Don't be blinded by theorists and a lying press.

Faber is bringing out my *ABC of Economics* in a few weeks.

Metevsky is definitely Zaharoff, so far as the facts could be ascertained at the time—none of them essentially contradicted since. Tho of course he stands for a type and a state of mind; and an error in detail wdn't invalidate him.

There is satire in the *Iliad* and the *Odyssey*. I cannot believe that satire is in itself alien to epos. Nor do I think you meant to imply that it was.

There are only three main planes. The Provence merely a part of perspective. Vide any painting with distance in background, as distinct from stage scenery *on* different layers of cardboard or hangings.

Best div. prob. the permanent, the recurrent, the casual.

I wonder how far the *Mauberley* is merely a translation of the *Homage to S.P.*, for such as couldn't understand the latter?

An endeavour to communicate with a blockheaded epoch.

Every effort toward independent pubctn. is worth while. When you have been through more, you will understand my ferocity *against* little

————, each unimportant in himself but ultimately being sources of typhoid. A little dung in the well, no importance . . . but undiseased water a public need. You young, and more especially the chaps who were young ten years ago, don't yet realize how much little pimps and edtrs. have done yew wrrrrong. No use weepin over the past. *But* kill Smith and Son; kill Richmond of *Times* ———— *Sup.* and all the rest, *Observer*, etc.

Note that the Fleet St. press is not yet open and that for 20 or 30 years four old bigots of Smith and Son have practically controlled the distribution of printed matter in Eng.

I recommend *New Eng. Weekly* for economic discussion (overlook most of its lit. opinion). Also C.H.D. remarks on education near beg. of *Warning Democracy* very useful even outside econ.

Enough for one morning.

You might in considering England, consider what writers have been expelled through impossibility of getting 30/ bob a week from the brit. publishing system. And the men who have upheld, caused, etc., that state of things. Whether you are "technically a gent." or whether any of the Makers are contemplating a vie des lettres, profession of writing etc.

253: To John Drummond

Rapallo, 18 February

Dear Mr. Drummond: I continue. 1. I don't remember whether you were referring to *XXX* as if it were the whole poem because we agreed that that wd. be the better "policy." I take it you know that it is only the first large segment of "about 100."

Your selections very good. Also "everything relating to everything else."

What is Leavis? He recently sent me his "Primer."

P. 45, personal love poetry neither in Cantos nor in any Epos . . . even (say) Beatrice in the *Commedia*.

Only a fragment of Zuk's article was pubd in *Criterion*. Complete French version in *Echanges* and Italian in *Indice*.

2. Other pt.: A critical manifesto is being planned in America. I don't know why the kilted Scots and effete Britons shd. wait for Hollywood and the PEE-raries.

"Not so much crit. as creat." on yr. title page.

I dunno how you feel about Eliot's evil influence. Not that his crit. is *bad* but that he hasn't seen *where* it leads. What it leads TO. Attention on lesser rather than greater. At a time when there is imperative need of a BASIS, i.e., what ole Unc. Wm. Yeats called "new sacred book of the arts." Something, or some place where men of good will can meet without worrying about creed and colour etc.

At any rate, that is what is behind the proposed manifesto, which has not been sent to editors (like W. C. Williams, Eliot himself, or other who have regular pulpit . . . not that some of 'em mightn't have signed). At any rate, the signers to date are: Zukofsky, Bunting, Marianne Moore, E.P. I forget who else has been invited. One can assume a few more. However, even the locus in which it will appear is still a bit uncertain.

I am sending you the gist of it. If you people want to manifest along the same lines, don't wait for the Am. pubctn. Might be more effective coming from a new group. You wd. say that news has reached you of an analogous manifesto being prepared in the U.S.A.

Seems to me "Co[ntemporaries] and Makers" as good a place as any for the move to come from. Heaven knows we have been waiting for over ten years for a sign of life in Britain.

Substance of manifesto:

1. The critic most worth respect is the one who actually causes an improvement in the art he criticises.
2. The best critic of next rank is the one who most focuses attention on the best work.
3. The pestilence masking itself as a critic distracts attention *from* the best work, either to secondary work that is more or less "good" or to tosh, to detrimental work, dead or living snobisms, or to indefinite essays on criticism.

254: To Langston Hughes

Rapallo, 18 June

Dear Hughes: Thanks very much for "Scotsboro Limited." As for the case itself. I don't know that my name has been used on any protest, and I don't know that my name or anyone's name can be of any use. I believe the American govt. as INTENDED and as a system is as good a form of govt. as any, save possibly that outlined in the new Spanish constitution, but no govt. can go on forever if it allows the worst men in it to govern and if it lends itself repeatedly to flagrant injustice.

There is no doubt in my mind that the extreme Southern states are governed by the worst there is in them.

I can't see how the "left" can make anything save confusion until it can think more clearly about economics, though it is no more ignorant of them than any other group or party.

All of which you are welcome to quote if you think it will do any good. I am not hiding my opinion.

255: To John Drummond
[postcard]

Rapallo, 3 December

As the beastlier segment of yr. nation which concerns itself with printing books, does about its best to keep mine out of the country, it seems to me that you (presumably as Saul of Tarsus) might be advised not to quote more than 2 Cantos gross, I mean not more than say 150 or 200 lines altogether; and that you might give a better idea of the poem by shorter and scattered quotations. Most Cantos have in them "binding matter," i.e., lines holding them into the whole poem and these passages don't much help the reader of an isolated fragment. . . . More likely to confuse than help. . . .

256: To Harriet Monroe

Rapallo, 9 December

My Dear Ole Harriet: Ignorance is the bane of Chicago and the whole blasted continent.

"Carnal" and "uterine" as used in my letter are simple LEGAL terms, technical legal terms, that you wd. find in the most proper English as late as Jefferson's time—meaning relations on mama's side and relations on papa's side of the family. And if America hadn't just discovered sodomy, thanks to high-brow papers and *Vanity Fair*, you wdn't have suspected Fred. II, who was certainly not given that way. Pier della Vigna was secretary of the Sicilian Treasury (or equivalent). Like some of Mr. Harding's cabinet he cheated and stole the public funds, difference being that he was executed instead of receiving national honours.

At any rate, fer God's sake let Z— see the original text of my letter and send an UNEXPURGATED copy to T. . . . I don't think even it will make the obtuse middle-aged young man *think* . . . but no use shielding him from the chance since I have taken the trouble to write it.

Send him this paragraph also, s.v.p.

1 9 3 3

257: To William Bird

Rapallo, 15 January

Deer Willyum: When t'ell 'ave I ever putt on the "high" or triple tiYiara in addressin' you??

I am deeply interested in yr. biYography which as uzul does you credit. I observe that you are a follerer ov Alex Hamilton, whereas T.J. is my cherished forebear.

Have you had Douglas' last pamphlek, which contains one misprint: a plus fer a x or somethin'??

The Vols. Cantos unforchoonately are not sold, but I will remit if you like, or will cheerfully spot up the binder's fee, and remit when the sale (IF) occurs. If you are under slight shortage, I will cheerfully remit at once.

Yaas, I remember baptisin' Mont. Is he in jail or out at the moment?

Agreein' fer sake of argyfaxshun that state is protector of privilege, WHOSE b—y privilege?? Why not spread it out a bit so'z to include somebody not on the inside credit Federal Reserve gang graft?? Vide C.H.D. on the kulschurl heritage! Sfar as I see, the technocrats either don't know, or they are dodgin' the econ. issue (tactfully riz by W.B. in his remarks on the Injun Ocean). — — — —

Great pity you don't take to licherchoor. The merit of yr. privik correspondence in *spots!!*

As fer yr. final pp., that is about the kind of mess that has been trespassin on my phantastikon for several weeks. Just a bloody or merely disorderly disorder with no sense, no thought, no ideas, no program, no sense of organization *any*where in the bloody lotuvum. Do you expect Col. Louse to dictate before or after the collapse?

Is Mont or anybody on the spot considerin' any noo mushroom to rize from the ashes?

Any objection to my quotin yr. epistle (without sayin who wrote it, or over yr. siggychoor, if you prefer)? If I get round to doin a narticle on the woild at large.

Re Comité des Forges: What is yr. op. re the followin inf. recd: Seul *le Petit Parisien*, *Pet. Journal*, *Journal*, *L'Oeuvre*, et les journaux d'extrême gauche. *Populaire*, *Humanité*, sont libres de tout controle financiel de la part Comité des Forges. Il peuvent avoir des contracts avec des journaux commandités par la comité d'un pt. de vue d'affairs (publicité) mais ceci n'entravent pas leur liberté. —/—/

258: To WILLIAM ROSE BENÉT

[William Rose Benét had planned an anthology in which the poets were to choose their own poems and comment on them. Pound had refused to join in, and Benét, thinking that he considered the fee insufficient, cabled that he would himself meet any difference in fee, that William C. Williams and Wallace Stevens had already sent material, and that he hoped Pound would reconsider. Pound's reply follows:]

Rapallo, 23 January

Dear Mr. Benet: I appreciate your kindness in cabling but I am afraid I shall have to be even more explicit in my answer.

I think you have done too much harm, as asst. edtr. of the *Sat. Rev. Lit.*, from year to year pouring poison into or onto the enfeebled or adolescent Amurkn mind; or at any rate doing yr. and Canby's damndest to preserve mildew. . . .

That may be Greek to you. I have no proof that you or C. EVER make the faintest effort to understand anything whatever outside yr. own set of fixed ideas and conveniences. Yr. weekly never opens up to what I consider decent opinion or sound criticism. You accept the worst infamies of American imbecility and superstitions without a murmur, or without any persistent effort to clean up the mess.

Yr. proposed anth. is merely another effort (however delicate) to shove over more god damn'd sob stuff, personal touch, anything, absolutely anything, to shield yr. booblik from fact, what is printed on page.

"Circumstances under which it was written" are no excuse. Author's sentiments re poem after it is written, etc. Browning explained the matter in words of one syllable or at least in very simple language.

At any rate I think I shd. forego the 25 dollars for the sake of critical integrity.

Do you understand this letter?

The foetor of the *Sat. Rev's* critical effort to uphold the almost-good and the not-quite-dead and the fear of facing the demands made in my *How to Read!!*

How the deuce do you expect me to swallow all that for the sake of a small sum of money?

259: To E. E. Cummings

Rapallo, 6 April

Dear Cummings: Somewhere or other there is a l'er ov mine saying I want to include yr. trans. of Aragon's *Red Front* in an anthology Faber is bringing out in London. Share out and small proportional advance to contributors: Bill Wms., Marianne, etc.

1. Because I want it. (Also want a few poems of yrs. not already known in England, preferably poems that have not been included in published vols. (mag. printing don't matter), or in my *Profile* (if I repeat from *Profile* it will look as if there lacked abundance of prudukk).

2. Because I think it may be the only way to get the *Red Front* printed in Eng. (tho' that may be error) or at any rate as good a way as any immediately available.

3. I want to ram a cert. amount of material into that sodden mass of half-stewed oatmeal that passes for the Brit. mind. Or at any rate . . .

Thank either you or Covici for *Eimi*.

I dunno whether I rank as them wot finds it painful to read; and if I said anything about obscurity, it wd. fare ridere polli—in view of my recent pubctns. Also I don't think *Eimi is* obscure, or not very; BUT, the longer a work is, the more and longer shd. be the passages that are perfectly clear and simple to read. Matter of scale, matter of how long you can cause the reader to stay immobile or nearly so on a given number of pages. (Obviously NOT to the Edgar Wallace virtue (?) of the opposite hurry scurry.)

Also, despite the wreathes upon the Jacobean brow,[1] a page two or three, or two and one half centimetres *narrower* (at least a column of type that much narrower) might solve all the difficulties. That has, I think, been tested optically, etc. The normal or average eye sees a certain width without heaving from side to side. May be hygienic for it to exercise its wobble, but I dunno that the orfer shd. sacrifice himself on that altar.

At any rate, I can see

"he adds, unhatting and becoming his raven mane,"

but I don't see the rest of the line until I *look specially at it.* Multiply that 40 times per page for 400 pages. . . .

Mebbe there IS wide-angle eyes. But chew gotter count on a cert. no. ov yr. readers bein at least as dumb as I am. Even in Bitch and Bugle I found it difficult to read the stuff consecutively. Which probab. annoys me a lot more than it will you.

At any rate, damn glad to have the book and shall presumably continue taken er chaw now here n naow there.

I suppose you've got a Brit. pubr. for it? Or possibly Cov. has a Lunnon orfice by naow?

Otherwise . . . yr. opinyum re advisability of putting a few into anth. as horse d'overs or whetters. As few xmpl. p. 338.

Oh well Whell hell itza great woik. Me complimenks.

P.S. Please try to reply suddenly re anthol. as Faber is weepin' fer the copy and I want to finish the fatigue before I go up to Parigi (address Chase Bank there after May 5th), but please answer this note to this Rapallo address.

260: To Agnes Bedford

Rapallo, April

— — — — I do NOT want "Tos Temps" sung in a translation. The HOLE point of my moozik bein that the moozik fits the WORDS and not some OTHER WORDS. . . .

The meaning is just the usual. Point of Sordello being that he can get life into what any other troub wd. have made a flat cliché. . . .

It is first strophe, purely conventional meaning. AND NOT TO BE SUNG OR PRINTED IN ENGLISH.

The toodle oot of the dicky bird, BUT perfectly lyric, and the ultimate mastery of his medium.

[1] The reference is to S. A. Jacobs who supervised the production of *Eimi*.

261: To John Drummond

Rapallo, 4 May

Dear Drummond: 1. I have writ the *N.E.W.* to correct one minor misapprehension on yr. part re structure of *XXX*.

2. Yesterday I got note from Pollinger saying he cdn't place *Mercanti di Cannoni,* and I sent up a curse to Orage which I hope he will print.

3. I am using yr. selections from *XXX* in my Faber anthology, as they wanted me to include something of my own.

This note starts from paragraph 2. It is not an isolated instance. WHEN bloody ever a book appears on the continent that is of ANY interest it is apparently impossible to get a translation pubd. in Eng.

Frobenius, Cocteau's *Mystère Laic,* the *Mercanti.* Apparently NO difference what the subject or the kind of book, suffice it that the book is fit to read or at any rate the kind of book that I buy and lend to my friends for the sake of improvin' their conversation or damagin their bloody iggorunce. . . . And the inevitable answer is that brit. publishiter can't make money on it. Thinks he can't. After a decade's delay Faber apparently is trying to get my own stuff into print. . . .

Damnd if I see anything for it but a new heave by the young, your elders are no more use than a barrel of wind.

It is apparently impossible to get reprints of antient works. Let that pass, the contemporary work stands in greater need of being printed IF you expect to live your next twenty years in bearable country.

Heaven knows *The Egoist* wasn't a model publishing house, but it did at least print *The Portrait of the Artist, Prufrock, Tarr,* and *Quia Pauper Amavi* and wd. have pub. *Ulysses* but all the printers refused.

The *Mystère Laic* was printed in *Pagany* (N. York), but ought to be issued sep. *and* in England.

You may see my remarks re *Mercanti.* Orage will have told you of Cockburn's *The Week,* sort of private news service, to supply defects, lack of honesty in daily press. Same need for books pubd. on continent. The publishing *trade* won't do it for you. What "group," body, corpse or whichever you can evangelize, I dunno. But it must be TIME for a new heave of some sort.

P.S. If you people at Cam. can do anything in the way of a nucleus, I'll do what I can to bring in the scattered and incongruous units of my acquaintance.

I don't know whether there is any use trying to combine international elements; Von Unruh and Haas, here; Williams, Zukofsky, Serly in N.Y. —both trying to start printing, but they wdn't have an eye to specifically British needs. . . .

I dare say you know all the inhabitants of yr. island who might be interested.

Apart from Orage and *N.E.W.:* Stokes, Cockburn, Rodker, Wyndham

Lewis (possibly . . . oh yes, mebbe), Eliot (passively), several members of the fair sex, D. R. Young, town counCilOr of Kinross, the somewhat savage and wholly impecunious Bridson raging in the back streets of Manchuster. Even Flint who *ought* to be made to be useful. Some younger man might smoke him up. He seems now draped in grief over ole 'Arold's tombstone. Never at best distinguished for energy and initiative. Ernest Rhys has no objection to there being a bit of life in letters, though he is utterly impotent when it comes to arousing Messieurs Dent. Still, just as well to know what centenarians will refrain from sabotaging an effort on principle. —/—/

262: To Harriet Monroe

Rapallo, 14 September

Dear Arriet: I know you hate like hell to print me, and that an *epic* includes history and history ain't all slush and babies' pink toes. I admit that economics are *in themselves* uninteresting, but heroism *is* poetic, I mean it is fit subject for poesy.

Also re my Christmas carol: *damm* it all, the only thing between food and the starving, between abolition of slums and decent life is a thin barrier of utterly damned stupidity re the printing of metal discs or paper strips. 30 years ago people didn't know. It is a complex *and* as simple as Marconi's control of electricity.

Anyhow Van Buren was a national hero, and the young ought to know it. Also this canto continues after the Adams. Printed separate, it will be clearer than if I pubd. 35 and 36 next.

Consider that Van's autobiography lay unprinted from 1860 or so down to 1920, probably because people who knew of it were too god damn stupid to understand it.

Anyhow the crush of crisis, and Frankie getting into a jam, *now* that he has seen and admitted half the truth in his *Looking Forward*, CAN'T keep the Van B. out of print any longer. Whoever can think, ought to be made to do it *now*. (Damn my reppertashun fer writin pretty sentimengs.) As there are a few clean and decent pages in the nashunul history, better print 'em. And Van B. was one of 'em. —/—/

263: To T. C. Wilson

Rapallo, 24 September

Dear Wilson: On ye compleat aht of ye schoolmaister.

Yr. letter to surface. Teaching damn sight easier way of earning living than hackwriting. No need to "stagnate." I didn't during the 4 months they stood me. I don't say Crawfordsville didn't cram on hours or misery, but nowt unbearable. You aren't a hundred years old. Plenty of time for you to tank up and fit yourself for Europe, Asia or Africa or wherever-whither.

Secret of teaching is a bit theatrical. Simply act the best prof you have known. The irritation of fools won't come from stewddents *but* from the "orthorities."

Anybody who can penetrate the text-book ring wd. confer a blessing. Small manifest on that subject somewhere. Gaston Paris wrote text-books, and France had some sort of culture and amenity. Also *the* most paying line, after religion. One text-book cd. keep you in Europe for life. Am inclined to offer you 25% of whatever I might get out of a text-book if you succeeded in inserting *me* into the text-book racket. I don't say it wd. be easy, but keep it in mind. . . .

Tenny rate, stagnation comes from inside; and not from circumst. Clearer idea you have of *what* you want, greater prob. of getting. But never waste time filling in details. That bitches it. −/−/

264. To Mary Barnard
[postcard]

Rapallo, 29 October

Age? Intentions? Intention? How MUCH intention? I mean how hard and for how long are you willing to work at it?

Rudiments of writing: vide my pubd. crit. Rudiments music??? My unpubd. and mostly unwritten crit.

Contents?? "Lethe" the best because there is more IN it.

What magazines do you refer to? Young uns that don't pay or the old fungus that has been putrifying on nooz standz fer 40 year?

Nice gal, likely to marry and give up writing or what Oh?

265: To T. C. Wilson

Rapallo, 30 October

Dear Wilson: It wd. be abs. *useless* to send the poems to Eliot. He don't even like the best of *Active Anth.* or "admit" any of it, save him, me an' Marianne.

I don't think there is any chance for *any* yng. feller making a dent in the pubk. or highly select consciousness by means of pomes writ in the style of 1913/15. An thet's flat and no use my handlin you with gloves.

I do not believe there are more than two roads:

1. The old man's road (vide Tom. Hardy)—CONTENT, the INSIDES, the subject matter.
2. Music. And I am slowly gettin round to a few formulations, shocked

largely by the god damn ignorance in which I have lived, and which wuz inherited from the generation of boobs who preceded me.

−/−/

266: To William P. Shepard

Rapallo, 23 November

Dear Doc Shepard: −/−/ If you, by the way, want to keep the students interested in contemporary French writing, there is after 10 years an awakening in Paris. Give 'em *L'Abominable venalité de la presse* or René Crevel's *Les Pieds dans le plat*. Apart from which, I spose they have already had Cocteau. There are also Albert Londres' *rapportages*. *La Chine en folie*, the best of 'em. Young Rostand has done a bad play, *Marchands de canons*, vilely written, but with decent intentions. Polaire was very good in it. I don't seriously suggest anyone shd. read it, but it marks the turn from irresponsible snobism to constructive effort, or re-awakening of consciousness and conscience in France.

Dif. between H. James and that ouistiti Proust. Pr. gives himself away in pref. to Morand's first book. The little lickspittle wasn't satirizing, he really thought his pimps, buggars and opulent idiots were *important*, instead of the last mould on the dying cheese.

Ten years ago Gaby Picabia came into studio and saw *Notturno* on my table and lifted an eyebrow; I picked up a current Proust and said "Well . . . ?" She answered "Eeh, voui, vous avez raison."

Gabe at any rate had the "sperit ova man in him," (and incidentally some of his later writings are dam good *as* writings, laconism, no frills and pantalettes, tho' of course he is likely to drop back into it at any moment).

Incidentally the grease and fugg of England and the kowtow of their supposed aht reached an apex this spring. Elgar (if you know whom I mean? Sir Ed. O.M.) on being introduced to the Princesse de Polignac (before Menuhin concert) opens conversation with hoarse whisper: "Hyperion won." (Condensed biography of the lady on request. However, as friend of Strawinsky, she was not deeply impressed by Ed's dogginess.)

And so forth. −/−/

1934

267: To T. C. Wilson

Rapallo, 7 January

Dear Wilson: −/−/ Bill W. prob. one of four. You can't throw out either Yeats or Possum yet. And old BinBin looks as if he might have found the light *at last* after 45 years' labour. That punk C—— displays more ignorant stupidity in half a page than any known living animal except U——.

Pore old M........ Doin his damndest. Been running after Farrar to get my 31/41 printed. . . . Damn it all, he ought to be encouraged. Yet: vast difference between deriving, showing influence, being influenced *and* simply spoiling a job. I don't think he is "accomplished," just facile. So god damn easy to do a thing badly or approximately or loosely *after* it has once been done with precision. Like all these people doing Picasso mandolins, with no regard to the shape.

A guy named Collis is beating up the Britons. Wants me to edit a mag again. I have replied that if he will bother, I wd. edit an annual (not a magazine, but an annual anthol. Not the same gang each year. If he swings it, I shd. want to see a batch of yr. mss. in say about 6 months' time. Also yr. views on yr. contemporaries and worthy confrères.

My tentative scheme: to weed or omit elders in *Active Anth.*; to look to Cambridge Left (Drummond, etc.), Bridson, Oppen (if energy don't fail), T.C.W., an unknown M. Barnard (??? nothing assured), Collis, if possible; Rakosi capable of anything more???

I don't think at my age it is a suitable job. I mean one CAN'T select the next generation as one selects one's own, but it seems almost the only knot hole for new writers to get thru. *Act. Anth.* really clearing off arrears of the past 7 years. Ought to be something younger and fresher.

Has Laughlin written anything? Apart from a few things in *Hoot* and *Advoc??* Any rate, he's in no hurry, and I needn't worry. He's got two mags to spread in. But I do distinctly want guidance from younger man IF I take on the job.

Surely Bunting and Bridson must be better than Eliot's deorlings. Tho I dare say Auden and Bottrall (*not* Spender) are among young England's best dozen. Can't remember the names of those guys at Cambridge (England), but thought they were awakening, as the neogeorgians are NOT.

That snipe ....s. Ain't man enough to answer, but has adopted a good deal of information contained in private letter. I spose thet is the yitt coming thru. (Don't be an anti-Semite, and don't mention this, as it is better to have him cleaning the sewer than clogging it).

Kemp, Goodman, Madge (at Cam.)—list discovered. –/–/

268: To Sarah Perkins Cope

Rapallo, 15 January

–/–/ One of the most valued readers seemed to find the Cantos entertaining; at least that's what he said after 20 minutes, with accent of relieved surprise, having been brought up to Italian concept of poetry: something oppressive and to be revered.

Skip anything you don't understand and go on till you pick it up again. All tosh about *foreign languages* making it difficult. The quotes are all either explained at once by repeat or they are definitely *of* the things indicated. If reader don't know what an elefant IS, then the word is obscure.

I admit there are a couple of Greek quotes, one along in 39 that can't be understood without Greek, but *if* I can drive the reader to learning at least that much Greek, she or he will indubitably be filled with a durable gratitude. And if not, what harm? I can't conceal the fact that the Greek language existed.

Ole Binyon, by the way, has just made a rather interesting trans. of Dante's *Inferno*, carefully exposing all the defects of the original. Much better than exposing a set of defects *not* in the original.

269: To Laurence Binyon

Rapallo, 21 January

My dear Laurence Binyon: If any residuum of annoyance remain in yr. mind because of the extremely active nature of the undersigned—(it is very difficult for a man to believe anything hard enough for it to matter a damn *what* he believes, without causing annoyance to others)—anyhow . . . I hope you will forget it long enough to permit me to express my very solid appreciation of yr. translation of the *Inferno*.

Criterion has asked me for a thousand words by the end of next week, but I am holding out for more space, which will probably delay publication for heaven knows how long. When and if the review appears and if it strikes you as sufficiently intelligent, I shd. be glad thereafter to send you the rest of the notes I have made. Minutiae, too trifling to print. But at any rate I have gone through the book, I shd. think, syllable by syllable. And as Bridges and Leaf are no longer on the scene, the number of readers possessed of any criteria (however heretical) for the writing of English verse and at the same time knowing the difference between Dante and Dunhill is limited.

I don't think one ever suggests an acceptable emendation but one does occasionally put one's finger on a slip or a momentary inattention or finds the spot where another man can tighten up his idiom.

I was irritated by the inversions during the first 8 or 10 cantos, but having finished the book, I think you have in every (almost every) case chosen the lesser evil in dilemma.

For 40 pages I wanted you to revise; after that I wanted you to go on with the *Purgatorio* and *Paradiso* before turning back to the black air. And I hope you will.

I hope you are surviving the New England winter. There is a savage young man named Laughlin (Jas.), ———— who may or may not be attending yr. lectures. Possibly too diffident to present himself or possibly thinks his opinions too heretical to make conversation agreeable. If you are meeting individual students, he is one worth bothering about.

270: To Mary Barnard

Rapallo, 22 January

Dear M.B.: Do understand that at yr. tender age too much criticism is possibly worse than none.

Routledge promises to bring out my *ABC of Reading* by April or thereabouts. That contains *part* of the lessons. —/—/

There is so little Sappho that that won't take long, after you buy a crib. I personally think Homer the best Greek. But that don't mean you are warned off the grass re either Aeschylus or Alexandria. . . .

A university without the Lavignac Laurencie is a *farce*.

You hate translation??? What of it?? Expect to be carried up Mt. Helicon in an easy chair?

Write yr. own ticket. *Invent* some form of exercise that don't depend on the state of yr. liver. Obviously an EXERCISE means something that tires *some* muscle.

"*Lai*" starts with something nearly a bad Sapphic line. Try writing Sapphics. And NOT persistently using a spondee like that Blighter Horrace, for the second foot. If you really learn to write proper quantitative sapphics in the Amurikan langwidge I shall love and adore you all the days of my life . . . eh . . .

provided you don't fill 'em with trype.

I suppose *The Dial* was dead before you came? Do you know what is wrong with a rag like *Hound and Horn?* How much do you dislike it, and why? This is not a necessary question, but *Dial* and *H and H* typify a certain *kind* of danger to educated American young.

Much more important that you should *like* something than that you shd. dislike. . . .

That's all I manage for the moment.

271: To Robert McAlmon

Rapallo, 2 February

Dear Bob: Here we are again. My usual rôle of butting into something that is not strictly my business. But I think both you *and* Hem have limited yr. work by not recognizing the economic factor.

Lot of damn rot and "psychology," people fussing with in'nards which are merely the result of economic pressure. Sort out the cussedness and the god damn idiocy which people *keep* after the pressure is removed and the meanness etc. due to A) immediate need; B) habit begotten of need and worry (plus reaction, booze etc. when the blighters can't stand staying conscious a minute longer).

I think the whole of egoistic psychological nuvveling is gone plop because the people who go on imitating Dostoiev. and the whole damn lot of 'em *won't* look at the reality. I.e. what was economics, or inevitable 30 years ago, is now just plain god damn stupidity, and people not having the guts to think *what* the monetary system is. Hell knows the neo-communists won't. They think the revolution is GOING TO BE in 1918 in Moscow.

Lot of psychic bellyache *not* a problem any longer, any more than man being melancholy for lack of a pill. Just as damn silly as dying of thirst in an attic because some kid has turned off the water from the basement.

People too lazy to examine the facts are not intelligent enough to write interesting books (reduced to bulls and memoirs depending on personalities).

And thass *that.* J.J. drunk no more dam interest than anyone else drunk . . . or rather that is an exaggeration. Still I do think any character in a Simenon "tec" w[ould] probably make a better fardel to be carried upstair[s]. An so forth . . .

272: To T. C. WILSON

Rapallo, [*? February*]

Dear Wilson: —/—/ *Why* the hell I was born patient, gord alone knows. You mightn't think it, but when I lose patience something is LOST. It ain't that thur waren't any.

Farrar is doing 31/41, but holding it back, God blast it, till autumn. Ought to have been in print last Nov. or at any rate before Roose took over the Fed. Res. deposits.

Bill's worst work is in the 1921/31 Collected. But there is some damn good stuff there. After all, the footchoor can leave out the slop. No, he ain't better than pore ole Possum, and we damn well need 'em *both.* —/—/

When I see foist issue of McCoon I can tell better what's needed.

EPITAPH

As 'Arriet Monroe approached her eightieth birfday
The — — — — Foundation thought it wd. be safe to entrust her
with the destinies of Amurikan poesy.
They had never had faith in her stability during her
earlier period
            when she was only 60 or 70.

Emend — — — — to Bulluwubby, and Coon can have that jem fer hiz maggyzeen.

273: To Mary Barnard
[postcard]

Rapallo, 23 February

Baloney dollar makes postage ruinous here.

The only book of any use on rhythm is Greek section in vol. I *Encyclopedie de la Musique*, Laurencie et Lavignac – – – –. Sold separetely, I think it cost about 65 francs. No price mark on it. I don't know how much real use it wd. be . . . but I know *nothing* else of any use. I have never worked on it or with it, but it contains intelligent remarks. What they call solfège, or savoir divider une note, is the job. Whether text book is any more use than a text book on tennis or trapeze-work, I doubt. Precision in KNOWING how long the different notes take in a given place. Tell

♫♫ from ♫♫ .

I suppose learning to play a Mozart melody, and seeing how it is written. Never mind the polyphony.

Certainly *don't* worry about *h and h*, periodicals, etc. That part of letter O.K.

There aren't any *rules*. Thing is to cut a shape in time. Sounds that stop the flow, and durations either of syllables, or implied between them, "forced onto the voice" of the reader by nature of the "verse." (E.g., my *Mauberley*.) Only stick to sapphics, till you can send me good ones.

274: To the Princesse Edmond de Polignac

Rapallo, [? March]

My dear Princess: Thanks so much for the Janequin. The next step is to see whether I can entice the Savona singers to sing it (overlooking the old-fashioned nationalism in La Guerre).

Settles one point, anyhow, namely that the sort of verbal values in the Arnaut Daniel have been completely thrown overboard in the Chant des Oiseaux, for sake of counterpoint, etc.

The Marignan seems finally to dispose of Marinetti's illusion that he had invented something. I am afraid the fantasia you liked was more Münch than Ign; I misunderstood his handwriting and thought it was merely from something outside the Chilesotti collection. I knew he had worked on the Trésors d'Orphée before coming here.

Gerald Hayes says the Oxford Press is sending me their edtn. of Wm. Young, whom he (Hayes) proclaims meraviglie e miracoli. The radiators have arrived, and I hope they will be connected for your convenience if you again honour us.

275: To Laurence Binyon

Rapallo, 6 March

My dear Laurence Binyon: I am all for your going *on* with it, as you have begun at the bitter end. I have had proofs of the *Criterion* article, so suppose it will be in the next number. After you have seen it, I will send the marked copy; for the minutiae. I don't think it (the copy) wd. be much use without the article.

You have the *main* quality. One can read the book as a book. The rest is now hardly more than a matter of proof correcting.

By "inversions" I meant any word out of its normal place. Thank heaven you didn't bother about [it] at the start. Concept of Engiish word order didn't exist in D's day anyhow.

The one footnote I shall add, when I reprint, is from Lord Bryce, who was more intelligent than either of us and saw that Dante MEANT *plutus*, definitely putting money-power at the root of Evil, and was not merely getting muddled in his mythology. –/–/

Inversions of accent, as you call 'em, are *dead right* (that will all be clear, I think, from *Criterion* article).

All your work on Oriental art is bound to profit you when you get to the lighting of the *Paradiso*. Not one hour of it but *can* go into the rendering. One's preparation for a real job is possibly never what one does when one thinks one is preparing.

P.S. I wonder if you are using (in lectures) a statement I remember your making in talk, but not so far as I recall, in print. "Slowness is beauty," which struck me as very odd in 1908 (when I certainly did not believe it) and has stayed with me ever since—shall we say as proof that you violated British habit; and thought of it.

276: To Felix E. Schelling

Rapallo, April

Dear Doc Schelling: As one of the most completely intolerant men I have ever met, the joke *is* on you if you expected to teach anyone liberality.

As for my being embittered, it won't wash; everybody who comes near me marvels at my good nature. Besides, what does it matter to me, personally? I don't get scratched by it, but the howls of pain that reach me from the pore bastids that are screwed down under it and who have no outlet, save in final desperation writing to someone in Europe.

A letter from a state university this A.M., along with yours, from a man whom I never heard of till he wrote me two months ago; assured me that the American college, univ. etc. are farther gone than I (E.P.) think.

I have never objected to any man's mediocrity, it is the idiotic fear that a certain type of mediocrity has in the presence of any form of the *real*. And the terror of newspaper owners, profs, editors, etc. in the presence of *idea*. I have documents stacked high, from men in most walks of life. Proved over and over again. No intellectual life in the univs. No truth in the press. Refusal to look at *fact*.

It is nonsense to talk about my being embittered. I've got so much plus work going on that I have had difficulty in remembering what particular infamy I wrote you about.

As for "expatriated"? [Bunk.] You know damn well the country wouldn't feed me. The simple economic fact that if I had returned to America I shd. have starved, and that to maintain anything like the standard of living, or indeed to live, *in* America from 1918 onwards I shd. have had to quadruple my earnings, i.e. it wd. have been impossible for me to devote *any* time to my REAL work.

You subsidized drifters can talk. But can you, a man with a decent culture, lie down in peace with Nic Butler as titular head of the country's intellectual life? The man who, apart from all his obvious grossness, has sabotaged the Carnegie fund. Not one damn cent of the half million a year that [it] costs the people has been spent on investigating the economic *causes* of war. Do you like it? Will you look at it?

The author of Helen's underwear is the arbiter of American music. Tell that to yr. talented brother.

What little life has been kept in American letters has been largely due to a few men getting out of the muck and keeping the poor devils who couldn't at least informed. And then when one did hand the American publishing world the chance to take over the lead from dying England, the bastard wouldn't take it.

English edtr (p.c. arrived this A.M.) sic: "Real hardsip (sub-rosa) nobody really capable of writing here!"

"HELP! America." God damn it, look at the facts. What I have done right down to this year. Got *American* authors printed abroad when the foetid American publishing system won't print 'em in America, because the filthy money won't flow, because the profits to Judas aren't sufficiently probable and tempting. If there were not a hundred American writers younger than myself who are grateful to me for services rendered you might have some grounds for talking about "HELP!"

No, doc, it won't do. You ask anyone who has met me or any one of a hundred correspondents about my being embittered. Disgust is one thing, but letting it get into one's own private Anschauung is another.

For every lid you think I shd. tolerate, there are a hundred good guys screwed down *under* that lid (whether in la vie intellectualle or in the accounting system).

You ain't so old but what you cd. wake up. And you are too respected and respectable for it to be any real risk. They can't fire you *now*. Why the hell don't you have a bit of real fun before you get tucked under?

Damn it all, I never did dislike you.

277: To Sarah Perkins Cope

Rapallo, 22 April

Dear Sarah: It is *like* a Murkn college to decide that Eliot is a critic (and then NOT have *The Criterion*)—especially as his poetry is what matters.

I have corrected the final proofs of my *ABC of Reading*, and that may save you part of yr. Mawrterdom.

I mentioned some books in *Instigations*. I wonder what is "available" and what you have read already. Try Browning's *Sordello*. Are you still young enough to read ole Uncl. William Yeats? Or at least to tell me how it strikes the young and tender of yr. generation?

I don't know why you shd., at yr. time of life, take up all the ugliness that the generations before you *had* to *write* in order to cure.

New sculptor loose on the roof, and marble dust dappertutto. Vide seal.

Get *New Democracy* which is the only *contemporary* paper in America. – – – – We have got to clean up the economic mess; and your generation has got to understand how much of life can be cured by a very simple application of economic sense to reality (reality today being ABUNDANCE of material wealth), poverty being an anachronism and *all* the god damn capitalist psychology being a disease that has eaten in thru every interstice of the mind. Distorted the vision of us that are supposed to be furthest from money. How much of capitalist literature can have a meaning in 1950, I don't know. No one now writing can do anything of real interest unless they perform a few acts of mental hygiene. Mostly as simple as brushing one's teeth or using iodine on a cut.

My generation needed Rémy de Gourmont. Yeats used to say I was trying to provide a portable substitute for the British Museum. I think *Instigations* WAS the university for people who were getting educated in 1920.

We ought to modernize the economic scene during the next three years, and then *stay* civilized. Music up to Rapallo level, and a little good art and letters.

I ought to know what you have already read. B. Constant's *Adolphe, Daphnis and Chloe*. How *can* one know what the next generation will like? There is one list of books in my *How to Read* and another in my *ABC*. There are a few things out of print. Golding's translation of Ovid's *Metamorphoses*, CERTAINLY . . . and being an institution of learning yr. Eng. prof. will never have heard of it; though it was good enough for Wm. Shakespear. *And* any dept. of English is a farce without it. – – – –

278: To John Drummond

Rapallo, 30 May

Dear D: – – – – Re Anthl. of Exposures. Suggest you discuss it with Orage. More likely to get it printed as a series in *N.E.W.* than in a volume (or at any rate, than if you try it first as a collection). *A.R.O.* about off his nutt with trouble in finding live copy.

Damn people wasting my time wanting information. Wish *some*one would attack the – – – – museum. They try to blackmail foreigners into giving them free copies; and absolutely – – – – on all living authors. I don't think you will find first edtns. of Cantos there either. Just the same as the peedling Tate Gallery refusing Epstein's *Birds* as a gift—which mattered; and presumably buying his later tosh at high figure.

Theory of bugwash society: that writers and artists are *not* to be sustained.

Egoist was Harriet Shaw Weaver, – – – –. Titular edtr. Dora Marsden who wrote the front pages on "philosophy" and left the rest free to letters. As nearly as I remember, I got them to appoint Aldington sub-edtr. and later got Eliot the job, though I remained unofficially an advisor without stipend. I think the files will indicate what I was responsible for, and at any rate I served as katalytic. H.W. deserves well of the nation and NEVER *turned away* anything good. Also the few articles she wrote were full of good sense. She amply deserves Eliot's dedication of whichever book it was.

No, of course the – – – – Museum hasn't *The Little Rev.* and they will have hell's own delight of a time to get it *now;* and any – – – – you can heap on 'em will be personally appreciated. Suggest you apply to the Duckegg of Marlborough (as the publication of Joyce after Consuelo subscribed promptly truncated my social contacts in "them quarters." Poor dear couldn't have it in the house wiff her growing sons (aged, if I remember rightly, about 18 at the time). That's American refeenment fer yuh).

Of course, J.J. never saw proofs of either *Eg.* or *L.R.Eg.* always secretive about circulation. Think it ended with 185 subscribers and I imagine *no* newsstand or store sales.

I have *L.R.* here, but your bloke wd. have to see it on premises. I am not trusting it inside a country run by unadulterated – – – – and which stole 500 copies of the French edtn. of *Ulysses* and then blackmailed the importer into silence. Said *if* he continued to complain about the theft they wd. "get him somehow," meaning crab his further publication of anything. *That* is the spirit of England, especially of Brit. licherchoor, the *Quarterly Review,* Sir J. Swire, etc., the whole – – – – lot: *Observer,* Richmond of *Times,* etc.

Nos. 1 and 2 of *This Quarter* can be consulted in Rapallo, but not very interesting.

Despite *The Egoist's* having been necessary to print Joyce, W. Lewis, Eliot and a lot of my stuff that Orage would *not* have in *The New Age*, I wish the young wd. rally round *New Eng. Weekly*. Orage must be 60 by now. Can't expect complete flexibility, and he has to concentrate on what he understands. Nevertheless, *much* better than the new credit mags, which are more tolerant of stray opinions. And while he is stubborn as a mule, a little persistence usually makes him see the *best* of what he don't follow, though he won't give way on the almost.

At any rate, he did more to feed me than anyone else in England, and I wish anybody who esteems my existence wd. pay back whatever they feel is due to its stalvarrdt sustainer. My gate receipts Nov. 1, 1914-15, were 42 quid 10 s. and Orage's 4 guineas a month thereafter wuz the SINEWS, by gob the sinooz.

279: To Mary Barnard

Rapallo, 13 August

Dear M.B.: Practical (or not) matters touched in this A.M.'s note.

Re mss. I think you have as good a chance as anyone of the young.

I don't know whether you have seen *Active Anthology* (Faber, oh damn 7/6 shillings, so I suppose prohibitive in the U.S. unless some liBerry!!!)

Routledge have pubd my *ABC of Reading* at 4/6 and the Yale Univ. are doing an Americ. edtn. Apart from what you might get from those vols. (the *A.A.* certainly *not* a model . . . but informative . . .) I don't know what *others* of yr. age are doing. Can only give estimate of intrinsic, etc.

As you have got that far, I don't know what you can be TOLD. Given the contents, what more can be done?

Technically you can study music. And apart ça, I think it is mainly a question of WHAT, not how.

There *is* a slight stiffness or old-fashionedness. . . . The language is still literary ("beholds" and "wenches" are not live speech). All of which is *very* slight, in the given case, but cumulative . . . and damned hard to escape. Landor's marmoreal??? Etc. Etc.

Re Gugg. make yr. Greek metre plan as *impressive* as possible. Throw in a lot of technical terms: Sapphic, Alcaic, etc. (with the correct spellings, etc.)

Rousselot is dead. I don't know if the College de France phonetics dept. is going on with the phonoscope experiments. However, that wd. give you excuse to pass thru Paris en route to Greece (where I don't imagine there is *any* real work to be done, but the Guggs. always have excuses for travel).

Do you want to send yr. stuff to Marianne Moore, with request for criticism? From someone *not* so much in sympathy with the contents.

— — — —

I am sending the unpubd. ones to Eliot. He is slower than coal tarrr and I don't suppose I shall get any action or answer out of him, but he is due here in October, IF, etc.

I *still* think the best *mechanism* for breaking up the stiffness and literary idiom *is* a different metre, the god damn iambic magnetizes certain verbal sequences. The lovely Mrs. Whatshername who died. What her name, married Benét. Wylie (Eleanor) etc. Different rhythm texture. Or take Helene Magaret—don't seem to *go on*. Don't worry about *lightness*. You ain't an Amy Lowell. Shall the gazelle mimic the hippo. "Be yerrsellf!!" I've forgotten yr. age. But it's O.K.

I have all, I have, confound it, to forge pokers, to get economic good and evil into verbal manifestation, not abstract, but so that the monetary system is as concrete as fate and *not* an abstraction etc. . . . Is all I can do. I can't think out the answers for anyone else.

I don't see any other occupation for you than work on metre, rhythm, melodic line. And to set round watchin' and waitin'.

You are probably more abundant than such of the younger males of yr. generation, as I know of, but then . . . what do I know about the comparative dynamisms.

The definite *vacancy* is in melodic validity. There *is* definitely a place open and waiting.

Nobody can DO anything about their contents anyhow; it either is or isn't. —/—/

280: To LAURENCE BINYON

Rapallo, 30 August

Dear L.B.: When one has finally done the job and found the *mot juste*, I dare say violent language usually disappears. Rubens' technique (at least in one painting about 4 ft. square) is not stupid. I dare say I damned him for the whole groveling imbecility of French court life from the death of François Premier to the last fat slob that was guillotined. —/—/

And when one has the mot juste, one is finished with the subject; and American magazines come round 20 years later to ask you to be paid for recollecting it.

Nic. del Cossa is now, I believe, considered the chief responsible for the Schifanoja frescoes. And I have since seen some Tura's corrupted by the Rotterdam or gotterdam dutch, or tinges with hell smoke.

And my use of "idiotic" is loose. You are quite right about that. Have always been interested in intelligence, escaped the germy epoch of Freud and am so bored with *all* lacks of intelletto that I haven't used any discrimination when I have referred to 'em.

There is another essay in the new Faber vol. dealing with Guido's relations (to Eliz. Eng.). I will ask 'em to send it you (shd. be out in Sept.). Also in "Date Line," the introd to the vol.

A lot of my prose scribbling is mostly: "There digge!" Plus belief that criticism shd. consume itself and disappear (as I think it mostly does in my *ABC of Reading*).

Ballate and Canzoni mainly for music. Sonnets ceased, I think, to be for music; hence ultimately a drug on market and defective in certain sensibility. I have set a lot of Villon and a good deal of Guido (more of that another time, or viva voce).

P.S. Power and speed to second Cantico.

Let's say Rubens' *interests* were limited; a lot of the life of the mind, and a deal of the best of it, unknown in his entourage?

281: To Mary Barnard

Rapallo, 18 December

Dear Mary: I was certainly right in telling you to work on sapphics. Metric work, your only rock to keep from being submerged in "conditions," Canby's weekly flux, etc.

Keep at it.

Have a care against spondee too often for second foot. The tension must be kept, and against the metric pattern struggle toward natural speech. You haven't *yet* got sense of quantity. And if you *had*, it wd. be something too easy to be worth wanting.

"I am rich" is as near as "rich am I," the *long* wovel makes the syllable long, and a syllable that is open and easily sung long fits a long space, perhaps better than a short vowel with heavy consonant load.

Sculptor*s* (plural) wd. perhaps be better language, and O.K. to end strophe. "I send forth ships" (well, I dunno, "I send ships forth." All those syllables are *long*).

"*Lai*," I am emphasizing, present impression is that metrically it is your best to date.

"*Lie adept*." Several adjectives don't seem to do much. What happens if you *remove* "courteous," "suave," (gusto a second noun) "No one," for "none." "to pass" for "to the passing," and "dipping *of*" (*ing* and *of* useless syllables; every syllable shd. have a reason for being there). —/—/

If you think well of any of these suggestions, please write direct to T. C. Wilson and ask him to make 'em on the mss.

Am passing 16 poems for the anthol. Omitting everything already used in College Vurrse. (Not sure, mebbe there are one or two more in ms.) Drummond is looking over.

Anyhow, you're bein' the starr border and I hope you won't *flop* like H. M......, and apparently the B..... goil is a floppin' already, unless Wilson has merely got a poor sample.

At any rate yr. in the runnin fer the star lady purrformer and the young lads need a stronger parental hand than they want.

You go on CHAWIN at them Sapphics, with an Alcaic strophe on Sundays. Remember the SWAT must strain against the duration now and again, to maintain the tension. Can't have rocking horse Sapphics any more than tu TUM, iambs.

282: To W. H. D. ROUSE

Rapallo, 30 December

Dear Dr. Rouse: I did not suspect you of wanting the advertisement, but to make up for American defects one has to participate in the annoying virtues of one's tribe. It is barbarous, but there it is. If a thing is good, the bdy. murkn wants to *do* something about it (often before he quite knows what it is).

The border line between "gee whizz" and Milton's tumified dialect must exist. (Dante, in *De Volgari Eloquio*, seems to have thought of a good many particulars of the problem.)

I must have been obscure if you thought it was *long* words in the Greek that bothered me. I may feel a gap between Homer and the dramatists greater than that which really exists.

Negroes in America love polysyllables and used to assemble most marvelous collections of unexpected syllables.

I have now read the "Adventures" straight through with gt. enjoyment, and clearer view of what you were doing. I don't know whether my actual notes on minutiae wd. interest you or not? If so, I can send up the volume. Or summarize, as you like.

I hope *The New English Weekly* will invite you to say something about the campaign for live teaching of Greek and Latin. That wd. come better from you than from me.

There are more questions in my head than I can set down with any apparent coherence.

Along with direct teaching of the language, is there any attempt to teach real history? "Roman mortgages 6%, in Bithinya 12%."

I have been for two years in a boil of fury with the dominant usury that impedes every human act, that keeps good books out of print, and pejorates everything.

Need for terminology, for articulation of terminology (for control of language). Decadence of thought, due to lack of observation of words. English contempt of literature and all the arts and 50 years of worse contempt in the U.S.A. It all goes into the kettle, and the broth is thin. It may be an illusion that the Middle Ages tried to define their terminology. Certainly the last half century did not.

Have you any explanation for the obsolescence and decline of Gk. and Lat. studies after, let us say, the Napoleonic wars?

Or, taking it from another angle, do you see in Brit. education during your time a reason why the country tolerates a governing class that can't see that: Work is not a commodity. Money is not a commodity. The state has credit. The increment of association is not usury?

Until Latin teaching faces the economic fact in Latin history, it may as well leave out history. History without econ. is just gibberish. My generation was brought up in black ignorance. Wherever one looks—printing, publishing, schooling—the black hand of the banker blots out the sun. An enlivening of classic study can come and come very quickly if the teachers will try to understand the question of the new tables. "There digge." We have been taught sham history, *à vomir.*

What I am trying to get at is, given the economic inferno that one has been through, trying to teach an elite and the present distracted writer cursed for every allusion he ever made to Greek or Latin, surrounded by people who complain that they can't "understand" a passage, for the simple reason that something Greek or Latin is mentioned.

Granted the bulk of the sabotage and obstruction is economic and nothing else, there is the fact to be faced that the modern world has lost a kind of contact with and love for the classics which it had, not only in the 18th Century and in the Renaissance (part snobism), but throughout the Middle Ages, when in one sense it knew much less.

And life is impoverished thereby.

"The truth makes its own style." But education has been so rotten at the core, so falsified that every learning has fallen into contempt. (*Latin Teaching* No. 2, June 1934) Mr. Croft seems to me an idiot (speaking of frankness). His kind of parroting seems to me exactly what does keep people from studying the classics and keeps school boys from believing what teachers tell 'em. Meaning in more curial style, that with that sort of animal teaching and with that kind of mind eternally eligible for jobs in schools, one *must* have some communication of the classics to living man that is independent of schools.

Some auxiliary means of teaching the intelligent boys who, being interested in locomotives at the age of 10, find Crofts insufferable but are not of necessity hermetically sealed against literature at 19 or 30.

Have I finally got round to my plea: for some means of communicating the classics to the great mass of people, by no means foreordained to eternal darkness, who weren't taught Greek in infancy?

Eliot remarked of G. Murry (or however he spells it): "He has erected between Euripides and the reader a barrier more impassable than the Greek language."

The "Adventures" will be given to half a dozen people whose interest I have aroused in the *Odyssey* and been unable to slake, as they are all too sensitive to read the tushery provided by "adorned" translations, though they might stick a couple of pages of Pope and a dozen or so of Chapman. Can you augment it? Can you keep the drive of the narration and yet put back some of what you have skipped? What happens if you go through it again, making as straight a tale for adults?

I take it the book of my essays to which you refer (cursed literary sentence) is *Make It New.* I wonder if you have seen my try at a text book (*ABC of Reading*)? Or whether it wd. infuriate you if you did?

Coming back to your letter (it is plain I have *not* wanted to be in England for years, but I would now like to be within talking distance) about strong words and small children, I wonder if in natural state they are shocked . . . or only after having used the words themselves *and* [been] reproved for it. . . .

What you say about Greeks in part Italian today. Small child at Sirmione saying "ci sono anche più depositi." Someone had dug into a few Lombard graves and left 'em open.

As to *plain* words: I wonder if it isn't part of writer's duty to clean them. A beastly writer can and often does defile his whole vocabulary, without least violence to correct syntax.

On page 6 you have the node. All real narrative writing (the secret of Edgar Wallace, to emerge from your (presumable) groves) is great modesty. As long as the narrator can keep his mind on his story and not think about his waistcoat or whiskers.

"Spade" for gelded she-dog gives place to "bitch," which oughtn't to be any worse than mare, cat female of Tom-cat or gatto maoulador, and so forth. Cock can not be mentioned in America. All Americans are shocked by the English use of it to designate male chicken and stay so until they have been some time in Europe (at any rate all pre-prohibition Americans).

From my first outpour. To repeat that about Binyon: do you know him? He needs you. I need yr. criticism more than you do mine. Nobody has taught me anything about writing since Thomas Hardy died. More's the pity.

1 9 3 5

283: To Henry Swabey
[postcard]

Rapallo, 24 January

— — — — You are quite right on the Atys element in all Anglo-Educ. Ref. my Cavalcanti *Rime* (partially reprinted in *Make It New*). Might note also that *New English Weekly* is giving more space to letushope live writing as such. At any rate, Eliot and I prob. going into some sort of advisory board (whether publicly or unpublicly).

Want new blood. Also I want (privately) news of state of opinion, etc., in let us say Durham (which is a place like another). Being out here. I have more *time* to reflect on such items than blokes in an office can. Don't worry about what you have been told you *ought* to think, but spill out what you *do* think and you may serve me as an extra eye. I need about 400. Also need counterweight; letters to *N.E.W.* office, to counteract resistance of the hang-backers. Trying for W. H. D. Rouse, Ogden, etc. In fact, want *all* the live minds. Don't worry about what I know; take a chance on my *not* knowing everything. Will do me no harm to hear the same news twice. Suggestions as to what hornets' nest thinks a lit. weekly (with economic drive) ought to be and do.

284: To E. E. CUMMINGS

Rapallo, 25 January

Waal; my deah Estlin an consort: You coitunly are a comfort inna woild
thet is so likely to go aphonik. An wot with this bootshaped pennyinsula
sufferin from premature bureaucracy ANYHOW!! And we allus were having
such a nice quiet revolution (continual); all but the local hill-habitators
who are all out and bigod they won't have any more cow if they ain't got
freedumb to leave tubercules in the milk.

And so forth. Anyhow, the old line is beginnin to notice the new boys
in 40 lire neckties and a forrinoffice manner. And I hope it busts somewhere else, so'z the boss can git on WIFF it.

Anyhow, the poems is sent to Lunnon espresso with a prayer to print
all that can be print without pinching English printers, libitty-tea law being az iz. – – – –

England needs you. I am afraid my popular style is rhetorical, just
broad. Not very pointed.

To –– on England:

> Ye ha' ca'd canny on food and drink
> The bairns can na eat your blather,
> You'd buggar a horse for saxpence
> Or sell up your dyin' father.

Simple old-fashioned songs, I can no other. And anyhow, they wd. pass
over the head of the pubulace. Note "saxpence," Lowland Scots for "a
tanner."

In any case remember I'm oldern you are.

As for new dollar substitutes, old tradition dies hard. I saw one yester'
week hung on pine tree by the sea board. Such is the Mediterranean spirit.

And so forf.

285: To C. K. OGDEN

Rapallo, 28 January

English thought needed an Ogden
To lead it out of its hog den.

Respected OG: Instead of sending me *Basic Eng.* and *ABC* you have sent
me a mass of light licherachoor with such repulsive titles as *Carl and Anna*
havva banYana.

You c'mon hellup me galvanize *New Eng. Weekly.*

Ad interim, I have writ to two High and Mighty Romans.

You might send a bit of propaganda to Ct. Galazzo Ciano, under sec.

for Press; and Carlo Delcroix, himself; or Dr. Monotti, edtr. of *Vittoria,*
— — — —. Monotti works just under Delcroix and wd. show him the stuff.
With De Vechii at Ministry of Education there wd. be more chance of
action than with some aesthetic mossback, sentimentalizing over Dela
Crusca. Also Dr. Hugo Fack (Gesell's pubr.) — — — — is good ground and
I have already interested him.

I can't rewrite all Fenollosa's essay which is the *most* important item on
my list of what you don't know.

Re Frobenius and Bruhl. Intelligence is so . . . *rare* that when one,
onct in 10 years, finds traces of it, the fact shd. cause joy. Bruhl just a
professor. Frobenius *thinks*. Both of 'em wd. enrich sis What's-her-name's
culture and enlighten her a lot more than some of the 47 varieties of bone-
head whom she does mention.

I proposed starting a nice lively heresy, to effek, that gimme 50 more
words and I can make Basic into a real licherary and mule-drivin' language, capable of blowin Freud to hell and gettin' a team from Soap
Gulch over the Hogback. You watch ole Ez do a basic Canto. —/—/

286: To Arnold Gingrich

Rapallo, 30 January

Private. Dear Arnold: —/—/ To run *The Noo Yorker* gaga you need
Kumrad Kumminkz. Vide my *New Eng. Weekly* article. The Kumrad
has 70 poems thet nobuddy loves. And it za shyme he has to send 'em
out of the country. Not that I am sure London will print 'em. But still,
the cachet. To git the younger pubk there iz nuthin like Kumrad Kumminkz. I mean you got Hem's lots. Cummin'sh has the others. And where
t'hell is ole Will Wallruss Willyams?

Give my regards to hoff, I shur like his drawin' wot hazza lot the mugs
ain't agoin' ter see. That boy can—put the lies right where they beelong.

Waal, damm if I can see the diff between Hem tellin the bastids to *look
at the* etchings and me tellin 'em to *look* at the skullpschoor. But so iz it.
I admit when they look at them nice old-fashioned engravins they can see
a park bench anna brothel, and besides the bloke iz in jail. — — — —

A couple of bawdy songs from father Eliot wdn't go bad with the
electorate. I see he has written a play. Mebbe a few lyrics sech az:

> *When I was only a slip of a girl*
> *Wot couldn't eat more'n a couple of chops . . .*

or of course "Bolo," which I am afraid his religion won't now let him
print. — — — — Well thet wdn't do fer yr. family maggerzeen nohow. But
still he might supplement Rascoe, or etc.

And what iz gone wrong with McAlmon? The kid just playin' the fool,
or wotever? Too bad some of his best have been printed, though hardly
more than privately printed. I hope he ain't gone plumb to hell.

287: To C. K. Ogden

Rapallo, 7 February

ad interim. Respected Og: Compliments on "Idola Fori," and up to p. 48 where I now am (rising for an interval, a breath, etc.). I shall perform due salaams, etc. publicly. *After* a shot at sis what's her name, and commendation of Blondel.

I have yet to see that Richards is much use. (Willing to learn, but no need of concealing doubts now present.)

Have duly noted refs to Lev-Bruhl and Leibnitz on what he didn't know about ideogram.

Got to have you in *N.E.W.* if I am to keep them at it.

I take it my note on Basic will be in issue for 14th. If you see any way that my criticism can be more *con*structive than I am likely to make it, don't be backward about suggesting it, either in print or privately. I shall try to make it clear that I am all for building, mostly on yr. foundation.

Eng. print so smeared with personal sniping and clique politics that any definition of limitations or any definition whatever is likely to be taken as "anti-."

So far (provisional estimate), Richards started and more or less lay down on you. Blondel lectured and is serious character, and Miss Whazzername is a diligent pupil.

For the rest, you have done yr. damndest with the personnel you cd. find.

I shd. be grateful for notice of *any* serious thought in Eng. outside *Psyche* group. . . . Had you been possessed of my apostolic fury, you cd. have "sold" me some of it five years ago when I was trying to prod you into pubng Eng. edtn of Fr. Fiorentino. I still doubt if (as pedagogy, etc.) there is any Eng. introd. to history of philos. as clear as F.F. up to Leibnitz, or wherever the first edtn stopped. And maintain my suspicion that after Leib we have either trype or derivatives from material science (roughly speaking) . . . nothing a man with any real brain cdn't do better with half an hour's thinking than with mucking around with printed material, until you did yr. job of chucking out useless verbiage.

As Frobenius functions, I consider him interesting. Also I return to my emphasis on Fenollosa's essay, neither of which elements I have yet found in the Ortho. pubctns. I can't see 'em as destroying or invalidating, but definitely as augmentive.

I shd. also appreciate confidence of list of serious characters in England, if any known to you. My own, outside the field of economics, is very short.

288: To W. H. D. Rouse

Rapallo, 22 February

Dear Dr. Rouse: A week or ten days ago I made some notes on yr. first book but did not send them because I thought:

I. Most important thing is that you finish the new translation in your own way and own spirit, uncontaminated.

II. In any poem of length the *first* essential is the narrative flow. My sticking and probings might bother you.

Now Mairet writes me he has written you saying he thinks he can use the stuff *now*, about a page a week, starting next month (which I suppose means March).

I am therefore sending you the ms. sep. cov. registered.

289: To E. E. Cummings

Rapallo, February

My dear Estlin: Don't be more of a fool than nature has made you. Poor Mairet is doin' his damndest and can't risk suppression. England wd. certainly stop the paper the minute it — — — —. But once past the initial difficulty and once you get a real toe hold in that funny, o very, country, I don't think you wd. have difficulty in — — — — away to yr. — — — — content. In between book covers; and in de lookx editions. Ref to the Rev. Arnaut Daniel on the value of fast movers who like 'em slow (male as opposed to Mae's view).

I am, concretely, and without hyperaesthesia, aimin at an Eng. edtn of *Eimi*. And I think a delayed — — — — is worth that. (And the poem as pore Mairet did it, still retained quite a good deal of pleasure for the reader. . ∴.)

May I say to the rev. etc. and so forth E.E.C. as has been said to me (even thru years of greater etc. so to speak gulf stream etc.): you are not known in England. However bad for yr. feelings, this means that you aint' known either *much* or enough. Graves' bloomsbugg *ain't* enough. Tho I admit the company of bro. hoff will be more entertainin' than that of the prospective Ogden and whatever other bloody brits one can scare together, still it wd. be even more entertainin to bring hoff and the Archbishop together. Not that his Left Reverence has yet *N.E.Wd.*

Why don't them buzzards in Noo Yok play bro Tibor Serly's muzik? Stokowsky keeps *promising*, and then Tibor has to come here or go to Budapesth for concerts (hand made) or orchestrated.

At any rate buggar the castration complex. Mairet, Nott, Newsome have *not* got it. It is a plain question of the cop on the corner and a shut down of the works.

Whoa down yew skittish thoroughbred . . . and wait fer the steam roller to pass.

If we had Doug divedends we could print what we like *when* we got ready. This here in'erest in soshul credit ain't confined to pertatoes.

— — — —

290: To W. H. D. ROUSE

Rapallo, February

Dear Dr. Rouse: To come down to trifles, or perhaps they aren't. Certain words seem to me "literary," no longer living, no longer *used* in speech as I heard it during my 12 years in England. Never have I heard the word "flight" spoken, though one reads it in detective stories.

Poor old Upward had a lot to say about Athene's eyes, connecting them with her owl and with olive trees. The property of the glaux, and olive leaf, to shine and then not to shine, "glint" rather than shine. Certainly a more living word if one lives among olive yards.

I wonder if those blighters have sent you my XXX, or if they are waiting for the new 31/41. . . .

Do we say "courteous," or do we say people have "good" or "nice" manners?

"Kind sir, will you be angry" seems to me fairy tale. "Pardon me, sir, but I hope you won't be offended." . . .

Is it English or American to say "Is it yr. first visit" or "Is *this* yr. first visit"?

I don't know that one needs keep "Allow me to inform you" where the next phrase is clear, and the tone of voice carries the meaning (178).

"Oh well" not "Ah well."

I don't see that one *translates* by leaving in unnecessary words; that is, words not necessary to the meaning of the *whole* passage, any whole passage. An author uses a certain number of *blank* words for the timing, the movement, etc., to make his work sound like natural speech. I believe one shd. check up all that verbiage as say 4% *blanks*, to be used where and when wanted in the translation, but perhaps never, or at any rate not usually where the original author has used them.

Alas, as you are writing English, you can't call *them there bloody* gallants, "cake-eaters" or "lizards," "dudes," "gigolos," "young scum" (I suppose my native tongue is still more flexible than English: "good for nothing young sprigs," "fils à papa," "spooners," "saps").

P. 13. A. Won't all the *meaning* go into: "And put twenty oarsmen into the best ship you can find."

When I suggested your doing a translation with *all* the meaning, I didn't mean merely to put back *words*, or translations for words.

I thought that passage about Odysseus on the mast, under the cliffs, has more boy scout craft than you gave it. I thought the situation of Mercury and Calypso has more *inside* it.

???

"And Antinous Eupertheson answered: 'Telemachus has apparently spoken with one of the gods, and learned a great deal of rhetoric. I hope he will inherit the throne of his father's in Ithaca.' "

No use: I can't fit my sentences into your cadence, but the only way I can express what I am driving at is to put down some sort of scaffolding.

" 'Much as the idea may annoy you, I wd. accept it,' said Telemachus. 'There's no harm in being a king. Kings accumulate property, and are greatly respected. There are other Greek kings, one of them, a young one or even an old one might succeed the noble Odysseus, if Odysseus were dead, but in that case I shd. at least be master in my own house.' "

I wonder if the word "canny" (kenn?) wdn't be a useful word here and there.

The *theioio*: not sure you don't shock *me* for a change.

What about Zeus saying: "How can I forget Odysseus, the fellow is one of us," or "How can I forget Odysseus, who is one of us, one of our own kind," or "almost one of us."

"A man with a mind like that comes near to godhead"; "when a man's got a mind like that even the gods respect him" ("can respect").

291: To HENRY SWABEY

Rapallo, 3 March

Dear Swabey: Having wasted postage in endeavour to save it, mind begins to function.

Have noted young Engmn waste time in not getting started; as cf. Americans or Latins. Have seen Englanders footlin round at age of 32, having graduated at Oxon, and not knowin' what they mean to do. Don't matter much what job a man learns, so long as he *learns* it; *then* if he wants to change, he can do something different and do it well.

Plenty *use* for man now who goes into Church with eyes open. Say, having read Trollope's *The Warden* and knowing what he is up against. Church organization: any man patient enough to go into it, bear it, and *use* it cd. be of great use to his country.

This apropos yr. wanting Troubadours, but not indicating if you mean to use study directly to *make* your own metric, or just from general interest in kulchoor.

I strongly suggest you make a study of ecclesiastical money in England. Not numismatism; but to know what the Church issued, under what regulations; ratio metal value to currency value; whether Bracteates issued; paper, if any. When, if ever, did usury cease to be mortal sin? It still is in Roman and must be in Anglo-Cat. Let in for greed and forgotten from ignorance, probably. A start for a young man, and his ultimate reach often matter of knowing and being known by intelligent people *soon enough*.

"We" need a good study of church money, bishop's powers, etc. Most

suitable study for young cleric. Eccl. Soup-eriors wd. have to approve
. . . or look fools. Durham ideal spot to start work.

You understand, general study of any large subject is no good. But you
start any specific line, and as no one has sorted it out, you are bound to
gather a lot of general information and prob. remember the live parts of
it, as you never wd. if you were just studying history or ecclesiastical hist.

I imag. there is plenty of stuff pubd. re Vatican coinage. But like as not
no coherent study of English bishops'. Whole tenor of the acts; theories
on which; morals or theologies on which they issued circulating medium.
In fact, a way to meet all yr. elders who are worth knowing.

I believe Calvin was the black devil, but no means of finding specific
passages at this distance from reference library.

292: To W. H. D. Rouse

Rapallo, 18 March

NO NO! Doc: Here you are backslidin' on all your highly respectable
principles and slinging in licherary langwidg and puttin' yer sentences all
out of whack.

"Odysseus' boy jumped out of bed as rednailed etc. appeared thru the
dawn mist," or whatever; and if he reached for his six-shooter before
puttin' on his boots, *that* is a point to be made, as highly illustrative of the
era. A guards officer wdn't. But I reckon in Idaho in the 80's Blue Dick
or Curly might have. And for his feet, they ought to be well-kept, or
elegant or patrician otherwise they slide into book-talk.

Tain't what a man sez, but wot he *means* that the traducer has got to
bring over. The *implication* of the word.

As fer them feet, the blighter had been usin cold cream, the bloomin'
Bloomsbury knut!! — — — —

I will discuss eagles with my venerable parent, as he remembers when
an Injun brought old Abe into Chippewa. That eagle went all thru the
Civil War and is supposed to have squawked above battles and come home
with the regiment and been stuffed and then burnt when the Wisconsin
capital burned.

What about magic and augury and luck-finding eagle feather? I am
bone ignorant of the subject, but have vague feeling that something or
other, etc. . . .

I think the *openings* of the books need especial care. This first page of
book two is *bad*. I mean it is just translation of words, without your
imagining the scene and event *enough*, and without attending to the
English idiom. The "ΤΗΟΚΟS," I suppose central chair, if more than one;
king's chair.

People have been trying to translate this for 400 years. Can't be done
easy. Very definite sense: Telemachus growing up and asserting himself.
It is the vividness and rapidity of narration, three little scenes, all alive.

That is *writing*. I just don't think you've yet got it. At any rate I'd like to see a "rewrite" as if you didn't know the *words* of the original and were telling what happened.

Excuse this firmness, but hang it, anything else wd. be waste of both our time.

293: To T. S. Eliot

Rapallo, 28 March

KIYRypes!! I keep on readin at this Morterarium. Waaal, I suppose it is a just estimate of the mortician's parlour which is England. Wd. take me six weeks to weed out all the assinine statements. It wd. be nice if you wd. reserve say 4 pages per issue to tell the reader honestly what is fit to read. Hen. Miller having done presumably the only book a man cd. read for pleasure and if not out Ulyssesing Joyce at least being infinitely more part of permanent literature than such 1/2 masted slime as the weakminded, Woolf female, etc., my note on Hank ain't there. — — — —

However, gor ferbidd that I speak modest ever again about anything I find fit to recommend. If you print Brid. you can print Bunting's Firdusi, which certainly is good enou(bloody)gh fer 'em.

Re translatin': ole Rouse is getting stubborn, won't pay any attention to Aurora's manicuring or Telemachus' feet. Damn. And he might have been useful stimulus both to Bunt. and Bin. —/—/

> SONG FER THE MUSES' GARDEN
> *Ez Po and Possum*
> *Have picked all the blossom,*
> *Let all the others*
> *Run back to their mothers*
> *Fer a boye's bes' friend iz hiz Oedipus,*
> *A boy's best friend is his Oedipus.*

A li'l hard on Brid. and Co., tryin so hard, but still true enough to be stingy. Krypes, young England led by an udder. Madge who started extreme (ne c'est pas) doing the Bloomsbury bend. Contradicting what he has just said re Hazlitt, Cobbett fer the sake of a prospective 9/ and six pence.

Waal, anyhow, I have read mos' ov yr. muggyzeen fer onct and wish I cd. git at the bastids with a acid cleaner. I'm not being merely skittish and deskruktiv. Mairet is the only English contributor I can read with respect. (Oh well; the Binbin is about up to Browning's average verse, that's trans.) I mean among the blokes that are explaining something or crizisin'.

Nickerson is an ASS.

Read, as usual. All the damn brits got a layer of suet three inches thick over their wits.

On whole purty high average for a Lunnon wyper. — — — —

294: To W. H. D. ROUSE

Rapallo, 17 April

I don't know that I have been clear enough re *recurrable* epithets—either to be simple and natural so that repeat don't worry one, or else strange and part of definite intended stylization.

Glaux, owl, totem or symbolic bird (gods connected with the divine animals, as stupid bitch Hera has her bull eyes), glare-eyed, owl-eyed Athena.

The Apollo at Villa Giulia gives tip to Mediterranean gods; startling, sudden, none of that washy late stuff done by sculpting slave models, nor afternoon-tea Xtian piety. Gods tricky as nature.

"Wine dark" I shd. accept. It is outside northern belief, but tells something about Mediterranean water that has to be seen.

Blond Menelaus: small dark Pelasgians or Mediterraneans still believe in cuckolding large Nordic fatheads. Cucufier un anglais, etc. At any rate, he has blond temperament, not redhead but note that as language you can repeat carrot-top, sorrel-top, reddy, whereas hair colours sound literary. As black-headed, etc.

The Nordic Menelaus. As to character of Odysseus. Anything but the bright little Rollo of *Chambers' Journal* brought up on Sam Smiles. Born on po' misero, don't want to go to war, little runt who finally has to do all the hard work, gets all Don Juan's chances with the ladies and can't really enjoy 'em. Circe, Calypso, Nausicaa. Always some fly in the ointment, last to volunteer on stiff jobs.

295: To W. H. D. ROUSE

Rapallo, April

Dear Dr. Rouse: Sorry, but I am afraid I think the start of V. just plain damn bad. Careless, frivolous. Missed opportunities *all* over it.

Let's list the aims:
1. Real speech *in* the English version.
2. Fidelity to the original
   a. meaning
   b. atmosphere

No need of keeping verbal literality for phrases which sing and run naturally in the original. But, the THEOIO is strong magic.

The Argicide, Hermes, carried past, the movement with the wind takes the god into nature. It is raw cut of concrete reality combined with the tremendous energy, the contact with the natural force. The reality that becomes mere pompous rhetoric in Milton. The miracle of Homer is that great poesy is everywhere latent and that the literary finish is up to Henry James'.

I think I have already mentioned to you, or at any rate printed, Dazzi's surprise at the modernity of Cavalcanti. "What, paroles en liberté!"

I come back to my first opinion re the way to get the job done, namely that you shd. run on, in your own way, to the end and then go back and look more carefully at the meaning of each let us say phrase (not word) of the original.

I simply don't believe that any man could do the masterwork that a definitive English *Odyssey* should be at the speed you are going.

Who makes the living line must SWEAT, be gheez!

I appear to be the last living Rhadmanthus, Turco the Terrible and the only fool left on earth who calls down the mighty from their seats (and then watches 'em clinging to the tacks in the upholstery).

Process usually conducted in taciturn aloofness . . . indicated in cessation of correspondence.

Then I hear N. Angell is weeping in public that I birched him. (Evidence not yet to hand.)

296: To W. H. D. Rouse

Rapallo, 23 May

Dear Dr. R.: Yes, keep on sending it and don't worry about my *time*. What else have I? And what is money good for but to save TIME?

I can't translate the *Odyssey* myself.

> A. Am on a job (or perhaps two or three) that needs all the brains I've got.
> B. Too god damn iggurunt of *Greek*.
> C. When I do sink into the Greek, what I dig up is too concentrative; I don't see how to get unity of the *whole*.

I suspect neither Dante nor Homer *had* the kind of boring "unity" of surface that we take to be characteristic of Pope, Racine, Corneille.

The Nekuia shouts aloud that it is *older* than the rest, all that island, Cretan, etc., hinter-time, that is *not* Praxiteles, not Athens of Pericles, but Odysseus.

I keep nagging you, because a trans. of the *Odyssey* seems to me so enormous an undertaking, and the requirements include *all* the possible masteries of English.

A best-selling novelist said apropos my *Propertius* that he (the novelist) couldn't do anything like that, "I got no *depth*." When one starts to praise the *Odyssey*, very hard not to get rhetorical. The deep is so deep, like clear fathoms down.

Para thina poluphloisboio thalasses: the turn of the wave and the scutter of receding pebbles.

Years' work to get that. Best I have been able to do is cross cut in *Mauberley*, led up to:

. . . imaginary
Audition of the phantasmal sea-urge

which is totally different, and a different movement of the water, and inferior.

Hell! There is work *work* work all over the job.

The *first* essential is the narrative movement, forward, not blocking the road as Chapman does. Everything that stops the reader must *go*, be cut out. And then everything that holds the mind, long after the reading, i.e., as much as is humanly possible, must be clamped back on the moving prose. It is enough to break six men's backs, and if you hadn't *been there* in a sailing boat, I shd. lie down and surrender. . . . −/−/

297: To W. H. D. Rouse

Rapallo, 6 June

Dear Dr. Rouse: −/−/ I thought I *had* given plenary approval to Nanny and all yr. country idiom, any real speech.

Card just recd. Possibly you are Greek enough to take complete cynicism as part of divine equipment and that I am so Xtian that a lying god tickles my funny bone.

> *You a goddess ask of me whom am a god,*
> *Nevertheless I will tell you the truth.*

Goddess wd. know anyhow, so no use the habitual mendacity, put as many folds on it as you like.

Pickthall, who knows his Near East, said veracity is only valued where people are in a hurry and set value on quickness.

13 June

The chief impression in reading Homer is freshness. Whether illusion or not, this is the classic quality. 3000 years old and still *fresh*. A trans. that misses that is bad. Must get *new* combinations of words. I can't recall "patient protagonist" as occurring in English. I use this as example. A trans of meaning. I repeat Dazzi's scandal re Cavalcanti using "paroles en liberté" and also wonder about Aeschylus and syntax, whether editors haven't tried to put back too much.

Dear W.H.D.R.: Press of work and *disgust* with the abysmal filth of the world as piled up in evidence on my desk by the *Daily Post* has kept me off this job and I go on a trip next week.

A very sensitive American writer (undergrad) here present has gone thru yr. ms. He is getting ready to write good novels. Last night he objected at first glance that yr. ms. was full of classroom phrases, and *hopeless*, and why did I think, etc., etc.

298: To Harriet Monroe

Venice, 13 August

Editress *Poetry:* In the interest of truth affecting others, I ask correction of the most flagrantly and blatantly mendacious statement in G——'s August note: "Like Douglas he ignores the fact that labour is an integral factor in the denomination of money values."

This is crass stupidity on G——'s part. The "cultural heritage" is the accumulated fruit of labour, mental and physical.

The item in my volitionist statements beginning "If money is considered as a certificate of work done" ought in itself be enough to show that G—— (as distinct from the not less foolish London professor who has assumed the celtic patronymic) either does not want to learn anything, or is incapable of so doing.

The term *Arbeitswert* on the immortal issue of Woergl notes would also indicate a similar perception of a standard of value to have been in the consciousness of the Gesellite protagonist. Not of course that I accuse G—— of wanting to give a fair and honest statement of my economics. He joins the series of nitwits who since the autumn of 1909 have tried to turn the clock backward in dealing with my chronology.

Considering the anti-Fascist slogans of the Green Shirts on England, Mr. G—— also shows himself bolchevikly ignorant of the Social Credit Movement. Which is what one expects of him.

299: To John Cournos

Rapallo, 25 September

Dear Cournos: Are you in touch with any of these Rhooshun blokes you write about in *Criterion?* As there is no way of getting one grain of sense into Communists *out*side Russia, would there be any way of inducing any Rhoosian intelligentsia to consider Douglas and Gesell? Especially Doug. as a *phase* of Communism suited to countries already in a higher state of technical development than their own. Converging movements. Doug's distribution effective for technological phase whereas Russia started in agricultural condition.

Gesell providing the great implement for breaking grip of finance. Allow for conspiracy of bankers and the new 7% Russian loan. But get the idea to some decent bloke (if any exists). The only real one I ever met was O.K., but all American Communists are, as far as I can discover, absolute boneheads, tinhorn repeaters.

I note Mr. Gingrich has yielded. If you can find out anything that wd. be useful to me re that locality, do so.

300: To Basil Bunting

Rapallo, December

—/—/ The poet's job is to *define* and yet again define till the detail of surface is in accord with the root in justice. [Rot] to submit to the transient. But poetry does not consist of the cowardice which refuses to analyze the transient, which refuses to see it.

The specialized thinking has to be done or literature dies and stinks. Choice of the *field* where that specialized analysis is made has a percentage of relevance. In no case can constipation of thought, even in the detail, make for good writing. LUCIDITY. —/—/

1 9 3 6

301: To James Laughlin

Rapallo, [?5] January

No real literature will come out of people who are trying to preserve a blind spot. That goes equally for ivory tower aesthetes, anti-propagandists and communists who refuse to think: Communize the product.

Dear Jas: I suggest, in order not to over balance yr. pages with Ez, you take to using a brief like the above in most issues. In black letter if you think advisable. You can preach on same text when/if you want to.

I want information re what papers exist. *Cur. Controversy* I haven't seen. But I want a list of papers. Does the existence of *Herald Tribune* "This Week" imply that "Books" no longer bubbles?

Also if I gitta choinulist's ticket, lemme know what cheap hotelz iz in N.Y. where you don't git bumped off by gunmen.

The Kumrad, Mr. E. E. Cummings, *iz* back — — — —. You better see him. He wd. prob. sacrifice one of his bright inimitable but with difficulty saleable verses to *New Democracy*. Also his Frobenius haz bin interjuiced to Havid, the *Advocate* might be pipe for a bit of Joe Gould's *Oral History*. Or *N. Dem.* get a *good* bit.

Waal, I heerd the *Murder in the Cafedrawl* on the radio lass' night. Oh them cawkney woices, My Krissz, them cawkney woices. Mzzr Shakzpeer *still* retains his posishun. I stuck it fer a while, wot wiff the weepin and wailin. And Mr. Joyce the greatest forcemeat since Gertie. And wot iz bekum of Wyndham!

My Krrize them cawkney voyces! — — — —

302: To Henry Swabey

Rapallo, 26 March

Dear Swabey: As far as age 22. Bishops' money *very* interesting, and what a louse Calvin was. A pimp, not even a pornoboskos. I shall take steps toward noise toward hope of getting some of it printed.

2. My "Churrrch of Rrrome" article is good because my archivescovo went through it. "Saevos raffrenare equos." Not to change ideas, but effectively showing that I had dragged in several irrelevant remarks and that after all a man needn't try to say *everything* in one article. Article thence improved by omitting irrelevant sentences. I pass on this ecclesiastical wisdom. Latin mind a great comfort.

I. I suggest you cut irrelevant remarks on cinema; and stick to money. Though you might leave the remark on "better he had accepted fornication" or whatever it was. Don't try to write a sermon while doing a different job. There'll be plenty of Sundays later.

II. Sort out Calvinism from Church of England. Calvin is about 100% — — — —, but you shd. for teleological pragmatism (??) get the Church of England on the right side of aequitas as far as possible. Show that the bastards who are pro-usury are against at least some decent Anglican authors. That can be done by inserting a couple of paragraphs.

Calvin (? surely never part of England's religion?) haeraesiarchus putridissimus, etc. But on the other hand, the respectable Anglicans, Rogers, Andrewes (whom Eliot dare not disagree with), etc. I suspect Inge and Ingram are Calvinists and unfrockable. Let the bug-headed ape of — — — — cleanse his own brothel, etc. (Language to be softened before transmitted to the lowly and profane layman.)

Tithes don't really come in. They are a dividend (*not* a fixed rate, I think) paid for keepin up the cultural heritage, which is not limited to material things.

P. 25, final paragraph: law of 1624—Usury is an evil; above 8% it becomes a punishable criminal offense.

Will write to and try to unparalyze Mr. Eliot. Forget if you have met him.

There are 30 or 40 typing errors in this copy: single letters. Unfortunately I was reading lying down without pencil or cd. have corrected 'em. On last page you say "church" has not made distinction. It shd. be "English Church," as I think the Scarrrlett Wumman Rome has distinguished (in fact, you come to that further down the page). . . .

At any rate, good job; not yet perfect. But enjoyable reading.

303: To Joseph Gordon MacLeod

Rapallo, 28 March

Dear MacLeod: Bravo! I am damn sorry you have lost your capital because every farden in these days is a plank in the tiny raft that civilization was floating on. And yr. loss adds that much to my grudge against the damn tee-yater. But you probably saved your soul and lost yr. caste marks in the process.

You might note my article on the Church of Rome in *Soc. Credit* for March 20. Plus communist denunciation of me on March 17th in *New Masses*. Plus Italian Bank Reform and the penetration of half a dozen Italian reviews and the *Osservatore Romano*, etc., by Por and myself writing, if you like, post-Douglas. Corporate State, hierarchy of values, and Italy where a man damn well is *not* valued merely or even more than 15% (if that) for his money.

Damn, I saw some of the Centaurs and thought Faber promised to print it. The abandonment of you by Eliot, Adrian, and the non-contact with Faber's blue china and slush boys, iz all *plus* with me.

I won't argue with you over single sentence, of necessity obscure, until I know you have read my three books on econ: *ABC, Impact, Jefferson and/or Mussolini*, and my current notes and articles. Or till you assure me you know where the world has got to in fight against the big usurers, Westminster bank in particular.

The fine old word "an independence" meaning *not* to be slave to controller of credit. The "owner" damn well does *not* control the output of his factory. The market is lord and the bank (save in Italia) has a corner on money.

Hell, Eliot won't print me either, except when I am harmless (they have been trying to find something harmless for a year. Meanwhile Routledge, Nott and the yanks have had to print several items). And my book on money is held up, and the second vol. of the *Make It New* series has been split into segments.

Use or own. Damn it, I don't want to *buy* or *own* every hotel I stop in. Ownership is often a damnd nuisance, and anchor. It was my parents' owning a house that put me wise, and I struggled for years to own nothing that I can't pack in a suitcase. Never really got it down to less than *two* cases. Which is a *nuisance* and really a stigma of poverty. Given adequate purchasing power one cd. *own* less.

I suggest you try a little Frobenius.

The Gaudier head was finally howked out of Violet's garden, the worse only for a few lawn-mower scratches. It adorns the hotel dining-room on the sea level, as the facchini didn't feel equal to hoisting it, and we weren't sure the structure of the terrace wd. hold it.

Waaaal, regards to the lady.

And this is all the time I can take off "Savin' Europe" fer the moment.

I don't think Eliot can be blamed for 100% of Faber's actions. He is *caught* in the buggaring system of usury and that is that. He complains that "they" put him to cleaning latrines. −/−/

304: To T. S. Eliot

Rapallo, 25 April

Why dunt you NEVER talk TURKEY!

I don't mind earning the rent, but whazz use of a letter all full of irrelevance? If I interrupt the flow of soul, life of reason, luminous effulgence of internal meditation, stop playin tennis against Palmieri and, in general, lower the tune and the tenor of my life, I gotter be *paid*.

Why don't you say: "Will you do 10 quid worth of hack work?" I mean if that's what you do mean. − − − − I take it all I gotter do is to talk about Britches, not necessarily read the ole petrifaction? So *do* be specific. Rabbit Britches indeed!!! Whaaar he git the plagiarization of Babbitt aza name anyhow? And as it wd. stop my doing an article already begun on three blokes that aren't yet mortician's, I spose I cd. be allowed to make an occasional confronto between Britches' dulness and the serious unreadability of a few blokes that would write if they could, but at any rate don't pretend, like the buzzardly [lacuna] . . . proposed title of the article: "Testicles versus Testament." An embalsamation of the Late Robert's Britches. All the pseudo-rabbits: Rabbit Brooke, Rabbit Britches. Wotter hell. Your own hare or a wig, sir???

I spose I can cite what I once said of Britches? I managed to dig about 10 lines of Worse Libre out of one of his leetle bookies. Onct. And then there iz the side line of Hopkins. Couldn't you send and/or loan? In fact the pooplishers ought to donate a Hopkins and the Hopkins letters so az to treat Britches properly. Background for an article that wdn't be as *dull*, oh bloodily, as merely trying to yatter about wot he *wrote*.

Something ought certainly to be done to prevent the sale of Oxford Press publications. Thaaar I am wiff yuh. − − − −

305: To T. S. Eliot

Rapallo, 26 April

NO!! my dear Sathanas: On reflection I see that it wd. be whoredom, and not even en grande cocotte.

If the luminous reason of one's criticism iz that one shd. focus attention on what deserves it, a note by E.P. on Bridges wd. be a falsification of values.

I thought (cogitation, the aimless flitter before arriving at meditatio) that the cadaver might be used to feed young pelicans, or to do honour to the obese but meritorious F.

But more I fink ov it, the less honest does such a wangle appear.

It is not a case where one can merely throw Richardly Aldingtonian dirt. I can't think Britsches has enough influence to be worth attacking. I mean one hasn't the excuse, as one has with nine-tenths of your *Criterion* writers, all Murrays, – – – –, bastards, Normans, Angells, etc., that the vipers ought to be killed. The number of putrid pigs in England is so large that to dig up a corpse for reburial, especially a corpse of the null, wd. be inexcusable unless one were absolootly in need of feed within the fortnight.

I did not instantly expect to find the EVIL one lurking under yr. weskit. But so was it. –/–/

306: To Laurence Pollinger

Rapallo, May

To Rt. Rev. Pollinger: –/–/ The fee is due to *quality*. The stinkingest fourth-rate painter wd. get six times that for work requiring a 25th of the time and acumen. Don't you go running away with the idea poetry is sold by the acreage any more than painting.

The sooner the pubing world gets the idea that the few good poets have a monopoly on First Rate work, the sooner the London sewage system will function and distressed areas become fewer.

The whole of an anthology of that kind rides on the work of four or five authors. The rest is detrimental. Snipes could be made to pay to get into good company. Sharks catch suckers that way in far countries.

The mistake of my life was in beginning in London as if publishers were any different from bucket shops. Arnold Bennett knew his eggs. Whatever his interest in good writing, he never showed the public anything but his AVARICE. Consequently they adored him.

An utterly stinking social order does its damndest to extirpate the arts, and then howls for pity when an artist gets wise.

There is not the faintest reason to build on the false criteria implied in the Robert's anthology.

307: To Katue Kitasono

Rapallo, 24 May

Dear Mr. Katue: Thank you for your friendly letter of April 26.

You must not run away with the idea that I really know enough to read Japanese or that I can do more than spell out ideograms *very* slowly with a dictionary.

I had all Fenollosa's notes and the results of what he had learned from Umewaka Minoro, Dr. Mori, Dr. Ariga. But since Tami Koumé was killed in that earthquake I have had no one to explain the obscure passages or fill up the enormous gaps of my ignorance. Had Tami lived I might have come to Tokio. It is one thing to live on the sea-coast and another to have traveling expenses.

Your magazine will, I suppose, arrive in due time. Printed matter takes longer than letters.

Your technologists can perhaps follow what people suppose, *wrongly*, to be no fit subject for a poet (despite Dante, Shakespear, and various other excellent writers who have understood why a poet can not neglect ethics, and why an ethic which is afraid of analyzing the motives of actions is very poor sham). –/–/

308: To Tibor Serly

Venice, [September]

Dear TTT-borrrRRR: Yer damn right, them New Hungs *can* play the fourtett. I like Palotai vurry much. He can't say much and we have only my limping German. I wd. damn well like to have 'em in Rapallo. In fact am determined to go on with the Rapal. concerts, despite fact that I have no assets save what I can earn. And haven't yet sold the stuff I proposed to shove into 'em.

Pal. sez they wd. be passing thru Italy in Feb. You spose they wd. come for 500 lire and a night's lodging? I can't *tell* 'em the Gertlers did and would again. I don't honestly know which 4tet is the better. Palotai a better cello than Gertler has, I think. Eh bo? Both of the quarts played here last week. Hung. in Ferroud and Bartok Vth. Gertler in Honegger and Berg.

And say bo!! can yr. li'l friend Hindemith play the VI-olahhh?! I'll say he can *play* the viola.

Yunnerstand I can't even *offer* the 500 lire yet. All I can do is to ask you too write Pal in Magyr and ask if they wd. be insulted by the suggestion. I told him I wd. like to have 'em. The date wd. be at their convenience.

What I am doing now is to put together a project on which I might by a miracle raise the minimum necessary cash.

Onforchoonate incident. The Hungs wanted to *eat* at midnight. I have known Venice 30 years but never tried to eat a dinner at midnight. I know that all the good cheap restaurants, the family cookings, etc., close at about 9.55. Am afraid I got 'em stuck with some bad grub, but it was the only place I cd. count on being open. Not having any common langwidge, will you tender my tough apologies and hope they fergiv and ferget. The violer player yenned toward another place, where I thought they wd. git stuck a price. Mebbe they wdn't have been stuck but it is a place on the Piazza where I thought it wuz dangerous for working men like ourselves to risk a bill. – – – –

309: To Ernest Hemingway

Rapallo, 28 November

Waal, me deah Hembo: Glad to see you doing man's woik and spillin the dirt on Georges, etc., which don't lower me respekk for Benito but raises wot I have for E.W.H. Now why don't you use yr. celebrated bean another 24 minutes and got to it that *all* them buggarin massacres are CAUSED by money. What is money? How does it get that way?

Banks make 90% of all buggaring money, of all exploding gunrunnin gunselling jawbreaking and eviscerating and . . . amputating money that goes into buggarin shells for the bloody, was it a WAR. And if the . . . didn't want it, and if murder by the million and no fun and no . . . chance to kill the sonvabitch that profits by hiring some poor simp to likk you first, is all . . . economics and to the bottom of that to bitch the bastids is the job.

Old Lady Unveiled for a list of the chief cesspools. And a few good slugs right in Bro. Ging's home paper will tell a lot of poor kids WHO got the profits, for 500,000,000 corpses, at so much per kadaver. It is economic. Bikrist.

And the buggars back of the Bank of Paris are more worth killin than pussy cats, however titanic, that ain't got no guns to shoot back with, you god damn lionhunter. What wuz the pore brute doin' to you? But Mr. DeWendel, Deterding etc. that did NOT even make peace. . . .

Why not take a crack at 'em in the only god damn part where they FEEL—god rot their testicles—in their *wallet*, in the buggarin bunk account.

You seen a lot, and unpleasant; but WHY WAS IT? Because some sodomitical usurer wanted to SELL the godamn blankets, and airplanes. As I am trying to indicate in my poem. . . .

Also make Farrar send you the cantos. He's charged me for alterations, I mean he has charged the account all corrections as alterations. . . . So KID the buzzard that you are going to review it, or anyhow don't pay him.

310: To Eric Mesterton

Rapallo, December

Dear Mr. Mesterton: I write to you as the only responsible Scandinavian of my acquaintance, in confidence and not for publication over my name. — — — —

The S. Acad. ought by now to get round to seeing that Douglas and Orage *worked* for peace, whereas dozens of soupeaters merely yodel about it in hope of ha'pence.

As to the literary reward!! In fact several of 'em. Tastes differ. Merely derivative writers with active wives or popular success are *not* idealist in the profound sense of the endowment. Or may be that adjective was used in ref to peculiarly Scandinavian terminology of Nobel's epoch. Doubtless the average of recipients has been high, but some of the greatest and most honest craftsmen, the most persistent battlers for truth have been omitted.

The carving a thesis in eternal beauty or in lasting verity!!!

Hardy, Henry James among the missing.

Sinc Lewis certainly *less* idealist than the author of *The Portrait of the Artist* and *Chamber Music,* and NOT in same category as author of *Ulysses.* O'Neill a post-Shavian derivative. Why not *Green Pastures* while they were about it?

Of course the American so-called Academy is a blot on God's sunlight. I don't suppose O'Neill was recommended by them any more than Sinc Lewis. But the existence of a mass of infamy like Butler invalidates U.S. official recommendations.

I write this in confidence, *not* to be used with my name, as I imagine any foreign interest or interference wd. breed resentment and opposition. Perhaps one shd. keep hands off; on the other hand, the sheer material force of the Nobel Award could be of such great use intellectually and morally if applied where it wd. stimulate greater and more incisive search into truth. Surely that also is a permissable form of Idealism. Shaw himself a mere louse in comparison with Hardy, Joyce or H. James. And Lewis and O'Neill less than G.B.S. Have always thought poor old Upward shot himself in discouragement on reading of award to Shaw. Feeling of utter hopelessness in struggle for values.

I suppose Gourmont never had a look in.

But you can *not* set O'Neill against Cocteau's *Antigone.* Not commensurable. Someone ought to get these ideas or this sense of values into the Swedish language. It ought not to come as from a foreigner. Though no harm in citing it as a kind of opinion which foreigner might hold. Indeed it might even be as implied from published criticism.

311: To Gerhart Munch

Rapallo, December

Dear Gerhart: Do you know Hindemith well enough to be able to find out what is the minimum he wd. take to give an all Hindemith program here with you (or with you and Olga, if there is a trio)?

I hear he is coming for the Florentine Maggio musicale so he wd. be passing near here.

I told you he had been invited to organize *all* the music in Turkey for Kemal?

Reports from Germany now hot, now cold. One, that the Ministerium likes him; 2) that his wife is a Jewess; 3) that he was-is-was-isn't, etc. banned and his name ordered kept out of press, etc.

I think the New Hungarian Quartet is fixed to come. As I wrote they and Hindemith highlight in Venice Biennale, with the Gertlers whom we had here two years ago. That item in case he wd. feel he was [not] in good company apart from you.

312: To Agnes Bedford

Rapallo, December

It is the next *Music and Letter* that I am in. I think it is called Jan. issue. And the estimable editor REGRETS my deleting a line wherein I referred to GIORDANNO as a garbage can. (Age, m'deah; AGE, I am getting mild and tender—I delete.) . . .

Music and Letters (Mr. Blom) appears to be too intelligent and "right" (from my pt. of view) to last.

What of other music pubctns? I am rather ready to *write* and have a go at building up reception of the Villon. Critical campaign for intelligence—rights of the word etc. Aiming at really putting over the Villon and Cavalcanti. But also to bring in vogue of Young, Janequin (already under weigh) etc.

And poke into the operatic blokes (XVI etc.) who meant well—(I am yet too dam iggurant to know what they really did). What is Rosing up to? Still too damn lazy to learn the words of anything? I don't mind how *good* his stage sets are—all helps and don't matter. . . .

Read Cocteau (I spose you do anyhow); read some more if you haven't all of him.

I don't know whom else. Simenon was superior Wallace, but is finished, I think.

313: To Henry Swabey

Rapallo, 19 December

Dear Swabey: Can you find out from the Bishop of Durham *who* it was who stopped the Church enquiry into the nature of money monopoly, credit and economics? The Church Assembly made a first move; it dissociated work from employment.

The Archbishop of York did not object. Or at any rate sent me a brief acknowledgement of my compliments rendered *very* informally on that occasion (postage due, I admit, as only a few Englishmen recognize that countries not under English domain require a different postal rate from the home countries), but still . . .

In the present crisis it matters somewhat whether that stoppage came from the friends and familiars of Messrs. Morgan, Norman, etc., or from the ecclesiastics who have some interest in religion. You as an intending parson have a right to know whether you will be expected to obey yr. bishop or something more centralized and mysterious. —/—/

1 9 3 7

314: To T. S. Eliot

Rapallo, January

Eminent Udder, S.C.D., etc.: −/−/

> *There onct wuzza lady named Djuna*
> *Who wrote rather like a baboon. Her*
> *Blubbery prose had no fingers or toes;*
> *And we wish Whale had found this out sooner.*

This exaggerates as far to the one side as you blokes to the other. I except *Ladies' Almanack*, which wuz lively. Marianne is scarce an exuberance, rather protagonist for the rights of vitrification and petrifaxis.
− − − −

315: To H. L. Mencken

Rapallo, 24 January

My dearly beeluvved Hank: Wot you say is mostly so, but why try to bluff yr. venerable friend that you have *read* any serious work of mine for a decade??

Who the hell cares about Doug. schemes? The job of a serious writer is to dissociate the *meaning* of one word from that of some other which the pore boobs think means the same thing.

Obviously until blokes can *define* the word "money" and ten or a dozen more words occurring with equal frequency in econ. writing, their writing will be tosh and their readers remain in same stew they were to start with.

The act of dissociation can just as well, or better, take place re something daily, and concrete as re something in a washed-out Impressionist painting.

What you go on doing is thumping an unreal effigy and callin' it Ez. − − − −

316: To Ronald Duncan

Rapallo, 27 January

Dear Duncan: I am for it IF and BUT. I am for it IF you have really looked over the ground, tried to coalesce with such extant efforts as *New English Weekly* and *Music and Letters* (Eric Blom). To both of which this note can serve as personal introduction.

I take it you are under 40 and that my experience as editor, as part of edt. boards, etc., *can* be useful, whether it is immediately applicable to yr. case or not.

Naow lemme tell yuh!! A successful (intellectually) review is made by a small compact group of writers. Should be at least four. Have you got four? Three is a bit scanty. *The Little Review* had four. The *Mercure de France* had 30 more or less. *The English Review*, when it lived, had really three generations—stratified groups with 4 or six in each. But F.M.H.F. was unbusinesslike.

Yunnerstan, my affairs are such that I must be paid *something*, even if it is only ten bob or two guineas. To write without being paid *now* (given my circs) is sheer self-indulgence on my part and avoidance of duty on my part.

How many of the writers whom I read with respect and/or interest are you *willing* to include? (Most of 'em wd. also require from ten bob to 2/2/-, though at least one wd., I believe, let you have stuff for nothing. Possibly two, though the 2nd should not.) Heaven knows there is *work* for a live monthly magazine. And also I wd. be willing to put a good deal of energy into the *right* one. —/—/

317: To W. H. D. Rouse

Rapallo, January

Whoops! And do I *envy* you. I *do*. That is the proper way fer a bloke ter know iz Greek. Here I am spendin 24 hours readin the *De Vulgari Eloquoi* which is also badly needed in a sloppy and slobbering world. Man perambulates triplex, seekin: the USEFUL (this he does in common with vegetables), the DELECTABLE (in company with the animals) and the HONESTUM (where he ain't got no company unless it's the blinkin hangels).

Obviously this is not Homer, but it is a comfort after an age of Wells and Jas Douglas. —/—/

And yet again, I have never read half a page of the *Odyssey* without learning something about melodic invention. — — — — The more a man goes over a real writer the more he knows that *no reader* ever read anything the first time he saw it. — — — —

318: To F. V. Morley

Rapallo, February

Waaal, Cetus be Grumpus: — — — Annas fer your epistle. Do I gitt you? Faber's lament for not commissioning *ABC of Reading*, but wanting something more comprehensive. The monkey's tail, let us say? Wot Ez knows, all of it, fer 7 an sax pence. O'Kay by me. — — — But the proviso that I can *revise* the damn thing from time to time as I get wiser. And that it don't need to be full of padding an sawdust.

THE NEW LEARNING (Paideuma being too long a word for
the public)

Introd.

Introd. on what Ez don't know.

Part I. METHOD (digest of the Analects)

Philosophy: history of same. Guide being Fr. Fiorentino. Plus a few scraps what he didn't know.

Licherachoor: restatement of *How to Read* and *ABC Reading*. (Not repeat, save of one or two essential summaries.)

Economic element in history and/or the *conception* of history in living historians who are alive, with retrospect to Cl. Salmasaius an a few wise guys.

Mebbe sub-title "How to Learn" would be useful.

Mebbe it would sound safer to the Colleagues if one putt it:

METHOD

PHILOSOPHY (history of thought)

HISTORY (hist. of action)

Licherchoor and deh Awts, the flow-yer of civerlizashun. Contrasts between Hoccydent and orient. Racial elefunts necessary fer the whole of Kulchur.

How much does Ez git fer eggsposin hiz iggurunce? In the brass covered manner? And when do you want the mannerskrip to git to deh printers?? An how you gwine ter keep deh Possum in his feedbox when I brings in deh Chinas and blackmen?? He won't laaak fer to see no Chinas and blackmen in a bukk about Kulchur. Dat being jess his lowdown Unitarian iggurunce. . . . — — — —

319: To Laurence Pollinger

Rapallo, February

My dear Larripol the Hipol: Fer Whale's own sake and fer the diggity of letters he should be made to pay up somfink on signing, but not to have that mean that he merely cunctates and putts off signing fer sax

months. I don't type anudder woid till this is settled. Even if only 20
quid. — — — —

> A contract time the Hippol's eye
> Should never blink, nor nodding head be hiz'n,
> But to Gug Faber's wiles reply:
> "By whales! the price is rizn."

Waaal, if you ain't still got that de Schloezer, gorrknoze whaaarrr it iz
got to. Mebbe it would be better by itself, not with my adjuncts. Mebbe
the Whale is loaded up to his plimsoll mark anyhow. I should hate to
think of him down below thaar, overbarnacled and crusted wiff pearl
oysters so'z he'd snuffocate and die of not breathing. — — — —

320: To F. V. Morley

Rapallo, February

Waaal, Whale my Cetus: As I was billyduxin, along come the Polehanger
with a concrete, which I answers by this postum, but to save stylistic jem,
I also send you the "turn this the udder way hup."

And me already a-sailing into what the Greek flylozzerfers *ain't* by comparison with Kung-fucius.

I suggest *The New Learning* as a be'r title than *Guide to Kultur*. The
public mightn't take the Guide idear seereeyus. However, if your public
is rough you kin call it the *Guide to Kulchur*, so long as you don't call it
the Gide.

Waaal, now about printin' bits as we go along: I mostly don't care, and
not likely that I could serialize very much of it. . . . — — — —

321: To Laurence Pollinger

Rapallo, February

Dear Pol: It reads like a mystery story to me. Anything Butch [Mont-
gomery Butchart] does without upsetting you is O.K. with me. As to M.
Beerbohm, Max never told me anyone had given him that kt. hd. I knew
he got a doctorate from the wild Scots.

I don't advise you to waste time on *that* question. Butch wrote me he
could get a thousand quid on the proposition and I asked *could* he.[1]

I should like to know as it would be a fair measure of the god damned
drivveling idiocy of the swine of [lacuna] make a writer's life difficult.
The French have a word of five letters and the Eng. one of four.

---

[1] He could. An American publisher offered £500. English offers died with this
letter. The proposition? *The Life and Times of Max Beerbohm*, by Ezra Pound.

It is *not* a book I should *offer*. I can conceive almost *no* circumstances under which I would write it.

It is very difficult to be understood. — — — —

Obviously if the sons of hell put up a million for copying the dictionary one *might* feel justified in doing it. But I should not feel justified in asking P., Pol. and H. to run round London trying to get a million on that proposition. Do I make the nuance clear? — — — —

322: To Henry Swabey

Rapallo, 22 February

Dear Swabe: Why tax money? Why just not issue ⅛th? Hell!! the main purpose of money is to *distribute* goods, food, etc. A govt. must spend, on roads, police, etc. The tickets issued must *not* be for amount in excess of available wanted goods. Hence need of some cancellation mechanism. They mustn't simply multiply and accumulate. (Doug's is not very comprehensible to the layman.) Gesell's is the *simplest* possible. Properly used it means *no* debts lasting beyond the productive powers of plant created by expenditure. (As in cases where money is borrowed by govts. to build things that perish, while creating unending taxes and indebtedness.) Etc.

It don't so much matter what you *call* a thing so long as you know what you mean and can communicate that meaning. Phobia at the term tax can be excessive.

I should like the Trollope pamph. on Palmerston if obtainable at reasonable price. — — — —

323: To Ronald Duncan

Rapallo, 10 March

Dear R.D.: Motto? Duncan hath banished sleep.

I think second number had better be the W. Lewis, not the Cummings. Cummings should take longer to prepare, and W.L. is "more familiar to your readers." The Landor-Lewis, Crabbe-Cummings merely alliterative couplings in first draft of idea.

The Lewis gives *you* chance to examine London as at moment of your own birth. Say the unknown London 1909 to 1914 or '17. *BLAST*, Lewis in *BLAST*. 1912, quarter of century back. Books already there; about 1914, files of *Egoist. Dubliners*. Lewis' *Tarr* (original version), *Portrait of Artist*. These three are known. But the *BLAST* stuff is not. Lewis' position, etc. You, Auden and D. Tom could all have a say re the *constructive* element or the pre-constructive destruction needed.

Re Cummings, etc., and America: I think you better invite Jas. Laughlin to act as American edtr. or correspondent or whatever. Make it clear that you can *not* introduce all the writers in his Nude Erections. That you prefer to do a good job on the best of 'em. That Hiler and Cummings are all the English traffic will *stand* during first six months. That you want him to do the short article on Cummings' poetry. That anything else he does will have (for reasons of space—32 pages official total, even if you at last moments run to more)—anything else from him will have to be limited to 200 word notices of events, i.e., books that mean. That he has 200 words a month absolutely free of yr. editing and that you want a page (500 words or whatever yr. page holds) and don't imagine you will find it unusable. But that 200 words per subject is all that wildcat editing can get over on the suet-headed Brits.

In the case of Cummings: I think you shd. do article on *Eimi* yourself. That someone should notice Cummings' play *Him*. Laughlin do the poems, esp. *No Thanks*. Auden on Com. would also be interesting. Eng. view vs. J.L. And that D. Thom. should do article on the whole Cummings. Or alternate you and Thom. on *Eimi*. Thom. do social significance of *Eimi* and you the general survey of the lit. I want you to read the *Eimi* yourself, whoever tackles it. Cummings' position with large public is due to *Enormous Room*. Known in N.Y. for the play and the ballet on Unc. Tom's Cabin (*Tom*) and the *E. Room*. You can announce the Cummings number in the Lewis number. Or vice versa *if* you can get the Cummings ready for No. 2. But I always tend to run too far ahead of pubk. interest. — — —

324: To Hilaire Hiler

Rapallo, 10 March

Dear Heelair: At last a guy with some brains is startin a maggerzeen in Eng(of all places)land. As he had the sense to come down here from Marseilles for 12 hours in order to consult the high and final EZthority, you can see he knows eggs.

Every three months is an art number. We think the first ought to be a Hiler (as most unknown in Lunnon), the second a Leger based on the mass of L's work, which nobody realizes until they see at least that Teriade book, *Cahiers d'Art* F.L. 1928.

Young Dunc (no relation of Isadora) will nacherly get over to Paris to get hep to what since.

For the Heelair number you orter say a few words. (*Short*, everything short.)

First real mag since *Little Review* (if you except *transition* and *Exile*, which were each partial in one way or other). At any rate kid has got sense and is *quick*, not Brit. suet.

For third art issue, I see nowt better than Ernst-Dali-Arp-Mirò. But if you got ideas as to anything, *tell* us. I dare say a W. Lewis would be better *if* Lewis will show sense and collaborate. At any rate, that wd. precede the sur's, *if*, etc.

If you got any better line, tell papa.

Dunc. very amused at you n me being two rejects from *The Little Review* swan song in 1924.

I think he has picked the few live wires in London and done it very well. Nacherly English ain't *very* lively but some is less dead than others. *And* the mag will be small, at least to start. No need of *transition* crap or Jheezus in progress. I am about thru with that diarrhoea of consciousness. Why ain't I called it that before and not in a private epistle? All I thought of when I last saw J.J. was: "in regress."

I dunno who in Amurka except you and Cummings and young Laughlin?? (the latter as correspondent). Eng. traffic won't carry the whole of the prairies.

Bill Wms. will be respected, and IF *Mule* really gets printed, them young lads can *shout*. At least they will read *Am. Grain*. They at least know that sur-r ain't news. That it was already made in 1923, etc., which their concurrents do *not* know. In fact, I think it's a good bed.

Can you send that catalog of yours and some *unpublished* photos of later work (as many as poss., saying which could be reduced if necessary). — — — —

325: To Katue Kitasono

Rapallo, 11 March

Dear Katue *Kitasono:* All right! Kitasono is your family name. We occidentals are very ignorant. You must *tell* us, patiently, even these details.

The poems are splendid, and the first clear lighting for me of what is going on in Japan. The *new* Japan. Surrealism without the half-baked ignorance of the French young. —/—/

Dear Mr. Katue: The most galling part of my ignorance at the moment is that I haven't the original text of the *Odes*. Pauthier was a magnificent scholar, and I have his French to guide me in Kung: *Ta Hio*, the *Standing Fast in the Middle*, and the *Analects*. I have also an excellent English crib with notes for these works. But the English version of the *Odes* is intolerable and an old Latin one unsatisfactory.

Can you find me a cheap edition? I say cheap; I mean good and clear, but not fancy. If it has a translation into some European language that would help and one would need to use the dictionary only for the interesting words.

Tami Koumé had a satisfactory edtn. of the Noh plays. The kana I cannot use. But I do recognize more ideograms than I did.

Impossible to write ideogram with a Waterman pen. I am doing a little essay, starting my next book with a note on 王名 and 以貫之, the first very clear, the latter interesting in its context.

Translations of the *Odes* are so bare one thinks the translator must have missed something and very annoying not to be able to see *what*.

With Sordello the fusion of word, sound, movement is so simple one only understands his superiority to other troubadours after having studied Provençal and half-forgotten it, and come back to twenty years later.

When I did *Cathay*, I had no inkling of the technique of sound, which I am now convinced *must* exist or have existed in Chinese poetry.

Does VOU include a critique of Japanese past poetry as a whole? A position from which you look at Chinese poetry, Japanese poetry gradually freeing itself from (? or continuing) Chinese, as we continually sprout from or try to cut away from, or reabsorb, resynthesize, Greek, Latin?

There are here too many questions.

326: To John Lackay Brown

Rapallo, April

Dear Mr. Brown: Fair questions. When I get to end, pattern *ought* to be discoverable. Stage set à la Dante is *not* modern truth. It may be O.K. but *not* as modern man's.

I certainly do *not* deny individual responsibility. I do deny the right of any man to shut his mind and accept the unmitigated — — — — of the present econ. system, artificially maintained by the most god damned — — — — and liars.

I don't expect, in the end, to have introduced ethical novelties or notions, though I hope to light up a few antient bases.

The Protestant world has *lost* the sense of mental and spiritual *rottenness*. Dante has it: "gran sacco che fa merda." The real theologians *knew* it.

Part of the job is *finally* to get all the necessary notes into the text itself. Not only are the LI Cantos a part of the poem, but by labeling most of 'em draft, I retain right to include *necessary* explanations in LI-C or in revision.

Binyon has shown that Dante needs *fewer* notes than are usually given the student.

You are very right that Blackmur et sim. do *not*, etc. If Yeats knew a fugue from a frog, he might have transmitted what I told him in some way that would have helped rather than obfuscated *his* readers. Mah!!!

Re your p. 2: that *section* of hell precisely has *not* any dignity. Neither had Dante's fahrting devils. Hell is not amusing. Not a joke. And when you get further along you find individuals, not abstracts. Even the XIV-XV has individuals in it, but *not* worth recording as such. In fact, Bill Bird rather entertained that I had forgotten which rotters were there. In his edtn. he tried to get the number of .... correct in each case. My "point" being that not even the first but only last letters of their names had resisted corruption.

Person looking for gibberish is welcome to find it. A Wimmin maun ha her will.

42-51 are in page proof. Should be out any day. I believe they are clearer than the preceding ones.

Doing a note on Hardy (Hardy's *Collected Poems*) for my next prose outbreak. Now *there* is a clarity. There *is* the harvest of having written 20 novels first.

Take a fugue: theme, response, contrasujet. *Not* that I mean to make an exact analogy of structure.

Vide, incidentally, Zukofsky's experiment, possibly suggested by my having stated the Cantos are in a way fugal. There *is* at start, descent to the shades, metamorphoses, parallel (Vidal-Actaeon). All of which is mere matter for little ....rs and Harvud instructors *unless* I pull it off as reading matter, singing matter, shouting matter, the tale of the tribe.

If you have *Polite Essays*, you will see note to effect that economics always *has been* in the best large poetry. Bank money wasn't so vital to Odysseus. — — — —

327: To F. V. Morley

Rapallo, 9 May

Waaal Whale: I dun finished *reading* my bukk, and there is a few phrases which mebbe iz libellus. — — — — I hereby give permish to omit the names of bloody lice like .....r or .....n, when they occur in indiscrete circs. Yuh git me?

Nacherly I talk about interesting subjects fer 360 pages out of the 370 (my loose typescript), but kulchur occurs in or above the stinking manure heap, and can not be honestly defined without recognition of the dungheap. Don't let this worry you into thinking I spend much type space mentioning lice. But Harry Stotl, *he* mentions POLITIKE, etc.

Of course I talks erbaht deh Buck Hare and other di*ver*sions. Can't spend me hole time on Arry. — — — —

I got some reflexshuns on deh Possum, co's of co'se he's kulchurd az hell. O long about his ducksun to Sam Johnson's *Vanity*. Waaal, naow I axs you is Sam Vanitied??

An I hope you won't fink I overdid Aristotle, cause I got to do somfin so't of thorough, fer to kork up deh *end* (deh TELOS or termination). Can't just go butterflying round all deh time.

I hope you all wasn't xpektin a *sad* book.

328: To W. H. D. Rouse

Rapallo, May

Dear Doc Rouse: Sorry; but England *never* wanted to see her face in a mirror other than a pink one of her own making. Foreign opinion of your country is not and never will be English opinion, and a great many Eng.

characteristics neither attract Latins *nor* the stock that left Eng. in the seicento.

Even so dispassionate an observer as Miss M. Moore writes: "I dislike Eden and Baldwin as much as if I knew them personally." I know the great Eng. pubk. loves smugness and the great passion of the majority is for a boot, any damn boot, to lick. It comes out even in visions. Well, pass that. It is a wasted prelude. And we get no further. After 12 years in London I wrote a couple of cantos.

And I get letters from various Englishmen who do *not* agree with your views. I personally doubt your objectivity. You have too many decent instincts to register certain kinds of filth. I wdn't in normal course set you to catch the considerably more than thief and considerably less than human who infests part of yr. island.

Also you can *not* sell me Pindar, and you can't sell me a dialect that never was spoken and never will be. The classicists have fouled their own bed. *Once* the classics could be studied in certain extent. But to try to take up room in a full life that is needed for Chinese and for Frobenius researches, is no go.

A man can read a thousand or 5000 or whatever books, but to suppose that they will be the *same* 1000 or 5000 after new treasure is available than there were in 1500 is to relapse into habit.·

I will back you and Homer in any international Olympiad, but I won't be loaded up with Mr. Pindar.

And I never heard any nurse or farmer say "for by thee on the sea swift ships are steered" or use any such constructions in daily talk. That is the choctaw that has driven Greek out of the schools.

There is too much unexplored Chinese, and what one gets out of it is too interesting to leave one time for this rhetoric.

When you get my *Guide to Kulchur*, you will probably curse me with the black currse of the O'Tooles.

Anyhow, lasting gratitude for Golding. — — — —

I hope my lambasting of Arrystotle will arouse a little *real* interest as distinct from the bureaucratic exploitation.

I don't see what I could do of *use* to the Loeb Library unless I do a review (i.e., 70,000 words or thereabouts) on the *whole* of it. And heaven knows I am *not* going to buy it. I can of course do potty little notes on new volumes, but that means contenting some damn muggyzeen editor and arguing over each vol. and getting it away from the usual hack reviewers. I could do the Loeb as (but more fully and 20 years more maturely than) I did Henry James' collected edtn. I don't mind having the stuff on loan *if* transport is paid hin and zuruck. But a real volume that would *sell* the library or part of it to a larger public, would imply cutting pages of the recommended authors. At least possibly so. And the lenders might object. On the other hand that could be obviated. I could indicate excerpts by page and line. However you better suspend judgment till, when, or if Faber do the *Guide*.

What I should do would be a long essay, criticism of Greek and Latin cultural heritage *confronted* by post-Renaissance knowledge of subjects not familiar to Pico della Mirandola. The Classics, not vs. "the moderns" as in 18th Cent. shindy, etc., but their place in a plenum containing XIXth Century Europe, the Orient, prehistoric art, Africa, etc. In short, in a *full* culture, with cinema and modern mechanics. Not merely overawed by high-sounding reputations nor squashed by disbelief in the past. – – – –

No, I will *not* help you reinflate Pindar. I left a beeyewtiful folio, Greek and Latin, of P. in London. Call me bdy. barbarian. I do *not* believe Pindar was the 67th part of Homer. All right as dilletantism for a bloke that knows Homer backwards by heart. . . . But I would rather you spent the next decade *revising* your *Odyssey* and your *Iliad*.

329: To Michael Roberts

Rapallo, July

Dear R: What I am trying·to get into yr. head is the *proportion* of ole T.E.H. to London 1908 to 1910, '12, '14.

Hulme wasn't hated and loathed by the ole bastards, because they didn't know he was there. The man who did the *work* for English writing was Ford Madox Hueffer (now Ford). The old crusted lice and advocates of corpse language knew that *The English Review* existed. You ought for sake of perspective to read through the whole of *The Eng. Rev.* files for the first two years. I mean for as long as Ford had it. Until you have done that, you will be prey to superstition. You won't know what *was*, and you will consider that Hulme or *any* of the chaps of my generation invented the moon and preceded Galileo's use of the telescope.

Don't think that I read *The Eng. Rev.* then. I did *not* lie down with the Wells or read *Tono Bungay*. Nothing to be proud of, but so was it. I was learning how Yeats did it. I believe that T.E.H. (if you dig up ms. you can verify) referred to "the pavement grey" (or "gray"; don't remember his spelling). He had read Upward's new work. I didn't till I knew Upward. And I suppose I am sole reader of all Upward's books, now surviving. I spose there is a set in Brit. Mus., and it might be possible for you to borrow my set, if you are in London.

I believe Hulme made Mrs. K[ibblewhite] and Flint do a good deal of the sweating over the actual translations of Bergson and Sorel, having got his slice on the options. I remember Flint glumpily talking about Hulme as a "dangerous" [? man, which] I take to mean that he had colluded Frankie into doing something useful. To T.E.H. at least.

Frankie is *another* study. You ought also to remember who were still alive in those years, and on whom young eyes were bent. The respectable and the middle generation, illustrious punks and messers, fakes like Shaw, stew like Wells, nickle cash-register Bennett. All degrading the values. Chesterton meaning also slosh at least then and to me. Belloc pathetic in that he had *meant* to do the fine thing and been jockeyed into serving, at least to some extent, a – – – – order of a pewked society. But *not*, as I felt, liking the owners of the – – – – pile.

Of course for those years London was *Strand Magazine* romance to young foreigner. Dare say Mike Arlen Kiljumji was the last rrromantic in Alladin's cave. — — — —

330: To Katue Kitasono

Rapallo, 23 October

Dear K. Kit: Your very beautiful book has just come, and I have started *trying* to read it, though some of the type forms are not as in Morrison. — — — —

The poems *look* as if you were going in for some extreme form of simplification, at greatest possible remove from Chinese elaboration. *Not* that I have been able to read even a single sentence at sight.

I take it no one has tried to make poems containing quite so many simple radicals. But my ignorance is appalling and my memory beneath contempt.

331: To W. H. D. Rouse

Rapallo, 30 October

Dear Dr. Rouse: Hupward an' honward! I am very glad my language was violent, and nothing is lost. You spend a lifetime and establish one dimension of the *Odyssey* which d—n well needed to be estbd. My friend F. spends 60 years listening to the sound of different-sized English sentences. Binyon takes 70 years to get cured of Milton. All of you get your rewards; and each his own, not the other fellow's. And at any rate I don't keep one opinion for you to your face and another for use among writers who don't *like*, etc., etc. The hardest job for the critic is to know when a writer is exhausted by an effort and how long it takes him to get back elasticity enough to revise a given job. F. M. Ford wasted 40 novels, as I see it, excellent parts merely buried in writing done at his second best. And so forth.

What is Curzon's *Oriental Series*, and isn't it the place to get a few *results* for the essential Chinese classics?? I have just finished a longish essay on Mencius. I am not setting up as an authority on Chinese, but it might save a decade or so to know of a series that could use results when attained. I shall have to go East some time. The new photo processes make it possible to reprint the Legge at a human price. Study certainly held up when the first books a man wants cost 20 quid. Thank heaven I have what is probably a Shanghai'd (pirated) edtn. of Kung and Mantse, and have managed to get the *Odes* from Tokio (a very bright lad there who runs a better literary magazine than the Occident is now providing or at least wider awake).

Is there an available prospectus or catalogue of Curzon series? What does it aim at? Certainly the Legge inter-page version of Kung, etc., ought to be available at a possible price; the Curzon could go on from there. I should think the Legge a *monument*, and real aid to comprehension cd. be furthered rather by warning the student what it is and what it is not than by trying to do new edition in English in a hurry. The *only* way to learn Chinese is interlinear or inter-page. Awful waste of time hunting characters in dictionary.

The Oxford Univ. Press ought to be fried in oil and Milford and his filthy gang stuffed down the jakes. Of all the farces, of all the misapplication of name, etc., that is the damndest fake in England. The Soothill Analects is just Legge with a little face cream smeared over it. *No* new donation, no new digging into the original at all. Just Soothill's ideas re slightly more re-feened langwidge than Legge. — — — —

The Loeb *is* a serious publication.

Law of diminishing returns ought to be restated or set against a law of *increasing* returns in study. There is more kick in ideogram for us, and for the next century of the Occident than in any other study. Or if that is a silly way of saying it, say than in any other study until you get down down down to bedrock—where almost no one ever *does* get.

The best thing I got out of the Loeb was the fact that between the *Nicomachean* and the *Magna Moralia* (ought to be called the *longer* not greater) the damn Greek lecturers had just slid over Aristotle's teXne in the list of components of kinds of intelligence. That was the beginning of the end. I doubt if anything but injection of Chinese studies can *cure* the results of that dessicated highbrowness.

P.S. I don't doubt the Curzon committee will be hypnotized by the superstition that all books in a series must be in uniform format, and that the inclusion of a photostat reprint of Legge wd. be *the* sin against the Holy Ghost. But even this form of superstition is subject to comment.

332: To W. H. D. Rouse

Rapallo, 4 November

Benedictions: No, I am not cursing you fer not makin your kings talk like gangsters. —/—/

Where the translation can be improved is in dimension of inflection of the voice. Possibly *no* change of vocabulary required, but the greater variety of intonation and of sentence movement. The indication of tone of voice and varying speeds of utterance. In that, Homer is never excelled by Flaubert or James or any of 'em. *But* it needs the technique of one or more life times.

I dare say (in private) that the use of slang is merely a sign of imperfect technique. The slanger *wants* to get the real sound of speech as spoken, and can only get near it by using the expression of the moment. *Limited,* this view, by fact that the god damn iggurunt often think they are using vulgah and slangy eggspreshuns when they are using words right out er Bill Shxpr, such as "boosing" or "bowsing," etc. Look at *Pericles:*

> *Faith, she would serve, (pause)*
> *after a long voyage at sea.*

The cadence is so well-taken that even the archaism in the first word doesn't dim the naturalness of the *sentence.*

1. words
2. sentences and movements of same——

two parts of writin'.

I come back to Ulysses the *toff*, liftin his imaginary highhat as he comes out of the underbrush.

My forebear is 78 or 79. Hard to get him to read the story again so soon after he has read it. Or at any rate, I haven't yet got any new comment from him.

Yaaas, Curzon: stuffed (if ever was one) shirt *would* putt his protegés onto them damn Hindoos and *omit* the more valuable languages.

Isn't it time *you* wrote some memoirs? Old Legge bristling with Protestant prejudice?? [lacuna] notes accompany my texts of Kung and Mang Tse. But vurry good learner. Oh *yes.*

Your impressions of these blokes probably more interesting than Sanskrit curleycues. After all you have lived thru one of the stinkingest periods of world history on into a dawn of sorts. I feel sure Butchart wd. welcome some reminiscences. *If* you putt 'em in *current* language. No man escapes a "bosse professionel" (or however the frawgs spell it). Greeks, I believe, had the decency to spell as it sounded to 'em, even if on two sides of the same street. Bloke said to me yesterday: nine separate dialects in Genova. Not a highbrow bloke, but an ex-marine, as we were coming from tennis. —/—/

333: To Gerald Hayes

Rapallo, 30 November

Dear G.H.: I am aiming my muzikfest for the first week in Feb. Hoping to give rather more of Whittaker's 12 new Purcells than W. seems to think advisable all in a lump.

Now about Jenkins: I think I asked you once before, just as you were in confusion of moving house. I hope to have three trusty fiddles, Münch at piano, a cello, and at a pinch the members of an untried but recommended quartet. Is there anything of Jenkins (or enough for a whole evening) that could be played as it stands?? Say I have it photo'd white on black 3½ by 4¼ inches—would that be legible? O.R. could then copy out the parts. *Preferably* not more than three fiddles, keyboard and cello. Probably *no* keyboard in original. Do any Dolmetschers want to dechifrer the basses (if so it be) or rejuice something for disponible instruments? I know nowt of Jenk, save what you have told me. Münch should provide the new Vivaldi, and stick to that job.

Heaven knows there is enough. And with the Purcell, we shall have representation proportional to Englyshe, *but* may as well interjuice Mr. Jenkins if it is possible.

As I haven't yet a projector, the small but not millimetric photos would save time. I don't mind spending a bit *if* it is to effective and immediate end.

Can you tell me who publishes Dowland? Or have 'em send catalog *if* anything possible for 3 fiddles and/or edited to fiddle and keyboard.

P.S. I seem to remember 3 vols of Lawes' songs. Thought it was modern edtn., but may have been in Brit. Mus. Songs, not instrumental stuff. Have never seen any instrumental Lawes.

334: To James Joyce

Rapallo, 8 December

J-J-J-Jayzus me daRRRlint: The ribbon iz pale and the carbon brighter and dis is deh feast of the angel or whatever, so you better have the carbon as the angel stops the sale of typink ribbuns. . . .

NOW: about Haupy. I *will* NOT. And fer various reysons. . . . NO sane man *likes* wrappin up parcels. It wd. do you no bloody good. Miss Yunkmans is married and Mr. Yauwner is no longer wid him (meanin wid Haupy). His Missus likes paper and string and standin in pust offices as little as I do.

Send the bloody book *here,* and when his nibs gets here I will lay it on the café table before him and say the grreat Jayzus James the Joyce in excelsis, rejoice in excelsis, wants the Xmas angels to sign it.

Like what Gabriel said to Mary (or vice versa) in Fra Angelico's pixchoor. He sez: "I waaaant that." Or rather *she* sez, "I WANT that in WRITIN'."

335: To Montgomery Butchart

Rapallo, 11 December

Dear Butch: −/−/ And now to *both* of you, *disobedient* (which don't matter) but naif (which *may* matter).

All successful magazines are sold below cost. At any rate at the start, and later if they succeed (sez Pat the oirushman). *Town and Country* tenpence to produce (this was years ago), yearly profit 20 thousand quid.

You are competing with *Night and Day* and other mags at 6 pence. The way to *exist* and put yourselves over is to calculate how much you can afford to *lose* for one year, or two years, or yearly; and try to cut down that loss slowly. You can *not* sell at 2/6. The blurb was *not* sales talk. The mag isn't here yet, so this crit. is preliminary.

If it cost you 1/6 per copy (for *how many?????*) to produce, you lose 50 shillings on every hundred copies sold direct; plus postage, plus 32 shillings *if* you sell at 8 pence to the bookshops. If you can sell 200 copies and distribute 100 as publicity, you are *on the map*. If you can sell 400, you are flourishing, at the cost of:

　　　　150 shillings for free copies
　　　　200 to 300, say 300, for copies sold.

If you had sent me estimates, clearly, I might have been in posit to see how to save some of this. Damn it, *BLAST*, its enormous mass, sold at 2/6. 20 quid is a small ante for a new group of writers. A small real loss better than a large one with a carrot of hypothetical profit before nose *if*, etc. Which is not.

Anyhow, loss for first year *inevitable*. Depends what you can afford to lose, how much per number. . . .

. . . with which kind woidz I await the arrival of *Tnsmm*. — — — —

Damn it, *when* the thing has a name, you can put up the price of back numbers. We didn't put up price of *Little Review*, but *if* it had been necessary, we could have done so.

Reid has arrived here.

What else?

I have no drag with Gotham Bk. Mart. Laughlin wrote quite clearly that your proposal to him was *idiotic*, that he cd. *not* sell *Tns* at a dollar. The "Book Mart" has infinitely less optimism and never *bought* any books from me. Wanted 'em on sale or ret.

Miller has considerable talent. Ultimately bores me, as did D. H. Lawrence. But that is private. In fact, I oughtn't to be dragged into giving opinion even to you and request you to keep it under your hats. I am *not* the general reader; and Miller is too good for them. I mean more than they deserve; and I wish him luck. Certainly comes just after the real writers of whom there are .... (numeral left blank).

Céline don't interest me at all, but what of it? Who does? —/—/

336: To Montgomery Butchart and Ronald Duncan

Rapallo, 2nd episl, 11 December

Dear B n D: Waaal wunners will nevuh cease. Mebbe I wuz wrong; at any rate, glad I got it off my chest this A.M. cause mebbe I would have hesitated.

But it *can't* sell for more than 75 cents in the Eu. S. Ah.

I congratulate you on the format. Mebbe you have pulled it off. Banzai. Eljen. Very clever the wire top and Cummings' end-on page. We shall see. Mebbe my morning note was just senile doubt.

The Johnstone looks active. At any rate *useful*. Of course, it is Ernst and Arp, unless the colour is something else. Mah!!! Looks 1938 anyhow; or at least 10 years nearer 1938 than anything else in Eng. $-/-/$

I suspect Bob McAlmon is still yr. best bet for short stories. At any rate, try to connect him. Possibly via W. C. Williams. Unless you got a better line of communique.

That stiff cover and end-on paper, a great light. Cover good. Denys Thompson probably useful as medium of contact with outer world. None of the rest touch it.

Ask Eliot for a brief and *un*printable poem. Or ask me *officially* to ask him.

Suggest review of Wyndham L's *Doom of Youth* in No. 2, with inquiry into cause of its withdrawal, *if* it was withdrawn. $-/-/$

I have read Dunc's Scene I. Thass O.K.

Mont O'Reilly's promised ms. not here yet. He wrote he would prefer it to the old one I have (M. O'R, pussydonym fer W. Andrews).

Anybody can be asked, on evidence of first issue. Zukofsky and Bunting can't diminish the appeal.

I was praps trying to be tacktful and leave a chance for public adhesion-isiveness. . . . Waal, goobye to awl *that*.

As *noble* extinction faces us, may as well have all the living on the contents list. Includin ole Bull Wlms *if* he can do a ringer. But *not* to be repd. by an inferior half-hour.

Young England: serious characters comprise the venerable Butch (almost disqualified as over age limit), one other kenuk, the black Scot, and Mr. Swabey. Can he write a brief essay or whatever for No. 2? Anyhow, there is about awl ole pop's ideas or as Butch asks: "criticize in anny waye."

Cocteau should be honoured; so shd. any frog or Parisite. To be asked in.

It is good enough to sell when it has become a rarity, and impurities are not there to rot it. I guess yew boyes have pulled one.

337: To T. S. Eliot

Rapallo, 14 December

Waaal my able an sable ole Crepuscule: It tain't often I has the chanct ter invite yer, but there izza bloke, as they say here, "in gamba," and he wanssa rouse all the mudfrawgz of the Camasco an he sez: Will the Possum rite a piece saying just and *plain* wot he fink a styge (notta stooge) playe orter be.

He pays somfink, not much acc. Threadneedle standards, but you cd. sell the piece later in the orryginal wiff the kudos of its havin been requested an published nearer the centres of European culture. Dew yew git me? It needn't be *long*, as I know you're lazy. But also it needn't be in that keerful Criterese which so successfully protekks you in the stinking and foggy climik agin the bare-boreians. Dew yew git meh?? I spose the answer is: lanwidg of Agon sustained thru a lively and brefftakink axshun to a Tomthunderink KlimuXX. However, you can say wot you like (not in epistolary, cause they cdn't translate *that* wiffaht losink somfink, but in Queen Eliz's and rhe Pos's English). — — — —

1 9 3 8

338: To Carlo Izzo

Rapallo, 8 January

Absolutely my first free moment.

1. "With Usura the line grows thick"—means the *line* in painting and design. Quattrocento painters still in morally clean era when usury and buggary were on a par. As the moral sense becomes as incapable of moral distinction as the ....p of ....y or ...t .....n or ....n, painting gets bitched. I can tell the bank-rate and component of tolerance for usury in any epoch by the quality of *line* in painting. Baroque, etc., era of usury becoming tolerated.

2. "Praedis": I don't care how you spell your wop painters, and I don't know whether A.P. was from Predi, Predo or Predis. Never been to his home town.

3. St. Trophime, in Arles, civilization entered that district before L. Blum and Co. got control. Better keep frog spelling, there ain't no church of S. Trofime.

4. "Eleusis" is *very* elliptical. It means that in place of the sacramental — — — — in the Mysteries, you 'ave the 4 and six-penny 'ore. As you see, the moral bearing is very high, and the degradation of the sacrament (which is the coition and *not* the going to a fatbuttocked priest or registry office) has been completely debased largely *by* Xtianity, or misunderstanding of that Ersatz religion.

"Ad" is certainly better than "per," but neither translates the "for" which means "invece di," "per le rite Eleusiniane," "dalle rite." Hellup!! English is halfway between inflected languages and Chinese.

I am not sure that "Tollerando usura" doesn't *sound* better and give the force better than "con." "With" in English derives from Ang-Saxon and has oppositive aroma. As in "withstand" meaning "stand against." I don't mean that it means "against," but "Tollerando" has a sonorous body that helps the line.

"Behest" (last line) very strong imperative; probably not indicated in dictionary. But I think stronger than "cenni."

All of which gives you *more* trouble. Ma che.

You could leave the "*con* usura" in various places, but I think "tollerando" better in opening line and in line 2 for the repeat. Also the choice between the two ("con" and "tol.") gives you more freedom.

"Mountain wheat": they say *here* "di montagna" not "monte," which is also associated with hockshop.

"Demarcation" is intellectual. It is also boundary of field if you like, but demarcation is universal. The bastid Cromwell and – – – – Anglican bishops and bankers obscure every hierarchy of values.

"Tagliapietra" (?? not man who breaks stone, but the artifact).

A. de Predi is O.K., if that is where he came from. I wonder if he was da Prato?

??? "Pietra *viva*"?? Whazzat mean? San Zeno architect also *cut* a lot of the stone pillars himself and signed one pair (group with knots of stone).

"Fu San Trophime" would keep your rhythm. I think in Italian you need "la Chiesa" both for churches in Arles and St. Hilaire, or Poitiers. Otherwise it could mean the blokes themselves and not the ecclesiastical munniments. – – – –

"Weave gold in her pattern": in Rapallo Middle Ages, industry of weaving actual gold *thread* into cloth.

"Nessuna apprende più l'arte di tolerare con filo d'oro." Damn wop language has only one word for thread and wire????

"Grembo"?? How refined! "VENTRE"??

What is "ceppi"?? "Brought palsy to bed." I.e., palsied old man. Shakespear's language is so resilient.

Next line I think you have done well.

"Hanno condotto donne da conio ad Eleusi" seems to me to get the drive. That does give the sense of profanation.

"In *convivio*" better than "messa"????

I don't like plural in "cenni." –/–/

339: To OTTO BIRD

Rapallo, 9 January

Dr. Ot. B.: – – – – Bout 3 days ago I luk thru me foto col. I sez: "Blast ole Gilson, five years and nowt done." Only rush of work saved me the postal charge of writing him to say "Wotter 'ell!! Send 'em back if you can't get action." Write me as fully as you like. I think I have printed most of what I know about Dino.

Have you the Cicciaporci edition of Guido? Firenze, Nicoló Carli, 1813. That has a good printed *Italian* version of the Garbo commentary, which of course your thesis can not ignore. Will serve as check-up on the ms. Cicciaporci really the best editor of Guido.

In return for my answers to whatever you don't know and I might, I suggest you gather any available information re Scotus Erigena, trial of Scotus Erig., and his condemnation. Was it merely for some fuss about the trinity? Does Gilson know aught abaht it?? Where *is* Gilson, if he ain't in Toronto?

If you (in parentheses) have any *poems*, send 'em to *Townsman* – – – –, saying I asked you to do so. They are out for quality not quantity, and could, I think, use you. If they don't go bust, they cd. also print brief resumé of yr. beliefs re the del Garbo, if and/or when you have any.

Which reading are you dealing with? The one I fuss over or another one?

Send me anything you like up to 20 pages. Better, yr. ideas on two or three sheets, unless I ask for further light on partic. points.

Young Danl Cory is workin on epistemology. You might also connect with him. His opinions cd. enrich a thesis and concentrate our fire. I don't find his address at moment, but you could get him via *Criterion* (my name as introd.). If letter via *Criterion* don't reach him, I will indaginare his ubicity.

The edition of the commentary should *of course* include reprod. of the photos. — — —

I shd. think the Italian version shd. *also* be included. Plus deciphered or still better *diplomatic* printing of the text with *all* the abbreviations. And an English version with notes.

What about yr. passing thru Rapallo, if various books not in local library?

There was a bloody great sprawlin edtn of commentaries, Garbo-Colonna-Rossi in parallel cols. Don't seem to be in bookcase and forget name of editor. Might trace it if you don't. You do *not* want it till the *end* of your studies, as it is more confusing than otherwise and not pertinent to del Garbo. Good thesis wd. deal with *Garbo;* a thorough job on *that* would be more use than a wallow in the wake of whoever it was did the sloppy correlation of G. with the others. Adding, as I remember it, *no* light.

My preference is for Avicenna. But the *early* printed editions are more likely to retain traces of what the XIII Century *thought* Avic. meant than are modern ones (or *one*).

Waaal, son. How'z your Arabic? We can use a Arabiker. Bunt'n gone off on Persian, but don't seem to do anything but Firdusi, whom he can't put into English that is of any *interest*. More fault of subject matter than of anything else in isolation.

And so forth.

340: To Ronald Duncan

Rapallo, 17 March

If you want to plan or want advice, better come on down here. Glad to see you in anny kase. As to strategy:

1. Butch didn't distribute No. 1 promptly.

2. When you first talked in the year XIV or whenever, the proposal was *four* footed. Dunc., Den Thom., Auden, and Ez. That cd. have tentacled. Cutting off contacts, the problem is other'd. If I am to serve the mag. instead of the mag doing certain jobs that are useful to me, that is O.K. but it is *other*.

For instance to get it reviewed, I should have to take a different line. Not simply the concrete fact which the buggars *won't* understand *any*how and wd. hate if they did.

Problem of my rent, also. I cd. put a different end on the René Crevel article I am getting ready for *Criterion*. That might catch a few eyes.

I come back to things *effected*. There were Gaudier and Lewis, or vice versa, plus me. There was before that my then recent headlines in 1909-1910 *plus* a clear program of three points *plus* a small nucleus of actual poems (H.D., Aldington, one of Bill Williams which were distinct from the stuff lolling about in 1911).

Neither of yr. warblers have written to me. Mebbe more tactful of Mr. Bridge's pupil to *not*. After all Bridges means more jobs and pay than I do; also ils n'aiment *pas* les idées nettes. – – – –

I think the reason I loathe all stage stuff is that it is split. I can stand quite bad theatre *in* the theatre, but when I read Shxpr I don't think of stage, I think of people. Anything that asks the reader to think of effect or how it wd. be on stage distracts from reality of fact presented. Even if it does appeal to the ballet russe or charlotte russe instincts of the bee-holder. Means the author not obsessed with reality of his subject.

Possum, by the way, thought your second scene not up to first.

After all there *were*, in London, dining circles or a *weekly* meeting of us and periphery. There was circulation from room to room in at least going concerns which wrote and published. It was a sort of society or social order or dis-order. If young men funk that sort of thing, I don't see what resonance they can expect; it is sting without sounding board. Admitting *all* the to put it mildly *im*perfections of the race of nuvvelists, of teas; but to edit, to speak *to*, to *aus*gaben, as distinct from meditatin' on the old umbilicus??? *If* that mechanism isn't used by the young they got to invent some other. If no donkey cart, a wheelbarrow. – – – –

341: To James Taylor Dunn

Rapallo, 12 April

Dear J.T.D.: –/–/ Also once again: when I am *not* writing Cantos, I do not care a hoot how much I am *edited*. I am not touchy about the elimination of a phrase. When I edit other people, I cut out what I don't want. When I *am edited*, I give the editor similar leeway. That is what *editing* is. The writer provides the ammunition and the editor shoots it *toward* his target. –/–/

342: To T. S. Eliot

Rapallo, 16 April

Waaal Possum, my fine ole Marse Supial: Thinking but passing over several pejorative but Possumble—oh quite possumbl—interpretations of selected passages in yr. ultimate communication, wot I sez appealin to you for the firm's interest, on your return from your Pasqual meddertashuns iz:

For review copies of *Kulch* (to git it circd. despite mutilation of the title), *Criterion* better try H. Rackham, M.A., Christ's College, Cambridge (England), as he would know somfink about the las' chapter. Tell him *we* spose it is the most careful (*his* edtn or the Loeb (or Low*ebb* classics) edtn) the Nic. Ethics has had. He would prob. do a damn *dull* rev.; but as wiff Gilson, dull review, *but* after five years young Bird is put onto the Dino del Garbo.

If Rackham is too stuffy, I spose ole Danl Cory is the only bloke wot would *think* about the more serious passages in the woik. It would have to be over a pussydonym cause SantyYanner would sack him if he said anything good about the book. And speakin of pussydonyms:

> *Sez the Maltese dawg to the Siam cat*
> *"Whaaar'z ole Parson Possum at?"*
> *Sez the Siam cat to the Maltese dawg*
> *"Dahr he sets lak a bump-onna-log."*

−/−/ To eggsplain about 3 *Lat. Poets.* I wrote *h*enquiring, then I gits the buk, hence change of venue. However, *if* you want about six lines, I will add 'em to the Golding. Don't bother to ans. this. I can say a woid about the Plautus and not sell the other two essays. Thus maintainin *your* friendly status with Routledge. −/−/

343: To Laurence Binyon

Rapallo, 22 April

Dear L.B.: You seem to have a good start (Canto I) and to be worried by Canto II, lines 1 to 50.

How *much* revision do you propose to make in the proofs? How *much* slashing and damning do you *want* me to attempt? We're not out for collaboration and rewrite à la E.P. Is it any use my making definite suggestions where I see *other* ways out than those you have chosen? E.g., *if* in II, 12 you use "remain" instead of "stay," there are two rhymes for II, 10 and 8.

Do you often enough take the third of the terza rima and work back to the first, or do you clutch and cling to the first rhyme you get and try to revise inside that set of rhymes?

You have very considerably improved the final line of the Canto in revision (ink).

Page 22, line 2: "chooses" is better than "*doth* choose." All these "does" and "doths" bother me.

Then Canto III runs rather better.

Also: how nearly exhausted are you with the job? Have you been *off* it long enough to come back fresh?? I mean the time between your last looking at it *before* it went to the printer and now?

First flaw I hit is also in the original. Question of these similes which compare several or many people to one, "uom," etc. Whether this is or was accepted rather as the French "on" (as in "on dit," which we translate "they say") I don't know. It always catches me up, to me a perfectly *un-seeable* comparison. I should incline to use a plural on supposition that the reader will read your English and only glance at the Italian when in doubt.

No use my counting the difficulties overcome. At this juncture the only thing that matters is those *not yet* overcome. The question is *when* to tackle 'em. I think you ought to finish the job, with the *Paradiso*. How *much* fault do you want me to find *now?* How much will it be useful for me to go after with hammer and tongs?? (D.A.)

Blast the blighter's syntax: he is all full of backsided clauses, etc. You can't shed the lot of 'em. But . . .

This *Purgatorio* is one hell of a job. Can you give me any hint as to what can be of most use to you *at this time?* I think the job enormously worth doing.

Later:

I am inclined to say in desperation, read it yourself and kick out every sentence that isn't as Jane Austen would have written it in prose. Which is, I admit, impossible. But when you *do* get a limpid line in perfectly straight normal order, isn't it worth any other ten? To limber your muscles, get out of certain kinks whereinto you have been drawn solely by terza rima and the length of the lines, would it be any good your reading Browning's *Sordello?* Have you ever read it? Or Crabbe? And then coming back to your verse.

I hesitate to make definite suggestions re particular words, as it might hamper you. One can never emend another man's work, or hardly ever. One can only put one's finger on the emenda.

Would you feel utterly immoral if you used an occasional 8 syllable line, where at present you have used fillers? or even 9 syllable?

I now proceed to Canto IV.

P.S. I am writing all this because I think people who do not know the difficulties of the job will be down on these minutiae like a pack of wolves. And the fact that most of 'em won't recognize the merits won't help it.

344: To LAURENCE BINYON

Rapallo, 25 April

Dear L.B.: Your virtues can be left out of this. There are enough of 'em, and several most admirable pages. All that counts at the moment is plugging a few small leaks that could be plugged quickly in proof-correcting. *Canto I:* line 121, Italian misprint, "mio" should be "noi."

Look again at the English from "before her" to "melting dew" [ll. 116-121]. "Melting"???

132, the "esperto" recalls "POLUMETIS," Odysseus' skill. Not crafty
enough to get back. Might improve the "essayed" and "knew."

Canto II: 32, "other sail *than*"??

37, I don't like "did allume." Or

59, "if that they knew it."

63, ??? "strangers" rather than "pilgrims"?? Hang the "even as." Also
80, "did I enlace."

94, "chooses" wd. serve quite simply in place of "doth choose."

106, "Those who."

Canto IV: 3, "raccoglie," "concentrate." It hooks up with the "bianco" in
Guido's "Donna mi prega" and the melody that most draws the
soul into itself. Re also line 11.

13, you might get "experience" at the end of your line and not "did I
acquire."

25, San Leo usual with cap. L.

33, the "to need" clumsy at end of line.

Canto V: 47, "even with the" etc. Drat that "even."

62, still worse; "*this my* guide." Damn it all, one does this sort of
botch at the age of 16.

101, "did give." (I am only swatting the "dids" and "doths" where
they have particularly hindered me. In the long run you flow
sufficiently to carry one over them. Thank Gawd fer that.)

Canto VI: 17-18, I know the orig. is "quel de Pisa," but it don't stick out
like "he of Pisa." Why not "the Pisan"? What about dropping
the "the" before "good Marzocco." Just a blank rest in place of
unaccented syllable. Perhaps this raises too many questions
about the convention of metric used. Shakespear did a lot of
funny bizniz with extra syllables, and it hasn't completely
bitched his sales.

36, "dost consider." Unnecessary at this point.

45, orig. "*fia*" not "sia." "Make" rather than "be." More active verb.

109, "cruel *one*." Nasty form; and Elizabethan might personify with
"cruelty." Am not sure this fits your [lacuna].

114, put the "me" behind the "befriend"??

127, "Florence" has a hasty squishy sound. "Fiorenza" or "Florenza"
gives one's teeth a grip.

Canto VII: 24, orig. is "*dal*" not "*del* ciel." "*Of*" not "from." I think it has
definitely different meaning here, not merely an indifferent substitution. Dant's emphasis on these things much greater than if
Dean of Canterbury were doing it now. Also the "from" is
ambiguous, tho not likely to be mistaken to mean "moved me
from." "Heaven's" virtue seems to me stronger in movement.

31, I dunno where. "Babies" is right; or if it is "muliebra" (*vide D volg.
eoloq.*) vurry hard for an ang-sax to deal with swaddling clothes.

37, "both followed all the others."?? Possible improvement in word-
order here?

44, "ascendy by night cannot be done"? This improvable.

Canto IX: 28-60, O.Kay, cheef. This is one of the good ones.

　75, "like in a wall some crack that it hath got." Try again.

Canto XI: 86-7, "gran disio del' eccelenza" (private kink of my own) that "desire of excelling or beating someone else" is the meaning, not the "desire of perfection." Our "excellence" is almost a synonym with "goodness." As the whole poem is one of fine moral distinctions, this dissociation is worth making.

　92-3, might be redone.

　94-126, Good, very good. "Naught but a wind's breath," etc.

Canto XII: 3, "dolce" always a sticky sweet when so translated. "Gentle pedagog"? Giver of easy instruction. Chance for a find, rather than taking jujube.

　(Your preceding note [lines 1-2] gives sense of Dant bending in the yoke *with* the other bloke.

　　　　　"We moved together
　　　　　　　like oxen" (plural)

It don't give proper visibility.

　　　"I went with him bowed; and we were like a pair of oxen."

The suggestion of original and Dant suggestionné into leaning over is magnificent. You had the amazement at the shadow very well a few cantos back.)

　9, "scemi" is very colloquial. I suspect the first time it ever got into literature was here. It is what nurses and mothers say to small children being bad and stupid: idiot, little monkey, you ass. Borné; I don't quite know what to do with it: Stupified, loggy, drugged. I don't know where our "shame" comes from; haven't an etymol. dic. here.

　21, damn the "*doth* spur." [lacuna]

　Page 139, have a go at last ten lines [XII, 82-93], from "Reverence over face." "Atti" are, I think, "movements." "Disse" is accented on first syllable. I know the vowels and general sound are like "he said," but "saying" would throw the line better. Line before, simpler word-order is easy to get. In fact, I think this is a passage where you weren't at your widest awake.

　It continues on p. 141 [line 98], "above the forehead." Angel wiped it *off* his forehead.

　102, I haven't ref. books but Rubicon is over by Rimini. I suspect it is again San Leo and not San Miniato. Maybe you have authority at hand. Rubicon cert. richer in associative value, Caesar, etc., than "Rubaconte." Don't for garZake take my word for this. It is the kind /of thing I muddle, and the Rubaconte may have nowt to do with Rubicon.

Canto XIII: 3, very dubious of improvement by "evil offstrips."

　50, "was cried" rather bothers me.

　76, "Sage *one*" grits my teeth. Damn these "ones." [lacuna] A joke even among the "tedeschi lurchi" who have no sense of language etc.

93, damn the "if that I hear." Meaning "if I hear," "if I hear that"??

107, don't like "guilty blot."

119, don't like "bitter steps of flight."

118, I think a good verbal order is attainable here.

Canto XIV: 10, "never yet known." Lines 10 to 16, word order improvable.

92, if Reno is Rhine, would give better sense of place. I don't know that it is; you probably have proper books of ref.

97, here a lot of chance of simple improvements. "Good" before Lizio not interesting, but *"Harry"* Mainardi improved sense of particular.

103, "my" not *"mine* eyes."

104, "Guido of Prata" gives elision of vowels. Better sound than "Guy"??

118, "Pagani will do well" [in place of "well shall do the Pagani"].

122, "does well to bear no son."

126, "hath our converse." "Our converse has." No need of inversion.

133 to end, a lot of unnecessary tangles in the order. "He to me spoke" is as bad as some of pore old Henry Newbolt. The original is in natural order. "He said to me." ??"By *who*" or "by whom." "I shall be slain by whomever finds me." Not "findeth" in any case.

That is as far as I have got with the grappling hooks. Hope some of this is some use to you. Will next proceed with XV to XVII.

345: To WILLIAM P. SHEPARD

Rapallo, April

Dear Bill Shep: I am going thru proofs of Binyon's translation of the *Purgatorio.* I want to reinforce all I said of his *Inferno* in *The Criterion* (reprinted in *Polite Essays*).

Binyon sheds more light on Dante than any translation I have ever seen. Almost more than any translation sheds on *any* original. Cavin Douglas and Golding create something glorious and different from the originals.

I strongly suggest use of Binyon in place of Temple edtn. for introducing student to the *Commedia.*

Also as Binyon tells me the *Hell* was a flop from sales side, I think Modern Language Assn. should be stirred. Binyon is going on to the *Paradiso*, but the revised edtns. of *Inferno* and *Purg.* would be blocked and needlessly delayed if some one don't battistrade a bit.

I expect to whoop in *Broletto.* Apparently B's Italian friends are saying he has got Dante's tone of voice (not the way I should have put it) and his English half-wits telling him terza rima is *unEnglish.*

346: To Laurence Binyon

Rapallo, 4 May

Dear L.B.: Glad you are bearing up. The more I look at Canto XVIII the more I am reminded of the soldier's letter in "Cantleman's Spring Mage" (ref. "Dear Ma: This war is a fair buggar."). Here goes.

Page 207 took all of yesterday's paper. — — — —

30, possible literality. "Endureth in its matter" gets rid of an adjective, always a pleasant act. "So mind enters desire when possessed" more literal.

Middle page is *good*.

49, the scholastics will scalp you for changing "substantial" to "essential" unless you have an utterly perfect alibi. All technical terms, nobody can understand them without either notes or preparatory study.

67, "get to bottom of reasoning." I daresay yr. version is pretty good.

78, "like a big bucket's bottom" wd. get rid of clause "that were aglow)." — — — —

79, as to "against heaven": Uncle Wm. Yeats not being at hand I don't know whether this is astrologic retrograde. It don't matter to *me*.

113, "One of those spirits said then" (or "spoke then"): "Where we 'go.'" No need to invert.

Then it seems to flow or I get lulled.

Canto XIX: 35, "begone" or "move on." Literally "come on." Which is a bit too colloquial. — — — —

112, if the line ends . . . "in want" and the next line begins "Of God." Quite easy to do this and the original does. Even with a repeat for emphasis:

"*I was miserable, I was a soul in want*
Of God. Here thou seest what my forfeit is,
Here for greed thou seest I pay my account."

When some one is speaking I think one has right to at least Shakespear's technique and license in the line.

117, "Il monte": I am not sure whether the term "monte" was already current for hockshop. I think there is pax pawky dig in the word. Whether this mount is more specific than "the mount," I don't know.

119, if you end it with "down-cast," I think a more impetuous rhythm is possible, and without tangle. And that it suits the movement of the original. I won't bother you with my guess for the whole line. Danger in my longer emendation is to lose *your* tone. Can't have change into an idiom that sticks out and falsifies a whole passage.

123, "So justice here to earth forces them bend" wd. eliminate an-
    other damn "doth."
Then she rides to page 233. — — — —
   106, "ghiotta" (and the cumulative effect of the original wording)
    seems to me wd. justify a more interesting adjective than
    "avaricious" which I find weaker than "avaro" *anyhow.* "Gold-
    guzzling," "swilling." I know the "ghiotto" is not the adjective
    attached to Midas in the Italian. I am talking of effect of the
    passage as a whole. And I find your line with "avaricious" *too*
    ti tum ti tum ti tum ti tum ti TUM. Might even be from that
    blighter Milton. *Also* it has two nouns chaperoned by two ad-
    jectives: Mr. and Mrs. Gosse in front, etc., etc. Whereas the
    Florentine apothecary has a noun on its own in the front half of
    line! and the swilling M. in the second half.
   131-2, I am tempted. Mebbe if I do a pseudo-Chaucerian 2 lines it
    will set you to something in key.

> "*Before Latona there her nest had made
> Wherefrom she hatched two eyen heven clere.*"

Or "of hevene clere." — — — —
And so to DINE.
Benedictions.
It's a grand life.

347: To LAURENCE BINYON

Rapallo, 6 May

Seconde Fytte

Dear L.B.: Cantos XXIII and XXIV pretty clean; say toothbrush rather
than rockdrill needed. — — — —
Canto XXIII: 39, I very much doubt "leprous" for "squama." "Scrofula,"
    "King's evil"??
Most of this page [269, ll. 28-60] is very good. Browning would have
liked it, if you don't mind my suggesting this, you being possibly an anti-
Bob.

   73, I wonder if it would be worth putting "*will*" in Italics. I think one
    has right to all sorts of printing dodges to clarify or make easy
    the reader's path.
   94; "Barbagia in Sardegna." One gets a feel here for this order in place
    names, even in family names. "Sardinia's Barbagia" don't seem
    either English or Wop and, worse, it suggests a person as much
    as a place to unwary reader.
   97, again this problem of the "dolce." I wonder if a simple "*my
    brother*" would be as good here?

100, what does your commentator say about "pergamo"? All my Dante books are strewed along from London to Paris.

107, "avergonate": "girls" better than "ones." I loathe these pronouns. The Italian adjective being feminine is translatable by a feminine noun. The "ones" is bad anyhow, and don't translate gender of the original. "Girls," "sluts," etc., all permitted here and all more visual than a colourless "ones."

128, is your Italian "sia" or "fia"? The "fia" as printed is infinitely more interesting. Christ *made* in the mass, and Beatrice, as theology, made in Paradise. My text also reads "fia," I won't swear I am right, but there is more interest in this interpretation. Dante's words often contain a precision that one passes over. E.g., the "sanno" for Aristotle as distinct from "intendendo" gives one chance to distinguish between cold intellect and real understanding.

Canto XXIV: 4, I have meditated on "eye's pits." I think you are probably right.

28-60, particularly satisfactory "Io mi son un che quando." COMPLIMENTI !!! And the chances of going flat just *there* were so many.

61-93, relapse into inverting.

69, "longing's prayer" I particularly do *not* like. "Leanness and (their) longing they were." Perhaps a bit Langland, but you have used that tone now and again. Heaven knows the reader will welcome short sentences wherever you can give him them. — — — —

99, the marshalls are I think more interesting than Wellingtons and Bluchers. A "marescallo" or "mareschalcho" up to at least 1450 was a *"master blacksmith"* and knew all about horses. *Il Libro del marescallo* is one of the jems in the Malatestiana at Cesena. As Dant calls Arnaut Daniel "miglior fabbro," so here I think he is paying a similar honour: The Craft and not the military pomp. And the "fabbro" to Provence would balance. There are several of these echoes in the *Commedia.* The Provençal wherein Arnaut speaks and the Spanish suggestion which I noted in my review of your *Inferno,* for example. (Proportional honour to the classics.) There is the "cavalchi" on the first of the terza, to keep the illuminated capital effect. In Arnaut the use of several words suggestive of the same picture is characteristic. — — — —

All the above are trifling save the "fia" and the "master smith"—that I should also make smoother by a run-on:

<pre>
                              . . . "those two
        Mareschalchi" . . .
        master smiths   (etc., rest of line)
</pre>

348: To Laurence Binyon

Rapallo, 8 May

Dear L.B.: I give you nearly a clean bill and a number of bull's eyes on the rest of XXV and XXVI. Some *very* neat work. The "sfumature" are so slight that I shall not bother to list them now. I might come back to 'em when you have finished the *Paradiso*.

Canto XXV: 113, omitting the "and" you could keep "cornice." I rather like it because Dant characteristically uses definite places and here the road along the mountain-edge is definitely a cornice—word still kept for French Riviera: "corniche"—and does, I think, carry specific picture to at least certain % of readers. "Ground beats up" is good, all the same. – – – –

Canto XXVI: 67, "Highlander" is excellent: in fact, you have got going. 117, the "parlar materno" is usually taken to be Provençal, the mother tongue of troubadour art, Sicilian and Bolognese being descended from it. "His tongue" or a change of a syllable. "Wrought better in our mother-tongue than I" would keep your metre. It is a trifling matter; I am less sensible of exact number of syllables; I would be worried if "cornice," for example, was put where "ground" is in XXV. However, applause. I don't think even old Wubb and Whhosia can hold out against these two canti, though "Rien que la bêtise humaine donne une idée de l'infini." I at any rate have never taken in these canti properly before. Dust on me blinkin' 'ead!! Oh well, when I get to *som* of this Escalina, I will write you on one or two other topics, not Dantescan, to give you a breather before you start aviatin' through the merrygorounds. I think you have broken the back of the opposition, apart possibly from some of the bloomink theology up aloft. Tom Aquin., etc. I forget what he and Domenik have to say, but reckon it's teasy.

Canto XXVII: 18, "accesi" is "lit" and therefore still burning. I think there is chance of improvement here: archaic "brennt." Sprained accent in "ardent," "cerement" and the great number of words ending in "-gent" or "-ment," "unspent," etc., "indument." – – – –

MAGNIFICENT FINISH! Utterly confounds the apes who told you terza rima isn't English. "Coppices" is very English.

Occasionally a word is *used*. There is an ideogram in one of *The Odes* (sun over horizon) that is *used*. The beauty here would *only* have been got by using terza rima. Lascia dir gli stolti who don't see it, and who have been for two centuries content that *technique* went out of English *metric* with Campion and Waller. Any respect for art and any care for the technique is unEnglish in the sense your bastardly friends employed the term.

For XXVIII: Bravo, Bravo, BRAVO. Nothing to mark, one or two queeries. Line 12 "casts" is possible for "casteth"; I don't know that I prefer it. Good emendation or correction that you have made on next page. P. 331, printer has used a defective letter "d" at end of "checked." In fact, there are *no* questions, nothing but O.K. repeated in my margin. This part of the job is *done*. Immensely worth doing.

In Canto XXIX: Nothing a man writing a critical article could find fault with unless he were a low crab. However, I am not writing a critique but going over the text with a microscope.

>   24, "Eve to rue" might be improved, but I shdn't bother about it now. — — —
>
>   95, "even."
>
>   107, "has" for "hath." Possibly in another position.
>
>   114, an "as" to avoid two "so's." — — — —

These are all too trifling to bother with, and you have spent more thought on it than I have.

I do, however, prefer your "supreme Hippocrates" [line 137] . . . Miltonism tho' it may be. . . . A good one. Possibly whimsical of me. . . . I think Eliot would prefer your emendation. At any rate we are on ground of imponderabilia.

349: To Laurence Binyon

Rapallo, 12 May

Dear L.B.: XXXII starts off rolling and nothing for me to get my claws into. Possibly "my eyes" in line one, saving "mine eyes" for 93, where I think it is right. I believe an opening shd. be as near normal speech as possible and a heightened or poetic diction can be slid into later if necessary or advisable.

>   44 and 46, I dunno about "Gryphon" and "griped" so near together, sound, etc.
>
>   48, a "thus" would seem better to me than "so." And at the end of the line, I am not sure about sense. I don't know that it is "all things"; "every good" would not arouse discussion.
>
>   50, "brought it to rest" would avoid the "halted" which don't seem to me the verb juste. You might halt a company. Otherwise seems intransitive verb. I mean the general feel of it is intransitive. And even if captain "halts" a regiment the sense is "commands it to halt."
>
>   63-4, "strain complete," "eyes severe": two inverts. "Whole of it" would avoid the first and I should look for way of ending one line with "severe" and starting the next with "eyes." — — — —
>
>   94, I don't know whether you are stunting with "very ground." Seems to me Dant meant "*true* ground," with rather more emphasis and association of ideas than a philologically correct "very" quite gets.
>
>   95-6, and I don't *know* whether the bloomink chariot was bound "by" or "to" the bi-natured yannymal.

Then you do a *very* neat bit of work.

105, "evil living men" seems nearer meaning. "Profit the *evil life*" might mean the opposite?? — — — —

151, I queery sense in your "she be owned." Surely the Italian means "no one should take it from her."

"Shoot quick glances round (??Verb better than a "with" for vividness.) Shooting

154, then you come to the *only* line of really *bad* poetry I have found in the whole *Purgatorio*. "But when she rolled on me her lustful eye" might be Gilbert and Sullivan. Positively the only line that is out of the sober idiom of the whole of your translation. Like Omerus he SLEPT. Moderate verb and adjective wanted. And may be better order if the "head to foot" preceded "paramour." — — — —

149, I suppose the "sciolta" means with her clothes undone. J'ai perdu ma ceinture, etc. . . .

Canto XXXIII: Very good down to line 81. Beatrice talking in crossword puzzles anyhow; so you have done well not to alter the original order of the words. The DXV counted as DVX, etc.

81, I thought "it" was simple printers' error for "is," but even that won't take the sense. The seal does not alter the image or figure impressed on it.

> *"With unaltered image of the seal impresst"*
> > *"Under seal's power*
>
> *Takes an unaltered image"*
> > *the unaltered image*
> *"Takes the unaltered figure on it pressed."*
> *"Holds an unaltered figure," etc.*

Certainly the wax *is* altered by the figure. Or do you think that he means the wax stays wax? In which case the reader needs that stated clearly:

> *"As wax stays wax under the seal impressed"*
> > *under the form impressed*
> *"As wax stays wax under the seal's power*
> *And takes the figure that seal has pressed."*

110, etc., GOOD. Very good.

121, reverse of usual situation where Italian has gender and English hasn't. Dant has cleverly avoided a gender in the simile. I wonder whether or not one should say "would herself"??? In various places "beauty" can in two syllables replace "fair lady" if you want room to turn round. Here it would permit you this and more things beside. — — — —

129, "well-nigh spent" is, I think, definitely bad for "tramortita." But you may have a good dictionary that justifies it. I should have taken it to mean "wholly petered out," but am not sure.

133-5, the "da essa preso fui" terzet not a maximum.

136, possible alternative for "more writing there were more space." All these possible alternatives are unimportant, but sometimes loosen up a clutch to consider an alternative.

Once again my thanks for the translation. And there are damned few pieces of writing that I am thankful for. The minute comments are no more than noticing a few nutshells left on the tablecloth post convivium. Nobody has had such a good time of this kind since Landor did his notes on Catullus. Or at least I don't think you can find any record of it.

And now, Boss, you get RIGHT ALONG with that *Paradiso* as soon as you've stacked up the dinner dishes. Why don't the twins do some work? Banzai, alaILA!

350: To JOHN CROWE RANSOM

Rapallo, 15 October

My Dear Ransom: Thanks for announcement. On the face of it, it wd. seem that you mean to fill a *long* felt want. I imagine I had better see the first issue before merely looking into my owne heart and typing.

So you exclude matter that is also appearing in *The Criterion?* Do you want to relieve pressure on Mr. Eliot's space? (For example, he is probably writing in anguish over an article of mine more or less on René Crevel, and if that were cared for in *Kenyon,* he might then have to go into crisis over some of my more active efforts at saving "Europe" and/or civilization.)

Another point on which I wd. almost invite editorial comment in the review itself, arises from yr. phrase "complete essays." After a certain "time" or let us say more definitely after an author has put forth a certain bulk of exposition and proved a certain quantity of serious purpose, backed by published results, should he be constrained to produce the "complete essay" on every or even on most occasions? "complete" essay on any of the topics whereon he is most qualified to speak? A physicist wd. be allowed very brief addenda to what he had hitherto shown.

Surely one of the first jobs for a critical review or tribunal is to decide *who* has earned the right to such informal and condensed expression. This is not the same thing as Mr. Eliot's "plenum," but it is a belief that runs more or less parallel with it. . . .

Another need perhaps greater or more immediate in sociological discussion than in criticism of the arts, is a loose-leaf reference system of vital essays or articles printed during the present couple of decades.

I can illustrate this more clearly in the economic domain than in the literary. Such articles, for example, as Delaisi's in VU No. 380, on the regents of Banque de France, and *The New Age* editorial on assassination in 1926 ought not to become inaccessible.

An analogous need in a review of letters wd. apply to articles of valid interest that get lost or are indeed stillborn and permanently hidden in technical and special reviews published by learned societies, language associations, etc. Once in every three or five years some of these reviews print something of more than philological interest.

We are hamstrung by a fear of being miscellaneous. The book-trade, accursed of god, man and nature, makes no provision for *any* publication that is not one of a series; and masterwork is never one of a series, neither is vital invention. It has its place in the historic process, which is far from the same.

As final enquiry: are you ready for a revival of American culture considering it as something specifically grown from the nucleus of the American Founders, present in the Adams, Jefferson correspondence; not limited to belles lettres and American or colonial imitation of European literary models, but active in all departments of thought, and tackling the problems which give life to epos and Elizabethan plays, without rendering either Homer or Bard of Avon dry doctrinaires?

The style of Justinian is not necessarily of less interest than that of the *Pervigilium Veneris* or of Augustine's purple.

351: To Katue Kitasono

Rapallo, 10 December

Dear K.K.: Thanks very much for *Cactus I[sland]*. I have copied the lines on Wyndham L. and am sending them to Duncan. I don't yet know enough ideogram to form an opinion of the original; and, of course, have no idea of its sound.

I suppose a world of perspective is inhabitable and one of approaching projectiles is not.

Have just seen W.L. in London. His head on duck; he has done new portrait of me. You can judge the two worlds when you get a photo of it, which I will send when I get one. The Wyndham drawing (done about 1912) that I have brought back is better than the Max Ernst that Laughlin introduced here circuitously. The Max that I had from him (Max) seven years ago is very fine. In fact, it goes away and the other Max approaches revolving.

If I don't send this brief note now, it will get lost in a mountain of papers.

1 9 3 9

352: To Ronald Duncan

Rapallo, 10 January

Dear Ron: Did *you* kill *The Criterion?* Wot will pore Robbink doo gnow?

> *Who killed Cock Possum?*
> *Who bitched his blossom?*

> > *"I," said young Duncan,*
> > *Sodden and drunken, "I bit* The Criterion."

> > *"I," said ole Wyndham,*
> > *"I bloody well skinned 'um."*

> > *"I," said Jeff Faber,*
> > *"I the worse neighbor*
> >   *I tightened the puss-strings."*
> > > ??
> > > ??

353: To Ronald Duncan

Rapallo, 17 January

Dear Ron: As you haven't given me Uncle Igor's address (or, if you did, I can't find it) you might forward this.

The Hall is at their disposal, père et fils, for anything they care to do. This *is* a pleasant part of the coast, rains and cold *should* be over in a week or so. There is *no* population and I can't draw money from the air. A fee for Strawinsky fils; yes, if it be moderate. *If* their glory is strong enough to draw a public from Genova or Pekin or Marseilles, they are welcome to the total gate receipts. I will splurge away in the *Mare,* and Cuneo is ready to go for the rest of the press. Genova papers always have noticed our concerts; before and after.

As you know the only overhead is the ten lire to porter and the cost of programs. This family can cover that as their reward for admission.

Dear Ron: Will you send on the original of this (the above) to Igor or Stanislas (or however he spells it)?

Sorry Thompson is Leavising. But can't be helped. I shan't answer and it wd. be better if some one less de la famille than Drummond could be found to do it.

Peroni very busy. Don't write even to me. At least nothing but cheques recd. for months.

I don't see that Belgion can start *Criterion*, nor Read, esp. in view of Possum's express remark to contrary.

What is *he* (T.S.E.) up to? If anything?

Thompson can't be worse than Mairet in *The Crit.*??? Or can he?? Only opinion I shd. like to see is Rackham's (Rackham, editor of Loeb edtn of *Nicomachean Ethics*), but as Morley cut my *main* point, even that wd. be conditioned. Still I could and would answer Rackham with pleasure. Final part of *Kulch* shd. be correlated with my "Mencius" in summer *Criterion* and the point re difference between *Nicomachean* and *Magna Moralia*. Which I would go into if asked.

I can't think of any other controversial ground in the book. The other discussions wd. be mostly pointing out the *ignorance*, such as Mairet's re that detrimental Lao Tse and clumsy inance cf. of Arist and Plato to Lao and Kung (mere tosh).

P.S. You could of course *invite* Rackham, saying Thompson has missed the *whole* point of the book and that his (Rackham's) answer, attack or whatever on the final section is the only one E.P. has any respect for.

— — — —

354: To Ford Madox Ford

Rapallo, 31 January

Dear Fordie: Friends of ole Bull [1] is a good idea (I spose yours) for a country so lousily *low* that everything is run on personality. — — — — A "sort of" Academie Goncourt *could* be used as prod to the useless Institute of Letters (whereto, as item for the Friends of Yam Carlos, you can say I nominated the said Yam Carlos within 24 hours of my own admission, but the sap-headed nominating kummytee did *not* put his name with Walt Disney's when it came to the annual recommendations). THAT body, if seriously criticised, Murry Bulter strangled and Canby educated or drowned, *could* be useful, at least in getting certain things reprinted. –/–/

355: To Hubert Creekmore

Rapallo, February

Dear H.C.: Copy of *A Lume Spento* supposed to exist in Treasure Room, Harvard Library (also possibly, but not sure, in Hamilton College Library).

God damn Yeats' bloody paragraph. Done more to prevent people reading Cantos for what is *on the page* than any other one smoke screen.

Don't bother about jejune attempts. Nothing worse than digging up all

[1] Ford initiated "The Friends of William Carlos Williams"—a circle devoted to the discussion and dissemination of Williams' work.

sorts of immaturities. Masses of uncollected stuff in unknown magazines, also in Italian; nothing yet done with my Italian notes and criticisms.
————

I don't have to *try* to be American. Merrymount, Braintree, Quincy, all I believe in or by, what had been "a plantation named Weston's."

Vide also the host in Longfellow's "Wayside Inn." Wall ornament there mentioned still at my parents'. Am I American? Yes, and buggar the present state of the country, the utter betrayal of the American Constitution, the filth of the Universities, and the ————— system of publication whereby you can buy Lenin, Trotsky (the messiest mutt of the lot), Stalin for 10 cents and 25 cents, and it takes *seven* years to get a set of John Adams at about 30 dollars. Van Buren's autobiog not printed till 1920.

An Ars Poetica might in time evolve from the *Ta Hio*. Note esp. my "Mencius" in last summer's *Criterion*. And as to "am I American": wait for Cantos 62/71 now here in rough typescript.

Literature rises in racial process. No need of letting off steam about process. You belong to the human species, you don't have to *do* anything about that; you can't become a kangaroo or an ostrich. Take all known family stocks from about 1630 via N. Eng. or Quaker whalers, landing I believe in N.J. Could write the whole U.S. history (American hist) along line of family migration; from the landing of *The Lion*, via Conn., N.Y., Wisconsin (vide *Impact*), to Idaho.

Ole Bull Wms. a mere dago immigrant. Finest possible specimen of course.

When are you going to make the place safe for *natives?* Or to hell with *safe;* when are you going to make it or permit it to be made a fit habitat?

For Ars Poetica, gorrdamit, get my last edtn of Fenollosa's "Chinese Written Character." Vide my introduction.

Yes, do better than that squiff, that femme ouistiti and lowest degree of animal life (apart from Cambridge Eng. profs) ....r. That pamphlet a laboratory specimen. Evidence for the condemnation of American teaching system if ever was one.

I believe that when finished, *all* foreign words in the Cantos, Gk., etc., will be underlinings, not necessary to the sense, in one way. I mean a complete sense will exist without them; it will be there in the American text, but the Greek, ideograms, etc., will indicate a *duration* from whence or since when. If you can find any *briefer* means of getting this repeat or resonance, tell papa, and I will try to employ it.

Narrative not the same as lyric; different techniques for song and story. "Would, could," etcetera: Abbreviations save *eye* effort. Also show speed in mind of original character supposed to be uttering or various colourings and degrees of importance or emphasis attributed by the protagonist of the moment.

ALL typographic disposition, placings of words *on* the page, is intended to facilitate the reader's intonation, whether he be reading silently to self or aloud to friends. Given time and technique I might even put down the musical notation of passages or "breaks into song."

There is *no intentional* obscurity. There is condensation to maximum attainable. It is impossible to make the deep as quickly comprehensible as the shallow.

The order of words and sounds *ought* to induce the proper reading; proper tone of voice, etc., but can *not* redeem fools from idiocy, etc. If the goddam violin string is not tense, no amount of bowing will help the player. And *so* forth.

As to the *form* of *The Cantos:* All I can say or pray is: *wait* till it's there. I mean wait till I get 'em written and then if it don't show, I will start exegesis. I haven't an Aquinas-map; Aquinas *not* valid now. — — — —

356: TO WYNDHAM LEWIS

Rapallo, 3 August

Dear Wyndham: I have buried pore ole Fordie in (of all places) *The XIXth Century and After*. Only hole left. And an inadequate oration as they had room for "under 1500" and by the day after the day, etc. An I think you make a beau geste and putt a penny on the ole man's other eye. No one else will.

Kussed as wuz in some ways, when you think of Galsworthy's England, etc., etc. And for ten years before we arruv I spose he had *no* one else to take the punishment from the frumpers. Wuz agin the "mortisme" of our venbl. friend Possum, and in short, virtuous as these things go in a world of Gosses, Royal Acc., etc. He did *not* regard prose as mere syntax. −/−/

Waaal, I am sorry you wuzn't in Washntn, and I hope you meet Uncl George [Tinkham] before he gits too tired of it awl. Nothing much else vurry paintable, though I can interjuice you to the Polish damnbassador, Patocki. Nice chap, but got Polish awt on the walls.

Why don't you dig up Angold? Nearly as bad a correspondent as you or Mons. Eliot.

Daily paper in Greenwich, millionaire suburb outside N. Yok, open to Ez. You might find it useful means of communication with some of the pubk if you go over or if you want to print anything there. They favour a lit. page by Ez. But the financial prubblum!!!

Also I onnerstand Barr (Mod Art Mus) is lookin for *early* W.L. Damn, I told you not to waste them drorinz. I might poifekly well have pinched the lot, and sold 'em for yr. bean-y-fit. Blue gal reposin at my left. Full of characteristics that wd. prob distress you. . . .

If you see Eliot, take a monkey wrench and find out *what* the hell Morley means to do in N.Y. (if anything save sink into the damnbience).

There is also a lot of my econ. writing available when young whathis-name gets back. I fergit wot you told me about Allen Unwin or why the blighters never print me.

Couple of young lads think them essays *ought* to be available. Dunno if you can turn them onto any deaf ear???

357: To Ronald Duncan

Rapallo, 6 August

Dear Ron: Have just had time to dig yr. *Pimp, Skunk* [*and Profiteer*] out of mash of papers brought back from U.S.

Yunnerstand I know *nowt* about teeYater. Hunks of Shxpr *bore* me; I just can't read 'em. Despite me admiration fer other hunks.

I think you have made very considerable technical advance. See no reason why Dukes shdn't do it. I know nowt about teeyater and dramedy. For Dukes it might be called "*Our* England." I think you shd. go find *out* what ole Fordie wuz drivin at; and eschew Mr. Eliot's affected and arty-ficial language. I also think you might cut, but don't know where. Some of the speeches may be too long. I, at any rate, tend to skip, as in 99% of the crap offered by novelists who want to be licherchoor. I read the opening half-line of a p. However yr. action does occur, in the harmony of the three poops. The language *intended* to be *their* cliche is O.K. as that. *Butt:* I can't hear the voices at other times. *If* you can cut *all* phrases that aren't alive and all that don't carry *on* the action.

Waaal, waaal, it's easy *saying* that. And so forth. Mebbe it wd. be mostly O.K. if spoke on the bleatink styge.

I enc. note for next issue, if you can stand that.

358: To Henry Swabey

Rapallo, 2 September

Dear Swabe: If for any reason postal communications are interrupted, will you please correct the proofs of my *Cantos*, now in press at Fabers? Do the best you can, a few misprints in a first edition won't matter, and better to get the book through the press somehow than to have it hung up indefinitely.

359: To Douglas McPherson

Rapallo, 2 September

Dear McPherson: There is plenty of room for a new mag. You can see from my note in *Townsman* "Statues of Gods" why I welcome parts of yr. manifesto. I, also, hit that note in *Front*, a Dutch left paper, some years ago.

But you must realize *first*, that the actual output of good poetry is *very* small. I shd. like to see a 16-page anthology (as review of past 7 years) possibly as a start for *Pan*. Were I forced to make one I shd. have to go into retrospect as far back as my own *Active Anthology* and take Bunting's "Northern Farmer" and a few other pages of him, plus a couple of Angold's satires, which you can find in *New English Weekly.* — — — — Plus a few poems by Cummings and a token payment of ten lines quoted from my new *Cantos,* just to show I exist. If you can find *six* pages outside that lot, go to it.

Note that Ron Duncan — — — — has found no poetry; Laughlin has found no poetry; Angleton has found one poem of Cummings' which I have been able to quote in *Meridiano di Roma.* Note that people only have to make *large* collections (*N. Directions* for ezampl) when there is lack of live material. Vide my *Catholic Anthology* (same thing) back in 1916. Faut de mieux.

But there is crying need for a small magazine "like *The Little Review* of 1917-19" that will fight and will include *all* the mental life of its time. *Furioso* omits polemic so no use for this. Duncan is on this job for England; there is a specific American fight that is not his job.

First: The *only* American book that *needs* reading is Overholser's *History of Money in the U.S.* — — — — Were I editing a Little Review or were I foreign editor of one on terms such as I had with *The L.R.* in 1917-19, I shd. quote the whole 17 points of the Ikleheimer circular from it. Ought to be on wall of every schoolroom.

2: There is the fight both against mercantilism (the syphilis of all American univ. teaching, the official — — — — fed to all American students) and against the bolshevik, as per Vanguard, Lenin, Marx, Trotsk, etc., at 10 cents and 25 cents in edtns of 100,000. Can't efface it. All one can do is to show that it is "old stuff" because of *omissions.* What is *needed* is 60 or 80 pages of *selections* of gists of the writings of Adams, Jefferson, VanBuren, Jackson, Johnson. Plus such data as Overholser gives. You can't run volumes of the founders' series in a small mag, but you can demand 'em, and *damn* the lights out of the sons of bitches who aren't getting 'em into print, i.e., all these Hist. profs.

3: There is the specific fight against the dryrot and redflannel in American letters, all the snotted subsidies, all the official crap. Neither Laughlin nor *Furioso* is doing the job. If the god damned big endowments had been founded to *impede* arts and letters, they cdnt have been much more efficient. They run to about 97% now.

If you care to use some of the things *Poetry* has suppressed in the past decades??? etc. Might be of use.

There is a job to be done, things to small for me to show interest in, which are yet a damnd nuisance and *no* encouragement or help to yr. generation.

Compare the Phelps, Dillon, Hillyer, whoosis and whoosis, damn if I can't remember their names, with the men whose point of view is *excluded* from the goddam colleges *and* subsidized reviews. . . .

America does *not* pay me 500 dollars a year and I imagine Williams and Cummings get even less for their writings. Is *that* any use to you young??

Re yr. extension of contents: The *real* work of a time is never done by more than four or five people with a fringe of occasional compositions. I suspect inclusivity. I think a man can be more *use* by picking what he really believes or wants and delousing his forebears.

At my age a man has too many olde lang synes. So difficult to kick old friends in the fyce when they get sloppy. I have, but very few do. Anyhow, you are too young to be tolerant. Pick the best from us old buzzards; don't load up with tepidities.

When I go onto a tennis court I don't want the young to send me a soft service even if I am the oldest living purrformer except Gustav of Sweden. Why shd. a writer want it soft from young critics? Naturally, a hard service gets a hard return. One wants a hard ball *in* the court; i.e., pertinent to matter in hand.

360: To Tibor and Alice Serly

Rapallo, October

Dear Alice and Tib: Here at least is a "Flea" that the audience can understand when sung.¹

I take it "hagy" is two syllables in the original, sung to one *a*. I have put two syllables to *a* in "god-it," "break-the." For "break the" you could have "break almost all the" and the "the" a mere "grace note"; and to sing "on the in" as a triplet; especially as both "thes" are on the same note (*g*). At any rate, the thing can be *heard*, and the emphasis of the singer comes on words that take an emphasis of meaning. Also certain almost rhymes in original are akin to the English "bit," "with"; "light," "out"; "floodlight" and "headlight."

No, I had rather you didn't send the sonata to a publisher. I don't see a market, I would rather begin with something I am more sure of, i.e., where I can defend the setting of *words*.

Waaal, thanks fer that nice licherary description of the pleasures of travel in Frawnce. D. keeps sayin' "If I had only known they were next door on Lake Annecy. . . ." — — — —

Re Buck Flea: "Buck" keeps the "B" of "bo" and the accent. "*Ram* flea" might be easier to sing, but not so good for the rise from *a* to *o* in the first "BOha" and the mouth closes on "buCK." At any rate this is as good as can be done in the time.

The slight changes in duration value of words from one verse to another are characteristic of folk song and keep it from being monotonous. "Ram flea" might get slurred and the meaning lost. You don't say it was

¹ *By god-it was a* | BUCK FLEA | *An' the damn thing* | BIT *us*
Dinner TIME | *supper* TIME, | *he was always* WITH *us.*
Had he eyes this | BUCK FLEA? | *Had eyes like a* | HEAD-*light.*
Did they GLARE? | *Did they* FLARE? | *By god like a* | FLOOD-*light.*
Had he claws that | BUCK FLEA? | *When he came to* | BITE *us*
He had CLAWS | *to break-the* WALLS | *on-the inside and* | OUTSIDE.
Had he belly? | BY GOD | *had he lights and* | LIVER?
Had a GUT | *that would* HOLD | *all the Danube* RIVER.

"*he* flea" till the 3rd strophe, but I reckon the male of the species is understood and that a *boha* of this natr wuz a buck or, if you like, a *bull* flea.

If you want to send me word for word translation of the original not taking any count of the music, I'll see if I can make any improvements.

In the second and third stanzas "buck" seems to me better than "bull." "Buck" and "bite," "light," etc., make better zyzogy than a soft sound like *ll* of "bull." And so forth.

I sent you the Siena program? Or did I forget to do so?

If I get to N.Y. in the spring, we might work up some of my Vivaldi reductions. Better stuff for publisher, I think, than that sonata on my opera basis.

361: To HENRY SWABEY

Rapallo, 31 October

Dear H.S.: −/−/ Kung and Mencius do not satisfy *all* the real belief of Europe. But all valid Christian ethics is in accord with them. In fact, only Kung can guide a man, so far as I know, through the jungle of propaganda and fads that has overgrown Xtn theology. The mysteries are *not* revealed, and no guide book to them has been or will be written. −/−/

362: To DOUGLAS MCPHERSON

Rapallo, 3 November

Dear McPherson: I got up an hour ago with intention of writing to you and to Eliot.

1st to suggest you apply quote from "Last Oracle" (Swinburne):
"Not a cell is left to the god."
or the Gk.: éipate tô basileî pése daídalos 'eulà 'eukéti PHoïbos 'eXei kalúban.

2. to Eliot re reprinting, etc., etc., which might do for *Pan* though I hadn't thought of that till I got yr. letter.

If I am to be foreign edtr., I have got to know a *lot* more about the practical running of the mag. I can't be any use unless we are sure of a year's run. Printing bill assured. And the possibility of paying a small sume for exceptional contributions.

In case of *Little Review:* The printing bill was *supposed* to be assured and I had 750 dollars per year, for foreign editing and contributors. It went $25 a month to me (i.e., $300 the year) for editing and 450 to contributors. I was contributor to French issue and to H. James issue. I had the choice of half the contents. That latter stipulation I don't now need or want. I haven't time nor the conviction on points where I might disagree with you. I.e., yr. interest in writers seems to extend further than mine and I don't see you jibbing at anything from Cummings, Eliot or whomever else I might suggest. It is now *you* who are seeing the volume of unprinted stuff needing publication.

To be of use as advisor I shd. have to know how many pages per month you can print. 32 seems a good number. I mean it is enough for *my* purposes. I want for my personal use 2 to 4 pages. I mean I could *do* something with a regular monthly fire of 2 or 4 pages. All got to be calculated beforehand.

I ought to be paid for Cantos and what wd. have been *Criterion* articles were the *Crit.* still in existence.

Might calculate 2 Cantos and 2 essays a year?? Apart from monthly notes or editorial?

I don't propose to deal with dead matter and negations. In fact, the younger generation ought to do the killing and carrying away of corpses. I've got my time cut out now for positive statements. My economic work is done (in the main). I shall have to go on condensing and restating, but am now definitely onto questions of BELIEF. Re econ: I can depute the rest to Overholser. Nobody *knows* what I have done: *Brit. Union Quarterly*, *Rassegna Monetaria*, etc. It has still got to be diffused, distributed, put into popular education, etc.

I don't think a mag can in 1940 be *contemporary* unless it faces the question of race. Any mention of Chinamen being different from Sweedes or Portuguese will lead to a charge of anti-Semitism. You haven't yet answered me on that point. You've got to know where yr. money comes *from.* . . . And the problem of short term credits keeps several offices mum. Different races *believe* different formulations.

If I am to be part of the staff, either you've got to be really free, or you have got to be based on some formula that I can accept. The more we get clear *before* starting, the less time and ink will be wasted later. So far I can't think of any disagreement by me to anything you have written. *But* you probably don't realize how much you have left vague. In fact, only with *age* does one realize the degree to which *all* human expression is polybiguous.

Yes, the Rev. Swabey is damn good man, one of the Few. But he is a curate, and I think he wd. in *Pan* be better employed on economics than on religion. He knows more about it; esp. some of the Church of Eng., etc., writings on usury, etc. He set out to teach father Eliot a few about Lancelot Andrewes. After all, *Pan* isn't Xtian, and there are, my arse!, enough Xtn publications. Let us have at least "a page to the god." However, O.K. to have him on Dante vs. Landor; he'd have got $50 from *Criterion* for it.

The surviving members of the human race are so far as I know (omitting several that wd. be useless or unavailable to *Pan*) Ron. Duncan, Angold, now in the army, Swabey, Overholser, Cummings, Bunting (probably unreachable), Wyndham Lewis (must be paid. Now in America. Anything not Hellenic unless Hephaistos be come), T. S. Eliot, despite his languors and cats (anglo and pseudo). −/−/

The minute you proclaim that the mysteries exist *at all* you've got to recognize that 95% of yr. contemporaries will not and can not understand *one* word of what you are driving at. And you can *not* explain. The SECRETUM stays shut to the vulgo. And as H. Christian said years ago re catholics: "For god's sake leave 'em *in there* (i.e., church). If they weren't in there doing that, they wd. be out here pour nous embêter." –/–/

363: To A. B. DREW

Rapallo, 7 November

FABERS, Production Dept.: Re yours 1st inst., details of proofs.

Canto appears in heading where it is intended to be read aloud (if one is reading aloud), so please retain it on page 88.

The one thing that is *not* wanted is uniformity in lots of places where a variant is *intended*. This also goes for hyphens in Chinese words. No need to go into all Lin Yutang has been writing on how to help Europeans remember Chinese names.

Your letter evidently posted before you had got my page proofs.

I put in the page numbers for the Cantos. The contents is grouped under the cantos. Can't very well be sorted out as to pages as the topics are frequently spread or used on various pages. – – – –

Page 30: variations of "can not" are O.K.

"Ouan soui" O.K., with or without hyphen. Spell it "banzai" if you prefer. Sound changes from one dynasty to another. Etc.

The TçIN can stay as is.

Likewise "TAOzers." I want in every way to get into reader's head I am speaking disrespectfully of Taoist.

French accents: Do please correct them.

At what degenerate period did an "E" get into "acquaduct"? I don't care how you spell it.

"Nutche" can stay either way.

On 97: The hyphen certainly STAYS after "up-." That is essential to the meaning, though you might *add* another hyphen after the) and before "held"; sic: ")-held," if you think that is clearer. I dare say the second hyphen would be more amusing and clearer: "up-(as they say)-held."

109: "Quarrell." O hell, put in as many hells as you like.

Page 125: The Moses Gill referred to, as in individual capable of suing for libel, is DEAD. Of course the race of him exists, but he is both Aryan and Shumarian and Palestinian; nevertheless, the race, including its Aryan members, is not a person-at-law. If you mean you *wish* all of him were dead, that is up to you.

134-5: You can use accents as in yr. Frog dictionary and spell him Richelieu. Same goes for Séville and état.

P. 155: lines 2-3, yes, the repetition is intended.

157: "erected" is correct.

158: you can lard in some lines of three or four dots ... . in the Latin if you like. I can't put in a whole page of Cicero's prose at that point. Got to abbreviate.

172: yes, do as you like; accent and cap.

Schuyler is DEAD. Hamilton's god damn father-in-law. Dead for a hundred years; and if you believe in hell, you are ad lib. to think he rots.

182: spell 'em as you like.

Idem 184.

Don't be "sorry." I am truly grateful for the care spent on these details.

Will get back the remaining page proofs as soon as possible, i.e., as soon as I can give 'em due care. They came this A.M. along with yr. letter.

364: To RONALD DUNCAN

Rapallo, 7 November

Dear Ron: You complain for specific and general ignorance of India. For two dozen reasons I strongly suggest you offer yr. services to the Ministry of Information on just that topic. Whether they accept the offer, is their lookout. But I hope you will make it. *Very* few people have *any* idea of both sides. A little clarity could be very useful and yr. having been useful cd. be useful later to you. Take my own case. I loathe and always have loathed Indian art. Loathed it long before I got my usury axis. Obnubilated, short curves, muddle, jungle, etc. Waaal, we find the hin-goddamdo is a bloody and voracious usurer. Maybe Ghandi isn't, but nobody else has been to see him. From what you told me, I can see separate villages, life as of herd of wild animals in Africa: no main structure to the country, *nothing* to satisfy European, Rodam, J. Adams sense of the state. You might cast some light on that. Mebbe it is agin their natr.

At any rate, the Rhoosian immolation on machine would seem further from their disposition than even red-coated England. And the Bolshie profanation of sacred, etc., etc.

Then for Mohammeds: they are O.K. on usury, but damn'd useless again for European man. They had a few centuries, Avicenna, etc. I am told: "Oh yes; that was all *non*-Mohammedan root, Persia, etc., squshed out by their stinking near eastern fanaticism. Sperit that built the Pyramids *without* the constructive sense to build anything. Abstract art." Vs. which: the Alhambra, Taj (by Italian workmen), etc.???

Anyhow, I can see a lot of useful work that you cd. do somewhere along that line. You can start as if telling me. I probably can see as much as the general pubk. My objection to English Raj? has been that they have preserved a lot of the unfit. Bad as eugenics. All of which is prob. iggurunce.

I knew some nice chaps came with Tagore in 1911-12, but haven't *done* anything, and Rabi himself poifikly *hopeless* re statal sense, etc.

Rushing to post.

P.S. Abstract better than distortion.

365: To George Santayana

Rapallo, 8 December

Dear G.S.: I, on the other hand, am convinced that Venice is a perfect place to pass the winter, but I don't suppose you will have the complacency or even the inertia to stay there till the 26th inst. or practically speaking the 27th.

You have obligingly finished the *opus* at the earliest date I cd. read it. I have also got to the end of a job or part of a job (money in history) and for personal ends have got to tackle philosophy or my "paradise," and do badly want to talk with some one who has thought a little about it. There is one bloke in England, whose name escapes me, who has dropped an intelligent aside in a small book on Manes. Otherwise you are the only perceivable victim.

Apart ca, did I quote T. S. Eliot to "Old Krore" who was "surprised to see" me at a meeting of the Aristotelian Soc. in, I suppose, 1916. "Oh, he's not here as a philosopher. He is here as an an   thro   pologist."

The venbl Corey so put the fear of gawd into me re yr. wanting to be left in peace to finish the Opus that I had the decency not to introduce serious subjects into our first conversation.

Do give notice if same is likely to be henceforth permissable. There are one or two gropings in my notes to Cavalcanti and one or two Chinese texts whereupon sidelight wd. be welcome.

Might tear up the carpet, perhaps along the line: We believe nothing that is not European.

Xtianity is quite lousy with non-European influences but all of it that is respectable is either indigenous or put there by hard work from the time of St. Ambrose down to the sell-out, when the usurers got hold of the papacy and the conclaves no longer believed or even had clear idea of their own dogmas.

I am not insisting. I am wondering how far this is correct. Nuisance not to have Migne on the premises as mere reports of Erigena look as if the interest may have been painted on by the writers of the reports. Gemisthus Plethon's polytheism evaporated when one got near it.

If I don't get to Venice in time to see you, I hope you (and the volatile acolyte?) will get to Rapallo.

1 9 4 0

366: To Otto Bird

Rapallo, 12 January

Dear Bird: If you are still plugging at that thesis, I think you will find a good deal of interest in J. Scotus Erigena, vol. 122 of Migne.

No use my bothering you with partic. refs. until I know what you are doing. Also one ought to read the whole thing esp. the commentary of the pseudo-Dionysus. So far I don't find the text backs up various statements I have read *about* Erigena. I want corroborations on various points. Often a hurried reading fails to find a "denegat" at the end of passage. A lot of nice ideas start in one's own head that can't be attributed to J.S.E.

Another point in *all* study of Patrologia and mediaeval philos or rather a whole system of examination is *wanted*. I suggest you will write interestingly if you start sorting out the elements as to source or probable source; and suggest *four* categories:

European (say Greek)
Roman
Jewish
and North European, Scotus, Grosseteste, Albertus de la magna, etc.

My present feeling is that *all* Biblical influence is merely rotten so far as the thought is concerned. Very probably I exaggerate. But justice and measure are Roman. The admirable tradition may start with Ambrose and last to Antonino. The Greek is fine. The European good.

Met a bloke who had been in East studying Mohammeds. He said they invented *nowt*. Anything good in 'em derived from Greece or Persia or somewhere. This to be taken cum grano and then some. Anyhow, I shd. like a sort out of at least *two* lots of concepts: The *European* and the *non-European*.

Re Cavalcanti: Erigena certainly throws doubt on various readings: *for*mato and *infor*mato, etc. I wonder whether lots of copyists didn't each emend the text to suit their own views.

I at any rate have got to digest Erigena and then review the whole "Donna mi Prega." And I shd. like a fellow-traveler.

Did I send you a few questions re need of a monthly magazine and what you cd. do for or about one?

Is Gilson on the premises? Has he got any hunches re European and non-European categories?

367: To George Santayana

Rapallo, 16 January

Dear G.S.: It is good of you to write at such length. Responsus est:

1. Premature to mention my "philosophy," call it a disposition. In another 30 years I may put the bits together, but probably won't.

2. Chinese saying "a man's character apparent in every one of his brush strokes." Early characters were pictures, squared for aesthetic reasons. But I think in a well-brushed ideogram the sun is seen to be rising. The east is a convention; the west ideogram hasn't the sun in it. Not sure whether it may be sheepfold (this guess).

One ideogramic current is from picture often of process, then it is tied to, associated with one of a dozen meanings by convention. Whole process of primitive association, but quite arbitrary, as: two men, city, night = theft. — — — —

Not the picturesque element I was trying to emphasize so much as the pt. re western man "defining" by receding: red, color, vibration, mode of being, etc.; Chinese by putting together concrete objects as in F's example:

red	cherry
iron rust	flamingo

Am not sure the lexicographers back him up.

Sorry you had those grubby pages. A few nice ideograms would have reconciled your aesthetic perceptions.

Have I indicated my letch toward *teXne*, and do I manage to indicate what I conceive as kindred tendency? From the *thing* to the grouped things, thence to a more real knowledge than in our friend Erigena (whose text I have wheedled out of Genova)—nice mind but mucking about in the unknown. *Damn* all these citations of Hebrew impertinence or whatever. Erig. *had* a nice mind, full of light and had perceived quite a lot. It's the fussing with nomenclature by absolutely ignorant arguers that gets my goat.

The decline of the West occurred between the *Nicomachean Ethics* and the *Magna* (or fat) *Moralia*.

I believe the venerable Dan C. was annoyed by the frivolities of my *Kulch.* I don't know whether it wd. serve as better answer to part of yr. question that what I can knock out in ten minutes. Not sure the book is still in print. Danl might think ill of you if you descended to borrow his copy.

I am trying to get my American publisher to reprint the "Mencius." But don't think it contains much more on the present point (or diafana).

At any rate, Fenollosa has delivered us from the godawful translations of Chinese poetry that preceded him. And there is a place where that rising sun ideogram in one of the poems in his anthology once and forever is a sort of "l'alba tan tost ve." However, this is getting too complicated.

Next A.M.: Your remark about my remark on "values remain" being dogmatic. Liddell gives "dogma, what seems true to one, an opinion." But "dogmatikes, belonging to opinions or maxims; maintaining them." I have always had an impression of an "ought" hanging about the word. I could say "values recur" (or I don't mind "remain"), but let it stand as an observation gathered from particular cases.

The ole W. of Bab. certainly and for long time has used her dogmas in the sense of something the sheep *had* to accept. Not as any "seems" but certainly as "maxim ex cat.," etc.

368: To T. S. Eliot

Rapallo, 18 January

Waaal, naow, me deer protopheriius: −/−/ I am sorry yew missed the outlook from the Palazzo, but it got so goddam cold we emigrated to a steam-hot and damn good eatin pension. And don't worrit about more *money*. I kin feed yew for a couple of weeks. And over a decent amount you cd. pay up after the war if any. Anyhow, don't stop for a mere matter of money. Come erlong fer St. Valentine's day or any other respectable Pagan feast.

I may go to Rome the fust pt. of Feb. I cd. lend you Italian money for about a week in Rome. Can't offer that luxury as a invite wiffout fewcher recompense. −/−/

And Spencer has the laff on Bastun; as they fired him, but Cambridge, England, wanted him. To which place he couldn't get. Jas sez it is first time Cam. Eng. has tooken a prof. from Cam. Mass. So HAW, bloody hawhaw. Minnethelaughing waters!!

I want a reprint of "Mencius" as soon as possible. Had a lot of jaw with Geo. Santayana in Venice, and like him. Never met anyone who seems to me to fake less. In fact, I gave him a clean bill. He has a low opnyn of yr. ole pal Irvink Babbitt, in which I suspect he is right.

I have now the text of Erigena, and *if* I could get hold of the recent publications about him, I could write quite a chunk. Not that I am letching to. Lot to connect wiff Cavalcanti's poem, if any more is wanted on them lines. Or allusions to Dant.

I shd. start rev. of mod. esp. of Erig. with Schleuter's Latin comment, dated Westphalia 1838. A bit special but *non*-political. Johnny Scot. "Pietate insignia atque hilaritate." Johnny had a nice mind. Omnia quae sunt lumina sunt. I haven't yet found anything that fits what I had read about what he thought, but it may be in the 600 pages double ocl. Migne, vol. 122.

You ought to be able to get tourist lire if you can come. Have you asked about that at the Italian tourist agency in Regent St.?? I shd. like to know, cause I cd. mention it if I am druv to invite anyone else in yr. distinguished place.

The Yanks are publishing a goddam series on Philosophers, beginning, i.e., begun, with Dewey. Santayana second. I could probably chew the ear off some of the fatheads.

Have you got Wyndham's Buffalo address? Why the hell don't the blighter write?

St. Ambrose is one of the blokes I keep on quotin'. However, if his birfday is past, I will have to await wiff anticipation. It is marked S. Vitaliano (which looks like a misspelling for "veal"; let's hope it is a fat calf). I never heard of the bloke, but he is on the orphans' calendar. And the 26th Saint PaulA (a lady martyr). How confusing your religion is anyhow.

What is the earliest date you cd. print a prose book? I want the "Mencius," and as Jas keeps selling the *Ta Hio* regular. . . . It would be about the same size. Or a trilogy: *Ta Hio*, "Mencius" and a note on Erigena. Probably about twice the size, depends on date. There is in the Zukofsky reprint of the first half of *Spirit of Romance* a 1912 note on sequaire of Goddeschalk, etc. The soft sort of stuff I then did. Pubd. in ole Mead's *Quest*. Seems such a waste to grind out new *prose* when there is such a lot of my stuff out of print. However, the mature omissions of a superior mind, the riper, the juicier, etc.—I get that angle also. I don't feel ready to knock off "The *whole* of Philosophy" in six months.

There is allus Claudius Salmasius' *De Modo Usurarum*. A serious author. And I have a Sextus Empiricus on the lot. Nice style. Voltairian finish. George nigh bust when I said I cdn't get a copy of Scot. Erig. but had managed to get a Sextus. Wot wiff ideograms and all, George *is* trying to *see* the connection. I have fed him the Cavalcanti and all is nice and cordial at the Hotel Daniele. In fact, if you were still an American I might propose a triumvirate. As *copain* I prefer him to some of yr. tolerated. —/—/

369: To Katue Kitasono

Rapallo, 22 January

Dear K.K.: I have you to thank for a very elegant volume. The drawings look as if an occidental influence had entered your life. "Decadence of the Empire." All I now need is a translation. As the poems are very short, don't bother to make it literary. If I had a literal version I might possibly put it in shape. Can't tell. Only a fraction of poetry will translate.

Did you use that bit of *Jap. Times* as wrapping on purpose? Or is it coincidence? First thing I see is "leg conscious Japan" which reminded me of Ito's first remark to me in 1914 or '15: "Jap'nese dance all time overcoat." Then I notice the ineffable Miscio in person, but not in voice, save in the remark on the fan dance and Sally.

I believe I could have done a better article on Ito than the *J.T.* interviewer. Did you meet him? The paper is dated October and says he was to return to America in Jan., so this is too late to serve as introduction, but if he is still in Tokio, give him my remembrances. I looked for him in N. York, but he was then in S. Francisco.

Mr. Masaichi Tani writes very good English, but he has missed a chance. His girls will have to be patriotic and "use Japan Knees"—whatever foreign clothes they obtain.

If you do meet Miscio ask him about "Ainley's face behind that mask," or his borrowing the old lady's cat. As to the photo in the *J.T.*, I can't believe even Hollywood and facial massage has kept him 18. Not 25 years later.

Do you know whether the *J.T.* is being sent me? It doesn't get here.

P.S. Did you see the *Hawk's Well*—is it any use in Japanese?

370: To T. S. Eliot

Rapallo, 1 February

To the affbl Protopgerius Wunkus: Gittin down to thet book. There is, so far as I know, no English work on Kulturmorphologie, transformation of cultures. Can't use a German term at this moment. Morphology of cultures. Historic process taken in the larger.

I know you jib at China and Frobenius cause they ain't pie church; and neither of us likes sabages, black habits, etc. However, for yr. enlightenment, Frazer worked largely from documents. Frob. went to *things*, memories still in the spoken tradition, etc. His students had to *see* and be able to draw objects. All of which follows up Fabre *and* the Fenollosa "Essay on Written Character."

There is a book of *patient*, and *How*, explanation to be done on this to get (in 80 years) it into the universitai head that history did not stop, better say historiography did not cease developing methods of Gibbon or ape or whomever.

Naturally history without monetary intelligence is mere twaddle. That I think I have conveyed to you by now?? But I bayn't sure you have grosp the other element in the growth of historiographic *teXne*. I should use both that distance from *Nichomachean* notes to *Magna Moralia*, along with various categories of Frobenius.

That I cd. start on now. I don't think I am ready for an analysis of Christianity into its various racial components, European and non-European. Think I should approach it in such a book—natr of belief, etc.

Note that I shd. claim to get on from where Frobenius left off, in that his Morphology was applied to savages and my interest is in civilizations at their *most*.

By way, ole pot-belly Wells writes me there is something in a book (on second reading evidently it is *his* book((or Work) *Wealth and Happiness of Mankind*. Seems incredible? Unlikely I can get a copy here or that it is sold at reasonable price or that he would ever get down to the brassier variety of tacks on *any* subject. Have you or Swabey or anyone ever seen or heard of the volume? — — —

371: To H. G. WELLS

Rapallo, 3 February

Dear H.G.: By a miracle I have got hold of yr. Hay Stack or serial review of the *Encyclopedia Britannica* (an uncertain work).

Waaal, you are pretty messy. Tho' you have some points in your summary of some one's book on P. Morgan. And one clause re money detaching people from soil and responsibility to same.

And as luck wd., I find you being merely the conceited half-baked J. Bull on p. 337. You *may*, if drunk, have chanced on a hysterical female; I have spent a deal of time in Italy and never seen a servant struck, tho' the barboy aged 16 did knock down the headwaiter for a fancied impoliteness on the part of the latter. Backward countries me arse!!

I have also see two females in combat in Kensington back street with admiring throng of refeen'd lower clawrs henglish and a comic male (about yr. build) telling one of 'em, the winner, "You 'adn't orter strike a wumman."

First observations in re way you *avoid* all the real authors, or at any rate so many of 'em No sign of Chas. Beard, for example. Naturally you are weak on Doug and Gesell because English do *not* read books by men younger than themselves or published after their own debuts. Butchart's *Money* would do you a world of good. But you cdn't have had that in '32.

Nevertheless if you are ass enough to consider Keynes a reliable writer, Khrrist and all – – – – help you. I think what it comes to is that you "established" guys never crab or mistrust any other Britisher who is in the gang. Krhhist, do you have yr. reading picked for you by the *Times Lit. Sup.*?? Keynes on H.C.L.: "*caused by* LACK *of* labour." In my hearing . . . An orthodox economist.

Of course, it ain't all yr. fault. Criticism is hard to get. I have had *five* real criticisms. I doubt if you have ever sought any. – – – –

If you wd. start any chapter with a *definition* (or the book)—with the definitions of the terms you mean to use. . . . No. Damn it, you use a good phrase and then you flop; you muff.

I don't at p. 348 see you facing the price gap. And Keynes is a louse, he is the kahal incarnate. And phrases such as "no other way" show incomplete knowledge. –/–/

Oh, hell, I've a vol. of Beard and another by Corey (with some facts in it). Is there any use my reading yours? I am not being paid to review it eight years late. I have no indication that *any*one ever has criticized it seriously to you or that your idea of criticism is other than the English current idea, i.e., part of publishers' advertising, a "review" by some Jackie S. who is paid to review it, because the publisher takes so much space (adv.).

But for affection's sake, I *will* read the damn thing carefully if you wd. like a careful criticism of some of the sloppy paragraphs.

372: To George Santayana

Rapallo, 6 February

Dear G.S.: Faber (the publisher) wants to know whether you would consider and on what terms you would consider, etc., a desperate attempt to save further generations from the horrors of past education.

All of which arises from my transmission to Eliot of your little story of Henry Adams "It can not be done." [1] Plus your further remark, "It doesn't matter *what* so long as they all read the *same* things."

The proposal is, if not beneath your dignity, and with the aim of getting out of our usuals, that you, Eliot (T.S., not his late cousin) and the undersigned should each, with malice or without, enjoy ourselves setting down either a method or a curriculum or both.

I don't imagine that we have *any* readers in common. We are regarded as the three Europeans of American origins or what not, or at any rate those who got out alive.

I had no such designs on your quiet when I entered the Daniele. I know that it savours of revivalism, etc.

On the other hand the shock of such a symposium.

Or as Eliot writes, "It is he (namely G.S.) who adds just the spot of respectability that makes (his phrase; I shd. say 'would make if,' etc.) the book queer whereas if you (E.P.) and me (T.S.E.) didn't have him I don't say we couldn't make the book just as queer, but the public wouldn't be so surprised."

I plead the missionary sperrit: GUILTY!!

I don't see why it shouldn't be as good or better a place to answer your critics (in that philosophical) symposium) as any magazine, etc. could or would offer. I do think it is an implement to carry your philosophy to readers who wouldn't normally read a volume labeled philosophy.

Faber is rushing ahead with "Has he an agent here (London)? We would want to handle American rights." All of which seems to me premature.

It is, hang it all, a chance to blast off some of the fog and fugg. I can see Eliot's reason and my reasons for welcoming the chance much more clearly than I can see why you should be bothered, but then on the other foot I don't see why you need be very greatly bothered.

Conjecturally you would regard curriculum or method as arising from a philosophic root, a scheme of values, and all you need do is attach a paragraph to that effect to whatever you happen to be writing. With as much or as little pugnacity, etc., venom or benevolence as the mood of the day dictates. Hell. Possum and I can't be as stuffy as some of the blokes now engaged in symposing on your beliefs. And the company would either excuse a lighter tone or gives alience to a greater gravity and suavity of (?) attack.

[1] That is, teach at Harvard University.

"What the exceptional y.m. ought to have the bare chance of learning in a university che si rispetta."

Length, amount, etc., would, I take it, be for you to dictate. Eliot and I to fill in whatever you chose to omit. My emphasis would be on economics, history, letters and possibly music. With my "Mencius" essay either in the vol. or implied.

I have *no* idea what Eliot would do, except that he agrees that the blighters should define their terms before spouting about this and the other.

Have I been clear? Faber invites a volume or triptych or however you spell it: G.S., T.S.E. and myself on the Ideal University, or The Proper Curriculum, or how it would be possible to educate and/or (mostly *or*) civilize the university stewd-dent (and, inter lineas, how to kill off bureaucratism and professoriality).

The Henry Adams anecdote is above price: it is your story and ought to be in the opening pages if not the opening paragraph. Anyhow, the idea arose from it.

I don't know what more I can say other than one more citation of Eliot's letter re the Faber committee: "They say that it ought to be a very queer book and it appeals to them."

373: To Henry Swabey

Rapallo, 7 March

Dear Swabe: You better twig the manifesto of the American Catholic Bishops and step on the gas. It covers a good deal, and yr. own potbellied bastid piscops are left at the post.

Don't bother re Wells. Have seen the book and had several notes from H.G., adorned with portraits. Reckon he never has and never will *define* anything. All his words indefinite middles.

Know nowt about Java or sadica marriage. What is?

Re European belief: Neither mass nor communion are of Jew origin. Nowt to do with that narsty old maniac JHV and are basis of Xtn relig. Mass ought to be in Latin, unless you cd. do it in Greek or Chinese. In fact, *any* abracadabra that no bloody member of the public or half-educated ape of a clargimint cd. think he understood.

The Cat. Bishops' manifest vurry long-winded.

What I meant re Doug was that there has been an absence of practicality, absence of consideration of *means* whereby state wd. arrange to compensate, etc. All par with the bloke who wd. just neglect to get LOGS for the raft. Everybody (especially the deracinés) dodging the job of doing it *on the spot; in* the place where they are. Hence, I spose, 151 votes vs. 15 thousand or whatever for some labour faker.

Glad of any good dirt on Tom Aquinas. A bad influence. Wrong type of mind.

374: To Ronald Duncan

Rapallo, 14 March

Dear Ron: On receipt of yrs. I promptly sat down and wrote you an article, but this A.M. it seemed too dull to be worth the postage.

I cd. pretty well swap my motto (see above) [1] for your "No taxes before the harvest." That is yr. best line out of four. I approve the aim of the others, but in practice some provision had to be made of the CENTRE. Nine fields system is O.K. — — — —

If you review *Cantos* and if Swabe does a comparison of the manifesto of the American Catholic Bishops' 68 points *with* the Papal Encyclical *and* with my *What is Money For?* that wd. prob. be better than any more of me. In other words, I am getting to age where at bloody last I occasionally wonder whether I don't talk too much . . . or at any rate to stop and ask meself: *is it useful* to say this or that . . . at a particular time.

I started yesterday's note with a line I had cancelled in ms. sent Swabe . . . *but!!!* reaction to remarks by other contributors, etc., etc., isn't printing matter.

Mass and communion not Jewish in origin. . . . What's use my saying *that* especially as I have *not* studied the Mass and am not absolutely sure what mightn't be tucked into it. Anything I said to Swabe can stand.

I suppose Austin is a pussydonym. Good poem.

Christianity is (or was when real) anti-Semitism, etc. What is the use of arguing (my arguing) with undefined terms. At any rate, I am off improvisations; at least for, I hope, a week or two.

Looks to me as if you had jazzed up Mr. Eliot's drumatik technique by having more to say. Rien ne pousse à la concision comme l'abondance d'idées.

Less the Bible is used for reading matter, better for Europe. If a race neglects to create its own gods, it gets the bump. Borrow yr. gods from a central bank and naturally you end in slavery and in moral — — — — and degradation. Would be mere waste of print to yatter about this.

The Cat. Bishops have assumed RESPONSIBILITY. Don't leave — — — — room in a urinal for the Anglicans or Arch-bs.

Protestantism is a usury politic. Well, *not* wholly. Believe Luther was against usury, and was anti-tax, at least agin sending tax money out of the country. What the hell is the use writing a dull article. No use my going off half-cocked on large subjects whereon I have not yet arrived at conclusion. Nothing in this note is ready for press. And to rewrite old articles makes boring copy.

The place to defend England is on the *land*. I am with you there.

Haven't you left a flat out of the miserere stave?

[1] Pound's stationery bore the following sentence from Mussolini: "Liberty is not a right but a duty."

Don't worry about the mysterium. There is plenty left. But not a sub-ject for polite essays. To hell wiff Abraham. Most of the constructive so-called Xtn ideas are out of the Stoics. In fact, I should suggest that *all* "Christian decency" is sheer stoic. I doubt if any single ethical idea now honoured comes from Jewry. But either one has got to do a Quarterly old style 20 page, down to the bottom based on 40 years continuous study, or let such a subject alone. At any rate, I have only finished my historic econ. section a year ago, and don't want to make wild statements. Questions no good at this time. Need *all* the circumjacent intelligence for immediate things.

Damn it all, I am a poek, partly a musician, i.e., in one corner up to a point, and a economist. I can't become an authority on another dept. in six weeks or even six months. Time is past for me to do interim stuff, and ex cathedra? NO.

Speculation is one thing; dogma another. And I don't think it oppor-tune to print speculation at the moment. May change my mind next week. I mean for *me* to print it, or write it for print. O.K. for you to dramatize.

Tempus tacendi. I don't know how long it will last. Might be a beauti-ful object lesson to Porterhouse [H. G. Porteus].

375: To Sadakichi Hartmann

Rapallo, 20 March

Dear Sadakichi: Two years ago I was elected to what I first heard H. James describe funereally as "a *body.*"

Naturally, they don't like it, but by dint of abuse the treasurer has printed a report recd. here this A.M. They are pouilleux with money. I mean from *our* sized view, not from the N.Y. view. Anyhow, they have a relief fund, not more than 500 a year to any one person.

Some of the painters may not be as lousy as most of the writers—never heard tell of most of either—but if you know some nice influential mem-bers, I see no reason why they shouldn't give milk. I can only think of two other qualified recipients; one may be dead and the other proud.

The sekkertary, oh Joy, is old Canby. But they say he ain't gotta bad heart; Seidel is at least a convivial sound. On the strength of the oysters to Walt (who died before the body emerged from the — — — — of time) you might git a sandwich. At any rate, this action is prompt. — — — —

376: To Ronald Duncan

Rapallo, 30 March

No, Ron: Chinamen not so simple as all that. Central field had to be ploughed, etc., and cultivated *first*. That job done, each of the eight families cd. attend to its own. Naturally any five or seven of them famblies wd. keep an eye on the one or three that *did not* do its stunt or stint of work in the ducal or state field. In fact, the mechanism for law enforcement right thaaar on the spot.

There was commutation to a tenth, for urban or at least for court, i.e., metropolis-capital city area.

Mencius remarks that reduction to $\frac{1}{20}$ means return to "dog and camp fire" state of society whereas above $\frac{1}{10}$th or $\frac{1}{9}$ is oppression. Bureaucracy, etc. $-/-/$

As to tax on non-cultivated land: why not go fascist and merely *cultivate* the damn land when the owners of latifundia fail to do so?

All taxes or fixed charges are from hell. A division of fruits is the proper mode. Tax on non-fruitful houses, libraries, pictures *no* use. It ends with everything in Lazard's cellar.

Tax? In money? Who issues the money?? The answer is *cultivate* the land; right of ownership shd. imply obligation to *use*. Ownership is a legal construction made by law and custom, not by geology. If you tax the Marquis, he merely borrows money; been goin on since days of Eliz. Farming out estates, etc. Invite the buggah to cultivate. If he don't, the county, township or whatever executive division, goes in and cultivates. Tax is merely a shifting of money, usually for sake of paying bugrocrats' salaries. It creates *nothing*.

A tithe; meaning SHARE *of the FRUITS, not* fixed charge, a percentage. An assurance to worker that if he produces he won't starve. Ammassi. If necessary. Have you got the Am. Cat. Bishops' manifesto?

As to teeyater: I dunno nowt abaht teeyater. Seems to me one needs a total social revolution before one can set up real festivals of *any* kind. Drama religious, but not costume historique. Essence of religion is the *present* tense.

Something might be done with fact (I mean seems to me fact) that *Catholic* church is *not* a stasis. I doubt if any modern Cat., stupidest priest in swamp village, believe the god damned muck that St. Cyril believed. All this damn near eastern squish is dead mutton, forgotten. Ordinary Cats. have *no* idea what Church once meant. Whether Roman Church can adjust yet again to what *anyone* really believes is another question. Anglicans don't *believe*. "Interferes neither with man's politics nor his religion." Etc.

377: To Ronald Duncan

Rapallo, 31 March

Dear Ron: $-/-/$ Blasted friends left a goddam radio here yester. Gift. God damn destructive and dispersive devil of an invention. But got to be faced. Drammer has got to face it, not only face cinema. Anybody who *can* survive *may* strengthen inner life, but mass of apes and worms will be still further rejuiced to passivity. Hell a state of passivity? Or limbo??

Anyhow what drammer or teeyater *wuz*, radio is. Possibly the loathing of it may stop diffuse writing. No sense in print *until* it gets to finality?

Also the histrionic developments in announcing. And the million to one chance that audition will develop: at least to a faculty for picking the fake in the voices. Only stuff fit to hear was Tripoli, Sofia and Tunis. Howling music in two of 'em and a cembalo in Bugarea.

And a double sense of the blessedness of silence when the damn thing is turned off.

Anyhow, if you're writin for styge or teeyater up to date, you gotter measure it all, not merely against cinema, but much more against the personae now poked into every bleedin' 'ome and smearing the mind of the peapull. If anyone is a purrfekk HERRRRkules, he may survive, and *may* clarify his style in *resistance* to the devil box. I mean if he ain't druv to melancolia crepitans before he recovers.

I anticipated the damn thing in first third of Cantos and was able to do 52/71 because I was the last survivin' monolith who did not have a bloody radio in the 'ome. However, like the subjects of sacred painting as Mr. Cohen said: "Vot I say iss, we got to svallow 'em, vot I say iss, ve got to svallow 'em." Or be boa-constricted.

Who publishes the Chinese farming book? Any use to me? I am too old to git out and plow, and besides all the fields here are terraced and worked by spade. However, I shd. purrfurr it to fishing; I ain't no piscator, not Ez. I thoroughly believe in plowin'. I have heard that to sail coastally or plow you fix yr. eye on a distant point or two points in a line. Anyhow, I can't plow till they make me a emperor, and no continent's yett bidding fer me soivices in thet line.

Of course Sweeney would be O.K. on stage. I think probably *all* dramatic writing makes a theatre; sets the scene, etc. That may be test of its being dramatic. Whereas undramatic writing *needs* a stage.

P.S. Bottrall'll do as good a review as anyone except possibly Possum.

378: To TIBOR SERLY

Rapallo, April

Dear Tib: Helluva job to get a complete set of programs. Only people who I care about having advertised are O.R., Münch (who has just hit the high in Germany: "one of the best if not the best pianist"), you, and the Hungarians.

In main outline:
1. June 1933: Mozart sonatas as per program sent sep. cov. 12 sonatas for violin and piano. The rest done privately so that a few of us heard the whole set.
2. Scriabine recital: 12 July (piano, Münch).
3. Autumn 1933-4: see programs.
4. Nov. 1933: Tigulliani concert in Genova.
5. Spring 1934: All William Young's sonatas, Whittaker edtn. Mozart sonatas repeated.
6. German music: Albert, Teleman, etc.

7. 1935 (I think). Serly, etc. That must have been Gertler IV. Bartok, third quartet.
8. 1936: Vivaldi.
9. New Hungarian 4tet.
10. Bartok 2 and 5. Also Ferroud, Boccherini.
11. Prog. Bartok, Haydn, Bartok (vide prog. eleven)

Oh, yes: in mention of Rapallo concerts, note the *laboratory* idea: intention to present the music, old *and* new, in manner that would lead to more *exact* estimation of the value of the compositions. Enough of *one* composer to show his scope and limits; his force and his defects. And then contrasts with Grade A stuff (see the early Bach concerts), with the modern or experimental.

Problem: *did* the Ravel stand it as well as the Debussy, etc.? The Bartok-Haydn maximum contrast, etc. Idea that a program is a whole: see later model in the Sab. 16th Sept. concert at Siena. Program constructed by Casella. Perfect model of prog. construction.

Note ours of 1933. Not indicating that Casella got it from us but steps in developing a demand *for* constructed program.

The improvement of Italian festival programs. Siena now proposes to do one composer or group of related composers, not merely mixed salad. Due mainly to O.R., but don't rub it in too hard, not tactful. Politeness to Casella will do you no harm. Easy enough to distribute the credit so as not to annoy anyone.

12. 1938: Purcell.
13. 1939: Mozart.

Note the *dates* of first Vivaldi manifesto here, 1936. And the fruition in Vivaldi week at Siena. Did I send you the Vivaldi big program? Oh well, better send it anyhow, with Olga's thematic catalog.

Our public performances suspended now for duration of war, but editing, dechifrage, of Vivaldi goes on. Reduction to two or three instruments —pyanny and one or two violins so as to try 'em out and see which shd. be written out in partitur for orchestra. However, the Siena week shows where a small push can lead. —/—/

379: To Henry Swabey

Rapallo, 20 April

Dear Swabe: Or pass it on to Ron. Not for me to muck into yr. internal politics, tho' don't see why I shdn't answer questions. Ron sent draft of reform charter. Too long and unreadable. Can't possibly get a whole mass of different ideas into *any* head. I shd. say it was time *you* started asking: *when* do the internal reforms begin?

I hear plowing has been left till too late. (Don't ask me. I am no aggy-kulchist.)

I shd. think a moratorium on taxes a better way to win than forced loan, esp. as anybody *knows* that Gesell can get the results with no damn loan whatsoever. Also general cry, "No tithes till after the harvest." That is basic. No honest man can object to that. Ron boggling about ownership. Damn this detail. The *use* of the land is what you want. I admit ownership now conditions this, but get the *root* and leave the twigs. A three idea program is all any group can cohere on. *If* on that. Cobbett thought the paaasuns fools to "tie tithes to boroughs." The idea "every man represented by one of his own trade" parallels protest against the rotten boroughs. All forms of disfranchisement can go under a general equation, but *when* will Brit. professional men *bother* to be represented by one of their trade? Apart from the lawyers who represent themselves first and clients afterward. I dunno with the P. Morgan? Biscops in the Lds. rep.——?

Anyhow, there are my three main clauses. Ron's objection to rabbits, seems to me wd. put up the back of the poachers' union, rural and slum Eng. having lived on rabbit fer this hunderd year (or is that fiction?).

380: To Henry Swabey

Rapallo, 9 May

Dear Swabe: The Bible should be read *after* the reader is literate. The poison, as intended, is and has for centuries been instilled into helpless babes. Obviously no man who had read either the classics or Confucius or even Brooks Adams would be infectable by the god-blithering tosh, low moral tone, black superstition and general filth dumped onto him. Whole thing a perversion. Which ain't to say there is no use in the Church.

All the Jew part of the Bible is black evil. Question is mainly how soon can one get rid of it without killing the patient. Some kind of reminder of the divine is desirable. Humanity being what it is, I don't see that one can start with a perfectly new and pure religion containing only what one really thinks decent. I mean as practical politics it may not be advisable.

Xtianity a poor substitute for the truth, but the best canned goods that can be put on the market immediately in sufficient quantity for general pubk. ??? I admit the problem is difficult. Mebbe best line is to get rid of worst and rottenest phases first, i.e., the old testy-munk, barbarous blood sac, etc., and gradually detach Dantescan light (peeling off the Middle Ages bit by bit, that bloody swine St. Clement, etc.) Omnia quae sunt, lumina sunt. — — — —

381: To Katue Kitasono

Rapallo, 29 October

Dear Kit Kat: Happy New Year. And for Kristzache get an idea of the relative value of *yen* and *lire*.

I have cashed yr. last postal order for 146 lire. Damn. That is about six dollars. The regular exchange of the dollar being at 19 lire to the dollar. But as resident foreigner, I can get a 20% bonus, bringing it to nearly 24.

Unless the yen has bust, it was worth about 40 cents, so that 34 would have been worth 13 dollars plus.

I don't mind putting up six or seven bucks to get the Sassoons out of Shanghai or damaging the opium revenue in Singapore (48% due to hop), but I should hate to have it used to scrag me rough-necked brothers from Iowa.

As I can't cash American cheques, save at risk of the Brits stealing 'em off the Clipper in the Bahamas and as nothing now comes from English publications, this thin line of supplies from the *J.T.* is, or *would*, be useful if allowed to flow in with proper (i.e., as at the source) dimensions.

If you can't get sense out of the postal system, fer gord'z sake try a *bank*. Must be some Italian bank with an office in Tokio??? Or the American Express Co. must exist and continue bizniz at least until or unless hostilities bust out. Which I hope they won't.

Cultural notes, possibly for *VOU*. Appearance of P. Tyler in *J.T.* reminds me that:

No editor in America, save Margaret Anderson, ever felt the need of, or responsibility for, getting the best writers concentrated—i.e., brought together in an American periodical. She started in Chicago, went to S. Francisco, then N. York and ended by publishing *The Little Review* in Paris. Evidently the *aim* was alien to American sensibilities.

The Dial might fool the casual observer; but its policy was *not* to get the best work or best writers. It got some. But Thayer aimed at names, wanted European celebrities and spent vast sums getting their left-overs. You would see same thing in American picture galleries. *After* a painter is celebrated (and Europeans have his best stuff) dealers can sell it to American "connoisseurs." —/—/

J.T. my last remaining source of information re the U.S. I don't even know whether Jas has got out the Am. edtn. 52/71 Cantos.

Itoh's book, *British Empire and People*, ought to be published *at once* in some European language. Possibly serialized in *J.T.*—or at least summarized. After all, in the Ban Gumi, the pacification of the country precedes the lofty reflection or plays of pussy-cology.

Great excitements last month: thought of going to U.S. to annoy 'em, but Clipper won't take anything except mails until Dec. 15. So am back here at the old stand. Thank God I didn't get as far as Portugal and get stuck there.

Pious reflections on my having spent 12 years in London, 4 in Paris, and now 16 or 17 in Italy. Which you can take as estimate, etc. etc. of national values. I dunno what my 23 infantile years in America signify. I left as soon as motion was autarchic—I mean *my* motion. Curious letch of Americans to *try* to start a civilization there or rather to restart it, because there seems to have been some up till 1863. I should *still* like to.

Have you ever had the gargantual appetite necessary for comparing the *J.T.* with American daily or Sunday wypers??? Or to consider what Japan does *not* import in the way of newsprint?? Oh well: don't. Let it alone. And get out another issue of *VOU*.

Any news of living authors would be welcome. Gornoze what's become of Possum and Duncan and Angold or the pacific Bunting.

Cultural policy of Japan?? Vide Ez' *Guide to Kulchur*, facilitated by Ez' system of economics, now the program of Ministers Funk and Riccardi. Tho' I don't spose they knew it was mine.

P.S. Re the U.S., vide my *Make It New*, Rémy de Gourmont's letter: "Conquerer l'Amérique n'est pas sans doute votre seul but." Funny trick of memory. I thought he had written "civilizer l'Amérique." That must have been in my note to him.

382: To Katue Kitasono

Rapallo, 15 November

Dear K.K.: −/−/ Ideogram is essential to the exposition of certain kinds of thought. Greek philosophy was mostly a mere splitting, an impoverishment of understanding, though it ultimately led to development of particular sciences. Socrates a distinguished gas-bag in comparison with Confucius and Mencius.

At any rate, I *need* ideogram. I mean I need it in and for my own job, but I also need sound and phonetics. Several half-wits in a state of half-education have sniffed at my going on with Fenollosa's use of the Japanese sounds for reading ideogram. I propose to continue. As sheer sound Dai Gaku is better than Ta Tsü. When it comes to the question of transmitting from the East to the West, a great part of the Chinese sound is no use at all. We don't hear parts of it, and much of the rest is a hiss or a mumble. Fenollosa wrote, I think justly, that Japan had kept the old sounds for the Odes long after the various invasions from the north had ruined them in China. Tones cannot be learnt at three thousand miles distance anyhow; or at any rate, never have been.

The national defence of Basho and Chikmatsu can be maintained by use of the Latin alphabet. If any young Tanakas want to set out for world conquest, on the lines of *Ubicumque lingua Romana, ibi Roma* (wherever the Latin tongue, there Rome) you will invade much better by giving us the sound of your verse in these Latin signs that are understood from the Volga to the West Coast of Canada, in Australia, and from Finland to the Capes of Good Hope and Horn.

English has conquered vast territories by absorbing other tongues, that is to say, it has poached most Latin roots and has variants on them handy for use where French and even Italian have shown less flexibility. It has taken in lashin's of Greek, swallowed mediaeval French, while keeping its solid Anglo-Saxon basis. It then petrified in the tight little island, but American seems to be getting into Tokio. Question of whether you want to "preserve" Japanese in test tubes or swallow the American vocabulary is for you to decide. −/−/

Throughout all history and despite all academies, living language has been inclusive and not exclusive. Japerican may well replace pidgin even in our time, but Japanese will never become lingua franca until its sound is printed in the simplest possible manner.

383: To Katue Kitasono
[postcard]

Rapallo, 22 November

Dear Kit Kat: Next time I have a bit of money from J.T., please take out for me a six months' subscription to the *daily* edition. I don't get enough news from the weekly. However dull you may think the paper, it is a d–n sight more lively than the usual dailies.

Have you had any news of Duncan or Eliot or anyone?

Bloke named Maraini (I have told him to see you, but forget what town he is in; may be half way up Fuji) seems to see *Meridiano* now and then. I wonder if your copies have come? They promised to send them.

1 9 4 1

384: To Katue Kitasono

Rapallo, 12 March

Dear Kit Kat: Have I asked, and have you answered: whether you have olive trees in Japan? And whether the peasants shake off the olives with bamboo poles?

The Janequin's "Canzoni degli Ucelli," Münch's version for violin, was printed in *Townsman*. I think I mention it also in ABC of Reading. J. born end of Quattrocento, about 1475, if I remember rightly. Otherwise these lines from a new Canto—or rather for a new Canto—can go to the VOU Club without explanation.

Lines to go into Canto 72 or somewhere:

Now sun rises in Ram sign.
With clack of bamboo against olive stock
We have heard the birds praising Janequin
and the black cat's tail is exalted.

The sexton of San Pantaleo plays "è mobile" on his carillon
"un' e due . . . che la donna è mobile"
in the hill tower (videt et urbes)
And a black head under white cherry boughs
precedes us down the salita.[1]
The water-bug's mittens [2] show on the bright rock below him.

[1] Italian for stone path in hills.

[2] If I were 30 years younger I would call 'em his boxing gloves. I wonder if it is clear that I mean the shadow of the "mittens"? and can you ideograph it; very like petals of blossom.

All of which shows that I am not wholly absorbed in saving Europe by economics.

Chronology: 1885-1940

1885 Born Hailey, Idaho, son of Homer L. and Isabel Weston Pound. Family moved to Pennsylvania eighteen months later.

1901-03 University of Pennsylvania.

1903-05 Hamilton College. Ph.B. 1905.

1906 M.A. University of Pennsylvania. Fellow in Romanics.

1906-07 Travel and study in Spain, Italy, and Provence.

1907 Instructor in Romance languages at Wabash College, Crawfordsville, Indiana. Resignation requested after four months (*see footnote, page 5*).

1907-08 Italy. *A Lume Spento* published in Venice, June 1908.

1908 London. *A Quinzaine for This Yule.*

1909 *Personae; Exultations.*

1910 *The Spirit of Romance; Provença.*

1911 *Canzoni.*

1912 London representative of *Poetry: A Magazine of Verse.* Published his translations of *The Sonnets and Ballate of Guido Cavalcanti.*

1913 *Ripostes.*

1914 Married Dorothy Shakespear. Edited the anthology *Des Imagistes.*

1915 *Cathay.* Edited the *Catholic Anthology.*

1916 *Lustra; Gaudier-Brzeska: a Memoir; Noh, or Accomplishment* (translations by Fenollosa and Pound).

1917   London editor of *The Little Review; Dialogues of Fontenelle* (translations). Edited *Passages from the Letters of John Butler Yeats.*

1918   *Pavannes and Divisions.*

1919   *Quia Pauper Amavi.*

1920   *Hugh Selwyn Mauberly; Umbra; Instigations.*

1921   Paris. *Poems 1918-21.*

1923   *Indiscretions.*

1924   *Antheil and the Treatise on Harmony.*

1925   Settled at Rapallo. *A Draft of XVI Cantos for the Beginning of a Poem of Some Length* published by Three Mountains Press, Paris.

1928   *A Draft of Cantos XVII to XXVII.*

1930   *Imaginary Letters.*

1931   *How to Read.*

1933   *ABC of Economics; A Draft of XXX Cantos.* Edited *Active Anthology.*

1934   *ABC of Reading; Eleven New Cantos, XXXI-XLI; Make It New.*

1935   *Jefferson and/or Mussolini.*

1936   *Ta Hio, the Great Learning* (translation).

1937   *Polite Essays; The Fifth Decad of Cantos.*

1938   *Guide to Kulchur.*

1939   Visited the United States. Honorary degree from Hamilton College.

1940   *Cantos LII-LXXI.*

Index of Names